Piping Traditions
of
Argyll

Piping Traditions
of
Argyll

BRIDGET MACKENZIE

A College of Piping Publication

© Bridget Mackenzie 2004

All rights reserved.
No part of this publication may be reproduced in any form or by any means without the prior permission of the publishers.

ISBN 0–9549380–0–3

British Library cataloguing in Publication Data.

A catalogue record for this book is available from the British Library.

This book is dedicated to Alex,
for forty years husband, friend, companion,
piper and fellow-enthusiast.
He got me into this.

Front Cover: Arthur Gillies, with Loch Awe in the background

Published by The College of Piping
(Principal Robert Wallace)
16-24 Otago Street, Glasgow G12 8JH, Scotland, UK
tel: +44 (0) 141 334 3587 • fax: +44 (0) 141 587 6068
e-mail: college@college-of-piping.co.uk • www.college-of-piping.co.uk

Typeset, printed and bound by Hugh K. Clarkson & Sons Ltd.,
Young Street, West Calder, West Lothian EH55 8HA

List of Contents

INTRODUCTION ix

MAINLAND ARGYLL
    Kintyre 1
    Knapdale 63
    Loch Fyne 73
    Mid-Argyll 90
    Nether Lorne 112
    Inveraray 119
    Loch Awe 163
    Oban and District 170
    Lorne and Appin 221
    Glencoe, Ballachulish, Glenorchy 241
    Glendaruel 267
    Dunoon and Cowal 277
    Morvern, Ardgour and Ardnamurchan 286

BIBLIOGRAPHY 310

INDEX OF PEOPLE 314

INDEX OF PLACES 326

INDEX OF MUSIC 333

List of Illustrations

Cover picture: Arthur Gillies, with Loch Awe in the background
Family Tree of the Earls of Antrim
Rock of Dunaverty, Southend
Limecraigs, Campbeltown
Drumdrishaig, Knapdale
Saddell House
Kilnaish Mausoleum
Family tree of Lachlan MacNeill Campbell
Dunskeig, near Clachan; view from Dunskeig
Robert Munro's Tomb, Falkirk
Kilberry Pipe Band, 1890s
Hugh MacCallum
George M. MacIntyre
Tony Wilson
John Wilson
Willie MacCallum senior and competitors at Campbeltown, 2000
Junior competitors at Campbeltown
Family tree of the MacAlisters and MacCallums
Kilberry Castle, South Knapdale
Archibald Campbell of Kilberry
James Campbell at Oban
Duncan MacLean, Ardrishaig
Archie Kenneth
Presentation of Archie Kenneth Quaich
Players at Minard, 1975
Duntrune Castle, near Crinan
Poltalloch House, near Crinan
Dalnahassaig, near Crinan
John Gillies
Gillies family tree
John Gillies with Scots Guards band
Gilbert Gillies
Frimley Band with Dr MacPhail
Frimley Band Certificate
Archie MacNab
Culfail Hotel, Kilmelfort
Line of the Campbell pipers at Ardmaddy
Sketch of J.F. Campbell
Drawing of Inveraray Castle in the late 18th century, and today
Portrait of the Marquis of Argyle
John M. MacKenzie

The 5th HLI Pipe Band
Painting of Donald MacPhedran
Family Tree of the MacKenzies, MacPhedrans and Rosses
Aultnabreac, Loch Achilty; ruins at Aultnabreac; Loch Achilty
Inveraray Pipe Band 1890
Inveraray Band with Lord Archibald
Ronnie MacCallum MBE
Duniquaich, near Inveraray
Arthur Gillies and Angus MacColl
Arthur Gillies after winning the Open Piobaireachd in 1993
Dunstaffnage Castle
The MacDougall pipers of Aberfeldy
Lerags, near Oban
Moleigh, near Oban; Moleigh farm buildings
Kilbride, near Oban
Kilmore Church, near Oban
Patrick MacDonald's grave at Kilmore; Patrick's gravestone
Dunollie Castle, Oban
Doorway of Dunollie Castle
Old pine tree in memory of Captain MacDougall
Red-throated Diver
Lochnell, near Oban
Old days in Oban
Birthplace of John MacColl at Kentallen
Kilbowie Cottage, Oban
John MacColl
Regatta in Oban Bay
Angus Nicol with the Duke of Argyll
View of the Oban Games
Oban Games in 1925
Neil MacLean
Wee Donald MacLean, Oban and Glasgow
Lovat Scouts at Balmoral
Winners at Cowal Games
Ronald Lawrie
Family tree of the MacFarlanes
Donald MacDonald junior
Glencoe
Family tree of the Lawries
William Lawrie, Ballachulish
John MacDougall Gillies, Glendaruel
5th HLI Pipe band with John MacDougall Gillies
Music and song of *Togail nam Bo*
Robert Reid

G.S. MacLennan
Funeral cortege of John MacDougall Gillies
John MacLellan, Dunoon
Norman MacLean

Most of the illustrations are photographs taken by myself or borrowed, with permission, from the Piping Times and from the archives of the College of Piping. The rest are acknowledged as far as was possible, but some I was given many years ago, and I do not know their origin. I apologise if I have infringed anyone's rights. Doubtless they will let me know.

MAPS
- Argyll and the Western Isles xiii
- Kintyre xviii
- Knapdale 62
- Nether Lorne 97
- Upper Lorne 171
- Cowal 268
- Ardnamurchan 286

Introduction

WHEN I COMPLETED A PREVIOUS volume, *The Piping Traditions of the North of Scotland*, complaints were made that the more southern areas of Scotland were being neglected, and I was galvanised into investigating Argyll. Strictly speaking, the term Argyll should be used only for the area now known as Mid-Argyll, and districts such as Kintyre and Lorne are not within it. But Argyll became the name of the county which stretched from Ardnamurchan to Southend, and this is how it is used here.

The intention was to include the traditions of the islands which used to be in Argyll, those lying to the south of Ardnamurchan, but this made the book so long as to be impracticable, and would have put the price beyond the reach of most pipers. Reluctantly, therefore, the islands have been separated from the mainland of Argyll, and two volumes are envisaged: this one, and a companion work, *Piping Traditions of the Western Isles*, which will include the islands north of Ardnamurchan as well.

The main aim of the series is to try to bring together and put on record some of the traditions of piping which are in danger of being lost, and to make some of the piping records easier of access. While I have named my sources at the end of each section, this is not intended to be a scholarly work, and I ask academic friends to refrain from reproaching me for avoiding marathon footnotes and obscure learned language. This book is for the pipers, and I hope that it is user-friendly, mildly entertaining, and sufficiently informative to be useful.

Some readers may find the historical or literary sections too heavy, but the lay-out should make it easy to skip these and try something more palatable. I have tried to leaven the lump of historical material by including a few frivolous items, purely for (possible) entertainment. The bad verse is my own work.

The sections on piobaireachd poems may be heavy going for many; I know they will be of interest to others, as I have had the comment that some pipers like them because they give dignity to piping in the literary world. Most pipers have no idea that piobaireachd poems exist, and perhaps this is a good place to give them an introduction.

The order of the sections of the text is geographical, working northwards from the southern tip of Kintyre and up the west coast as far as Ballachulish and Morvern; then it takes in the Ardnamurchan peninsula, which used to be in Argyll.

As in the earlier volume, the lay-out is in sections which are intended to be complete in themselves. And as before, this leads inevitably to a certain amount of repetition, which I think is preferable to endless cross-referencing. I apologise for any irritation this may cause.

Once again I have to stress that I have deliberately omitted pipers who are currently competing at the Games and in the bigger competitions. It might seem ridiculous to mention, let us say, Oban without an account of Angus MacColl, or

Campbeltown without Willie McCallum, but I am certain that a mention from me would not enhance their prospects, and it might well prejudice a judge against them. Once they have reached the stage of themselves becoming judges, fine, but not when they are still competing.

There is very little about the pipe band scene here, mainly because of my own ignorance on that topic. The book is long enough without my venturing into those perilous waters.

I know there are mistakes in this book. There are mistakes in every piping book ever written. I prefer to be told outright about them rather than pick up rumours, so would welcome any corrections or additional information – please send them to me, c/o the College of Piping, 16-24 Otago Street, Glasgow G12 8JH Scotland, UK. All letters will be answered.

One of the great pleasures of the earlier book was the amount of correspondence it engendered. Interesting letters came from all over the world, some of them from descendants of pipers named in the book, and I have been given a wealth of additional information. I welcome comments, with or without more information.

A problem with a book of this sort, drawing on local traditions, is that the information given to me may not be strictly accurate – but it does represent the tradition handed down. Should this be corrected, or left in the form in which it was received? What if one person tells me one thing, and another has a different story? I have done my best to reconcile conflicting accounts, but I do feel that I should not 'correct' local tradition, even if written records indicate that it might be mistaken. After all, even written records are based ultimately on information given locally, and often given to a stranger with no Gaelic, so that the official line may be equally misleading. So if you find what you think is a mistake, it may be that it is included here as part of what has been handed down locally, after being subjected to the distortions of time. Or, of course, I may simply have got it wrong.

A source which I have been unable to consult is the Oban Times, of which the back numbers date from 1861 onwards: unfortunately these old editions have been unavailable to the public for many months, indeed years, while their contents were being transferred to computer.

As before, I owe a huge debt to a number of kind people who have kept me right and have been generous with their information. This book was more difficult to assemble than the previous one, as I do not live in Argyll, and could not just step out of the house and talk to local people. I am not complaining, as Alex and I have been made to feel welcome all over Argyll, and have met with an enthusiasm for piping which matches our own.

Among those we have reason to be grateful to are the following, as well as a host of others, some of whose names I never even knew, though we shared a love of piping. In particular, I owe a debt to:

Nancy Black, Oban
Ronald Black, Peebles

Elizabeth Brownell, Grantown-on-Spey
Alistair Campbell of Airds
Jeannie Campbell, Glasgow
Jean Denham, Dunach
Arthur Gillies, Kilchrenan, Loch Awe
Neil Gillies, Barnton, Edinburgh
Charles Hunter, Oban
Archie Kenneth, Stronachullin, Loch Fyyneside
Colin Lawrie, Dunbarton
Graham Lawrie, Gartocharn
Ronald Lawrie, Oban
Archie MacAlister, Ardrishaig
Mrs MacArthur, Glenfeochan, Oban
Fred MacAulay, Inverness
Hugh MacCallum, Dunblane
William MacCallum senior, Campbeltown
Hugh MacDonald, Abriachan, Loch Ness side
Murdo MacDonald, Archivist, Lochgilphead
Murdoch MacDonald, Evanton
Nan MacDonald, Inverness
William M. MacDonald, Inverness
Charlie MacFarlane, Glenfinnan
Sheila MacIntyre, Kenmore, Loch Fyne
Stewart MacKenzie, Surrey
Duncan MacLean, Ardrishaig
Norman MacLean, Glasgow
Alistair MacLeod, Inverness Library
Dugald MacNeill, Edinburgh
Seumas MacNeill, Glasgow
Duncan MacPhedran, Wiltshire
Neil MacPhedran, Canada
Margaret and Alasdair MacPherson, Glenfeochan, Oban
Phosa MacPherson, Newtonmore
Finlay MacRae, Dingwall
William MacRobbie, Inverness
Kenneth MacTaggart, Inverness
Angus Martin, Campbeltown
Donald Morrison, Oban
Ian Murray, Edinburgh
Nigel Norman, Kilmartin, Argyll
Keith Sanger, Penicuik
Isabel Souden, Lochgilphead
George Stewart, Golspie
Katherine Stewart, Abriachan

Virginia van der Lande, Nottingham
Robert Wallace, Glasgow
Katrine Wilson, Campbeltown

Libraries and Museums:
Inverness Central Library, Reference and Family History Section
Edinburgh City Central Library
Oban Central Library
Motherwell Central Library
College of Piping Museum and Library

    My debt to all of them is unpayable. All I can offer is my thanks. Some of the people on the above list have unfortunately died during the time I have been preparing this book. My debt to them is still as great, so I have retained their names on the list, and I hope this does not give pain to their families.

DORNOCH 2003

In lists of tunes, the following abbreviations are used:
M = March
S = Strathspey
R = Reel
SA = Slow Air
GA = Gaelic Air
RM = Retreat March
H = Hornpipe
J = Jig
P = Piobaireachd. In giving the number of variations, I am following the practice of the Piobaireachd Society publications, which count the Urlar as the first variation. This is not the normal habit of pipers, who usually count the variations which follow the Urlar.

2/4, 6/8, etc. refer to the time signature of the tune

The number at the end refers to the number of parts in the tune

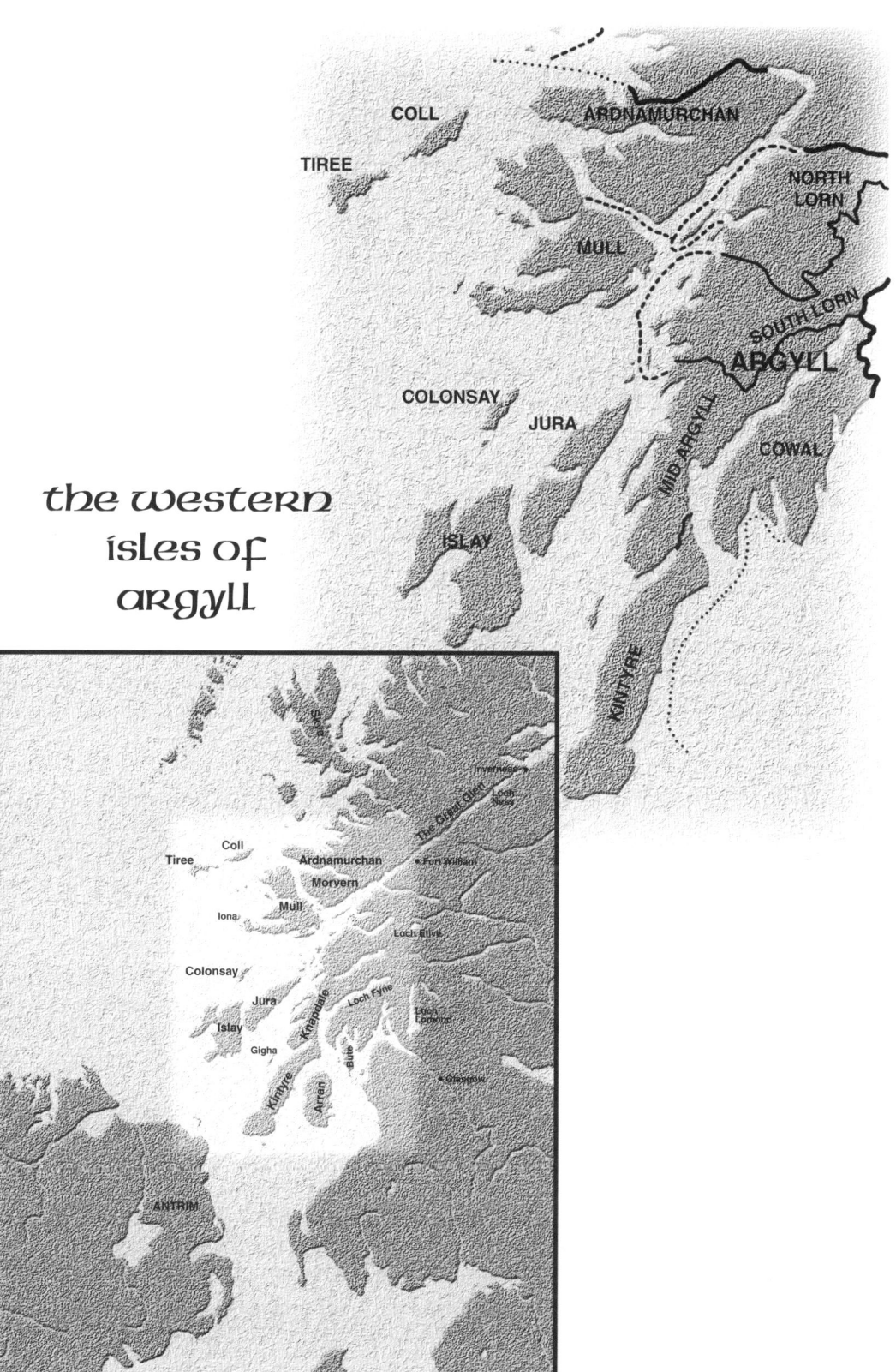

SOME TUNES ASSOCIATED WITH ARGYLL

See also lists of compositions by John MacLellan, Dunoon, Archie Kenneth, Angus Lawrie, William Lawrie, John M. MacKenzie, George MacIntyre, Donald MacPhedran, Duncan MacLean and John MacColl. Their works, apart from one tune by John MacLellan, are not included in this list.

Alastair McAllister S 2
Argyll and the Isles, by John MacLellan, Dunoon M
Argyll Is My Name (The Fisherman's Frolic) 6/8 J 2
The Argyllshire Volunteers March 2/4 M 4
Bonnie Argyll, by John Gordon 6/8 SA 2
Colonel Campbell of Inverneill's Farewell to the Argylls 2/4 M 2
Dr Ross's 50th Welcome to the Argyllshire Gathering, by Donald MacLeod 6/8 M 4
Glenorchy, by Donald MacLeod 6/8 J 4
The Hills of Glenorchy 6/8 M 2 or 3
The Lament for the Bishop of Argyll P with 3 variations (see below)
Loch Etive Side, by John Cameron 2/4 SA 2
Lochgilphead, by Colin McLauchlan R 2
Lochgilphead Fair R 2
McAllister's Dirk R 6
MacDonald of Sanda's Lament P with 8 variations
MacPhedran's Dream 6/8 M 2
Pipe Major Alex MacNeill, by Angus J. MacDowell 2/4 M 4
Ranald Beag, by Seumas MacNeill 6/8 SA 2
Seumas MacNeill, by Bobby MacLeod 6/8 M 4
The Lament for the Bishop of Argyll:

    The Editor's note to this tune, published in Book 15 of the Piobaireachd Society Collection, says that around 1740, an antiquary called Walter MacFarlane commissioned the writing of three volumes of manuscript of music for the harp and the fiddle. The writer was a fiddler and composer in Edinburgh, David Young, who transcribed the music as for the fiddle. Among the tunes are some which appear to be piobaireachd.

    The Lament for the Bishop of Argyll, which has been described as a 'proto-piobaireachd', that is, an early stage in the development of piobaireachd form, 'seems to possess the character, though not the typical structure, of piobaireachd'. The manuscript does not give the grace-notes, and the editors have published the work in both forms, as it appears in the manuscript, and with the grace-noting added. The editors add: 'A curious feature of this score (in the manuscript) is the fact that there are repeat dots at the end of each movement.' They omitted these on the grounds that they thought that 'each movement has an internal build-up and climax, the impact of which is likely to be dulled by repetition.'

A harp or fiddle tune called *Lament for the Bishop of Argyll* is in the Dow manuscript and in the MacFarlane manuscript (c.1742). It is not certain which bishop this was, but there are four possibilities: (a) Robert Montgomery, son of the Earl of Eglinton, died around 1558; (b) Neil Campbell, resigned 1608; (c) Andrew Boyd, illegitimate son of Thomas, Lord Boyd (an Ulster family), died 1636; (d) Hector MacLean, who supported Montrose and Charles I, and became Bishop of Argyll in 1680, died 1687. Hector seems the most likely subject of the lament. He married Jean Boyd, a granddaughter of Andrew (c) above, and they had sixteen daughters. One of his sons was Anndra Mac an Easbuig (Andrew the Bishop's son), who became a well-known MacLean poet. Andrew is mentioned as 'The harper's son in Mull' in an account of the depredations committed on the Clan Campbell; and he fought alongside Dundee at the Battle of Killiecrankie.

PIPERS FROM ARGYLL

Pipers referred to in various records as simply being from Argyll include:

LIEUTENANT RONALD CAMPBELL, DESCRIBED IN the Notices of Pipers as 'of an Argyllshire family' served with the 72nd Highlanders (Seaforth) in India and South Africa. His main interest to the piping world is the Journal he wrote in two volumes, mentioning pipers and piping in his regiment.

He belonged to the Grenadier Company of the 72nd, and in India, during the siege of Pondicherry in 1793, under a severe cannonade from the fortress, when the men were in a trench suffering greatly from the burning sun, Lt Campbell was told to direct the piper of the Grenadier company to 'play some Pibrochs to enliven the men. The moment the piper began, the fire from the enemy slackened, and soon after almost entirely ceased'. The enemy (the French) climbed on their battlements to listen, and 'seemed more astonished at hearing the bagpipe than we were with the Colonel's request'.

In 1806, in the Battle of Blawberg in the Cape of Good Hope, the men were pursuing the Dutch across country. Lt Campbell wrote: 'The troops halted for a time to rest, and in spite of the burning sun and extreme fatigue of the men (who had marched some miles through heavy sand), the Grenadier Company of the 72nd requested that the pipers might strike up 'Capper Feidh' to which they danced a reel, to the utter astonishment of the 59th Regiment which was close in rear'.

DUGALD CLERK, 1811-1877, a native of Argyll, who went to Edinburgh to become a sporran-maker in Rose Street. 'A sweet performer', he died suddenly when he was about to write a book of pipe music.

COLIN CAMPBELL, an Argyllshire man and 'a born piper' is described in the Notices of Pipers as a 'quiet respectable type of West Highlander'. He enlisted around 1854, 'when well up in years', in the 72nd (Seaforth) Highlanders, but never became Pipe Major although he swore he had been promised the rank, and he was often asked to replace the Pipe Major and play in the officers' mess. In the end he was so exasperated by his lack of promotion that he began to abuse the officers, becoming overexcited and pouring forth his grievances in Gaelic, until he had to be led away. This did not help his prospects. He was the youngest of five brothers, all excellent pipers.

DUGALD MACFARLANE, born in Argyll, lived in the late 19th century and was a prominent player of reels and strathspeys.

DUNCAN MACLACHLAN was a Nova Scotian piper of Argyll family. He was taught by Ronald MacKenzie, nephew of John Ban, in 1868, when Ronald was stationed in Canada with his regiment, the Seaforth Highlanders. Duncan was considered to be an excellent piper.

DONALD MACPHERSON from Glenelg became a policeman in Argyll around 1900, for some years before he went to Govan. He retired with the rank of Inspector, and died in Glenelg in 1935. He was a reed maker who experimented with a drone reed to avoid waterlogging. He was rated as a good player.

Marion Campbell, in her book *Argyll The Enduring Heartland*, mentions that her father, John Campbell of Kilberry, was friendly with the TOWNSLEYS, travelling people who had many pipers in their family. In summer, they did the rounds of Argyll, Ayrshire and Renfrewshire, 'following the harvest', as old Mrs Townsley put it, meaning not after the harvest, but following it around to be taken on as workers, as the crops ripened at different times, starting with the hay. While the men and the younger women were working on the farms, the older women and the children went round the villages, selling clothes pegs and renewing old friendships.

Living in Langbank, Renfrewshire, in the 1960s, I recall old Mrs Townsley coming every year with pegs, and staying for a cup of tea and buttered toast. Marion Campbell remembered the menfolk, whom I rarely saw: her father said the Townsleys had a better right to the land than he had himself, and he collected traditional airs from them. Certainly in Renfrewshire the musical Townsleys were often a feature of a summer train journey on the Glasgow-to-Gourock local line, singing traditional songs to pipe tunes.

Young JOCK TOWNSLEY was a piper, and Kilberry once came out of a meeting in Inveraray to find Jock on the green by the war memorial, playing *Bha Mi Aig Bhanais Air Bhail' Inneraora* (*I Was At A Wedding In Inveraray*, another name for *The Campbells Are Coming*). He was playing it in jig time, for dancers. Marion Campbell had an early memory of dancing, as a very young child, holding out the pleats of her first kilt and looking up into the dark-bearded face of Jock Townsley playing his jig.

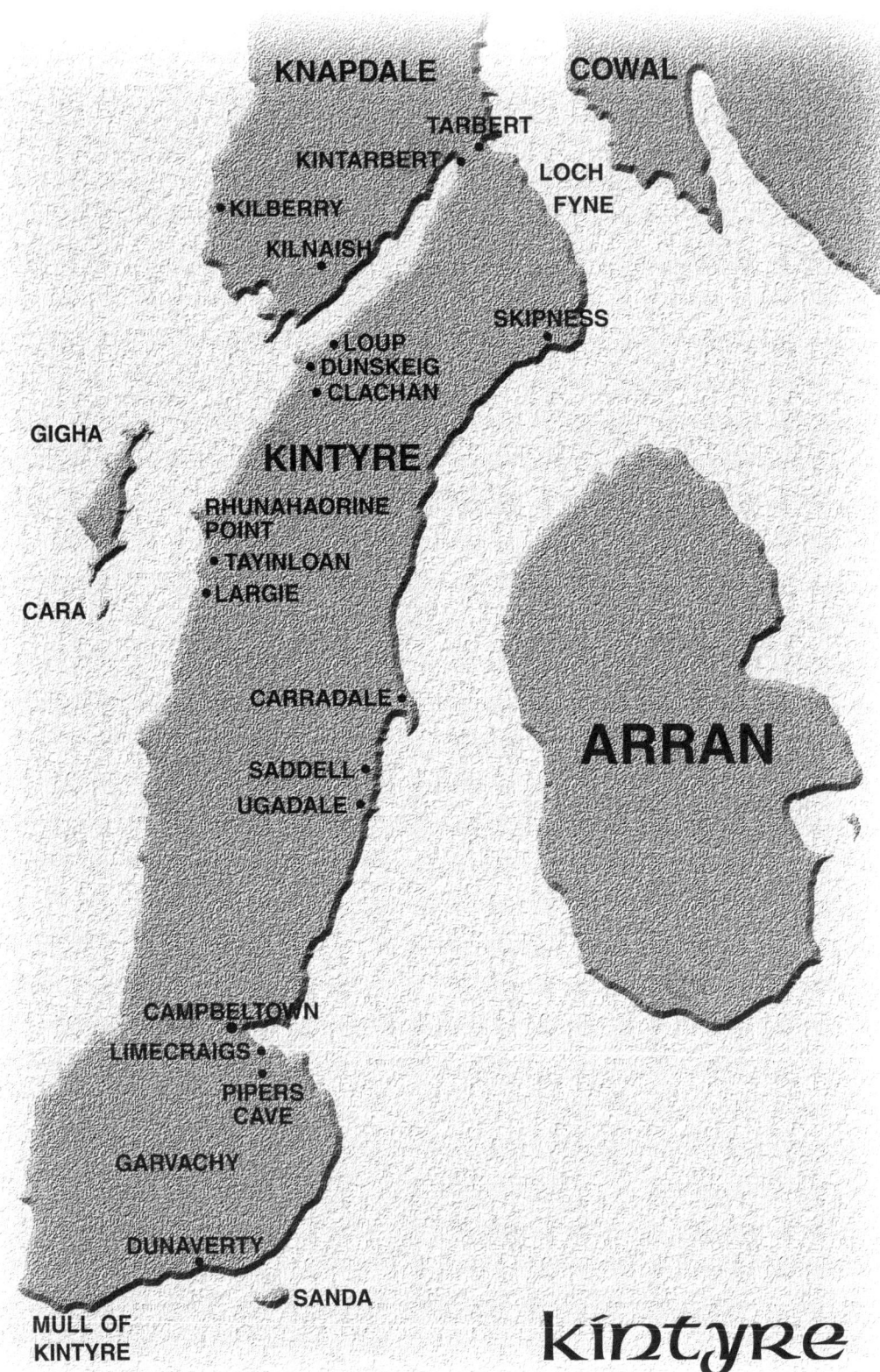

kintyre

TUNES ASSOCIATED WITH KINTYRE:
Campbeltown Kiltie Ball, by John MacLellan, Dunoon S 2
Campbeltown Loch 6/8 M 2
Captain H. MacNeal's Welcome Home from South Africa, by G.S.Allan, 1901 2/4 M 2
Dalintober, by Donald MacLeod 6/8 M 4
Glencarradale House, by George D. Taylor S 4
Hugh A. MacCallum, by Archie Duncan 9/8 RM 2
Kilmichael Glen, by W.J. Campbell 6/8 M 4
Leaving Kintyre P with 8 variations
MacAlister's Dirk R 4
MacCallum's Birthday, by Andrew MacDonald 2/4 M 4
MacDonald of Sanda's Lament P with 8 variations – see below
The MacNeals (or MacNeills) of Ugadale, by John M. MacKenzie 6/8 M 4
The Men from Dalintober, by R. Fleming 9/8 M 2
The Men Went to Drink (or *The Old Men Went to Drink*) P with 6 or 8 variations
Mrs Alex Wilson, by J. Wilson S 4
Mrs MacNeal of Ugadale, by G.S. Allan R 2
The Mull of Kintyre, by A. Duncan 6/8 J 4
Pipe Major Ronald MacCallum MBE, by G.M. MacIntyre HP 2/4 4
Pipe Major William Wilson of Campbeltown, by James Wark 2/4 M 4
Pipe Major Willie Wilson, by R. Fleming 6/8 M 4
The Road to Kintyre, by John M. MacKenzie 6/8 J 4
Ronald MacShannon, by Archie Duncan 9/8 RM 2
Round the Mull, by George M. MacIntyre 2/4 HP 4
Sandy Thomson, by J. Wilson 6/8 J 4
Sheila McMurchy's Dance, by James Wark R 4
Torisdale Castle, by J. Thomson 2/4 M 2
The Waves of Kintyre, by Archie Kenneth S 4

Leaving Kintyre is a piobaireachd work believed to have been a rowing tune, although some think it might be a rope-pulling shanty: presumably the difference lies in the size of the vessel and whether it was ocean-going or coastal. The work is found in its fullest form in the Campbell Canntaireachd manuscript of the 1790s, though Angus MacKay gives a simpler version. If it is an emigrant work, it must be seen along with *Beloved Scotland* and *Weighing From Land*. Such works were often played either on board ships leaving for the New World, or on the jetty as the ships set sail. Many of them seem to have been composed in the late 18th century.

A lawyer living in Tobermory in the 1840s left us a description of two emigrant ships lying there, one taking Protestants to the New World, the other Roman Catholics. Both vessels were around 600 tons, and the lawyer was full of pity for the 'poor creatures' who were due to leave. He said the Protestant emigrants were quiet and sober and had no pipers with them, but the Catholics were noisy and drunken, and had three pipers. They were from Moidart, 'sensible and savage looking fellows', and the agent in charge 'took care to keep them employed and amused with their preparations, piping and dancing'. It is clear that pipers were welcome passengers, as a diversion for the others.

The (Old) Men Went to Drink is a piobaireachd work with eight variations. Local tradition has it that the old men used to go up from Campbeltown district to drink at the inn at Tayinloan, a very old hostelry on the west side of Kintyre, at the place where the Gigha ferry comes in. The idea seems to have been that by the time they made it back to their wives in Campbeltown, they would have had time to sober up – unless of course they drank all the way home.

Fionn (Henry Whyte, himself an Argyll man) quoted a Gaelic song:

Tha na fir ag ol
Ann an Tigh-an-loin,
Uisge-beatha's beoir
Tha na fir ag ol.

Chaidh na fir a dh'ol
Ann an Tigh-an-loin,
Uisge-beatha's beoir
Chaidh na fir a dh'ol.

'The men are drinking
In the House of the Food,
Whisky and beer
The men are drinking.

'The men went to drink
In the House of the Food,
Whisky and beer
The men went to drink.

Tha na coin a tathunn,
Tha na fir a tighinn,
Tha na coin a tathunn,
Tha na fir a tighinn.

Chuid nach ol sinne dheth
Oladh na gillean e,
Dh'oladh na gillean e
Phaigheadh na gillean e.

'The dogs are barking,
The men are coming,
The dogs are barking,
The men are coming.

'Whatever we ourselves don't drink
The lads will drink it,
The lads will drink it,
The lads will pay for it.'

BACKGROUND

Any account of piping in Kintyre has to consider the strong influence of Ireland on the cultural life of the whole peninsula, and especially that of the parish of Campbeltown. The coast of Antrim is a mere eighteen miles from Kintyre, and the Glens of Antrim in particular had close ties going back to the 15th century. This means that the descent of many inhabitants of the Glens from the MacDonald Lords of the Isles, and from other related Hebridean families, cannot be ignored.

The combined legacy of Hebridean and Irish influences gave the music and poetry of Kintyre a special flavour. Islay and Gigha, and to a lesser extent Jura, too, felt this influence, and there seems to have been a two-way traffic, so that Kintyre was influencing these islands, and they were influencing Kintyre. Angus Martin, in his excellent book *Kintyre, the Hidden Past*, reckons that families emigrated from Ireland and then sometimes migrated back if times grew hard, and some went back and forth with new generations – the same surnames are found on both sides of the channel, to this day.

In earlier times the Kintyre men sometimes went over to Antrim to lift cattle, and took their pipers with them, according to Peter MacIntosh. One of the pipers was related to the Glens folk, and to warn them he played 'an original tune called *A mhnathan nan gline gur mithe dhuibh eirigh* ('Ye wives of the glens, it's time you would rise'), and this warned the women to guard their cattle' (see also Glencoe, below).

Campbeltown parishioners fell into two groups. One was those who had come over from Ayrshire, especially supporters of the Covenanters in the 1600s, escaping from the purges of Bluidy Clavers; they were to become a group to which many of the wealthier farmers and merchants of the district belonged. According to Peter MacIntosh, they 'added much to the morality and intelligence of the natives'. The second group were those who came from the Glens of Antrim, with a rich variety of musicians and poets among them. The Irish group were poorer in material wealth, and seem to have been wilder, less manageable and infinitely more talented (to make a sweeping generalisation).

The pipers in Kintyre, on the whole, belonged to the group of Irish / Hebridean extraction, and they included MacAlisters, MacCallums, MacMurchies, MacNeills, MacDonalds, MacLeans, MacKays, MacMichalls, McGeachies, MacKerrals, MacIntyres, MacQuilkans and Wilsons, all of whom probably moved from Antrim to Kintyre, sometimes by way of Islay or Gigha, over a considerable period of time. Peter MacIntosh tells of one Irishman of the late 18th century, called John Graham, who was 'simple but inoffensive, could play some tunes on the bagpipes and sing and talk wittily at times.'

Sometimes the Hebridean element in the Glens made the Scots in Kintyre feel more kindly towards the incomers, but a steady influx of impoverished Glensmen cannot have been entirely welcome. Martin says that many of the Irish arriving in Kintyre were 'not merely poor but quite destitute', and they became such a burden on the parish that some were given their fare back to Ireland, and deported. They were also blamed, sometimes with justification, for introducing disease and bad habits.

A brief account of the history of the Glens, necessarily simplified, may be relevant. It ties in with works such as the *Lament for the Earl of Antrim, Lament for Hugh, Lament for Samuel*, and the career of Donald Mor MacCrimmon.

Although there was constant and continuous migration and counter-migration of families between Kintyre and Antrim, the big change had been in 1399, when Iain Mor MacDonald of Dunyveg in Islay – a second son of one of the MacDonald Lords of the Isles – married Marjorie Byset or Bissett, heiress to the Glens of Antrim. This marriage changed the balance of power, shifting the focus from Islay to Antrim. The Glens opened up as a place of refuge for Hebridean MacDonalds and their allies, and some historians think that this diffusion of power led eventually to the weakening of the Lordship of the Isles. The MacDonalds were known as 'of Dunyveg and the Glens', and became enmeshed in the turbulent politics of Ireland, especially in the late 16th century.

As far back as the 12th century, Somerled of Argyll had a son Dugald, from whom the Clan MacDougall is descended, and Dugald's nephew, Somerled's grandson, was Donald, the progenitor of the Clan Donald and forebear of the Lords of the Isles. Donald was known as Donald of Islay.

It was probably a son of Donald of Islay, Angus Mor, who in the mid-1200s had a son Alasdair, and Alasdair was the founder of the family of the MacAlisters of Loup, in Kintyre. Some say Alasdair was Angus' brother rather than son, but, whichever he was, the date was around 1250.

Angus Mor's grandson John of Islay (Iain Ileach) was the first Lord of the Isles, who died in 1385, and he had two sons, Donald, second Lord of the Isles (died 1423), and Iain Mor, who married Marjorie Bissett. From this marriage are descended:

the MacDonalds of Largie in Kintyre (who had William MacMurchie as their piper in the 18th century);
the MacDonalds of Sanda (Archibald Mor and his son Archibald Og were both killed in 1647; see *Lament for MacDonald of Sanda*);
the MacDonalds of Colonsay, who drove out the MacPhees and seized Colonsay (*The Rout of the MacPhees*).

Coll Ciotach MacDonald and his son Alasdair MacColla were both embroiled in the Civil Wars of the mid-1600s. Alasdair made a savage march northwards through Kintyre and Knapdale in 1646, and it was probably Alasdair who was warned by his piper as he approached Duntroon (see below). Both Coll Ciotach and his son were killed in 1647.

Coll Ciotach's great-uncle was Sorley Buy. Buy is pronounced 'Boo-y', the name being an anglicised spelling of the Gaelic Somhairle Buidhe, which is sometimes translated as Fair-haired Samuel. He had married into the O'Neills of

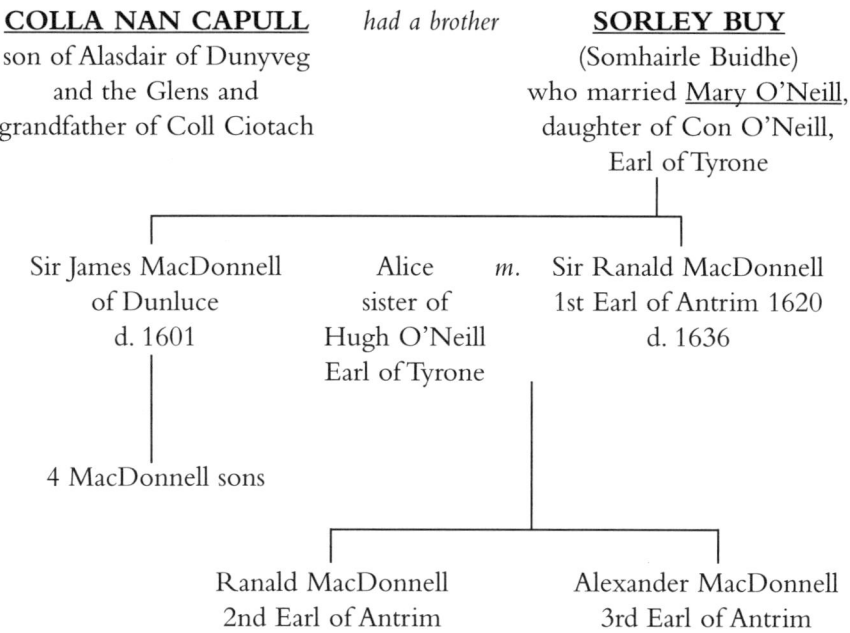

Family tree of the Earls of Antrim

Antrim and took an active part in the struggle to prevent the English invasion of Ireland. The two great Irish leaders were Hugh O'Neill, Earl of Tyrone, and Hugh O'Donnell of Tyrconnell. O'Neill's sister married Sorley's son, Ranald MacDonnell, who later became the first Earl of Antrim.

Sorley died in 1590, and may possibly be commemorated in the *Lament for Samuel*, also known as *Stewart's White Banner*. The two Irish Earls eventually surrendered and escaped abroad. Hugh O'Donnell died in Spain and Hugh O'Neill in Rome, in the early 1600s. It is thought that the *Lament for Hugh* might be for one of them; O'Neill may be the more likely because of a link with the Hebrides.

The *Lament for the Earl of Antrim* was probably made in 1636 for Sorley Buy's son Ranald, the first Earl, who was given the title in 1620. Linked to Hugh O'Neill by marriage, he was deeply involved in the struggle against the English. Irish sources say that the Hebridean MacDonalds joined forces with the MacLeods in the early 1590s to send a force of fighting men to Antrim, in support of the two Earls; but the MacDonalds had second thoughts, and withdrew their men. The Skye contingent came home, and in 1595 the MacLeods on their own sent a band of 500 highly trained archers to Hugh O'Neill. Fighting in Connaught along with the O'Donnells, they helped to raise the siege of Sligo Castle, playing a decisive part in the battle. A letter to the MacLeods from Lady O'Neill in 1925 confirmed that there is a tradition in the O'Neill family that one of their chiefs had been a great friend of one of the MacLeod chiefs, to whom the O'Neill gave a beautiful chalice, now known as the Dunvegan Cup.

The MacLeods also have a tradition that their piper, Donald Mor MacCrimmon, was over in Antrim in the early 1590s, learning music from the famous Antrim harpers. It is thought that harp music at that time had structural patterns similar to those of piobaireachd, and Donald Mor may have been studying the structure and form of it.

The tradition is vague and undated, and historians have found no documentary evidence of it – but this does not mean the stories are untrue. There are plenty of examples of a despised local or family oral tradition turning out to be acceptable to the establishment after all, when documentary or archaeological evidence is uncovered. Oral tradition should not be discounted.

It is, of course, not certain that the Lament is for the first Earl. His son, the second Earl, was known widely in the Highlands for his support of Montrose: he led a band of wild Ulstermen in Montrose's campaigns, alongside Alasdair MacColla. Although he was as well known as his father, he is less likely to have been the subject of a MacCrimmon lament, for the same reason that the *Lament for Donald Duaghal MacKay* is not likely to have been made by Patrick Mor MacCrimmon: the MacLeods of Dunvegan were doing their best not to become involved with Montrose and his ally Lord Reay (Donald Duaghal), for fear of offending the Earl of Argyll. They needed to keep in with Argyll who allowed them control of Glenelg, but only as a favour. So it was not likely that their piper would have made a public lament for the second Earl of Antrim, and it was almost certainly Sorley Buy's son, the first Earl, who was the subject.

Because of the close links with Antrim, this historical background would have been familiar to the people of Argyll, and especially of Kintyre. They would remember the hanging of the MacAlisters and the slaughter at Dunaverty in 1647 – victims' descendants were still living in the neighbourhood. Stories would be told on winter evenings, songs sung, piobaireachd played. History was not a written subject to be studied in school; it was part of the on-going life of the district, which went to make the people what they were.

This was also the background of the emigrant Irish population who over the generations arrived in Kintyre, bringing with them their own traditions and culture. It is interesting to trace the evolution of their names, the gradual anglicisation or 'Lowlandising' to a more acceptable, 'civilised' or recognisable form. Thus, the Irish O'Brolachan who came to Kintyre gave way to Brolachan, then 'Brolach or Browdie', and ended up as Brodie. MacMurchie found different forms, as MacMurtrie, MacMurphy or Murphy, and presumably when members of the family wanted to conceal their Irish origin, it was corrupted to Currie, a surname well-known in Ayrshire. The MacCallums reached Kintyre as MacIlchaluims, a name, once MacGillechaluim, which suggests that they had been in ecclesiastical life, possibly as monks or as servants to the clergy.

Some of the families with names which are clearly of Gaelic derivation may not have originated in Ireland but may be of Scots Gaelic origin, having moved south into Kintyre from further north in Argyll or elsewhere, whether mainland Scotland or the islands. Often it is not possible to tell for certain whether a name came from Ireland or from Gaelic Scotland.

It is clear that many solid Protestant Ayrshire families regarded themselves as paragons of respectability, and despised their wild Irish invaders as uncouth. Sadly, some of the Irish had to accept this judgement, especially if they were seeking employment, and they tried to emulate their neighbours, no doubt dropping their Irish-Hebridean musical talents as well. But enough of them took pride in their origins to preserve their heritage.

Some of the immigrants were unable to gain a foothold in Argyll, and took to the roads, joining a number of families who had suffered eviction in Argyll at the hands of the harsh landlords of the 19th century. A few settled in caves along the coast of Kintyre, and eked out a miserable existence, eating shellfish and seaweed, and depending on casual, seasonal farm work to make a poor living. Others obtained the use of marginal land on high ground: the weaving settlement at Garvachy, four miles south of Campbeltown, seems to have been the result of impoverished Irish immigrants seeking a desperate living. Some of the MacAlisters and MacCallums married into the very old Kintyre familes such as the Ryburns and the Flemings, to gain a toehold on the ladder of prosperity.

On the whole, the piping families were the poorer families of Kintyre, and there was little in the way of employment for them. One of the MacKerrals at Garvachy gave his occupation as 'musician' in the parish register – he made his living by playing the fiddle.

MacIntosh says that musicians were much celebrated and appreciated in Kintyre, and he mentions a man called MacPhee at Carradale, who was a renowned fiddler. Another name he puts forward is that of Donald Macandoirie (or Dewar), a blind man whose son became the Principal of Aberdeen College. This must have been the same family as the MacIndeors of Islay, well known as pipers. Donald was 'a sweet player on the fiddle, much respected, frequently employed and well remunerated', but he was exceptional. The occupations, if any, of most of the poor immigrants are not known, and some must have been in desperate plight.

The MacAlisters of Loup, a leading Kintyre family descended from the Lords of the Isles, had lived on the south side of the entrance to West Loch Tarbert, in North Kintyre, since the 1400s, and had played an important role in the history of the district. They maintained their own pipers, traditionally believed to have been drawn from their own kin, and this position as piper to Loup was heritable. The pipers lived at the farm of Dunskeig, between Loup and the village of Clachan, and tenancy of this farm seems to have been one of the privileges which went with the job (see below, MacCallums and MacAlisters).

MacDonald of Largie, at Killean, on the west side of Kintyre, opposite the island of Gigha, was a patron of music and had his own pipers. In 1745 these included a piper called MacLellan, and another, William MacMurchy, whose family was probably of Irish origin. William was also his bard, a most talented man who played the pipes, the fiddle and the harp, as well as being an accomplished Gaelic poet. He made a valuable collection of Gaelic poems, and it is said that he wrote down both the piobaireachd music and the harp music of his time. As he died in the 1770s, when the transcription of pipe music was very much in its infancy, he must have been a pioneer and was clearly a man of exceptional intelligence.

Peter MacIntosh tells a tale of the time in 1745 when MacDonald of Largie declared for the Jacobites and proposed to march with a force of his men in support of the Prince, the only Kintyre land-owner to do so. 'This came to the knowledge of Ceanntarbert [presumably MacAlister of Loup?] who sent word to MacDonald that if he intended to join the Prince he would meet him on the way in passing and that they would have a hot day of it and that few would remain to join any party. MacDonald saw it proper to alter his mind and send his men with Fir Chinntire (the Kintyre men).

'When they reached Inveraray, MacDonald's pipers played alternately: MacMurchy played *The Campbells Are Coming*. The Duke of Argyll, being in the company of other gentlemen at the time, took no notice of the tune that was played; but MacLeolan [MacLellan, the other piper to MacDonald] played *Fir Chinntire*, which the Duke immediately recognised, and said to the gentlemen present, 'Come, we must go out and welcome the Kintyre men'.

'The Duke gave a grand ball to the Kintyre men at Inveraray, the Duke himself dancing a high dance, and McLeolan playing; and after he finished the dance he said to McLeolan 'You are the sweetest player I ever heard, and you are the most ill-looking man I ever saw'. McLeolan replied, with a sarcastic smile, 'I think it was the same tailor that shaped us both' (a tactful way of saying 'No uglier than you').

'McMurchy was a superior piper and a good poet, but was grieved that the Duke did not take notice of him, and that he did not play *Fir Chinntire* also.'

They all marched to Falkirk – but were too late for the battle.

After the '45, it seems that William MacMurchy had a spell in the 77th Regiment – where he met John MacArthur, it is said. Was this 'the Professor' John MacArthur who went to live in Edinburgh, or his uncle, John Ban, father of Angus MacArthur of manuscript fame? Was this where William learned how to record pipe and harp music on paper? Or at least was it perhaps where he got the inspiration to attempt it for himself?

Peter MacIntosh also tells a tale which Neil Rankin Morrison associated with the Rankins. When William MacMurchy was living at Largieside, around 1750 or 1760, 'a superior piper and poet', he was visited by another eminent poet. William received him most respectfully, and played him a few tunes on his pipes. The gentleman saw there was some bread or scones toasting beside the fire, and as he got up to leave, he said:

Piobaireachd is aran tur
'S miosa leam na guin a bhais,
Fhir a bhodhair mo dha chluais,
Ba biodh agad duais gu brach.

'Piping and dry bread, worse to me than pangs of death, you man that deaved both my ears, may you never get a reward' (– which seems distinctly unmannerly in a guest). MacMurchy dropped the pipe from his mouth and said:

Stad a dhuine fan ri cial,
'S olc an sgial nach boin ri bun;
Tha mo bhean a t-eachd on chill,
Is ultach d'on im aira muin

'Stop, man, give ear to reason; bad is the story with no foundation. My wife is coming from Chil (Kilkerran, the old name for Campbeltown) with a load of butter on her back'.

MacIntosh goes on: 'The gentleman finding he had met his match (since William's impromptu verse was more skilful) returned and a friendly conversation took place until MacMurchie's wife came home with the butter'. The gentleman had a good feed of hot buttered scone, and left, wondering how a man like MacMurchie could live in such a remote place. Remote, of course, is a subjective term: if you live in Shetland, London is remote.

The MacMurchies were an Irish/Hebridean family who appeared early in Kintyre, and were a lasting influence on the cultural life of that part of Argyll. Keith Sanger thinks there was probably a link with the MacMhuirich family, famed for their bardic skills (see below), and the name MacMurchy may be a corruption of MacMhuirich.

Most of the music of the district must have been domestic, mainly heard at weddings, funerals and private ceilidhs; there can have been little opportunity for a piper to find employment. Up to the late 1770s, the position of Town Piper in Campbeltown, and probably in Inveraray, too, was held by pipers whose names are now lost, except for the last Campbeltown Town Piper, John MacAlister. His name was preserved by the historian of some 100 years later, Peter MacIntosh, who told us that John lost the job when in 1777 the Town Piper was replaced by a bell on the church. Other than the two posts of Town Piper, the only openings for pipers were either in private service, to the Duke of Argyll, MacAlister of Loup, Campbell of Kilberry, MacDonald of Largie and possibly a few others of the gentry – or as pipers in the local Militia Force or West Fencible Regiment, after the '45 Rising.

(see below, MacAlisters and MacCallums)

SOURCES
Angus Martin
Ronald Williams
J.Michael Hill
Peter MacIntosh
I.F. MacLeod
Keith Sanger

A PIPER'S SONG
My chanter had a plastic reed
(Black and yellow, yes)
It satisfied my every need
(Really well, oh yes)
It even played out in the rain,
In summer's heat it kept me sane –
So why have I gone back to cane?
Much more mellow, yes?

DUNAVERTY: *MACDONALD OF SANDA'S LAMENT*

Sanda is a small island off the southern tip of Kintyre, and the site of Dunaverty (Castle) lies at Southend, on the mainland of Kintyre, on top of a huge rock opposite Sanda. The castle was destroyed in the late 17th century. Dunaverty is pronounced with the stress on the second syllable: Doon–AV–erty.

Although Sanda is an island, this work is included with the traditions of mainland Kintyre, since Sanda was the Laird's title rather than his home.

Cumha Fir Sundaigh (*MacDonald of Sanda's Lament*) [Peter Reid's spelling Cumah may be a copying error, although the same spelling is found in other manuscripts] appears only in the Peter Reid manuscript of 1826, under that title, but it is known elsewhere as the *Lament for the Laird of Contullich, Cumha Fear Chunntulaich*, probably composed by Iain Dall MacKay, as one of his 'Munro cycle' works. From the dates of the different titles we have to assume that it was recycled (so to speak) by Iain Dall when he wanted to commemorate John MacLeod, the Laird of Contullich, who died in Skye in 1728. The use of an earlier work made for someone quite different is comparatively frequent: *Chisholm's Salute*, for example, appears to have started life as the *Lament for Iain Ciar* or *The Glen is Mine*, and was seen in other guises, too (see below).

The line of MacDonald of Sanda was descended from Iain Mor MacDonald, Lord of the Isles. Iain Mor's great-grandson John Cathanach, who was executed in 1494, had two sons, Alexander, from whom the Earls of Antrim were derived, and Angus Ileach ('of Islay'), who was killed in 1565.

When John Cathanach was executed, Angus Ileach was in Antrim, where his brother Alexander joined him. The clan history goes on: 'When Alexander at last received his rightful inheritance as fifth of the line of Dunyveg, he gave to Angus the lands of Sanda, Machairiach and others in Kintyre, near Southend'. These lands included the Castle of Dunaverty, in Southend, built high on a coastal rock.

Angus' grandson was Archibald Mor (Big Archibald) MacDonald of Sanda. He and his son Archibald Og (Young Archibald) were both deeply embroiled in the Civil Wars of the mid-1600s, and both were arrested by the Earl of Argyll in 1639, while in the company of two of the Kintyre agents of the second Earl of Antrim.

Not much is known of these two MacDonalds, father and son, but a statement made in July 1638 to the Sheriff of Argyll by the minister of Kilcolumkill in Kintyre mentions Archibald Mor, and makes it clear that he was illiterate and unable to read any of his correspondence. He had taken important letters to be read to him by the minister, concerning plans made by the Earl of Antrim, and the refusal of certain lairds to sign the Covenant. Sanda, mistakenly trusting the minister's integrity, told him too much, and his information about rebellion planned by O'Neill and Tyrconnell in Ulster was useful to their enemies, the Covenanters.

A report of the Battle of Inverlochy in 1645 has a curious note that one of the prisoners taken, from the ranks of the Campbells (who were abandoned on the field of battle by the Marquis of Argyle), was 'the Laird of Sanct McDonald in Kintyre'. This is taken to be a corrupt form of the MacDonald Laird of Sanda, and suggests that Archibald Mor may have been forced to fight for his Campbell captors. All of the prisoners taken that day were spared, 'being men of quality' and valuable for ransom or exchange.

Early in 1647, Archibald Mor of Sanda was free in Kintyre, and in command of a force of MacDonalds fighting for Alasdair MacColla and the cause of Montrose. General Leslie was advancing with the Covenanters across Argyll from the north, and in order to hinder his progress through Kilmartin, Kilmichael and Kilberry, a force of four or five hundred men was led into those parishes by Archibald of Sanda and Duncan MacDougall of Dunollie. In a 'scorched earth' attempt, they destroyed all settlements, houses and goods, and the burgh of Inveraray was burned down by MacDonald of Largie.

The following night Alasdair MacColla spent at Largie, on the west coast of Kintyre, before the Battle of Rhunahaorine nearby, which he lost. Alasdair fled to Ireland, and Archibald Og of Sanda went with him. The father, Archibald Mor, remained in Kintyre to take command of the remaining MacDonalds. He must have known that he stood little chance of survival, especially after the atrocities committed in Knapdale, but he covered the retreat of MacColla and Archibald Og by lighting fires after dusk. He had his piper play near the fires so that Leslie would think the rebels had encamped for the night; and then, leaving the piper playing, he withdrew his men in the darkness, to Dunaverty Castle, at the tip of the Mull of Kintyre. It is not recorded what happened to the piper.

What came next is open to some doubt: Leslie besieged the castle, where Archibald Mor of Sanda had some three hundred men crowded into a small building. Some say that Leslie offered quarter (mercy) if Archibald would surrender, but he refused, and so the offer of quarter was withdrawn.

In a preliminary assault Leslie succeeded in cutting off the rebels' water supply, and Sanda was forced to agree to give in, on promise of his men's lives. It seems to be generally agreed that his promise was given, but not kept, although pro-Covenanting writers deny that it was offered again. Whatever the background, the outcome was the same: around 300 helpless unarmed prisoners were brutally slaughtered. A few who were spared were sent to serve in the French army.

There is a story that Archibald Mor's infant grandson was saved by his nurse, Flora MacCambridge, who fled with him to hide in a nearby cave. Certainly the line of the MacDonalds of Sanda continued after the massacre. (For those who may be wondering, MacCambridge is an anglicised corruption of an old Kintyre name, originally Mac Ambrois, son of Ambrose).

Archibald Mor MacDonald of Sanda was among those who died, probably killed by being flung over the 80-foot cliff, though some of those thrown over were shot first, and many had their throats cut. Hector MacAllister of Loup and his two sons were hanged by the Campbells. A contemporary comment was: 'Heere was crueltie enough; for to kill men in cold blood, when they have submitted to mercie, hath no generosities at all in it'.

There is a tradition that these atrocities were carried out by General Leslie on the orders of the Marquis of Argyle, who seems to have been there at the time. One account says that Leslie hesitated for two days before giving in to the persuasions of others. Bishop Guthry's *Memoirs*, quoted in Volume II of *Highland*

ABOVE: *Dunaverty Rock, at Southend, in the early years of the 20th century. The castle was on top of the rock, and the bodies of many of the victims of the massacre of 1647 were thrown over the cliff (on the left side of the rock), which is about 80 feet high. The castle was destroyed later in the 17th century.* (PHOTOGRAPH BY KIND PERMISSION OF MARTIN, STATIONERS, CAMPBELTOWN)

RIGHT: *The cliff at Dunaverty.*

Papers 1240-1716, give a graphic (if not impartial) account of the massacre at Dunaverty: he says that General Leslie promised to spare the men if they left the castle peacefully, 'but having surrendered their arms, the Marquis of Argyll and a bloody preacher, Mr John Nevoy, prevailed with him to break his word, and so the army was let loose upon them and killed them all without mercy, whereat David Lesley seemed to have some inward check. For while the Marquis and he with Mr Nevoy were walking, over the ankles in blood, he turned about and said 'Now, Mr John, have you not for once gotten your fill of blood?"

The legal documents drawn up soon after the massacre put the figure of men butchered at just short of five hundred, but this figure was probably based on hearsay, and inflated by hopes of compensation. Around ninety of the dead were MacDougalls from Lorne and their supporters, many of them belonging to the Argyll gentry. They are listed by name in the legal writs.

The Notices of Pipers say that Alastair Mor MacDougall, hereditary piper to the MacDougall chief at Dunollie, Oban, composed a work called *Latha Dhunabharti (The Day of Dunaverty)*. This is a tradition preserved in the Dunollie family. It is possible that *Latha Dhunabharti* was the original name of the *Lament for MacDonald of Sanda*.

Archibald Og of Sanda, the son, was meanwhile with Alasdair MacColla's main force in Ireland. Archibald rose to the rank of Lieutenant Colonel, before he died in battle in Ireland, along with his leader, later in that same year, 1647.

According to the Notices of Pipers, 'it is said that the well known '*MacAlistrum's March*' was composed in [Alasdair MacColla's] memory and played at his funeral. It was 'much esteemed by the Irish', and is an unusual, wild air'. Does this mean the tune was composed in Ireland? By whom? Was it in the form in which we have it now, that is, a piece of Ceol Beag (Light Music)? Or was there a piece of piobaireachd of that name, perhaps with that name as its secondary title? And how was MacColla called MacAlistrum? What does the word mean? It has been explained as MacColla's Drum, but this is probably a rationlisation. Perhaps it was Mac Colla Struaim, son of Coll of the Armed Force, but this must be extremely doubtful. There is so much we do not know.

Seton Gordon, in his book *Highways and Byways in the West Highlands*, states that Archibald Mor and his son Archibald Og are both buried 'a few hundred yards from Dunaverty and near the public road where there is to be seen a small enclosure.' MacDonald of Largie is also buried here, according to Seton Gordon. Was Archibald Og's body brought back from Ireland? It seems unlikely, especially as his leader Alasdair MacColla was buried where they both fell, in Ireland.

Seton Gordon also mentions having spoken to a local man who told him about human bones being uncovered on the shore below the cliff. Shifting sand has revealed large numbers of human remains there, over the years.

The *Lament for MacDonald of Sanda* was almost certainly made to honour Archibald Mor MacDonald, one of many piobaireachd works composed in connection with the Civil Wars of the 17th century. *The Battle of Auldearn, Ewen of the Battles*, possibly *Black Donald's March*, possibly the *Lament for Hugh*, possibly the

Lament for Sorley (or *Samuel*), the *Lament for the Earl of Antrim*, the *Lament for the Castle of Dunyveg*, *The Rout of the MacPhees*, the *Lament for the Viscount of Dundee*, the *Daughter's Lament*, the *Piper's Warning to his Master*, *Sir Ewen Cameron of Lochiel's Salute* – all of these may not have arisen from the long struggle between the government and the crown, but a case could be made for each of them. And there are probably more.

It is not known who composed the *Lament for MacDonald of Sanda*. It could possibly have been one of the MacDougall piping family, or it may be a MacDonald work.

SOURCES
Old Parish Register for Campbeltown
David Stevenson
Bishop Guthry's *Memoirs*
Donald J. MacDonald of Castleton
Notices of Pipers
Seton Gordon, *Highways and Byways*

PIPER'S CAVE

To the south of Campbeltown, below a crag on the shoulder of Beinn Ghuilean, there is a cave known as the PIPER'S CAVE. This is one of the many such Piper's Caves found in the islands and on the mainland, all with much the same legend attached: in this one, the piper was thwarted in love, and decided to go in search of hell. So with his dog at his heels he marched into the cave, playing a coronach, and was never seen again. The dog, true to type, came out of a cave at Southend, seven miles away, with its coat singed off. How many bald dogs does it take before a new breed is declared?

An authoritative book on the caves of Scotland lists no fewer than 27 caves which have this story of the piper and his dog. I have been unable to find the origins of the story, but I suspect it may be in classical Latin or Greek literature. Or it may have its roots in an Irish tale.

DISPRAISE POEMS

A poem in 'Dispraise' of the pipes featured in a talk given by Professor Derick Thomson to the Gaelic Society of Inverness (see TGSI Vol IL) . The poem was made by the Gaelic poet Niall Mor MacMhuirich, probably in the early years of the 17th century, and Professor Thomson makes it clear that while the work has obvious links with Mull, its origins may have been in the Kintyre / Islay area, with strong influence from Ireland. Its title was *Seanchan na Piob o thus* 'the History of the Pipes from the beginning', a work of crude satirical humour, which briefly outlines how the pipe developed from a pig's bladder, and then goes on to mock two individual players.

Niall Mor Mac Lachlainn mhic Dhomhnaill was the grandson of a MacMhuirich who held land in Kintyre in 1541, and his *Dispraise of the Pipe* is the earliest of its kind that we know. The MacMhuirich family of filidhean (the top rank of the bards) may be related to the MacMurchies in Kintyre (see above).

There was a series of dispraise and praise poems, and Professor Thomson lists them:
1. a *Dispraise of the Pipe* made by Niall Mor MacMhuirich, sometime before 1630, when Niall was in his 70s;
2. a *Praise of the Pipe*, made in answer to Niall by Gilleasbuig na Ceapaich (Archibald of Keppoch), possibly around 1675, but certainly before 1682 (it may have been composed much earlier than this, but did not come to light immediately);
3. a *Praise* by Iain MacAilein (John MacLean, the Mull bard), in reply to 2.; it praises both Gilleasbuig and the pipe as an instrument;
4. a *Dispraise* by Lachainn mhic Iain (of the MacLean family of Coll), some time after 1715; it refers clearly to both 2. and 3.

The collection of Gaelic poems made by William MacMurchy in Kintyre (see below) in the 18th century included versions of both 2. and 3. (NLS 72.2,15 – Gaelic MS LXV)

Other poems about piping, or about particular pipers, include another work by Gilleasbuig na Ceapaich, about a piper whose uncle, Domhnall Donn of Bohuntin, made a similar poem himself. These both date from about 1680. In addition, in the mid-18th century, Alasdair Mac Mhaighstir Alasdair made a *Praise of MacCrimmon's Pipe* (*Moladh air Piob-mhor Mhic Cruimein*), and a little later, John MacCodrum made a *Dispraise of Donald Ban's Pipe* (*Diomoladh Piob Dhomhaill Bhain*). This last has an interesting verse about bad piping which uses canntaireachd phrases in an unusual manner:

    Nach gasda chuis-bhuirt
    A bhith cneatraich air urlar,
    Gun phrannadh air lutha,
      Gun siubhlaichean grinn,
    A'sparradh o-draochain
    An earball o-drochain,
    A'sparradh o-drochain
      An toin o-dro-bhi;
      Mal caol cam
      Le thaosg rann,
    Gaoth mar ghreann reota
    Throimh na tuill fhiara
    Nach dionaich na meoirean,
    Nach tuigear air doigh
      Ach o-theoin is o-thi.

('Is it not a fine laughing-stock to splutter away at a theme without playing of variation or lovely grace notes, ramming odraochan in the tail of odrochan, ramming odrochan up the rear of odrovi; a narrow crooked bag, half-full of slavers, a wind like the chill of frost through the squint holes that the fingers cannot cover, only ohon and ohi can be understood aright').

The poet goes on to describe the pipe's previous owners:

    Turraraich an dolais –
  Bha treis aig Iain Og dhith,
  Chosg i ribheidean connlaich
   Na chomhnadh le ni;
  Bha i corr is seachd bliadhna
  Aig mac Eachain 'g a riasladh
   Air slibh Chnoc-an-Lin;
   An fhiudhaidh shean
   Nach duisg gean,
  Ghnuis nach glan comhdach;
  'S mairg dh'am bu leannan
  A'chrannalach dhoinich,
   Chaite gran eorna.

('Melancholy rumbling – Iain Og had a spell of her [the pipe is feminine], she wasted as many straw reeds as would be a godsend to cattle; for more than seven years Hector's son had her, an apology for a mouthpiece, ill-using her on the slopes of Cnoc-an-Lin; the old wooden piece that gives no pleasure, the face with its dirty covering; woe to him who had the miserable wreck for a sweetheart, barley grain could be winnowed with all the wind that she needs').

Note the reference to straw reeds: boys in the remoter parts of the Highlands were still using these improvised reeds as late as the second half of the 20th century. It is likely that the straw in earlier times was from bere barley, no longer a common crop. Bere had a tough straw more suited for use as a pipe reed than modern straw would be.

Note also the use of the word *leannan* 'sweetheart' to denote the pipe, a common usage which must remind us of the title *MacCrimmon's Sweetheart*.

Another verse goes:

    Mu'n cuirear fo h-inneal
   Corr-bhinneach na glaodhaich
   'S inneadh air aodach
    Na dh'fheumas i shnath;
   Cha bheag a'chuis dheistinn
   Bhith 'g eisdeachd a gaoirich,
   Dheanadh i aognaidh
    An taobh a bhiodh blath;
    Riasladh phort,
    Sgriachail dhos
   Fhir an droch shaothair,
   Bheir i cheud eighe
   Ri seideadh a gaothair',

>Mar rongan ba caoile
>'S i faotainn a'bhais.

('Before the bawling light-headed slut [the pipe] can be put in working order, the amount of thread she needs would weave a cloth; no small cause of disgust it is to listen to her din, she would make your side cold where it was warm before; murder of tunes, screeching of drones of the poorly-employed fellow, she gives the first cry when her mouthpiece is blown into, like the rattle of a lean cow nearing death') – (William Matheson, *The Songs of John MacCodrum*, pp. 66-71).

The Donald Ban in this poem is not Donald Ban MacCrimmon for whom his brother made the great lament in 1745, but a local piper in Skye.

Professor Thomson says: 'We may look on the topic as a perennially popular one, taken up by bards of successive generations'. He traces the tradition back to early poems satirising bad harpers, including an Irish poem which uses some of the same wording as Niall Mor uses in his *Dispraise*. Several linguistic clues suggest that this type of poem may have originated in the Kintyre area, or in Islay, which may have had it direct from Ireland.

Some of the poems, especially the Dispraise works, are quite coarse and robust, even bawdy and obscene, with (more or less) witty invective, described as 'almost village poetry', scoring points on a personal level, often no more than crude abuse.

Niall Mor's *Dispraise of the Pipe* is not one of the more subtle attacks. It starts like this:

>Eatroman muice o ho,
>Air a sheideadh gu h-an-mhor,
>A'cheud mhala nach raibh binn
>Thainig o thus na dilinn.

('A pig's bladder, o ho, when blowing very greatly, the first bag was not harmonious from the very beginning').

>Bha seal re eatroman mhuc,
>Ga lionadh suas as gach pluic;
>Craiceann sean mhuilt 'na dhiaidh sin
>Re searbhadas is re durdail.

('There was a while with a pig's bladder, which was filled up from every cheek; the old skin of a wedder came after that with screech and buzzing').

>Cha raibh 'n uair sin anns a' phiob
>Ach siunnsar agus oan liop,
>Agus maide chumadh na fuinn
>Do'm [b'] cho-ainm an sumaire.

('At that time there was only a chanter on the pipe and one lip (mouthpiece), and a stick holding the tunes, which we call the drone').

Several verses of obscene abuse follow, and the poem ends with:

>Chuir Bhenus bha seal an Ifrinn
>Mar dhearbhachd sgeul gu fearaibh Dhomhain,
>Gur coranaich bhan is piob-ghleadhair

Da leannan ciuil cluas nan deomhan.

('Venus was for a time in hell, as proof of the story of the underworld, the keening of women at funerals and a clamorous pipe are the two most devilish sounds in existence').

This poem has been included to give an idea of the nature of some of these Dispraise poems, their crudity and their limited effectiveness. Even a trained poet of the calibre of Niall Mor was not able to make this type of poem acceptable as literature, and he abandoned the use of poetic, classical language in order to get down to the required level of obscenity. John MacCodrum, in the second half of the 18th century, made his Dispraise in more polished poetic language, and combined more wit and humour with a better knowledge of the pipe.

These Dispraise poems attacking the pipe in crude terminology are an interesting relic of the very old tradition of the pipe seen as a symbol of obscenity. This was common in England in the 16th and 17th centuries, where there was no tradition of serious, classical pipe music. There the pipers were classed with jugglers and acrobats as popular entertainers at fairs and such occasions, and they were open to mockery and bawdy comparisons. This was one reason why the Puritans wanted to suppress the pipes in England, with some success. In some parts, all that remains of the tradition is a silly giggle or a grin when the pipes are mentioned – and those who giggle no longer know why they do it.

It is interesting that even in the area where the serious classical music was probably created, this old tradition associated with the instrument was continued. We know that even serious pipers gave their pipes names with obscene undertones. The pipe was referred to in terms of femininity: being of the feminine gender in Gaelic, and having close contact with the piper's body, seems to have encouraged men to make the obvious comparison. Neil Munro, in his story *The Lost Pibroch*, spelled it out:

'He filled the bag at a breath and swung a lover's arm round about it. To those that know not the pipes, the feel of the bag in the oxter is a gaiety lost. The sweet round curve is like a girl's waist; it is friendly and warm in the crook of the elbow and against a man's side, and to press it is to bring laughing or tears'.

The 17th and 18th centuries were less cosy about it. The MacCrimmons had a famous pipe called the Oinseach, often translated innocuously as the Idiot, but Oinseach really means a half-witted female who squeals when you squeeze her. The MacRae pipers of Kintail had a pipe called Am Maighdean, the Virgin, and doubtless other equally suggestive names were found, around the country. This of course gave the Free Church good reason to attack the pipe, quite apart from the belief that music was the work of the devil anyway.

SOURCES
Derick Thomson, TGSI Vol IL, 1974
Gaelic Scotland
William Matheson, *The Poems of John MacCodrum*
Neil Munro, *The Lost Pibroch*

DUGALD CAMPBELL

THE POSITION OF PIPING IN Kintyre seems to have been strengthened in the second half of the 18th century by the presence of Dugald Campbell, once of Achrossan, later (after 1762) of Kintarbert.

Dugald's family belonged to Achrossan (also spelled Acharossan or Auchrossan), a small estate or farm on the east side of Loch Fyne, south of Strachur. He was a young soldier in an Independent Company in 1740, when some of these companies were amalgamated to form the Black Watch. Dugald was one of the original officers of the Black Watch, appearing on the first Muster Roll as an Ensign, in 1740.

By the time of the '45 he was a Captain. Promotion had to be bought with money, not merit, in those days, so his slow rate of preferment tells us that he was not wealthy. In 1746, after Culloden, when Jacobite fugitives were being rounded up on the west coast, 120 of the Argyll Militia were sent from Fort William, to join 80 regular soldiers under the command of the infamous Captain Fergussone of HMS *Furnace*. Dugald Campbell was seconded from the Black Watch to take command of the Argyll Militiamen, presumably because he was an Argyll man himself.

Dugald is credited with finding the Jacobite leader, Simon Fraser, Lord Lovat, who was hiding inside a large hollow tree in South Morar. Lovat at this time was over eighty, hugely obese and a sick man, suffering from the dropsy. He was pulled out of his hiding-place and put into a sedan (carrying-chair). As the soldiers carrying him set off at the run for the coast, where the prison-ship, the *Furnace*, was waiting, Dugald Campbell ordered the pipers to play *Lovat's March*, with which the old man 'seemed well pleas'd'.

Whether this order was given as a genuine tribute to Lovat, or as a mockery, we do not know. The Black Watch had special reason to hate Lovat, who had once commanded one of their Companies before he changed sides and unleashed his Fraser clansmen against them. Tribute or mockery, Lovat, who had the nerve to outface any insult, chose to take it in good faith. For all his faults, which were many, Lovat had a genuine love of pipe music, and was a good judge of piobaireachd. He had stipulated in his Will that all the pipers between Edinburgh and John O'Groats were to be invited to come and play at his funeral, all expenses paid. The invitation was never issued, since he was beheaded as a traitor.

On this occasion, he was not in the end taken away by HMS *Furnace*, either because he was too important a prisoner or on grounds of his age and illness (they would not want him to die on board, en route for London). Instead, he was taken overland to Fort Augustus, and later transferred south, to be imprisoned in the Tower of London, before his execution.

It is not certain what tune *Lovat's March* was. It may have been the 2/4 march now known as *Morar Sim* or *Morair Simi*, the Gaelic name for Lord Simon. Army tradition is that this March was composed to celebrate Lord Lovat's return from exile in 1719, but there is no hard evidence that it was known before 1800, though it could date from some time in the 18th century.

It seems more likely that *Lovat's March* was a piobaireachd work, possibly the tune which is called *Fraser's March* in the Campbell Canntaireachd manuscript of 1790. This work is not found elsewhere in any of the early collections, but Dugald Campbell knew it, and he knew his pipers could play it, in unison, and play it well enough to please old Lovat.

Who were these pipers with Dugald Campbell in 1746? There is a tradition that Donald Dubh Campbell, piper to the Duke of Argyll, was a piper to the Argyll Militia in the '45, and helped to round up Jacobite fugitives. He may well have been in Morar that day, and asked by Dugald Campbell to play.

John Gibson has suggested that the players might have been pipers brought by Dugald from the Black Watch, maybe his own personal pipers, maintained at his own expense. Another possibility is that they were pipers permanently attached to the Militia: certainly in the 1770s there were at least two Militia pipers based in Campbeltown, attached to the local force, then known as the West Fencible Regiment. It is perhaps less likely that this was the arrangement in 1746, but one thing is certain: there was no pipe band at this early date. Any regimental pipers had to be maintained by the officers. When Dugald gave orders to 'the pipers', there were probably only two of them.

There is confusion about the Argyll Militia regiments. When Donald MacDonald was described in 1811 as 'Pipe Major Argyleshire Militia Regiment', he was the newly appointed Pipe Major of a recently raised Militia Regiment which drew its men from any part of Argyll, but was stationed outside Edinburgh.

Limecraigs, where Dugald Campbell lived; he died there on New Year's Day 1788. The house was built in the early 18th century, and belonged to the Dukes of Argyll. Dugald was probably there by virtue of his position as the Duke's Chamberlain in Kintyre.

It was available for service anywhere in Britain, as required for the defence of the realm. Such Militia regiments were not intended for overseas service unless they themselves volunteered for it – and sometimes they did.

At the same time as the Argyleshire Militia was active, there was also a home defence regiment, the Local Volunteers, who were based locally for the defence of their own region. There seems to have been a local force, whether called the West Fencible Regiment or the Argyll Militia, permanently based in Campbeltown, and from about 1760 until his death in 1788, the commanding officer in Campbeltown seems to have been Dugald Campbell. His rank is uncertain, but as a local man and a veteran of the Black Watch, he was the obvious choice for the appointment. From the late 1770s, probably 1778, he was the Duke of Argyll's Chamberlain in Kintyre, and lived at the big house called Limecraigs, on the south side of Campbeltown. This residence probably went with the post of Chamberlain, though this is not certain. The house belonged to the Duke, and was sometimes used as a Dower House, for widows of the ducal family.

Dugald seems to have left the Black Watch in the late 1750s, when he was still known as Campbell of Achrossan. In 1761, Angus MacAlister of Loup was bankrupt, and his lands, which included Kintarbert, were sequestered and sold off. They were bought by his neighbour across West Loch Tarbert, Duncan MacMillan of Dunmore. The estate of Dunmore lies between Kilberry and Kintarbert.

In 1762, MacMillan separated the estates of Dunmore and Kintarbert, and sold Kintarbert on to Dugald Campbell. Dugald assumed the designation Campbell of Kintarbert, and became one of the Campbell gentry of Kintyre. A list of those of the landowners of Argyll who paid tax on their wheeled vehicles in 1785 includes Dugald Campbell of Kintarbert, paying duty on one two-wheeled carriage, which puts him quite low down in the hierarchy, but still indisputably a member of the Campbell gentry.

There was no big house on the Kintarbert estate, and this was fortunate for the piping world, as he made no attempt to build one, and seems to have remained in Campbeltown, where he was in the thick of local piping. Later generations of his family, notably his grandson Lachlan, lived in the mansion house of Saddell, beside Saddell Castle, on the east coast of Kintyre, but in Dugald's time that house belonged to another branch of the Campbells.

Duncan MacMillan of Dunmore, who had sold Kintarbert to Dugald Campbell, had a sister Geilis who eloped romantically with Hector MacNeill of Ardmeanish in the island of Gigha. These MacNeills were tenants of the farms of Drumdrishaig and Crear, to the north of Kilberry, and lived at Drumdrishaig. Hector's son, also called Hector, had the designation MacNeill of Drumdrishaig. He married Margaret Campbell, the youngest daughter of Dugald Campbell of Kintarbert, and their eldest son was born at Drumdrishaig in 1802, as plain Lachlan MacNeill. In later life he became Lachlan MacNeill Campbell of Kintarbert.

Lachlan's father, Hector MacNeill, was a Captain in the Royal Navy, and seems

Drumdrishaig, where Lachlan MacNeill Campbell of Kintarbert was born in 1802, as plain Lachlan MacNeill.

to have been a jolly fellow, kind to his elderly relatives and of a cheerful, generous disposition. A story is told of the days when he joined the Navy as a young Midshipman. When he left home, his mother, Geilis, gave him a Bible and made him promise to read a passage from it every day. When he came home on his first leave, she asked to see the Bible. She opened it, and showed him several banknotes she had put between the leaves. 'Oh, Hector, Hector' she said sorrowfully, 'I fear you did not keep your promise'. 'Oh, Mother' said Hector, full of contrition, 'I wish I had – I could have done with the money'.

Hector's kindly character comes through even in the dry legal documents in which he made sure his elderly aunts and female cousins were adequately provided for. In disposition he was unlike his Campbell connections, who had a mean, quite vindictive streak. Dugald showed himself to be a hard man, and in 1763, he was paid £1.7s.0d. for 'searching for, apprehending and committing to the Tolbooth of Campbeltown' two homeless Irish immigrants, whose only crime was homelessness. What to do with them next was the problem, solved by forcing them into the Royal Navy against their will. Dugald's grandson Lachlan inherited this hard streak, and proved to be a harsh landlord (see below).

Dugald Campbell had six children, three boys and three girls. Of the six, the only one who had sons was Margaret, the youngest. Her children were Lachlan (1802), Dugald (1807) and Isabella (1812). None of them married.

Dugald died at Limecraigs on New Year's Day, 1788, and his eldest son succeeded him as Campbell of Kintarbert. All three of his sons were in the army, and served abroad, but none of them had children. One of Dugald's daughters married Neil McGibbon, a prominent lawyer in Inveraray, but their children were all girls.

LACHLAN MACNEILL CAMPBELL OF KINTARBERT

Captain Hector MacNeill of Drumdrishaig (sometimes spelled Drumdrissaig or Drimdrissaig) married Margaret Campbell, youngest child of Dugald Campbell of Kintarbert. This was in 1801, and their elder son, Lachlan, was born the following year. He was born and brought up at Drumdrishaig, a farm on Loch Caolisport, a few miles to the north of Kilberry.

The farms of Drumdrishaig and Crear, close by, had been owned by the MacNeills until around 1700, when the Earl of Argyll made a deal with Hector MacNeill senior (Lachlan's grandfather) whereby the islands of Colonsay and Gigha were restored to the MacNeills, and the two farms in Knapdale reverted to the Campbells – but Hector continued to hold the two farms as tenant. He was designated MacNeill of Ardmeanish, on the island of Gigha, and it was his son Hector who took the name of Drumdrishaig.

When his father, Captain Hector, died in 1830, Lachlan became Lachlan MacNeill of Drumdrishaig. Eight years later, when the last of his three uncles died without an heir, Lachlan inherited his grandfather Dugald's estates, including Kintarbert, and immediately assumed his grandfather's surname, Campbell, becoming Lachlan MacNeill Campbell of Kintarbert. This carried with it the status of land-owner, as a member of the gentry of Argyll. He held two estates, Kintarbert and Saddell, the latter being on the east coast of Kintyre, with an ancient castle and a large mansion house. There Lachlan took up residence, and lost little time before making his presence felt.

He proved himself a harsh landlord. Between 1839 and 1848 he evicted 42 families from the Saddell estate – which was not densely populated – and he

Saddell House, near to Saddell Castle. Here Lachlan MacNeill Campbell lived after he inherited his grandfather's estates and designation.

brought a legal action against one of his tenants and a Campbeltown butcher, for the loss of a brown cow which was seen being driven away by a man, a woman and a small dog. The evidence was not conclusive, but the Sheriff was related to Lachlan, and the verdict was not in doubt: the accused had all their property sequestered and sold, before they were evicted and forced to emigrate, as they were now destitute. This cannot have endeared Lachlan to his tenants, but he may have been merely demonstrating his disciplinary qualities to his fellow landlords in Argyll.

As soon as he became a member of the Campbell landed gentry, Lachlan was appointed a judge at the national piping competitions in Edinburgh. He himself was a piper, which was unusual for one of the ruling classes. He had been a piper for many years, although it is not known who was his first teacher. It was not his grandfather, Dugald Campbell, who had died before he was born. He may have learned from one of the MacAlister pipers at Loup (see above), or possibly one of the MacMurchies taught him. There was an abundance of pipers in Knapdale and Kintyre during his boyhood.

Later, probably in the 1830s, he went to John MacKay, Raasay, for tuition. It is not known exactly when: John was in Eyre, in south Raasay, until 1823, when he moved to Drummond Castle. He left Drummond in 1830, and was given a house in Kyleakin, Skye, where he spent the rest of his life. It seems likely that it was at Kyleakin that Lachlan had his lessons. John MacKay died there in 1848.

Lachlan probably paid John generously for his tuition, and was rewarded, as were so many of John's patrons, by having a composition made and named for him. *Lachlan MacNeill Campbell of Kintarbert's Salute* appears in Angus MacKay's manuscript, dated 1836 in a note added in Angus's writing. At that time, however, Lachlan was still plain MacNeill of Drumdrishaig, so it would seem that the title was either changed or added in 1838, when Lachlan became Kintarbert. The work must have been composed at Kyleakin, which does suggest that that is where Lachlan was taught.

This Salute should not be confused with the work known as *Lachlan MacNeill Campbell of Kintarbert's Fancy*. This latter seems to be much older than the Salute, and may well have been nameless until it was taken up and played frequently by Lachlan. In the 1980s, Willie McCallum made it a favourite of his own, in similar style, and had it still been nameless then, it might be known today as *Willie McCallum's Fancy* (rather than *Lachie Thingie's Fancy*, as pipers tend to call it). We do not know who composed it, but it may be the work of one of the MacAlisters, or the MacMurchies, possibly Lachlan's own teacher.

Lachlan appears to have been a friend of John MacKay's son Angus. We deduce this from the existence of a bound volume of piobaireachd music, written out in Angus's own hand, apparently for presentation to Lachlan. It is indexed in both English and Gaelic, and bears a label on which is written: 'A rare and valuable Collection of Piobaireachd Music from Kintarbert', while another label on the back cover says: 'It is particularly desired that this Music Book be kept quite clean' and it is signed Cha(rles) Forbes, Broom Wood. Inside the back cover is the word 'Kintarbertt' (sic).

For a description of the Kintarbert manuscript by Roderick Cannon, see the Piping Times, July 1999 (available from the College of Piping, Glasgow).

This appears to be the manuscript copied by Duncan Campbell who was piper to Sir Charles Forbes of Newe, Aberdeenshire. The manuscript he copied was lost in the 1920s, but several careful copies of it had been made and were preserved (see Roderick Cannon, Preface to the Piobaireachd Society Collection, 1997).

The Kintarbert manuscript came to light in 1999 among several manuscripts of pipe music generously donated by Mrs Jessie MacLennan to the National Library of Scotland, after the death of her husband George. His father, G.S.MacLennan, may have inherited these manuscripts from his own father, Lt. John MacLennan, who served in the police forces of both Dundee and Edinburgh. It is not known how Lt. John came to acquire them.

Lachlan MacNeill Campbell's brother and heir, Dugald MacNeill, does not seem to have been a piper, and it was probably he who sold (or gave?) the manuscript volume to Sir Charles Forbes. The references on the book to 'Kintarbert' almost certainly refer to Dugald rather than to the estate, since neither of the brothers lived at Kintarbert (see above). It is unlikely that Lachlan himself would have parted with such a treasure in his own lifetime, as he was not short of money.

Sir Charles Forbes' piper, Duncan Campbell, was another pupil of John MacKay, Raasay, and a prize-winning player around 1835. He came from Foss, Loch Tummel, in Perthshire. When he had made a full copy of the entire manuscript, he then re-copied 61 tunes from it, perhaps for his own use.

As a member of the Campbell gentry of Argyll, Lachlan MacNeill Campbell became acceptable as a judge at the national competitions, though the upper echelons of society probably looked askance at his piping abilities. Just as they regarded any young man who danced well as a cad, the gentry would consider that being a good piper put him on a level with their servants. He judged at the competitions held every three years in Edinburgh as one of a large bench of some 15-20 judges, most of them drawn from the landed or titled classes, and many of them pretty ignorant of the music they were judging.

Lachlan was one of the few judges who were themselves pipers – Campbell of Kilberry said he was remembered in Argyll as a fine piobaireachd player – and he played both small music and Ceol Mor; from his contact with both John and Angus MacKay, he must have had an extensive knowledge of pipe music, and have met other pipers when he was at John MacKay's house. John was said to have more than 250 piobaireachd works in his memory, and never to mix them up. And his son Angus was an authority on both piobaireachd and light music.

Lachlan judged at Edinburgh in 1838 and 1841, and according to the Piobaireachd Society editors (Book 8), 'on other occasions, it is believed'. But he was not well, and by 1851, a doctor was resident in his house. Lachlan died at Saddell House in May 1852, a few weeks short of his 50th birthday. It is not known what his illness was, but it may have been tuberculosis, which did not discriminate between landlord and tenant, rich and poor. We know that Lachlan had been in poor health for some years, as James Robertson, writing his diary in Tobermory in January 1844, made a note: 'Captain Beatson says the drunken minister of Campbelltown is dead, and L.MacNeill Drumdrissaig is better'. Presumably Robertson continued to use Kintarbert's former designation after he had inherited the estate and taken the name of Campbell.

Lachlan was unmarried, and his brother Dugald succeeded to his estates of Saddell and Kintarbert. Dugald comes over as a gentler soul than his brother, perhaps inheriting his father Hector's kindlier nature. He did not take the name of Campbell, but was content to style himself Dugald MacNeill of Kintarbert. Some of his family called him MacNeill Campbell, but he did not favour this himself. He had followed his father into the Royal Navy, and like his brother, he never married. On his death in 1874, his sister Isabella inherited the estates, there being no male heir; she at once took the name of Campbell, and lived in some style at Saddell House, with a paid companion and a large household of servants, until her death in 1885. The estates passed to a Campbeltown merchant called MacLeod, who may have been a relative.

Lachlan, Dugald and Isabella are buried in a small chapel known as the Kilnaish Mausoleum (Gaelic Cill an Aonghais, Church of Angus). It lies on the north-west side of the road (B 8024) from Tarbert, Loch Fyne, to Kilberry, 200 metres northeast of the cottage of Kilnaish. Its OS reference number is NR 773614. The mausoleum which is now in a semi-ruinous state, is of 19th century construction, on the site of a church of early Christian origin.

Inscriptions, on plaques once fixed to the walls of the chapel, but now mostly on the ground, some of them broken, were recorded by Miss Marian Campbell of Kilberry, as follows:

1. HECTOR MACNEILL Esq of Drimdrissaig, died 30th March 1830, aged 76 (this was Captain Hector, Lachlan's father. Drimdrissaig is now spelled Drumdrishaig).
2. 'This and adjoining tablets to the memory of beloved parents and affectionate relatives was erected by Lachlan MacNeill Campbell Esq of Kintarbert and Dugald MacNeill Esq, his brother. 1845'.
3. LAUCHLAN MCNEILL CAMPBELL Esq of Kintarbert, died 2nd May 1852, aged 49.
4. MARGARET CAMPBELL, daughter of Dugald Campbell of Kintarbert . . . (illegible) . . and wife of Hector MacNell Esq of Drimdrissaig, died 12th May 18 . . in her 77th year (inscription partly illegible).
5. MALCOLM MACNEILL Esq, late of Jamaica, died Skipness 1815, and his sister, Miss MARY MACNEILL, died Campbeltown 1831. (It is not certain who these two were. They were of the same generation as Hector, 1. above, but do not seem to have been his brother and sister. Perhaps they were cousins).
6. ANN CAMPBELL, daughter of Duncan Campbell Esq of Sunderland (in Islay) and wife of Captain Duncan MacNeill, died 4th June 1778 in her 40th

Above: *Kilnaish Mausoleum, where Lachlan MacNeill Campbell of Kintarbert is buried, with other members of his family, is on the MacMillan estate of Dunmore. The two families were connected by marriage, and several MacMillans are also buried here. Lachlan died in 1852.*

Below: *Lachlan's plaque was one of several which fell from the wall and broke, but the incription is still legible, and there are plans to restore the building.*

year. (Duncan MacNeill was a brother of Hector, I. above)
7. JANET died 1766 3 months
   ROBERT 1769 23 months
   HECTOR 1770 10 months
   DUNCAN 1771 3 months
   HECTOR 1777 16 months
   (These infants were the children of Ann and Duncan MacNeill. Ann may have been passing on tubercular infection to her children in the womb. Babies were quite often born suffering from TB).
8. On a recumbent stone: round the edge 'Here lyes KATRINE BUCHANAN, spouse to Duncan MacMillan of Dunmore, who departed this life the fifth of March 1707 the 41 year of her age'. In the centre is an armorial shield, the initials DMM KB 1707, a skull and crossbones and other emblems.
9. On the walls are plaques in memory of Dugald MacNeill Campbell and his sister Isabella MacNeill Campbell, erected by MacLeod of Kintarbert in the 1880s.

The choice of the Kilnaish Mausoleum as the family burial place for the MacNeill Campbells is unexpected, as the chapel is on the MacMillan estate of Dunmore. It shows the strength of the links between the three families, MacNeill, Campbell and MacMillan, on the north side of West Loch Tarbert in the 18th and 19th centuries.

SOURCES
Stewart of Garth
Angus Martin
Wendy Wood
John Gibson
Sir James Fergussone
MacMillan history
Campbell papers
Marion Campbell
Murdo MacDonald, Archivist to Argyll and Bute Council, Lochgilphead
Angus Martin
Piobaireachd Society Book 8
Piping Times (R. Cannon)
Kintarbert MS
Will of Lachlan MacNeill Campbell

JOHN MACALISTER AND HIS DESCENDANTS

A distant relative of Dugald Campbell was a piper named John MacAlister. He was the son of the MacAlister piper to the laird of Loup, the laird being himself a MacAlister.

The MacAlister pipers' family descent is traditionally said to be the same as that

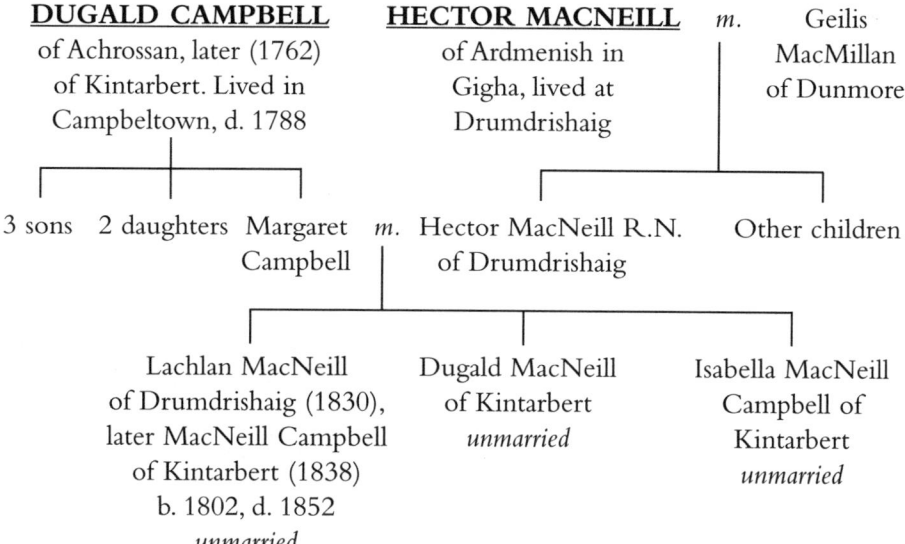

Family Tree of Lachlan MacNeill Campbell

of their laird, both able to trace their line back to the Clan Donald in Antrim, and before that, to the Lords of the Isles, based in Islay. If this tradition is genuine, the pipers were related to the Earls of Antrim, and to the Irish Earl Hugh O'Neill, prominent in the struggle against the English in the 1590s (see above).

The name of John MacAlister's father is not known, but the position of piper to Loup was heritable, and the pipers held the tenancy of the farm of Dunskeig, near Clachan, in North Kintyre. John was born at Dunskeig, probably around 1750; the exact date is not known, as the Register for Kilcalmonell Parish does not start until about 1780.

John had several brothers, two named in the Register as Angus and Duncan, and one somewhat dubious brother named in the Preface to Angus MacKay's collection as Donald, possibly a mistake for John. (The Preface was not written by Angus himself, and there are other mistakes in this section of it, e.g. it gives Joseph MacDonald's first name as John). There may well have been more brothers, and sisters, too: the Register for the 1780s is torn and fragmentary, difficult to read for the relevant period.

John went to Campbeltown, seeking a means to make a living. He was a piper, presumably taught by members of his family. He could not expect to take over as piper to Loup until his father died or relinquished the post, and meanwhile he had to live.

He put his skills to good use by becoming the Town Piper in Campbeltown; his duties would have been mainly on civic occasions, but his daily task was to play a curfew on the streets of the town every evening, to let the townsfolk know it was time to go to bed. But although John was an excellent piper, he was not reliable, being renowned for his heavy drinking. Around 1777, the burghers of

Campbeltown decided to instal a bell on the kirk, and do away with the position of Town Piper. Obviously it was cheaper to ring the bell for two minutes than to pay a man to play up and down all the streets for an hour – and John's unsteady habits must have made the decision easy.

So John was out of work, and he next appears in the records as a piper in the Militia, or West Fencible Regiment, the unit retained in Campbeltown for the defence of the district. The date of his joining is not known, but it was probably after 1777. He became 2nd Piper to the Militia, and Dugald Campbell was his commanding officer.

Right: *The tenancy of Dunskeig, a farm near the village of Clachan, in North Kintyre, went with the post of piper to MacAllister of Loup, who lived about a mile away. The position of piper was heritable, and the piping MacAllisters had probably held Dunskeig for several generations.*

Below: *The glen below the house at Dunskeig is fertile and sheltered, with access to the sea at its western end.*

The officers of the regiment were concerned that the 1st Piper, whose name we do not know, was not up to scratch, and John, the 2nd Piper, seemed to them a much better player. There was dissension, as some wanted to retain the 1st Piper as being dependable even though less talented, others advocating the promotion of the brilliant but unreliable John – and probably most of the officers were not at all certain of their own judgement of good piping.

The story is told in Peter MacIntosh's *History of Kintyre*, written nearly a hundred years later and drawing extensively on local oral tradition. He uses the terminology of his own time, referring to the 1st Piper as Pipe Major, which is not correct for the 1770s. There was a rank called Piper Major in one regiment, the Royal Scots, in the 18th century, but it was abandoned in 1764; it was in any case an officer's rank, comparable in some ways to Pipe President today, and a Piper Major was usually not himself a piper. MacIntosh uses Pipe Major simply to denote the 1st Piper.

The story as told by MacIntosh goes like this: the officers decided that a contest should be held to decide between the two pipers. 'They sent for Mac Cruiman, the chief piper of Scotland ' – this, if literally true, would have been Iain Dubh MacCrimmon, one of the two piping grandsons of Patrick Og (the other brother, Donald Ruadh, was in America at the time), but it is unlikely that they fetched Iain Dubh to Campbeltown.

We know there was a MacCrimmon piper living locally, listed in the Notices of Pipers as EY (HUGH) MALCOLM MacCRIMMON, 'late of Skye'. He died at Dalintober, Campbeltown, in 1822, and was born around 1737, so was probably in his forties at the time of the Militia contest. The Notices say 'it appears, from another source, that he was a piper', but does not name the source. It seems most likely that Ey Malcolm was the judge on this occasion. (Ey probably represents the Gaelic Aodh or Aoidh, which we now render as Hugh).

Peter MacIntosh goes on: 'A day was appointed, and a feast prepared, for the officers and for the great Mac Cruiman. McAlister was very fond of strong drink, so a sergeant was ordered to guard him lest he should get intoxicated; but a thirsty person is full of inventions, and McAlister managed to get half a pint of rough whisky, which he swallowed up rapidly, and became quite intoxicated so that he could not stand upright. The sergeant was affronted, and threatened to punish him, but McAlister held up his fingers, exclaiming 'Be not afraid, it is in the fingers, in the fingers, not the legs. Prop me up till I blow up my pipe, and then she will hold me up herself'.' (Pipes are always feminine in Gaelic, of course).

'The 1st Piper was then called to play in front of the house' (presumably Limecraigs), 'and then McAlister was called upon to play a piobaireachd, which he did, walking now quite steady. McCruiman said 'There is a piper, for the other man's music, I did not understand it at all'.'

So John MacAlister was made 1st Piper to the Militia in the late 1770s, replacing the man whose piping made no sense. It is interesting that this was the criterion used by MacCrimmon to judge the music – not whether the players made mistakes or went off the tune, but whether the interpretation made sense. Perhaps modern judging would benefit from this approach.

And with that rank, of 1st Piper to the West Fencible Regiment, John was sent to Falkirk in 1782, to compete in the big national competitions, newly started in order to encourage a revival of piping. The *History of Kintyre* says he 'went several times to Edinburgh in order to compete for the prize awarded to the best piper, but always returned unsuccessful in consequence of getting intoxicated on the day of the competition. At last his wife accompanied him, and by her great influence kept him from strong drink, and then he was successful . . .'

Peter MacIntosh was slightly obsessive about strong drink and intoxication, and his account cannot be right. For one thing, the early competitions were at Falkirk, not Edinburgh, and moved only later to Edinburgh; and they lasted three or four days, not one. And we know from the Preface to Angus MacKay's book that John won first place and was awarded the Prize Pipe at Falkirk in 1782, and that was only the second time the competitions had been held.

Once he had competed and come first, he could not enter again at Falkirk, as the rule was that an entrant could only improve his position. If he had come second, in future attempts only first place would be open to him, and once he had won the Prize Pipe, he could no longer enter. He had beaten the formidable MacGregor and MacArthur pipers that day in 1782, and had been declared the Foremost Piper of Scotland.

The following year he returned to Falkirk, to take part in a parade of all the competitors, past and present, to the churchyard; and the previous winners from the first three competitions played piobaireachd in unison among the gravestones.

One account says they played the *Lament for the Clans*, but another calls the same tune *Lament for the Children*. The Gaelic title for both of these is the same, *Cumha na Cloinne*, and it may be that the use of both translations is significant: was the work which we now call the *Lament for the Children*, for which title Angus MacKay supplied a suitable story – was this work made by Patrick Mor MacCrimmon under the name *Lament for the Clans*, not for the loss of his seven sons at all, but for the loss of 700 MacLeod clansmen and other Highlanders at the disastrous Battle of Worcester in 1651? Tradition has it that Patrick Mor was present at the battle, one of the few lucky enough to come home, and the lament may be the expression of his grief and feeling of survivor's guilt, in the aftermath. Sometimes Gaelic stories have a symbolic meaning (lost on most of us these days), and it is possible that Angus' story of Patrick losing seven of his eight sons was not meant to be taken literally but was a way of saying that the MacLeods lost seven-eighths of their clansmen at Worcester.

This recital in 1783 was not the first time that the Falkirk graveyard had echoed to the sound of piobaireachd played in unison. One of the graves there is that of Sir Robert Munro of Foulis, who was killed at the Battle of Falkirk in 1746. He had commanded a regiment of the government forces, who abandoned him when attacked by the Highland cavalry; he was cut down on the field of battle and left to die. Although he had fought against them, six Jacobite chiefs attended his funeral, and their six pipers played at the graveside a work said to have been called the *Lament for Munro of Foulis*. This is reckoned by some to be a setting of the work we now know as the *Lament for MacDonald of Kinlochmoidart*, a Jacobite leader who was cruelly executed in Carlisle after Culloden. It would seem that the composition, which we now have in two settings, was current in the mid -18th century, and was used at funerals, perhaps those of brave soldiers in particular.

As the pipers returned from Falkirk in 1783, 'many gentlemen' in Edinburgh thought it would be a good idea to hold a public entertainment in the form of an indoor competition to show off their skills – and that was the start of the Edinburgh competitions. At least, that is what we are told in what purports to be Angus MacKay's Preface to his Collection of Piobaireachd, written around 1838; but William Donaldson has shown that this Preface was probably written by James Logan, and is by no means the horse's mouth information we had supposed it to be. There is evidence elsewhere that there had been a great deal of ill-feeling about the judging at Falkirk that year, and many players said they would never go back there.

The Edinburgh competition or entertainment was held in Dunn's Assembly Rooms. In those days, preliminary heats were played, to weed out the poorer players and leave a hard core of finalists. John McAlister played *Cogadh no Sith*, War or Peace, presumably in the preliminary rounds, but did not win a place. Again, this account is refuted by William Donaldson, who quotes a contemporary letter which says that although John did turn up for the preliminary rounds (many did not), he was not able to play even one of the 28 tunes written out by John MacArthur and old Donald MacIntyre for the performers. The pipers appear to have been required to play from the script, and although Peter MacIntosh attributed John's failure to strong drink, it seems just as likely that he was unable to read the hand-written staff notation, having learned his piping entirely by ear.

Up to this time the format of competitions was that all the pipers played the same tune, each in his own setting, and the judges found this difficult to assess. The idea of having the music written down was to try to standardise it, and make the judges' task easier. The

Grave of Sir Robert Munro at Falkirk, where three pipers, including John MacAlister, played piobaireachd in unison in 1783.

writing of pipe music in staff notation was still very much in its infancy, and the crude attempts to write the music cannot have been easy to read, even for those players who were literate – and most were not. Things were made no easier by the fact that not only the pipers were affected by strong drink, but the judges and the committee were all intoxicated, too.

So the accounts conflict: Logan says John MacAlister played *Cogadh no Sith*, without success, while the contemporary account says he played nothing. This letter has a cryptic reference to John, calling him 'McAlister Finlay's Goad' – the meaning of this is unknown (John Finlay of Glasgow had been asked by the Highland Society to find them a suitable piper, and John MacArthur was given the post. The meaning of 'Goad' here is not clear). This time, in Edinburgh in 1783, John MacAlister was entered as Piper to MacAlister of Loup, and there is no mention of the Militia.

Around this time, he and his two brothers appear in the Parish Register for Kilcalmonell, listed for the first time as living at Dunskeig, near Clachan, in North Kintyre. It is about a mile from Loup, on the southern side of the entrance to West Loch Tarbert. It looks as if their father had died in the early 1780s, and the son or sons had taken over as piper(s) to Loup, with the tenancy of Dunskeig. It is not known if John's brothers were pipers, but it seems likely that they were. No more is recorded of John as a militiaman, and we have to assume that he peacefully drank himself to death at Dunskeig. No record of his death has survived.

He appeared twice in the Parish Register, as the father of two sons, Godfrey, born in 1788, and Ronald, 1790, both born at Dunskeig. There were almost certainly other children, but the Register is so fragmentary or illegible in the 1780s that their births cannot be traced. We do not know the names of John's mother or his wife, as that Register recorded only the names of the fathers of children brought for baptism and ignored the women.

John's younger son Ronald went to Campbeltown, as his father had done before him. He settled at Garvachy (or Garavachy), a poor upland farm in hill country about four miles south of Campbeltown, on the road over the hill to Southend. It is, or was, near the boundary between the parishes of Campbeltown and Southend. The name Garvachy appears in the Census records up to 1871, but had gone by 1881. It is marked on the OS two-and-a-half-inch maps, but not on the one-inch. The name is no longer used, and is barely remembered locally.

In the early 19th century, there was quite a community at Garvachy, where families eked out their meagre agricultural living by weaving. There are many references in the records to weavers at Garvachy, presumably weaving wool, mainly MacCallums and MacAlisters, who seem to have been there since the mid-1700s. When Ronald MacAlister went there from Dunskeig, he was probably joining relatives already established there.

Most of the Garvachy families were of Irish descent (see above), and they included, as well as MacCallums and MacAlisters, also MacMurchies, MacKays, MacMichalls, MacKerrals, MacNeills and MacQuilkans, many of them full of talent, both musical and poetic, and with a name locally for being a wild bunch of fighters and drinkers, what are known as 'hellers'. We are reminded of the MacLennans in the Black Isle in Easter Ross, who had the same combination of artistic talent and fieriness, and the same reputation. The families of Irish/Hebridean extraction in Kintyre intermarried extensively, and their lines of descent are interwoven like the serpent designs in a Celtic manuscript.

Ronald MacAlister from Dunskeig may have had a cousin of the same name, born in the same year, 1790, who married a girl called Janet Cordiner. It is not always easy to distinguish between these two Ronalds and their families. (I say 'may have had' because there are dark rumours of a bigamous marriage, and it is possible, though not proven, that the two Ronald MacAlisters were one man). The Dunskeig Ronald married Mary MacKerral of Garvachy – and it was one of her relations, probably her brother, who gave his occupation as 'musician' in the Register: he played the fiddle. Mary MacKerral, born in 1798, was the daughter of Malcolm MacKerral and Margaret MacGeachie.

Ronald and Mary had nine children: Margaret 1823, Janet 1824, twins Mary and Jean 1826, Ronald 1829, Malcolm 1831, Betsey 1833, Isabella 1835, and Agnes 1837. Four of the girls – Janet, Betsey and both of the twins – married MacCallums.

Twins were frequent in Campbeltown parish, and especially among the MacAlisters. The tendency was no doubt strengthened by the intermarriage of related families. Ronald's twin daughters, Mary and Jean (sometimes spelled Jane in the records) married MacCallums who were related to each other, and there had been marriages between members of the two families in the previous generation, so they were closely entwined.

The twin Jean MacAlister was married in 1852 to Neil MacCallum (born 1825), son of Neil MacCallum and Agnes Boyd. Neil senior was the son of Lachlan MacCallum and Jean Fleeming who belonged to one of the oldest Campbeltown families. The ten children of that marriage included James, born 1792, who in 1816 married Margaret MacDonald, daughter of Donald MacDonald the Edinburgh pipemaker and piobaireachd collector (see below).

WILLIAM MACCALLUM AND HIS DESCENDANTS

Jean's twin sister Mary married William MacCallum, and from this marriage is descended the entire line of great MacCallum pipers of the last two centuries. William was one of twelve children, including twins, born to Archie MacCallum and his wife Mary Ryburn. The Ryburns, like the Fleemings, were an old-established Campbeltown family.

We cannot trace the MacCallums in Campbeltown any earlier than 1725, but it is likely that they were originally from Ireland (see above).

William MacCallum and Mary MacAlister were married in 1851, and six children of the marriage are recorded, Mary 1852, Margaret 1857, Archibald 1860, William 1863, Malcolm 1867, and Ronald MacAlister MacCallum 1854. This eldest son was the grandfather of Hugh MacCallum and taught Hugh his piping.

He was the first of the two famous Pipe Majors called Ronnie MacCallum. His children were another Ronald MacAlister MacCallum born in 1880, Hugh 1882, Archie 1883, Marion 1886, William 1880. William, who married a MacMurchie, was the father of Hugh MacCallum.

Hugh MacCallum, his nephew Willie, and his kinsmen Ronnie MacShannon and Stuart Liddell, are only four of the many fine pipers who are direct linear descendants of the Foremost Piper of Scotland in 1782, John MacAlister; and, going further back, they may be descended from the MacDonald Lords of the Isles, and may have the blood of the Earls of Antrim in their veins (see above).

ARCHIE DUNCAN, born in Campbeltown in 1909, served in the Royal Scots Fusiliers as pipe corporal, from 1929 to 1936, and returned to serve throughout the Second World War. He later became ill, and was under the care of Mr William Sillar, an orthopaedic surgeon in Glasgow. In tribute to him, Archie composed in 1970 a 12/8 March *William Sillar, FRCS*.

Archie was an uncle of Ronnie MacShannon, and in 1973, he composed a Retreat March *Ronald MacShannon*, to honour one of the family's many fine young pipers. He similarly commemorated Hugh MacCallum (see below). Other works by Archie Duncan include:
Armstrong's Welcome 4/4 M 4
The Dhorlin 9/8 RM 4 (The title refers to a shingle bar of land connecting Davaar Island to the mainland, at the mouth of Campbeltown Loch).

THE MACMURCHIES

BOTH OF RONALD MACALISTER'S SONS at Garvachy married girls called MacMurchie or MacMurchy. Other spellings of this name include MacMurtie, MacMurphy and even Currie (see above), and opinions differ about the pronunciation of the 'ch' in MacMurchy: some of that name say MacMurchy with the ch as in 'church', others use the Gaelic ch as in 'loch'. Keith Sanger thinks the name may be a variant of MacMhuirich, the name of a line of famous bards in Argyll. There are many instances of marriages between MacMurchies and MacCallums – Hugh MacCallum's own mother was a MacMurchie.

The MacMurchies were a family of great talent from way back, celebrated as pipers, poets and harpers in Kintyre. One of them, William MacMurchy, was piper to MacDonald of Largie in 1745, and he was well-known as a Gaelic poet and as a harper. He made a collection of Gaelic poetry, his own and that of other bards, and is said to have written down piobaireachd music, as well as the harp music of his time. We do not know whether this would have been in the form of canntaireachd vocables (in words), or whether he was using staff notation. His musical manuscripts have been lost, though his Gaelic poetry has been preserved; this may suggest that the music was in canntaireachd vocables which would look like gibberish to a non-piper and would perhaps be more likely to be thrown away.

As William MacMurchie died in the 1770s, he must have been one of the pioneers in the writing of pipe music: none had yet been published, although the young Joseph MacDonald, on his way to India in 1762 had written his *Compleat Theory*, and his brother Patrick was soon (1784) to publish his book of *Highland Airs*, with four piobaireachd works in staff notation, transposed as for the violin. William MacMurchie presumably knew nothing of these, and so, we assume, had no model, any more than Joseph and Patrick had, and, just as they did, would have had to work out a system for himself.

Around 1790, Colin Campbell wrote the Campbell Canntaireachd manuscript of some 169 piobaireachd works in canntaireachd vocables, surviving in the two volumes of a possible three. This may have been part of a movement in Argyll to record and preserve the traditions of pipe music. It is clear that William MacMurchie was a man of the highest intelligence and full of initiative. Keith Sanger, who is the authority on the MacMurchies, thinks that William may have been the piping teacher of John MacAlister – after his father.

MacMurchies were living at Garvachy in the early 1800s, and their musical genes went into the MacCallum blood, along with those of the MacAlisters.

In the late 1890s, when the young Archibald Campbell of Kilberry was waiting to hear if he was to go out to India to further his legal career, he amused himself by forming a small local pipe-band at Kilberry. The pipers he recruited included three MacMillan brothers, one of them Angus MacMillan from Lergnahensian, two miles to the south-east of Kilberry, close to Dunmore; he had been piper to the Dowager Duchess of Argyll, and was an excellent player of light music. His brother Neil was described by Kilberry as 'a country player', and the third brother, Duncan MacMillan, also joined the band. These MacMillans had links with South Uist, their grandfather having been born there. Another piper was Sandy MacNeill, coachman and chauffeur at Kilberry, a 'good orthodox player of MSR and a competent fiddler' said Kilberry. His daughter married a cousin of R.U.Brown, Balmoral.

Another of Kilberry's players was John Carruthers, 'a good player on the right shoulder'. He was a brother-in-law of John MacColl, and the son of the farm manager at Kilberry. And there was a John McFater, who lived a mile to the north of Kilberry, described as 'a very gifted player for dancing, with thoroughly unorthodox fingering' – does this mean he played the so-called redundant A in his Taorluath movements? Or was it an open C that offended Kilberry? John McFater's mother was one of the MacAlisters of Dunskeig, presumably descended from John MacAlister, the 1782 Prize Pipe winner, or from one of his brothers (see above).

Later, a piper called John MacMurphy (a corruption of MacMurchie) joined the band, but Kilberry said he was 'conspicuous for his inability to step along with the rest', that is, he could not march while playing, and had to be drilled into shape for the march to the bonfire marking the Queen's Jubilee. All went well on the day, to Kilberry's surprise, but he soon found out why: 'John MacMurphy had been walking along with his pipes under his arm, because by a special intervention of providence his reeds had slipped into the bag as soon as we started'.

At New Year, the band was sometimes supplemented by 'the likes of John MacColl', as Kilberry put it – if John MacColl can be said to have had a like. No doubt he was visiting his wife's people at Kilberry Farm for New Year.

This small, local, short-lived band gives us a glimpse of the piping talent available in an area of very few square miles, way out in the country in Argyll, at the end of that century. These MacNeill, MacMillan and MacMurchie pipers were all connected to the MacCallums and MacAlisters in Campbeltown.

Kilberry Pipe Band, raised by Archibald Campbell in 1898. The pipers are, left to right: John McFater, whose mother was of the piping MacAlisters of Dunskeig; John Black; Angus MacMillan; John Carruthers, brother-in-law to John MacColl; Neil MacMillan; Sandy MacNeill. Seated is Archibald Campbell himself.
(PHOTOGRAPH BY KIND PERMISSION OF THE COLLEGE OF PIPING)

DONALD MACLEAN

IN 1790, A PIPER FROM Campbeltown, Donald MacLean, decribed as being 'from Kintyre', competed in the big national competitions in Edinburgh, and won third place, playing what Angus MacKay (or James Logan) recorded as '*A Favourite Piece*'. This was the old name, used by English speakers, for what is now called *MacCrimmon's Sweetheart*; it has always been called *Maol Donn* in Gaelic, though no-one is entirely sure what this means. Until about 1850, or a little earlier, the name *A Favourite Piece* seems to have been used by English-speakers when it was played in competitions, but even today, many non-Gaelic-speaking pipers continue to call it *Maol Donn*. It has been claimed that it was originally a Kintyre tune, with no connection to the MacCrimmons at all.

Five years after gaining third place in Edinburgh, Donald MacLean again featured in the prize list, coming second in 1795. He seems to have been offered the position of Piper to the Highland Society of Scotland in 1798 – if indeed this is the same Donald MacLean, which is not entirely certain – and he held the post for the next 35 years, until his death in 1833. In 1798, his son, also Donald MacLean, came third at Edinburgh, playing as a boy piper in the adult competition. He was thirteen years old.

Donald MacLean (senior) was married to Mary MacCallum, a great-aunt of the William MacCallum who married the twin Mary MacAlister (see above). Donald's genes went into the MacCallum line.

We do not know where or how Donald MacLean learned his piping, but when he was a boy, Dugald Campbell was living in Campbeltown, and it may well have been through him that Donald's talent was fostered. The MacAlisters and the MacMurchies may have taught him. We just do not know. Very little is known of the organising of piping tuition, other than boys being taught by their fathers, uncles or grandfathers; in a few cases we hear of a promising young piper being sent by his laird or chief to a piping 'school' or 'college', such as those of the MacCrimmons, MacArthurs, Rankins or MacDougalls – and sent sometimes from considerable distances, and at some expense.

A piping school was not an educational establishment as we would use the term today. It would not have a building or organisation of teachers; tuition was in the instructor's own home, and it was a 'school' only in the sense that he might be teaching a group of pupils in a class together, and they would be resident with him, or living locally, for several weeks, months or even years, at a time. There is no evidence of such a school in Kintyre, and we have to assume that a piper like John MacAlister learned first from his family, then from whoever was available, possibly William MacMurchie.

DONALD MACDONALD

IN 1811, THE SECOND PRIZE at Edinburgh went to Donald MacDonald from Skye, described as 'Pipe Major Argyleshire Militia'. That year, three of the five prize-winners were militiamen, and these were not from the local militia regiments but from the forces mobilised all over the country against the threat of invasion by Napoleon Bonaparte. These regiments were locally recruited, but were stationed anywhere in Britain as needed, and the Argyleshire Militia in 1811 were near Edinburgh.

Donald MacDonald, born in Glenhinnisdale, in North Skye, was taught his piping by the MacArthurs, probably in Edinburgh. He later published his well-known *Collection of Ancient Piobaireachd* (1820). He had been in the Caithness and Rothesay Volunteers, which had been disbanded in 1802. He had set up as a pipe-maker in Edinburgh, and when the Argyleshire Militia Regiment was re-formed in 1811 and stationed in Lothian, outside Edinburgh, he was well-placed to accept an appointment as their new Pipe Major. He seems to have relinquished the position to his son John in 1816, but continued in the regiment as a Piper. In 1817 he advertised his piping Tutor, describing himself as 'late Pipe Major' of the Militia Regiment, and that same year he competed as 'Piper, Argyleshire Militia Regiment' – and won the Prize Pipe.

In May 1816, a girl called Margaret MacDonald, described in the Register as Donald's daughter, married James MacCallum, one of the Garvachy MacCallums. Both are described in the Campbeltown Register as being 'of this Parish'. It has recently (2004) been discovered that Donald was living in Campbeltown, some time between 1802 and 1811.

There is a record of a daughter of Donald MacDonald living in Edinburgh as a widow after her father's death, and it seems that she and her unnamed widowed sister were then in need of financial help. Margaret may be this missing sister; she married in 1816, and her daughter Mary was born in Campbeltown in October 1817. After that, all three, James, Margaret and Mary, disappear entirely from the records.

James was described in the Register as a 'seaman'. At this period a distinction was made between a seaman and a fisherman, and between a seaman and a Royal Navy sailor. So it looks as if James was a merchant-seaman, possibly working on a ferry or cargo boat plying between Campbeltown and Glasgow, or up the west coast. Or perhaps he was on an ocean-going vessel, and away from home for long periods. In those circumstances, his wife Margaret might well have joined her family in Edinburgh – or she may have gone there after her husband's death. We do not know when or where he died.

James was an uncle of Neil MacCallum who married Jean, one of the twin daughters of Ronald MacAlister (see above), so he was a collateral ancestor of the MacCallum pipers. It cannot be claimed that the blood of Donald MacDonald is in the MacCallum line, but Donald is there in the family tree, along with Donald MacLean and John MacAlister. The MacCallum family seems to have had more than its share of top-class pipers, related by blood or by marriage.

In the 1820s a piper named Donald MacMichall appears in the Register, giving his occupation as 'piper' with no indication of what sort of piper, military or otherwise. He was a son of John MacMichall and Katherine MacArthur, of Garvachy, and he married Mary MacAlister, daughter of Ronald MacAlister of Garvachy, probably the cousin of Ronald from Dunskeig. Donald MacMichall had three sons and a daughter; it is not on record whether any of them was a piper, but it seems likely enough.

The Taylors from Skipness were well-known in Kintyre for their piping, and founded another piping dynasty. They, too, married into the MacCallums, and were associated with the Wilsons, an important piping influence in the district as players, and especially as teachers. The Wilsons were related to John MacColl, Oban, and the Carruthers family, and John M. MacKenzie learned his piping from the Wilsons (see below). They, too, married into the MacCallums.

An Irish family, the MacQuilkans, also married into the MacCallums, bringing with them their piping genes and a wealth of talent in all kinds of music.

The MacPhedrans from Knapdale, who had connections with John Ban MacKenzie in Ross-shire (see below) and were good pipers in their own right, married into the MacCallums, but this was quite early, in 1815 and earlier, before the MacKenzies married into the MacPhedrans, so none of John Ban's family genes are in the MacCallum blood.

It is clear that the MacCallum pipers in Campbeltown had piping genes from many sources. Close contact with the MacAlisters in particular was greatly to their benefit, and their Hebridean/ Antrim descent from the Lords of the Isles must have brought with it talent in music and poetry. It can be no surprise that a family with such a heritage has produced so many first-class pipers.

The MacAlister piping link was continued in 1844, when John Thomson, piper to Alexander MacAlister of Loup and Torrisdale, competed in the last of the Edinburgh competitions and was placed fifth, playing the *Lament for Donald Ban MacCrimmon*. We assume that John was a forebear of the piping Thomsons of Campbeltown (see below).

SOURCES
OPR Kilcalmonell, Campbeltown, Killean, Skipness, Gigha
Census Campbeltown, Kilcalmonell
J. Michael Hill
Peter MacIntosh
Highland Society Records
Angus MacKay / James Logan
William Donaldson
Geoff B. Bailey
Angus Martin
Keith Sanger
Hugh MacCallum
Roderick Cannon (edition of Joseph MacDonald's *Compleat Theory*))
Piping Times (Kilberry's Band)
MacMillan History
Notices of Pipers

HUGH MACCALLUM

LISTING HUGH MACCALLUM'S ACHIEVEMENTS BECOMES tedious, a seemingly endless litany of awards and dates, but what an impressive career lies behind the dry figures. He won the Gold Medal at Inverness in 1967, following it up with the Gold Clasp in 1972, 74, 77 and 85. The Gold at Oban in 1972 led to innumerable awards of the Senior Open Piobaireachd – playing in Argyll seemed to relax him, and his performance of the *Lament for Hugh* in particular is still mentioned with admiration. It also won him the championship at the Glenfiddich competition in 1978. Since his retirement to the bench, where

Above: Hugh MacCallum in his heyday, competing in Skye in the 1960s, in front of judges Angus MacPherson and D.R.MacLennan. (PHOTOGRAPH BY COURTESY OF THE COLLEGE OF PIPING)

Left: Hugh MacCallum

he is a respected judge, his mantle has fallen on his nephew and pupil, Willie MacCallum.

Archie Duncan made a 9/8 Retreat March in 2 parts, called *Hugh A. MacCallum*.

In 1998, Hugh was the speaker at one of the lunchtime lectures run by the University of Strathclyde in the Ramshorn Theatre, Glasgow. His subject was 'The Development of the Competition March', and he played his own illustrations. Ian K. Murray was there, and remarked that Hugh succeeded in 'holding the interest of an audience comprising both the knowledgeable and the curious.'

Ian Murray went on: 'The development of the march was traced from the time when Scottish Regiments required to have music to march to on the first proper roads – they adapted songs, airs and dance music – through Angus MacKay's transformation of *Miss Forbes, Farewell to Banff* into the significantly more demanding *Duke of Roxburgh's Farewell to the Blackmount Forest*, Hugh MacKay's influence on the composition of the march (*Crags of Stirling, Charles Edward Hope de Vere,* etc.), Donald Cameron's eclectic approach to composition, the impact on competitions of William MacLennan who died at the age of 32 but achieved fame as an artist, architect, piper and dancer in his short life, John MacColl, without whose compositions the repertoire would be markedly poorer, down to Donald MacLeod who showed that even with nine notes it was still possible to create fresh melodic marches.

'Hugh also mentioned many other composers some of whom composed only one or two marches but which are still played to this day and made special reference to G.S.MacLennan who, according to some competitors of the time including John MacColl, over-embellished his tunes. Three memorable points were made by Hugh: – that when the march was first developed it was seen by piobaireachd players as pop music; that at one time the playing of 2/4 marches had become such a craze that it was seen as threatening the playing of piobaireachd; and thirdly that the tempo of march playing had increased over the years (G.S. MacLennan and Willie Ross played a part in this) but in recent times there had been a noticeable deceleration in the tempo. The audience at the Ramshorn were invited to time Hugh's playing which resulted in a calculation of 68-73 beats per minute depending on the tune played.

'Hugh played a wide selection of marches. His playing on an instrument you would die for was, as it always was, unflamboyant but beautifully crafted. I found *Inverlochy Castle* and *Dr E.G.MacKinnon* particularly attractive . . .'

It is not often that a player of Hugh MacCallum's standing will speak in public with such knowledge, thought and authority, and his opinions always command respect. His talk was clearly enjoyed thoroughly by those with the experience to appreciate its value.

Hugh holds a special place in piping legend: it is said that when a suspect was arrested after the lifting of the Stone of Destiny from Westminster Abbey and imprisoned in Saughton Gaol, Edinburgh, Hugh went to stand outside the prison gates. There he played the piobaireachd *The Unjust Incarceration*, as his personal protest.

PETER CAMPBELL

AN EDICT OF EXECUTRY ISSUED in 1812 names Angus Campbell, a sailor in Greenock, as executor to his late brother, Peter Campbell, piper in Kintyre, 'who lived at High Aird, Saddell', which is corrected to 'in Carradell'. Nothing else is known of Peter, but it is clear that piping was his occupation, not merely his hobby. *[I am indebted to Angus Martin for this reference, taken from the records of the Commissary Court of Argyll, Bigwood, p.453]*

PETER REID

THE MAIN SOURCE OF INFORMATION about Peter Reid is the Notices of Pipers. We have to assume that this passage was written by the original compiler of the Notices, Lt John MacLennan (father of G.S.MacLennan);

he was a younger contemporary of Peter Reid, and probably knew him in Edinburgh and Leith. He wrote:

'Peter Reid 1801-1881. A native of Campbeltown, where he was well educated. Was a very melodious piper. He became clerk to Bailie MacPhie in Leith, and on the landing of King George IV on his memorable visit to Scotland, Reid, R.W. Hume and John Wood played on Leith Pier while the King was landing, at 12 noon, on 15 August 1822. They then played up to the King's Park and at the grand procession to Holyrood Palace.

'From the nature of his employment, Mr Reid did not compete at all, but he left a large MS of music from which we can learn he had a firm grasp of the subject. He was a well formed man, of a pleasant temperament and kindly disposition. He often officiated as judge at Highland Gatherings, and his decisions were always looked upon as thoroughly satisfactory. He died in Glasgow, and his remains are interred in Sighthill cemetery'.

It is not clear where he received his education; if it was indeed in Campbeltown, he cannot have been better educated than his local contemporaries, though he may have made better use of his instruction. We know from his death certificate that his father was a 'crofter master', and there can have been no question of a private education. It is not thought that he attended university or college, but went into the commercial world at an early age, after leaving Kintyre to become a clerk in Leith.

'From the nature of his employment' probably means simply that he worked a six-day week, and was thus prevented from competing on Saturdays or weekdays, and of course no competitions were held on Sundays. Many competing pipers were employed on big estates whose proprietors maintained pipers and entered them for competitions, in order to increase their own prestige. These pipers were not only given time off to go to the Games or the big national competitions, but were equipped by their employers with full Highland gear, including good pipes, and given financial backing for their travels. This was denied to players such as Reid, and unless they were men of leisure, with ample wealth of their own, as well as time to spare, they could not compete. By the time Reid had risen far enough up the tree to be able to have his Saturdays to himself, he would have been too old to compete, and became a judge instead. The big Edinburgh competitions were ended in 1845, and Reid would have been judging at the Highland Games within reach of his home in Glasgow.

He was known to pipers such as Angus MacKay and Lt John as 'Mr Reid', a designation normally reserved for the gentry. Possibly he earned this respect when he became a judge: most piping judges were drawn from the gentry, more for their social status than for their piping knowledge (see below).

From the 1820s on, Highland Gatherings were being established. William Donaldson (pp.89,97) indicates that the earliest were within travelling distance of Glasgow or Edinburgh, held at St Fillans, Dunkeld, Stirling and Strathearn. The judges for these Games may have been appointed by the Highland Society of London or Scotland, from the ranks of the well-to-do and the educated.

Roderick Cannon, in his General Preface to the Piobaireachd Society Collection, says that Peter Reid 'is said to have judged frequently at the annual piobaireachd competition in Edinburgh', but this may be a misinterpretation of Lt John's words. There is little doubt that the judges at the Edinburgh competitions came from a higher social caste than the middle class to which Peter Reid had climbed after leaving Kintyre. In *The Highland Bagpipe and its Music*, Cannon suggests that Reid was one of the few middle-class judges at the Edinburgh competition, the very beginning of a softening of the official attitude towards judges, but this seems unlikely, in the light of Lachlan MacNeill's experience.

Lachlan's experience seems clear enough: he was another fine amateur player, knowledgeable about piobaireachd, as was Reid, and he was of considerably better family than Reid. His father was a MacNeill of Gigha, his grandfather Campbell of Kintarbert, but he was excluded from the bench at Edinburgh until he himself inherited an estate and joined the ranks of the landed gentry of Argyll. Until 1838, Lachlan MacNeill of Drumdrishaig, a pupil of John MacKay and a friend of Angus MacKay, was not considered qualified to judge at the highest level, because his designation 'of Drumdrishaig' denoted the tenancy of a farm, not ownership of an estate. But when he inherited Kintarbert from his uncle and added Campbell to his name, he was appointed to the bench, and he judged in Edinburgh in the late 1830s and at the last of the Edinburgh competitions.

Peter Reid was not a landed proprietor but a crofter's son , and in Leith and Glasgow he belonged to the world of trade. Yet in Robert Mudie's contemporary description of the King's visit in 1822, Reid is described as 'a young man, the son of a gentleman', which could hardly be more specific. He may have had influential connections in Leith.

He seems to have been friendly with Donald MacDonald who was a pipemaker in Edinburgh, winner of the Prize Pipe, and compiler of a Collection similar to Reid's own. Reid may also have known John Ban MacKenzie and his son Donald, both of them outstanding pipers who visited Edinburgh to compete (see below). From Angus MacKay's references to 'Mr Reid', it seems that Angus knew him, too. These friendships, dangerous in the eyes of the Highland Society of London, might well have kept Peter Reid out of the judging world, as the Societies feared the increasing influence of the pipers, and would not have welcomed an alliance between them and an intelligent, educated, influential man from outside the upper classes.

Peter's death certificate in 1881 tells us that he had been a carpet manufacturer, and that he was living in Kersland Street, Hillhead, which in the 1880s was a district of well-to-do families, in the west end of Glasgow. Wealthy he may have been, but by Victorian standards not out of the top drawer: he might fairly be described as a Captain of Industry, certainly the product of his age in which a crofter's son could come to the big city and make his fortune – but he could not penetrate the closed world of the hereditary landowners.

The appointment of judges at Highland Games, as opposed to the big national competitions, was presumably not so rigorously controlled, and Peter Reid's reputation for scrupulous fairness made him a rare bird indeed, at any competition.

He must have established a reputation as a player at an early age, since he was only 21 when the royal visit had him piping the King ashore at Leith. Robert Mudie's account of the great day said:

'The royal barge now passed the pier-head, where three young men, the sons of gentlemen in Leith, struck up some national airs on the great Scots bagpipe; which gave a national note to those demonstrations of welcome and joy that seemed to have delighted his Majesty'.

The party of Personages from Edinburgh and Leith who were in the welcoming party to greet the King waited for his arrival in 'Mr Reid's bookshop' on the Leith quay-side. This business combined a bookshop with a lending library, and it is clear that the proprietor, from his designation as 'Mr', was regarded as a man of some standing. Was he a relative of Peter? It seems very likely.

We do not know when Peter left Campbeltown. It is possible that he was sent as a boy to Leith, and he may have been brought up, at least partially, by Mr Reid of the bookshop. Nor is the length of Peter's employment by MacFie & Co., Leith, known, but by 1826 he was in Glasgow, where eventually he owned his own firm of carpet makers. This was the time when Turkey Red helped to make Glasgow prosperous, and doubtless Reid's factory was part of that prosperity.

Born in 1801, Peter probably learned his piping before he left Campbeltown for Leith. His teacher may have been one of the MacAlisters, or possibly Donald MacLean, who later became piper to the Highland Society of Scotland, and had a boy of his own to teach.

Before Peter had moved to Leith, he would have had contact with Donald MacDonald, the Edinburgh pipemaker and competing piper, and he may have had lessons from him. Donald had been living in Campbeltown, and in 1816 his daughter married James MacCallum there: who knows, perhaps Peter attended her wedding, when he was fifteen.

Peter Reid put a date to his manuscript of pipe music, writing 'Glasgow 1826' on it, but he must have been compiling it for some time before that. He was then 25 years old, and we have to assume that at least some of the unusual settings he gives were learned by him in his Campbeltown years, so that they reflect the music played in Kintyre before the 1820s.

His collection is now MS 22108 in the National Library of Scotland, in Edinburgh. The manuscript is bound with a copy of Donald MacDonald's published collection which it appears to complement, as not many of the tunes in that collection are repeated in Reid's. Also included in the same binding is a collection of poems and songs.

The manuscript seems to have been known to some of the earlier editors of the Piobaireachd Society Books, who made notes on parts of it before returning it to its owner, presumably a member of the Reid family. It was then 'lost' until in 1970 it re-appeared, and the then editor, Archie Kenneth published this note in Book 13:

'Thanks to the generosity and initiative of Dr. Stewart Carslaw – a direct descendant of Peter Reid – this long-lost manuscript has been made available to the editors, and it proves to be of considerably more interest and importance than previous statements had suggested. Several questions are raised by the contents of this collection, as many of his settings are radically different from those of Angus MacKay and Donald MacDonald, or indeed from those known to occur in any other record. Perhaps the most obvious query is – What was his source, and whose teaching do these settings represent? They are often of distinct musical merit.

'Apart from these distinct settings of tunes known elsewhere, the manuscript contains one complete tune and two Urlars not known elsewhere; and rather interestingly it and the Campbell Canntaireachd alone record 'the *MacNabs Gathering*' and they both contain the same extra beat, the settings being practically identical. There is nothing else in the manuscript to suggest a common source with the Canntaireachd.

'A close study of the work shows that the Editorial Notes to certain tunes previously published in this series do not always describe Reid's settings accurately. It is hoped that this can be remedied in the course of reprinting the relevant books.

'As well as the musical content of his manuscript, Peter Reid has included a large quantity of light verse and quotations from Scott and other sources such as MacPherson's *Ossian*.

'The light verse appears to be contemporary and probably in part of his own authorship. In this section of the manuscript there are frequent references to John Bain, or Iain Ban – there is a poem in Gaelic – and it appears at least possible that the man referred to is John Bain MacKenzie. The date of the work (c.1820) is consistent with this hypothesis as is the content of at least one of the poems, one verse of which runs as follows -

> 'John Bain – John Bain- come oft- come fast
> Ere life's tree lose its fleeting leaves -
> On thy wind pipe blow its farewell blast
> And thy honoured frame the meeting leaves'.

'Assuming the identity of John Bain with John Bain MacKenzie, this certainly indicates that Peter Reid was on close terms with him at the time the manuscript was being written. It may be that some of these very distinct settings represent the versions played by John Bain MacKenzie'.

The verse is puzzling: it seems to refer to Reid's fears that John Ban was about to fall off his perch, or as he puts it, leave the meeting, as if John Ban was an old old man – yet Reid was only five years his junior. It seems likely that John Ban would not have been flattered (if indeed that is what it is saying).

In the General Preface to the Piobaireachd Society Collection, Roderick Cannon says (p.11):

'Several of the tunes in the early part of the MS have a note indicating that they were played by a particular piper to win a prize in the competition, and one of them is from Donald MacDonald, who won the prize pipe in 1817. The style of music writing in the MS is very close to that of Donald MacDonald.

'This MS was apparently not known to General C.S. Thomason until fairly late in his work, and several of the tunes in it are not included in *Ceol Mor*. It came to light in time for him to include Reid's version of '*The Laird of Contullich's Lament*' in the revised version of *Ceol Mor* . . .' (this composition is apparently another setting of the *Lament for MacDonald of Sanda* – see above).

Peter Reid's background was Campbeltown. He was born there on December 8th 1801, ninth of the eleven children of Hugh Reid (or Reed) and his wife Janet Longwill. Three of his elder siblings had died in infancy. Hugh was described as a 'crofter master' on Peter's death certificate, but the meaning of this is not clear. 'Master' may mean simply that he employed people on his croft, and that was probably in later life, after Peter had gone to Leith.

Peter seems to have been named for his maternal grandfather, Peter Longwill, who was probably the son of Patric Langwill, married in 1731 to Mary MacCallum, a collateral ancestor of the piping MacCallums of Campbeltown (see above).

Both the Reids and the Longwills were old-established families in Campbeltown parish, going back at least as far as the local records extend, into the 17th century. There was a family of Reids in Southend parish in which the name Peter recurs, in different Gaelic forms.

Both the Reids and the Longwills may have come to Kintyre from Ayrshire in the mid-1600s, after the persecution of the Covenanters there by Bluidy Clavers (otherwise known as Bonnie Dundee, or to pipers as the Viscount). Peter Reid seems to have had Ayrshire rather than Ireland as his background, and this makes him unusual among the piping families of Campbeltown.

Peter Reid married Margaret Stewart on 1st December 1831, when he was living in Glasgow. A son was born in 1833, and named Hugh, after Peter's father. A daughter Margaret followed in 1835, Jessie in 1838, and a son James Robert Reid in 1843. He was the informant for his father's death certificate, giving his address as 4 Linnvale Gardens, Hillhead, Glasgow – probably the former name of Lynn Gardens, off Great George Street, just around the corner from his parents' house at 33 Kersland Street.

Peter Reid died on December 26th 1881, at the age of 80. He was buried in Sighthill Cemetery, Springburn Road. His significance to the piping world is undoubtedly his manuscript, though his record as a judge whose decisions were always looked upon as thoroughly satisfactory probably makes him unique.

SOURCES
OPR Campbeltown, Midlothian (Leith), Lanark (Glasgow)
Reid death certificate
Piobaireachd Society Collection
Roderick Cannon, General Preface

Roderick Cannon, *The Highland Bagpipe*
John Prebble, *The King's Jaunt*
City of Edinburgh Council Libraries and Information Service (Andrew Bethune, Edinburgh Room)
J.W.S. MacFie
J.S. Marshall
R. Mudie
D. Robertson
John Russell
Joyce Wallace

ROBERT MACKINNON AND DONALD FERGUSON

ROBERT MACKINNON, BORN IN 1835, was a sucessful competitor in the 1870s and 80s. He was born at Glaonaig, near Skipness, in the north of Kintyre, south of Tarbert, Loch Fyne. Both MacKinnon and his grandmother's name, MacIntyre, are Kintyre names, but in 1861 he was working at the Erskine Ferry Inn in Renfrewshire. After he married in Erskine, he moved to Glasgow where he joined the 105th Glasgow Highlanders. He was at that time a Wine and Spirit Dealer. It was not until 1878 that he gave Skipness as his place of domicile even though he was still living in Glasgow.

James E. Scott said that Robert's piping teacher was his uncle, DONALD FERGUSON, who lived at Torrisdale, to the south of Carradale. A popular Kintyre song *Wee Donald Ban* was made for him. The relationship with Donald Ban is not entirely clear, as James Scott said that Robert's grandmother, whose name was MacIntyre, was Donald's mother. Presumably MacIntyre was the grandmother's maiden name, and she married a Ferguson, and her daughter married a MacKinnon.

Donald Ferguson was, according to his obituary in the *Campbeltown Courier*, for many years piper to John Hayes at Torrisdale Castle; he is described as 'one of the best known worthies of Kintyre' (an area rich in worthies), and around Carradale 'his services were frequently requisitioned for dance parties, etc.'

Angus Martin tells a story about Donald Ferguson. One day, he was out on the hill as a beater for a party of grouse-shooters. When they stopped for a refreshment, the beaters were told by one of the gentlemen that they should be aware that they were about to receive a particularly fine sample of the water of life, which was 'at least thirty years old'. When the whisky was finally dispensed, it seemed less than adequate a measure, by local standards. Donald held his up, squinted at it and observed 'Thirty years old, eh? My, but she's sma' for her age'.

An account, also by Angus Martin, tells of a Hallowe'en celebration, held 'old style' on November 12th, 1855. 'The evening was spent in ceilidh-houses at Torrisdale and Whitestone, where there was dancing to the pipes of Donald Ferguson and Neil Galbraith'. A ceilidh-house was a house known for its hospitality, music, song and dancing, where folk were always welcome to come in and take part. Certain houses in most Highland districts would build up such a reputation. This Neil Galbraith may have been a great-great-grandfather of John M MacKenzie (see below).

Donald lived to be over eighty, never married, and died in January 1896. He is buried in Brackley burial ground, a few miles to the north of Carradale.

The MacIntyres in Skipness were said to be related to Duncan Ban MacIntyre, the Glen Orchy bard, who in the late 18th century made a piobaireachd poem, *In Praise of Ben Dorain*. Duncan Ban MacIntyre also composed a fine Gaelic poem every year in praise of the national piping competitions at Falkirk in the 1780s (see below).

Robert competed at Oban in the very first Argyllshire Gathering of 1873, winning second prize in the piobaireachd as 'Robert MacKinnon, Kintyre'. By the following year he was 'Pipe Major of the Glasgow Highlanders', a post he seems to have held for four years. He competed with considerable success up to 1882. Jeannie Campbell gives details of his career, in her book *Highland Bagpipe Makers*: after being four times second in the piobaireachd, he eventually won the Gold Medal in 1880. He was an excellent light music player and an accomplished dancer. He was evidently a good player who could hold his own with such as John MacColl, Alexander Ross, Angus MacDonald and William MacLennan.

James Scott recorded that Queen Victoria expressed a wish to hear Robert play. Robert sent for his uncle Donald, and played his pipes in the royal presence, before giving an exhibition of dancing to his uncle's playing.

Robert married Annie MacDonald who came from Laggan, Inverness-shire. They met at the Erskine Ferry Inn, where Annie was a maid. They had three sons and a daughter, all born in Glasgow. He started his bagpipe making business in 1875, and his sons later joined the firm. His military bagpipe with full silver mountings cost £30, but half-mounted with German silver could be bought for as little as £8. Large pipe chanters were £1 each, pipe chanter reeds nine pence, and drone reeds three pence.

Probably related to Robert was William MacKinnon, who worked as a pipemaker at the same address in Glasgow, 3 Brown Street (see Jeannie Campbell, writing of William Gunn, p.37). William MacKinnon was born in Lanarkshire in the early 1840s, and may have been a cousin of Robert.

In 1884 Robert published a tutor and collection of light music, re-issued in 1898. He died of bronchitis in 1907.

GEORGE ROSS competed at Oban in 1890s. He was discharged from the army on 9 Dec 1901, having completed 24 years and 293 days service. He was born in 1858, and on leaving the army gave his intended place of residence as Campbeltown, and his trade as carpenter. (Piping Times, July 1991). He seems to be the same George Ross who was a Sergeant Piper in the Royal Highlanders, but there may be confusion with J.George Ross, Pipe Major in the Black Watch.

GEORGE M. MACINTYRE

GEORGE M. MACINTYRE WAS BORN IN 1918, and died in 1997. On his death, Iain Duncan wrote this tribute, which was published in the Piping Times in June 1997:

'The world of piping has suffered a great loss with the unexpected death of George MacIntyre on Tuesday 8 April.

'A native of Campbeltown, George was given his first lesson in piping by an uncle, John Galbraith. From here, he joined the Campbeltown Pipe Band, under the leadership of Pipe Major Ronald McCallum.

'In 1938, he joined the 8th Battalion Argyll and Sutherland Highlanders (TA) where he met Iain Lawrie, son of the well known Willie Lawrie. Iain not only helped bring George's piping technique to a very high standard but identified George's natural composing talent.

'On June 7th 1940, George was captured at St. Blimont, near St Valery in France, and was taken prisoner of war. He escaped camp on several occasions but each time was recaptured. In one of the camps he met up again with Iain Lawrie and in that same camp was the celebrated John Wilson. Although some camps had pipes and chanters supplied through the Red Cross, they were unfortunate to have neither instrument. Undaunted, the three would finger tunes on brush handles. It was in this camp that George composed his 4/4 tune *Hills of Argyll*, adding suitable words; a soldier yearning for home.

'After the war, he became a founder member of Campbeltown Ex-servicemen's Pipe Band.

'In 1964 George moved south to Corby where he lived for many years. There he became a close friend of Tom O'Rourke, who is immortalised in one of George's compositions. It was while living in Corby that he began to gain recognition as a composer of some repute. And as his compositions appeared in the infrequent publications of that time, and be played by the big bands, his reputation grew.

'In his own words, in a 1995 BBC Pipeline broadcast exclusively featuring George and his music, he became fed up living in Corby and yearned to move nearer to his home town of Campbeltown.

'An invite from Lt.Col. Gayre of Gayre and Nigg and Minard Castle provided the means, taking him back to Argyll and placing him no more than 60 miles from Campbeltown. For several years he lived at Minard Castle Lodge, George employed as piper to Colonel Gayre, and his wife Isobel employed as housekeeper in the Castle.

'During his stay at Minard, he published a book exclusively devoted to his compositions, and since then many more of his compositions have been included in new collections.

'On leaving Minard, he returned to Campbeltown where he continued active involvement in local piping, tutoring, adjudicating and, not least, composing; there remains a wealth of unpublished manuscripts.

'George seldom composed to order. He maintained tunes would just come out of his head. The titles would mostly have some association with the time and where the composition was conceived. There were many anecdotes surrounding the titles of his tunes. During his stay in Corby, a tune materialised one Saturday afternoon while visiting Tom O'Rourke, and he decided to name it after Tom's wife; the tune remained, in George's opinion, his finest composition. That tune was *Lucy Cassidy* and there are surely few pipers who would disagree with his opinion of this superlative hornpipe.

'George was the incumbent president of the Kintyre Piping Society and in1995 was presented with honorary membership in recognition of his considerable contribution to the world of piping.

'George was laid to rest on 14 April in Campbeltown's Kilkerran Cemetery, to Pipe Sergeant Ian McKerral's rendition of a touching slow air George composed some four years ago, the name of the tune, *Kilkerran*.

'To his family and devoted wife Isobel we pass our condolences'.

In 1993 the Piping Times published a letter from George MacIntyre about some plates which depicted a piper. George wrote:

'My mother had two plates exactly the same, in colour and design. They are now in the possession of my sister who lives in Norway. We go there every year, and I have always admired them. After reading the article in the Piping Times, I phoned my sister and asked if there were any markings on the back of the plates. She said there was a stamp on both of them which resembled a lover's knot. My sister who is 80 years old always remembered them being in my mother's house. If I receive any more information about the plates I will let you know'.

This was typical of George MacIntyre's enthusiasm for and interest in anything to do with piping, which seems to have been the mainstay of his life.

George MacIntyre's book, the *Minard Castle Collection*, published in 1986, was his own compositions, and proved very popular.

The Bank of Scotland in 1995 celebrated its Tercentenary with a composing competition, which attracted 173 entries, anonymously submitted from all over the world. The winner of the First Prize of £1,000 was George MacIntyre, with a 2/4 March (published in the Piping Times, May 1995). Nobody was surprised.

George MacIntyre's compositions include:

Alex Miller 6/8 J 4 pts
Andrew MacKay HP 4
Andy Warnock 6/8 M 4
Angus MacIntyre R 4
Archie MacMillan 9/8 M 2
Archie McArthur HP 4
Archie McLellan 6/8 J 4
The Bank of Scotland Tercentenary March 2/4 M 4
Bobby Anderson HP 4
Bob MacDonald 6/8 M 4
The Bugler R 4

George M. MacIntyre (left) beside Seumas MacNeill when the Bank of Scotland prize was presented, in 1995.
(PHOTOGRAPH BY COURTESY OF THE COLLEGE OF PIPING)

The Cheeper 6/8 J 4
The Chestnut Tree 6/8 J 4
The Cheviot Collie 6/8 J 4
Clan McSporran 6/8 M 4
Col. P.F.F.Gladwin, Minard 4/4 M 2
David MacPhee 2/4 M 4
The Desert March 4/4 M 4
Donald Beaton 6/8 J 4
Donald Campbell 9/8 M 2
Donald Gilchrist 4/4 M 2
Donald MacEachran R 4
Dora Watt HP 4
Dr Iain Michie 4/4 M 2
Glen Lussa 2/4 M 4
Hazel Thompson HP 2
Hills of Argyll 4/4 M
Isabel MacLean 6/8 J 4
Jean MacLean 6/8 J 4
John Barker 6/8 J 4
Johnny Jump Up 6/8 J 4
J.W. Benson R 4
Kilkerran S A
Kilmaho M 4/4 (see Piping Times April 1996)
The Librarian 6/8 M 4
Loch Gair 6/8 M 4
Loch Ruan 4/4 M 2
Lt.Col. Gayre, Baron of Lochore 6/8 M 4
Lucy Cassidy HP 4
Madam Gayre, Baroness of Lochore 6/8 M 4
McArtney's Horse Trough 6/8 J 5
Milldam Midges 6/8 J 4
Minard Bay 6/8 M 4
Minard Castle 3 /4 M 4
The Mull of Oa 4/4 M 2
Per Ardua 4/4 M 2
Pipe Major A.W. Wilson R 4
Pipe Major John A. MacLellan 6/8 J 4
Pipe Major R. MacCallum M.B.E. HP 4
Pipe Major R. Stewart 6/8 M 4
Pipe Major Tom O'Rourke 6/8 J 4
Robert Byrne 6/8 J 4
The Rocky Burn 6/8 J 4
Round the Mull HP 4
Sarah McRoberts HP 4

Sheena Cameron HP 4
Simplicity 6/8 HP 4
Three Wee Crows 6/8 J 4
Una McIntyre HP 4
Willie Crawford 2/4 M 4
Wrong Wedding HP 4

SOURCES
Piping Times June 1997 and September 1994
Pekaar

DONALD MUNRO is listed in Jeannie Campbell's book, *Highland Bagpipe Makers*, as a maker of Bagpipes and Highland Costumes in London, opening his business in Charlotte Street in 1926. He seems to have lasted until 1936 when Angus MacAulay took over, after Donald's death.

Donald came from Tarbert, Loch Fyne, and had taken over the Charlotte Street business after R.G.Lawrie gave up their London branch on those premises. Donald made the shop a centre for visiting pipers in London, and Jeannie says many received tuition there.

Donald Munro died in London in 1935.

WILLIAM THOMSON was a native of Campbeltown who preceded John M. MacKenzie as piper to the MacNeills of Ugadale. A pupil of John MacDonald, Inverness, he was a fine player, and one of his distinguished pupils was Ronnie MacCallum, MBE. He was for many years a close friend of John MacColl, the Oban maestro, and the two families used to share a house for the Argyllshire Gathering.

WILSONS

(*Based on notes received from Angus Martin*)

AS SO MANY WILLIAM WILSONS are confusing, I have numbered the generations. The Wilsons were a family of noted local pipers, descended from Antrim-born William II Wilson amd Ellen McAlister, who were married in Campbeltown on the 18th May 1861. They later went to live in Southend, the parish to the south of Campbeltown.

William's parents were William I Wilson, printer, and Emily Davidson; and Ellen was the daughter of Archibald McAlister and Janet Millen, in Campbeltown.

William and Ellen had a son WILLIAM III McALISTER WILSON, who in 1904 married Catherine McCormick (born 1873); she came from Ballycastle, Co. Antrim, the daughter of Andrew McCormick, labourer, and Mary Laverty.

William III was drowned in Campbeltown harbour on 6 May 1919, while coming ashore about midnight from a Royal Navy ship on which he had been playing the pipes at a 'function'. The local paper described him as 'a piper of recognised ability, and a frequent performer on the local concert platform. Piping was his one hobby, and a more obliging fellow with his art it would have been impossible to find'.

William III left four children: James 1905, William IV 1907, Mary 1910 and Archibald 1917. ARCHIE WILSON was killed in North Africa, in the Second World War, in the Battle of Longstop Hill. This is said to have been the last battle in which a piper led his comrades into the fight. Archie featured in the prize lists at Oban in 1939, and was considered a most promising player.

WILLIAM IV WILSON was a pupil of John MacColl, along with Willie Lawrie. He taught Ronnie MacCallum MBE, as well as his own son John and his nephew, Tony Wilson. William IV married a McKerral, who belonged to Campbeltown.

It is William IV who was commemorated by James Wark of the Strathclyde Police in his 2/4 March, *Pipe Major William Wilson, Campbeltown*, and by Ron Fleming's 6/8 March, *Pipe Major Willie Wilson*.

William IV's son JOHN WILSON, born in 1949, showed early talent as a piper. After winning many prizes as a junior, he fulfilled his promise by winning the Gold Medal at Inverness in 1968, when he was only 18. Fourteen years later, he took the Gold at Oban, in 1982.

For many years a piper with the Srathclyde Police Band, he was described in the Piping Times as 'one of the mainstays of the successful Strathclyde Police band of the 80s and 90s'. Since his retirement from the police, he has become a respected judge, and has resumed his career as a solo player, his playing having lost none of its crisp fingering and musical interpretation.

ANTHONY W. WILSON, born 8 August 1932, was the son of Mary McAlister Wilson, daughter of William III who drowned in Campbeltown harbour when she was nine years old.

The Piping Times for September 1994 published this tribute to Tony Wilson:

'The death occured on June 20th of Tony Wilson at his home in Campbeltown, Argyll. Tony was perhaps best known as hav-

John Wilson of the Strathclyde Police

ing been pipe major of Campbeltown Pipe Band when they accompanied Paul MaCartney on the record '*Mull of Kintyre*' which became the top selling single record for a very long time.

'He was taught first by his uncle Pipe Major William Wilson and played in the Ceann Loch (Campbeltown) pipe band under his direction. When he was old enough he joined the Scots Guards and played with the pipe band at home and abroad. Later he joined the City of Glasgow Police where he played with some of the outstanding solo professional pipers of the day.

'On his retiral he returned to Campbeltown and became involved very seriously in teaching young people. He was appointed part-time piping instructor to the local school and was responsible for a considerable upsurge in piping interest.'

Tony Wilson
(PHOTOGRAPH KINDLY LENT BY MRS KATRINE WILSON, CAMPBELTOWN)

William MacCallum, senior, Campbeltown, tells the story of the day when Pipe Major Ronnie MacCallum (the Duke's piper), was giving a lift to Ronnie Lawrie, Jock Leitch and Tony Wilson. They were 'buzzed' by a car driven by a young fellow, who overtook them on a dangerous bend, and as he passed, the Pipe Major shouted to him to slow down, he'd get there just the same. The young man took exception to this, and at the next traffic lights when they drew up behind him, he got out and approached their car with hostile intent. At once Jock Leitch, a large man, climbed out, followed by Tony Wilson, who was no smaller, but finally it was Ronnie Lawrie who sent him scurrying for his car, Ronnie being enormous and menacing. The youth vanished over the horizon without a word being exchanged. He probably thought Ronnie MacCallum was travelling with his three minders.

George M. MacIntyre composed a reel, *Pipe Major A. W. Wilson*.

RONALD FLEMING, an Australian living in Brisbane, but of Campbeltown origins, made a number of tunes, some with Argyll connections. They include:
Jimmie Strachan's Squeeze Box 6/8 M 4
Jimmy Johnstone's Fancy S 4
The Men From Dalintober 9/8 M 2
Donald Morrison's Welcome to Brisbane 6/8 M 4 (1978)

JOHN M. MACKENZIE, born in Campbeltown, was of a family belonging to Inveraray, and an account of him may be found below, see Inveraray.

DR FLORA MACAULAY

Dr MacAulay was born of a Hebridean family, but brought up in South Wales where her father was a G.P. She herself became a doctor, one of the first female orthopaedic surgeons.

She practised in the West Highlands, settling in Carradale, Kintyre, and spent her summers travelling round the Games and competitions, enjoying pipe music above all else. This interest was recognized when a tune *Dr Flora MacAulay* was made for her.

She died in 1994, and was buried at Southend, Kintyre. One of the Cups for which the junior pipers in Kintyre compete is named in her memory.

(*Based on a report by Lorne Cousin in the Piping Times*)

KINTYRE PIPING SOCIETY

The Kintyre Piping Society, sometimes (but mistakenly) known as the Campbeltown Piping Society, was started in 1951, mainly on the initiative of John M. MacKenzie. He formed a committee of local piping enthusiasts, of whom there were many, and they laid out the objects of the society: to encourage piping in Kintyre, to organise competitions, to stimulate interest among the general public towards piping, to run demonstrations of piping by expert players and to further the interests of piping and pipe music in every way possible. Like all societies in small communities, this one has had its difficulties but now appears to be thriving.

The first recital, in 1951, was given by John D. Burgess, and in November 1953 the College of Piping, with financial help from the Arts Council (those were the days), staged a night of first-class piping in Campbeltown, with Donald MacPherson, Tommy Pearston, Seumas MacNeill, John MacFadyen and Duncan MacColl. Since then the Society has had recitals and illustrated talks from most of the piping notables of the time.

George MacIntyre, piper and composer who had retired to live in his native Campbeltown, was given honorary life membership of the Society in 1995.

In 2000, to mark the tercentenary of the Burgh of Campbeltown, the Society ran a competition to which eight of the top pipers in the country were invited. This attracted sponsorship from local businesses, including the Springbank Distillery. The competition has proved so successful that it is now an annual event, held in the Argyll Arms Hotel in Campbeltown.

At that first competition, the players were Brian Donaldson, Willie MacCallum, Angus MacColl, Roddy MacLeod, Stuart Shedden, Gordon Walker, Robert Wallace and Greg Wilson. The joint Chairmen were Hugh MacCallum and Alistair Cousin, and the judges were John D. Burgess, Norman Gillies and John MacDougall. To the surprise of nobody, Willie MacCallum was the winner overall, with Brian Donaldson as runner-up. The competition was followed by 'a rousing ceilidh which went on well into the small hours', to quote Hugh

Competitors at the first Springbank Competition in Campbeltown, to celebrate the tercentenary of the Burgh.

MacCallum's report in the Piping Times. The chief organiser of the event was Hugh's brother, Willie MacCallum senior, a leading light in the society, who works indefatigably to further the cause of local piping.

HECTOR F. MACNEILL, (uncle of Dugald B MacNeill, College of Piping), who died in 1998 in his 80th year, lived in Campbeltown and was for many years Secretary of the Kintyre Piping Society.

The Society also runs Junior competitions, valuable for the youngsters' piping development, especially those who live in places remote from the big centres. The list of trophies for which the juniors compete reads like a Who's Who of Campbeltown piping: they include the Pipe Major J.M. MacKenzie Cup, the Dugald MacShannon Cup, the Archibald Johnston Cup, the Kintyre Society Cup, the Pipe Major Willie Wilson Cup, the Dr Flora MacAulay Cup, and the Pipe Major Ronald MacCallum MBE Cup.

Both Duncan MacColl and Alistair Fletcher have donated pipes which can be lent out to any junior piper who does not have his own. With all this help, and such enormously inspiring local forebears, the juniors of Kintyre must surely become the stars of tomorrow. Already they are making a name for themselves and for Kintyre in junior competitions such as Cowal and Gairloch.

Junior competitors in Campbeltown, 2000 – the stars of tomorrow?

In 2002, the newly-formed Kintyre Schools Pipe Band had its first full season of competing, and very creditably finished second to Lochgelly High School from Fife, having pushed their rivals hard throughout the summer. 2003 saw them sweep to further triumphs, winning the Schools championship and many other competitions.

The Senior Depute Rector of Campbeltown Grammar School, Mr Casey, paid tribute to the players, praising them for having brought 'immense credit to their community, their schools, their parents and themselves', by their behaviour as well as their playing. Mr Casey went on to refer to Pipe Major Ian McKerral as the driving force behind the resurgence of juvenile piping in Campbeltown. 'Without Ian at the helm, none of this would have come about. His drive and enthusiasm know no bounds'. He also paid tribute to Campbell Anderson who had brought the band's drummers from being complete novices to championship standard in under a year.

A recital of pipe music played by two leading pipers is held annually in Inveraray Castle, always well attended.

The music of the song *Campbeltown Loch, I Wish You Were Whisky*, made a popular hit by Andy Stewart, who wrote the words, was taken from the pipe tune *The Glendaruel Highlanders*, composed by Alexander Fettes. It was first made in honour of the family of John MacDougall Gillies (see below). There is also a well known pipe tune, a 6/8 march *Campbeltown Loch*.

MacCallum and MacAlister Pipers in Campbeltown

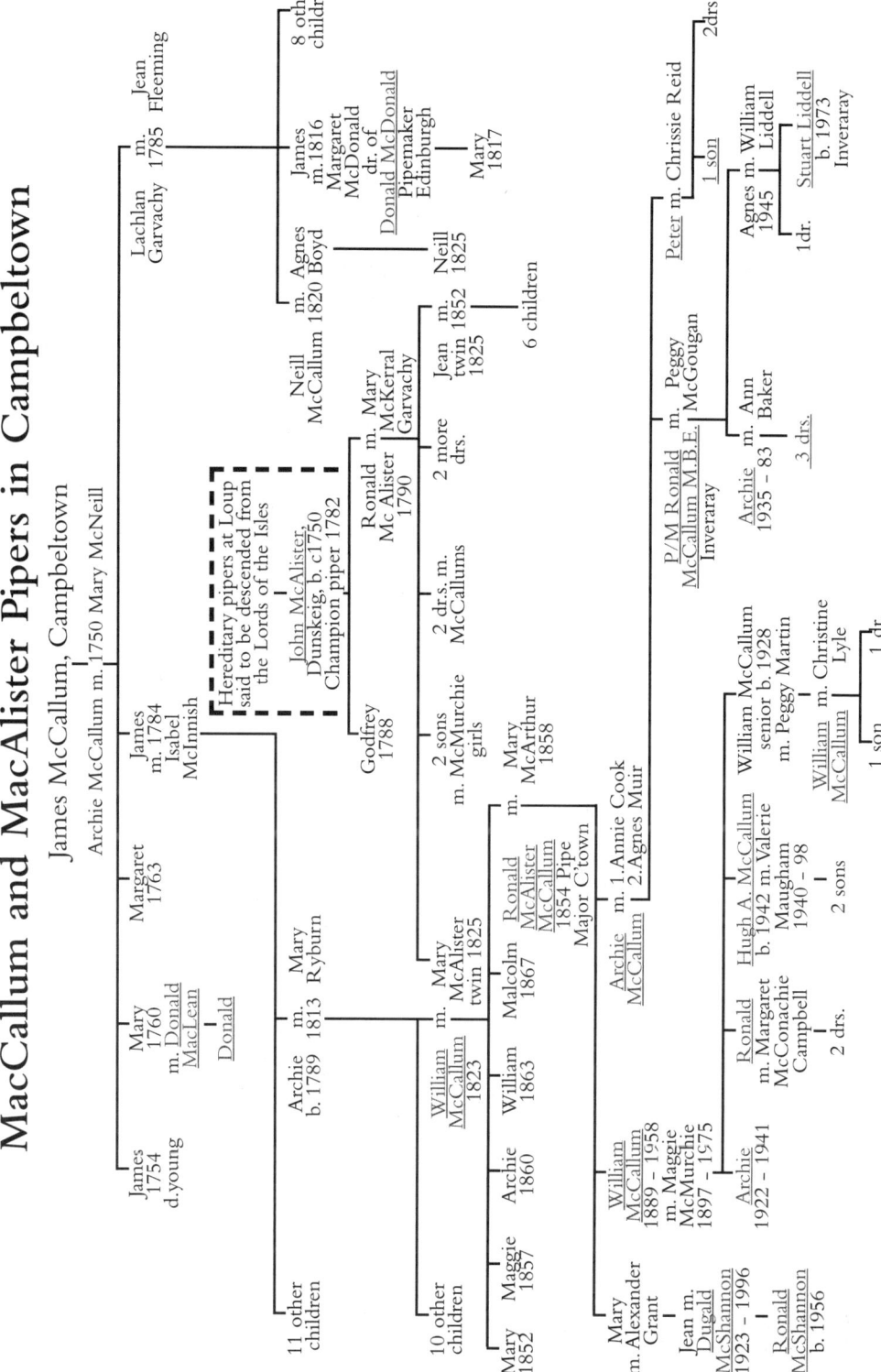

Family Tree of the MacAlisters and MacCallums

62 *Piping Traditions of Argyll*

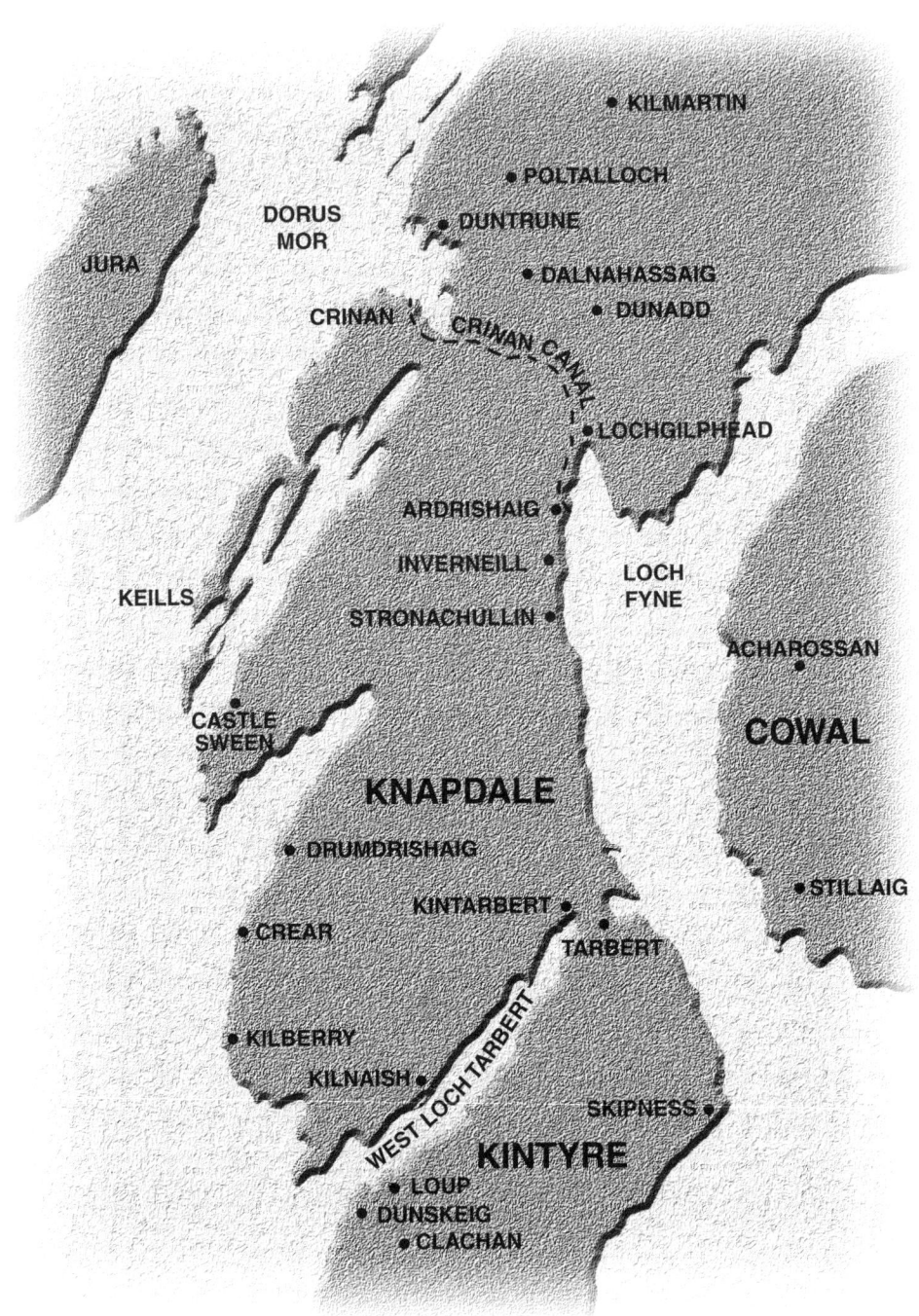

knapdale

Knapdale

KILBERRY

TUNES ASSOCIATED WITH KILBERRY INCLUDE:
Archibald Campbell of Kilberry, by John MacColl 2/4 SM
Kilberry Ball, by Robert Meldrum Polka 2
Kilberry Castle, by Archibald Campbell 2/4 M 4
The Lament for Angus Campbell, by Archibald Campbell P with 7 variations
Monkland Basin, by Archibald Campbell S 2
Mrs Campbell's Favourite Strathspey, by Archibald Campbell S 2
Mrs MacDougall ('s March), by Archibald Campbell 6/8 M 4
Reel, by Archibald Campbell R 2
The Road to Loch Sween, by R.Fleming 2/4 M 4
Robert Campbell, by Archibald Campbell S 2
Salute to James Campbell, by Archie Kenneth P with 10 variations

CAMPBELLS OF KILBERRY

ARCHIBALD CAMPBELL, 1877-1963, 'Kilberry' to the piping world. The Notices of Pipers give this account of Archibald Campbell:

'One of the foremost amateur players of his time, especially of piobaireachd. Youngest of three piping sons of John Campbell, (known as 'Big Jock'), 10th of Kilberry, Argyll. A pupil of Angus MacRae, John MacColl, John MacDonald MBE, Alexander (Alick) Cameron, John MacDougall Gillies and William Ross MBE.

'Entered the Indian Civil Service in the year 1901 and was latterly a Judge of the High Court in Lahore. Retired in 1928, and afterwards a Lecturer in Indian Law at Cambridge University. Was a composer and well versed in the theory and practice of the bagpipe, its history and the careers of notable pipers.

'Compiled with his brother, Captain JOHN CAMPBELL of Kilberry (also a good amateur piper), Argyll and Sutherland Highlanders, a collection of '*Ceol Meadhonach*, or middle music for the pipes', first published in 1908 and reprinted with additions in 1931.

'His services as a judge at piping competitions both in India and at home were much in demand. Was Honorary Secretary Music Committee, Piobaireachd Society for some years. Had access to the minutes and correspondence of the Highland Society of London regarding its piping competitions, and gave valuable aid in further completing these Notices. Principal editor of Books 1 to 8 published by the Piobaireachd Society, 1925-1939. His knowledge of the subject of Highland piping was profound.'

John MacColl made a Slow March in 2/4 time, with 2 parts, called *Archibald Campbell of Kilberry*. John's father-in-law was the farm manager of the Kilberry

Home Farm.

In 1881, the butler at Kilberry Castle was Alexander Ross, brother of Duncan who was at that time piper to the Duke of Argyll at Inveraray. They had been born in Contin parish, Ross and Cromarty, and may have been related to John Ban MacKenzie (see below). Alexander later became piper to Lord MacDonald, in Skye.

The Piping Times for December 1991 published an entertaining account, with a photograph taken in the late 1890s, of the Kilberry Pipers, a small amateur pipe band formed by Archibald Campbell when he was waiting to go to India (see above, MacCallums and MacAlisters).

In answer to a query from Rothiemurchus, Kilberry wrote in 1960: 'We used to have rather fun playing a band, without drummers, all over the roads on summer evenings... There is not a piper of any kind in Kilberry nowadays'. He named the players (see above), and said the band was started at New Year 1897, when they 'played down to the shinty ground' for the annual New Year shinty match. That was Jubilee Year, and they decided to play in the march to the bonfire, so evening practices were held in the garden at Kilberry. For a ball at Kilberry on January 12th 1898 (the Old New Year Day) 'eleven pipers played the carriage up to the barn'; it would have been twelve, but Sandy MacNeill was the coachman and had to look after the horses.

In 1898 'I had practices twice a week. All attended regularly...'. Archibald was away at Cambridge for a few months, but on his return he organized a competition, with prize money and a challenge medal raised from various friends and relations. The judge was Sir Douglas Ramsay of Banff. John Carruthers won the medal, and Angus MacMillan, piper to the Dowager Duchess of Argyll, won the Strathspey and Reel.

That same year Archie had been in trouble in college (Pembroke College, Cambridge) 'for playing *Her Golden Hair* about midnight for a lot of ruffians to dance to on the grass'. He also mentions an episode when he was staying with the Ramsays at Banff: 'I distinguished myself by playing the Long Reveille under the dining room windows when Sir James was reading prayers therein'.

1899 saw a band of twelve pipers at New Year, and 'a threesome by John MacColl, Sandy MacNeill and myself when after being soaked through and through, two hard games, and very vigorous dancing on the gravel, we played the Concourse from the house to the steading with the 93rd'. Hard games of what? Probably shinty, the traditional New Year game.

Home for the Easter vacation, he found the band going well ('Good playing at concert'). And in June, 'we had several practices of the band and used to march out about 9 o'clock on the long summer evenings dressed in the kilt while the whole population turned out to listen.'

In 1899 he took the Indian Civil Service examination, and although he did not leave until 1900, the pipe band took second place. James Campbell's account of his father's younger days ends: 'So let the last words come from Angus MacMillan, forty-five years later. 'Yes, we could play in those days and we hadn't a white hair in our heads. The old days were very happy when one thinks of all the harmless fun we used to have in the Pipe Band. Well, after all, we had our days'.

It should be borne in mind that Archibald did not start playing the pipes until 1894, and said himself that he did not attempt to be any good at it until 1897, when he was twenty, so several of the pipers in his band, notably John MacColl, John Carruthers and Angus MacMillan, would have been better than himself, though we would not guess that from his comments on their prowess, which he made in later life.

Archibald must have been remembering those days at Kilberry when in India in 1907 he formed a group known as The Seven Pipers of Simla, and a 6/8 march of that name was composed – one of the two composers was Major Kenneth MacKenzie Cameron, Major RAMC.

The seven were:

Major Kenneth M. Cameron; Mr Walter MacKinnon, architect; Lt.Col. A.C.B.MacKinnon, 9th Ghurkas (these two MacKinnons were Major Kenneth's brothers-in-law); General Sir Frederick Campbell; his son, Major F.C.G.Campbell, 40th Pathans; Lt.Col. John Campbell, 93rd Highlanders; his brother, Mr Archibald Campbell, Indian Civil Service.

Archibald had three sons, Angus, James and Colin, 'all above average amateur pipers'.

Right: Kilberry Castle, in South Knapdale, Argyll, several miles to the west of Tarbert, Loch Fyne. The Castle is the seat of the Campbells of Kilberry. It has now been classed as a building at risk, as it is falling into disrepair.
(PHOTOGRAPH BY COURTESY OF THE COLLEGE OF PIPING)

JOHN and ARCHIBALD CAMPBELL of Kilberry

THE NOTICES OF PIPERS HAVE this to say of John Campbell: '1872-1928. Eldest son of John Campbell, 10th of Kilberry. An excellent amateur piper who did much for piping. Served in the A&S H from 1890 until 1909 when he retired as Captain. Became Lieut Col. of the 8th (Argyllshire) Battalion shortly before 1914, and as such served during the War.

'Founded the Piob.Soc. in 1902, along with his brother Captain James Campbell of the 93rd; Captain Colin MacRae, formerly of the Black Watch; Captain C.A.H.MacLean of Pennycross, also in the 93rd; Captain Kenneth Cameron, an army doctor; John Campbell of Kilberry – this was the father – and James MacKillop of Polmont. They met in 1903 in Dowall's Rooms, George Street, Edinburgh, for the first meeting of the Piobaireachd Society. It had 14 members, including the Hon. Miss Elspeth Campbell, niece of the Duke of Argyll'.

The first Piobaireachd Society competition was held the following year, and in the piobaireachd the winner was John MacDonald (The original Gold Medal is now in the possession of the College of Piping Museum), with G.S.MacLennan second and William Ross third. But the year after that, 1905, there was trouble, and Captain John Campbell and seven others resigned, mainly over disagreements about publishing the music. Eventually it was all patched up, and throughout the years, the Campbells of Kilberry have been leading lights in the Society, Archibald being the Chairman of the Music Committee and Editor of the publications for many years. Professional pipers were not allowed to join the Society in those days. Nowadays they are more than welcome.

To mark the centenary in 2003 of the founding of the Piobaireachd Society, a book is to be published, recounting the history of the society, and it is not felt necessary to go into it here.

The Notices go on:

Archibald Campbell, Kilberry, pictured at Luss Highland Games.
(PHOTOGRAPH BY COURTESY OF THE ROYAL SCOTTISH PIPERS' SOCIETY)

'John brought out, with his brother Archibald, the *Kilberry Book of Ceol Meadhonach*, originally published in 1908, which supplied a want long felt by pipers, as there was no work devoted to that class of pipe music. Both he and his father were staunch friends and supporters of the professional piper, and especially of the regimental piper. A story is told which would relate equally well to either father or son. Inspecting the arrangements for the Argyllshire Gathering Ball at Oban, Kilberry noticed a door labelled 'Reserved

Knapdale

for Band and Pipers'. 'Here', he said 'Take down that notice and put up another one, 'Reserved for Pipers and other Musicians'.

The Piper Press in March 1998 gave in full the obituary of Archibald Campbell which appeared in the Oban Times in 1963. This was unlikely to be critical of the gentleman, for so long a doyen of the Argyll piping scene. It is quoted pretty well in full:

'Highland bagpipe music has lost its finest authority with the passing of Archibald Campbell, Kilberry, whose death occurred on April 24, 1963, at his home in London. He was 86 years of age.

'The third son of John Campbell 10th of Kilberry, he was educated at Harrow and Pembroke College, Cambridge.'

[This sets the scene: we are not dealing with your average Highland piping enthusiast, but one who came through Harrow and Cambridge, and later made his home in London (as a piper once said to me in amazement, about another player altogether, 'he lived in London *when he didn't have to*')]

The obituary continues: 'After leaving university he entered the Indian Civil Service in 1900 and after a distinguished career was appointed a judge of the High Court in 1921. Retiring in 1928 he returned to Britain and in the following year was appointed lecturer in Indian Law at Cambridge University, a post he held until 1941.

'Born and reared as he was in the north, Campbell of Kilberry had an intensive knowledge of all matters related to the Highlands. He is probably best known ... as an authority on his lifetime hobby of playing the pipe and its music.

'To this hobby he brought a first class brain, tireless industry, unlimited enthusiasm and proficiency gleaned from instructors of the highest qualification. Angus MacRae, John MacColl and William Ross were his mentors for ceol beag; Sandy Cameron, John MacDougall Gillies and John MacDonald for ceol mor.

'With this background he achieved a unique status in piping – not only as an acknowledged expert on all forms of playing, but also as a mine of readily available information on all matters directly or remotely concerning pipers and pipe music.

'His greatest work was no doubt in the renaissance of the piobaireachd cult, which may be said to date from the publication of General Thomason's *Ceol Mor* in 1900. But his knowledge and appreciation of other forms of music will be within the power of many to testify to – those whose playing he had judged; those who have read his many contributions to this newspaper; those who have sought his advice or opinion in private or in the friendly atmosphere of pipers gatherings; those who have been participators in the agile correspondence which he delighted to carry on with fellow enthusiasts.

'It was to piobaireachd, however, that his main work was devoted. His aim was to make his knowledge of this somewhat esoteric art available to others. To the extent that the present interest in ceol mor is due to the availability to all of books of authority. The credit for such a welcome state of affairs is largely his. [There seems to be an editing lapse here]

'The records of his achievements are two – the Piobaireachd Society publications dating from 1924 (Books 2 to 10 inclusive), and the *Kilberry Book of Ceol Mor.*

'The primary object of the Piobaireachd Society publications was to make available to pipers all information concerning the tunes selected which patient research among the authoritative manuscripts could produce. The secondary object was to provide pipers with one authoritative setting of each tune in easily legible staff notation.

'The system had its faults in that the printed settings have, with the passage of time, come to be regarded as ex cathedra directions as to the way the tunes should be played. The original purpose of submitting one of several possible and permissible alternatives has become obscure. The competition system, admirable though it is in many respects, has done much to develop the somewhat false reverence which is often accorded to 'Piobaireachd Society' settings.

'The main value of the books, however, is to be found in the notes. There lay the labour and the learning, and the information to be found in the notes is, and will continue to be, of indispensable assistance to enquiring minds.

'The *Kilberry Book* had a different purpose. The editor shed the mantle of an impartial disseminator of information and sought to present to the piping world a record of the style of playing of his three instructors . . .

'No one appreciated better than he the imperfections of staff notation as a medium for piobaireachd instruction. Indeed any intention to instruct beginners is disclaimed in the preface. But the work constitutes a noble attempt to suggest to the educated piper many of the subtleties of timing and expression which are the life and soul of piobaireachd playing.

'The following is an extract from a contribution made by Kilberry as a young man to the Oban Times of September 1903, under the title of 'The Passing of the Piobaireachd': 'The old tunes must be rescued and put where they can be heard and appreciated . . . but where are they? . . .

'Written or unwritten, they are there, noted in old books, scrawled on stray fragments of paper or engraved on the memory of some old-time piper. They are there today. Tomorrow they will be gone . . . Let the highlander look to it, lest his grandchildren and great-grandchildren curse him, as we would fain curse our forefathers for suffering to be lost what is already lost beyond recall' . . . The ardent enthusiast of 1903 had in his old age no reason for dissatisfaction with his services to the cause which he then championed.

'His three sons he tutored in the art and judging of piping – James today is one of the leading adjudicators. There is another son out in Kenya. Angus, a younger son who was in the Malayan Civil Service when the Japanese invaded Malaya, through his ordeal as a POW died a few years ago. His (Archibald's) wife predeceased him several years ago.

'By the death of Kilberry piping has lost a champion and one of its greatest figures, a wonderful gentleman to meet, seldom critical but always ready to give advice.

'We are unlikely ever again to meet anyone quite like Archibald Campbell of Kilberry'.

This obituary is unattributed, but the name of Archie Kenneth springs to mind as we read it, and he may have written at least part of it.

Archibald Campbell was not among the founder members of the Piobaireachd Society, formed in 1903 to fill the need expressed so passionately by his article in the Oban Times. He himself was in India, but his two brothers were deeply involved in both the founding of the Society and the ructions which followed, leading to their resignation from the Committee.

The obituary is predictably admiring of Kilberry, and reading the Notices about the Kilberry Campbells it is difficult to avoid the uncomfortable feeling that they were all busy writing in each other's praise, if not actually their own. There is little evidence that either John or Archibald was an outstanding player, indeed, Archibald's playing was described by one contemporary as 'ponderous', by another as 'wooden', and some commentators feel that Archibald's 'profound knowledge of piobaireachd' was to some extent a destructive force, as he formed theories about piobaireachd and sometimes distorted the music as found in the manuscripts and oral tradition, to make it conform to his own 'rules'.

William Donaldson's is probably the strongest dissenting voice. In his chapter on *The Piobaireachd Society 1902-1914* (pp. 282 ff), and in a later chapter *The Piobaireachd Society's Second Series* (pp.374 ff), he made several attacks on the music policies of the Society, speaking disparagingly of Kilberry's 'position of apparently unassailable power in piping'.

Donaldson points out that 'despite his high profile within the Piobaireachd Society, Archibald Campbell had limited personal contact with piping in Scotland. On his return from India, he settled in the south of England and kept himself informed through a network of correspondents. He had seldom heard John MacDonald play since before the Great War, but he was anxious to tap his knowledge and channelled a stream of enquiries through Seton Gordon'.

He wrote to Seton Gordon: 'It will be very helpful if you can send me anything else hereafter that J.M. may say about any tune'. It is thought that John MacDonald was not aware that his words were being used in this way, nor that Kilberry was privately dismissing him as an 'also-ran' who 'habitually broke down'.

In private correspondence John MacDonald was just as scathing about Kilberry. Once he wrote 'I certainly don't agree with any of his comments on the Camerons or Gillies, and I have had so much to do with him before he went to India and since his return that I am almost justified in saying he is untruthful'. Elsewhere he wrote about the *Little Spree*: ' A. Campbell says in the notes that Gillies preferred it with the rest on the first note. Gillies and I had a few words about this . . and I asked how he played it. His reply was that he didn't play the tune.'

William Donaldson presents Kilberry as a devious schemer who used piping as a means to build up his own power; he gives him little credit for his undoubted achievements, and, as always, the truth probably lies somewhere between the extremes of Donaldson and of the obituary.

Archibald Campbell's son James, himself a respected figure of authority in the piping world, has given us an interesting account of the publication of *Ceol Mor* after his father had retired to London. It eventually appeared in 1948, and in the 1980s, James followed it up with his two books of *Sidelights*, which were Archibald's notes on the tunes he had published.

The arrogance displayed by Kilberry in print has stuck in the throats of many, but it was probably a manifestation of his social background, his legal career, and his years in India. It would have been acceptable in his own time, though unpalatable now. Dugald MacNeill asks whether, if anyone else had done the job, he might not have been equally arrogant, or have become so.

This impression of high-handedness is to some extent ameliorated by his notes in *Side Lights on the Kilberry Book of Ceol Mor* (1984) and *Further Side Lights* (1986), which were his recollections of what had been taught to him by Sandy Cameron, John MacDougall Gillies and John MacDonald, Inverness. Published by his son James, the notes show how he reached some of his decisions as to the best setting or reading of a phrase, and he emerges as considerably more open-minded than he appears from other Piobaireachd Society publications.

Unfortunately some of the comments he made in private correspondence belie this apparent open-mindedness, especially in his attitudes to John MacDonald (see above).

In the *Sidelights*, he declares that John MacDonald 'justly merits the reputation which he possesses of being a most beautiful piobaireachd player. He is universally so described by all who know anything about the music. MacDougall Gillies is nevertheless his superior, incomparably so in knowledge and also as a player in everything but mere technique. There is far more feeling and expression in Gillies's rendering of a tune than in anything that MacDonald can produce ...'

No 'possibly' or 'it could perhaps be claimed' for Archibald Campbell. With him it was 'I think so, therefore it is so'. The voice of the ruling classes. I wonder how many would agree with his opinion as voiced above? Only MacDougall Gillies' pupils, and possibly not all of them?

Of his teaching, he said (p.4):

'I commenced to play the pipes in 1894' (when he was 17)' but did not start attempting to do so well till 1897, when I had lessons from Angus MacRae. From him I learnt two piobaireachd, '*Too Long in this Condition*' and '*MacLeod of Raasay's Salute*'. I had some instruction from John MacColl when he visited Kilberry in 1898 and 1899. My real piobaireachd education commenced under MacDougall Gillies about 1900, and since then I have never missed going to him in Glasgow as frequently as I could. When I was on leave from India in 1905 John MacDonald spent three weeks at Kilberry and I learnt from him for several hours a day. During my second leave in 1910-11 I went to Gillies frequently and finally in May 1911 Alec Cameron came to Kilberry for three weeks and I worked with him for six hours a day at least during the whole of that time. What I have put down in the score and in the notes is what I have been taught, not what I have evolved as my own ideas . . . . What I have tried to compile is some record on paper on how the tunes are played by my instructors, a task which few, if any, others have attempted and for which few are qualified by necessary training with pen and chanter'.

Even now, the arrogance peeps out: he assumes that because he is an educated man and has had a few weeks training from master-pipers (and how many learners can summon a famous teacher to their house for three weeks?), he is therefore qualified to put it all before the piping world. It must take supreme self-confidence. But this attitude is very much part of the times he lived in, when his birth entitled him to privilege not dreamed of today. Few others had the nerve to put their pens to paper, and there is nobody who has left us information of the kind found in the *Sidelights* – and those that did make a contribution had fewer qualifications to do so than Archibald Campbell. We have only to read the correspondence in the Oban Times, concealed under pen-names, to appreciate the clear thinking and lucid style of Kilberry.

It is electrifying to hear any pupil of John MacDonald, even one of only three weeks, describe his playing as 'perhaps a little rigid and wooden at times'. Later, he quotes Alec Cameron as saying that both Gillies and John MacDonald were beautiful players. Kilberry felt that MacDonald tended to cut the middle note in a run of three too short – this is sometimes said to be the style of Calum Piobair MacPherson rather than the Camerons.

The notes in the *Sidelights* are immensely interesting, and a debt is owed to James Campbell for putting them before us. His notes on the *Lament for Captain MacDougall* quote Robert Meldrum's comment on the last bar but one of the Ground, which has two 'extra' notes. In spite of Meldrum's instructions to play it exactly as written, Kilberry 'brought the bar into accordance with convention by removing the dots'. Whose convention? This is an example of theory taking precedence over tradition, and pipers resent the high-handedness, however well meant, of editorial confidence in his own ideas. Yet it is he who immediately points out other examples of 'something like an extra beat or half beat' being introduced towards the end of a ground, citing the *Lament for the Children, the Battle of the Pass of Crieff, the Bells of Perth* and *Isabel MacKay*, and concludes that 'This is evidently a peculiarity of the music' – so why emend *Captain MacDougall*?

Dugald MacNeill points out that every writer on the stave had slavishly followed bar-arithmetic, from Joseph MacDonald on, and Kilberry was following this tradition. His successor, Archie Kenneth, proved more flexible.

On page 53 Kilberry tells us that both of his teachers, Gillies and Cameron, told him the first variation of *Seaforth's Salute* should be played 'round', which he took to mean in 3/4 time, 'but I have been through this variation time after time with both of them and on the metronome as it is very difficult to get hold of . .' Not many good piobaireachd players would use a metronome, which seems totally alien to piobaireachd – but then, so do time signatures themselves (in my opinion).

Again in *Further Sidelights*, a comment like that on p.45 brings us up short: 'Most piobaireachds should be finished in a quarter of an hour'. Should? Can we lay down these rules? Indeed, should we?

We can forgive all this, however, when we read Kilberry on piobaireachd, in the Piping Times in 1995:

'It is certainly difficult music to understand, but in a well played piobaireachd on a well tuned pipe, sounds can be produced which are never heard in marches, strathspeys or reels, and which satisfy the ear of a skilled piping musician in a way that no other sounds can do.

'I suggest that . . . the piobaireachd form of pipe music was developed . . . for the purpose of bringing out from the instrument the most pleasing sounds of which it is capable.

'Piobaireachd is a product, not of barbarism, but of civilisation'.

That last sentence could be framed and hung on the wall.

SOURCES
Notices of Pipers
William Donaldson
James Campbell in the Piper Press and Piping Times

James Campbell at Oban in 1995, talking to Gordon Walker before the March to the Games Field. This is a characteristic portrait of James, who was always friendly with current pipers, and interested in their playing.
(PHOTOGRAPH BY COURTESY OF THE COLLEGE OF PIPING)

Loch Fyne

TUNES ASSOCIATED WITH LOCH FYNE AREA:
Ardrishaig, by J.A.MacLellan 1959 2/4 M 4
The Buntie, or the Glenfurness Blacksmith, by John Masson 2/4 M 2
Climbing Duniquaich, by D.C.Mather S 2 (Duniquaich is a steep hill to the north of Inveraray)
Colonel Campbell of Inverneill's Farewell to the Argylls 2/4 M 2
Dalnahassaig, by G.S.MacLennan S 2
Kilmartin Castle, by D.Campbell 6/8 M 2
The Lasses of Kilmartin R 2
Lochgilphead, by Colin MacLauchlan R 2
Lochgilphead Fair 4/4 R 2
Lochgilphead (Iain MacLeod), by Archie Kenneth 2/4 M 4
Lochgilphead Pipers' March, by Archie Kenneth 6/8 M 4

See also Inveraray

PIPERS ASSOCIATED WITH LOCH FYNE

ARCHIE MACDONALD from Invera (= Inveraray) competed at Edinburgh in 1786, and was placed third. He was described as 'late piper to the 78th Regiment'.

JOHN MACLAUCHLAN from Loch Fyne was a piper in the 74th Regiment (later the 2nd HLI). He fought in the Peninsular War in Spain, where he distinguished himself by his bravery under fire. When his pipe was damaged, he coolly repaired it in the thick of battle and resumed playing. He was killed in 1808, at Vittoria. He should not be confused with the John MacLachlan, from the same area, who was Donald MacPhedran's brother-in-law (see below).

ALEXANDER MCKELLAR or MacKeillor, from Loch Fyne, was a Pipe Major in the 78th Regiment (Seaforths), from 1860 to 1863. He served in the Indian Mutiny. He competed at Inverness in both 1860 and '61, but was not placed. He was known as a composer, and his works included his re-writing of *The Barren Rocks of Aden,* based on a tune originally made by James Mauchline of the 78th (1836-45), acknowledged to be much in need of improvement.

JOHN GRAHAM-CAMPBELL of Shirvan, near Lochgilphead, 'a talented piper and composer of reels and jigs.' He was an advocate who was badly wounded in the First World War. His son DUGALD was a good amateur player too, who compiled 'A Guide to the Judging of Piping', published by the College of Piping in 1954. John, known as Jock, was Archie Kenneth's uncle, being his mother's brother (see below).

CHARLES MAITLAND was well known as the Pipe Major of the Inveraray Pipe Band – see under Inveraray Pipe Band, below.

ELSPETH CAMPBELL, niece of the Duke of Argyll, was the daughter of Lord Archibald Campbell, founder of the Inveraray Pipe Band; she was herself a capable player, at the end of the 19th century. She was among the founder-members of the Piobaireachd Society in 1903.

JOHN MACGREGOR 'from a village on Loch Fyne' – see under Inveraray.

DONALD F. ROSS was the son of the doctor at Lochgilphead. He became a doctor himself, and was a good piper who won the Gold Medal at Oban in 1937. He was a pupil of Willie Ross of the Scots Guards. Ian C. Cameron said he returned from Liberia and Ecuador, to become a doctor in England. He was killed in a road accident, and is buried in his native Lochgilphead.

NIALL CAMPBELL from Strachur was a noted figure in the worlds of piping and of shinty in the 20th century. Born in 1919 he became a piper in the Argyll and Sutherland Highlanders, and on his discharge became personal piper to Sir Fitzroy MacLean, the owner of the Strachur estate where Niall made his home. He devoted much of his life to service to the community, and taught hundreds of Argyll children to play the pipes, as well as running the pipe band of the former pupils of Dunoon Grammar School. In 1986 he was awarded the B.E.M. for services to the community and to piping. He died in 1998, and five pipers from the Strachur Piping Association played at his funeral.

Two writers who were not themselves pipers but had an influence on the piping world were both associated with Argyll:

NEIL MUNRO (1863 – 1930), probably best known for his *Para Handy* tales, made frequent reference to pipes and piping in his novels and short stories, and especially in his tale *The Lost Pibroch*.

Neil was born in Inveraray, his mother being a housemaid, possibly in the Castle. His father was said to be a member of the ducal family, or one of their guests. His grandmother was from Loch Aweside, and he grew up as a Gaelic speaker in Inveraray, steeped in the traditions of the area. When he was 12 years old, his mother married the retired governor of Inveraray Jail, Malcolm Thomson, and Neil later started work, reluctantly, in a lawyer's office in Inveraray. In 1881, he left for Glasgow to pursue a career as a journalist.

He worked for forty years for the Glasgow Evening News, of which he became the editor from 1919 to 1924. He was widely acclaimed as a writer in his own lifetime, and was awarded two Honorary Doctorates, by Glasgow and Edinburgh Universities. He died at Helensburgh in 1930, and An Comunn Gaidhealach erected a monument to him at the head of Glen Aray.

His short stories are couched in a high-flown, almost hysterical, 'poetic' language, and are full of a mawkish sentimental romanticism. He gave this full rein in the Shieling Stories, but had apparently grown out of it by the time he wrote the novels and the Para Handy tales. His novels are written in a clear, controlled, narrative English, making good use of his knowledge of Gaelic and his detailed familiarity with the Highlands, and seem to some extent to be modelled on the adventure stories of Robert Louis Stevenson. They are a thoroughly good read, even today, and *John Splendid* in particular gives us an excellent idea of life in Argyll in the mid-17th century. It is especially interesting in that it is written from the Campbell point of view.

But in the Shieling Stories, he had indulged in a Celtic frenzy which is not acceptable to many modern readers. His story *The Lost Pibroch* is far too romantic and sentimental. Here the influence is more James Barrie than Stevenson, though he disliked Barrie as a 'Lowlander trying to create the romance of the Highlands'.

In 1896, *The Lost Pibroch and Other Shieling Stories* appeared, written as if they were folktales drawn from the oral tradition. *The Lost Pibroch* is about two pipers who appear in a small township and compete with the local blind piper, Paruig Dall. Finally, Paruig plays the Lost Pibroch, known to have an unsettling effect on the entire adult male population, and all of them then leave, abandoning the women and children to fend for themselves. It is a curious tale, and there has been much argument about its meaning. Is it an allegory of the dereliction of the old life in the Highlands? This seems the most feasible interpretation, though it is not clear why the families were left behind. Do they perhaps represent the fragile Highland way of life, with the implication of guilt on the part of the departing menfolk in giving it up?

The high-flown style no longer inspires great admiration: mirth is more likely to be the reaction, especially to the reading of extracts aloud in front of an audience. The first two paragraphs give us a flavour of the thing:

'To the make of a piper go seven years of his own learning and seven generations before. If it is in, it will out, as the Gaelic old-word says; if not, let him take to the net or the sword. At the end of his seven years one born to it will stand at the start of knowledge, and leaning a fond ear to the drone, he may have parley with old folks of old affairs...

'Today there are but three pipers in the wide world, from the Sound of Sleat to the Wall of France. Who they are, and what their tartan, is not for one to tell who has no heed for a thousand dirks in his doublet, but they may be known by the lucky ones who hear them. Namely players tickle the chanter and take out but the sound; the three give a tune the charm that I mention – a long thought and a bard's thought, and they bring the notes from the deeps of time, and the tale from the heart of the man who made it'.

This is only the start of the tale. They don't write stuff like that any more, and let us be thankful. I find it unacceptable, falsely poetic, positively damaging to the good name of piping. But it was much admired at the time it was published, when 'fey' was a term of admiration, and clearly it is wrong to dismiss it when it was so much a product of its age. Even as we laugh, we cannot fail to recognize the sincerity and the deep feeling of nostalgia in his work.

Perhaps that was the secret of his success: the lowland cities in the 1890s were full of expatriate Highlanders, and in them there was the perpetual nag of guilt and regret, a kind of shame at having left their own world. Neil Munro's Celtic poeticism must have touched a nerve. Today we are hardened, and the exiles have settled down, no longer missing the Highland life, proud of our roots but not longing to return. *The Lost Pibroch* supplied a need of the time, and it is wrong to mock it.

Had he written only the Shieling Stories, so sentimental, so earnest, he might be barely remembered today, but his journalism was widely enjoyed, and his novels, too. They are much more restrained in style, well-structured and lively. And of course his Para Handy tales endeared him to all Scots – and showed that he did have a sense of humour after all.

We should be grateful to him for using piping as a subject of his writing. How many works are there, fictional works as opposed to documentary travellers' accounts, which even mention piobaireachd, let alone name and describe any of them? Walter Scott did his bit, and between them, he and Neil Munro put piobaireachd on the literary map; all credit to them for that.

Neil Munro brought piping into other stories, *The Red Hand*, *The Secret of the Heather Ale*, *War*, and *The Oldest Air in the World* being good examples, all with the same pseudo-historic, over-romanticised descriptions. To what extent Neil Munro shaped later perspectives of piping is uncertain: surely he must have had a hand in forming the ambivalent attitudes of the modern press to piping, attitudes in which the ribaldry of the English meets the romance of the Highlands as depicted by himself and Scott, with uneasy results.

On the whole, the tee-hee approach dominates. The shriek of mirth which greeted a reference to the Piping Times on a television programme shows that civilisation has not yet penetrated far south. Maybe we should send a missionary.

HENRY WHYTE, known by his pen-name Fionn (Gaelic for White), wrote on Highland subjects, and especially piping. He lived in Glasgow, but was born in Easdale of a Mull family, and for many years had a house in Easdale. His book *The Martial Music of the Clans* (1904) became a classic, and he wrote the background historical notes for the piobaireachd works in Glen's Collection (1907) so that he was a fore-runner to Alec Haddow and Seumas MacNeill. He also wrote, probably as a young man, perhaps even a schoolboy, a Prize Essay on the Rankin pipers of Mull, which contains some interesting detail. This essay is now in the Tobermory Museum.

Both Neil Munro and Fionn belong to the period when the Piobaireachd Society was founded and began to publish the music in written form. All at that time seem to have been motivated by a feeling of panic, an awareness that unless someone did something, the old music would be lost – as indeed the old harp music has been lost. We may not entirely like what they did, but they did do something, and it was the best they could, according to their knowledge and resources at the time. Again we are guilty of sneering at their efforts, but could we honestly claim we would have done better, a hundred years ago?

DUNCAN MACLEAN

DUNCAN MACLEAN WHO NOW HAS his home in Ardrishaig was born on the island of Scarp, to the west of Harris, in 1918. A musical and talented man, he plays the fiddle and the pipes, and is also a landscape painter, linguist, poet and keen angler. As a piobaireachd player, he was largely self-taught, relying on books and tapes, after he left school and was living near Amhuinnsuidhe Castle, in Harris. He says the ghosts of his forebears taught him, and he plays on the right shoulder ('the natural way, it was the Highland regiments who changed it'). He found the teaching tapes of Donald MacLeod helpful, and later became a friend of Donald's. He feels he owes Donald a debt as his strongest piping influence.

As a young man he was not able to compete, as he was living on an isolated croft on Scarp, where the family worked four acres of land and supported themselves by lobster fishing. Later he was working long hours, before he went into the army. Before the outbreak of World War II, he was with the Post Office for three years, and was already beginning to compose pipe tunes. He did not attempt to compose piobaireachd, however, since he knew enough about it to appreciate it is more than merely a matter of finding a melody and putting variations to it. But his output of Light Music has been prolific, and he made many fine tunes. A born teacher, he has had several piping pupils, including his son Allan (see below).

On the outbreak of war, Duncan and his brothers Calum and Donald joined the 51st Highland Division, leaving home together on September 4th 1939. Duncan remembers looking back and seeing his mother at the door of the crofthouse, waving goodbye to her three sons.

All of them survived the war. They went first to TA

Duncan MacLean, at the age of 81, playing the chanter in his house in Ardrishaig, in 1999.

training, then Duncan was posted to the 4th Camerons. He recalls hearing Willie M. MacDonald playing *Bonnie Strathyre* in the barracks, and has never forgotten it. Another memory was of John Wilson, who in spite of having lost parts of his fingers as a boy was a fantastic jig player. Duncan treasures a memory of him tapping out a rhythm on a bren gun box with his tackety boots, before playing the *Lochaber Gathering*. They were waiting at Le Havre for transport to the front.

Their fighting career did not last long. Duncan, like so many Highlanders, was captured at St Valery, and spent the next five years as a prisoner of war. He worked as forced labour in coal mines and in a factory in Germany; these were not entirely wasted years, however, for Duncan has an amazing ear for languages, and came home a fluent speaker of French and German adding them to his native Gaelic, in which he is a considerable scholar, and the English he acquired as a boy. He has also added Italian, self-taught for his own amusement. All his life one of his pleasures has been translating Gaelic songs into English poetry, a gift which has remained with him into old age.

As far as piping was concerned, his five years as a P.O.W. were a blank. On his return from the war, he saw a lovely set of pipes in R.G.Lawrie's window in Renfield Street, Glasgow, and was prompted to go in and buy himself a practice chanter – all he could afford. He says that was him hooked again, and has been hooked ever since.

He then availed himself of the government scheme to offer college training to ex-servicemen. He took a one-year course in Rural Science and Geography at a college near Preston, and trained as a teacher. He taught for five years – 1950-55 – at a school near Nottingham, while doing research in Rural Science for Nottingham University. He recalls a night when his Nottingham landlord came into his room and saw the practice chanter lying on the table. 'What's that, Duncan?' he asked, 'Is it an umbrella?'

He was not well paid, and when he married a Harris girl, Peggy MacLennan, in 1953, they had to live on a weekly wage of £6, of which £3 went on rent for their rooms. Peggy was a lovely singer with a passion for Gaelic songs.

In 1955 they moved to a teaching post in Orkney, where they lived on the island of Egilsay for five years, before they had two years in South Orkney. The next move was to Lochaline, in Morvern. After that Duncan was the head teacher of a primary school near Stranraer, until finally he moved to a bigger school at Achnamara, in Mid-Argyll. He remained there as headmaster for ten years, until heart trouble forced him to retire, on doctor's orders, at the age of 60. He and his wife moved to Ardrishaig, where she died in 1996. Duncan and his son Allan now live in Brae Road, Ardrishaig.

ALLAN MACLEAN was taught his piping first by his father, and made good progress, having what is known as a 'photographic ear', that is, he can memorise and play back any tune he hears played once through. In the 1970s, John MacFadyen was holding weekly piobaireachd classes in Oban, and Duncan and Allan attended them together. Allan later competed locally with some success. He has an excellent ear for tuning. He works as a postman in and around Ardrishaig, and takes part in the piping life of the district.

After his retirement Duncan taught local boys, such as Archie McAlister from Ardrishaig, and he became a focal point for pipers throughout the area. He ran talks and classes for local youngsters, and when John MacFadyen and Professor Alec Haddow came to give a recital and lecture in Lochgilphead, they invited Duncan to come along as Guest of Honour. Steeped in piping tradition, he was a regular attender at the Argyllshire Gathering at Oban until very recently. His compositions, both published and unpublished, will stand the test of time, as his memorial.

His compositions include:

George MacLeod, Esq. of Harris M
Peter Ross, Esq. of Tarbert, Harris M
The Shores of Achnamara M
Miss Margaret Cunningham, Ardrishaig M
Memories of Archie Kenneth M
Miss Mary Kenneth's Wedding S
Pipe Major Willie Smith J
Willie and Lily Smith at Burwick M
Allan MacLean Esq., Ardrishaig RM
Donald's and Margaret's Wedding M (This is Duncan's nephew, Donald A. MacLean, who is a piper himself).
Audrey's Farewell to the Argyll Arms Hotel, Ardrishaig M
Nicol MacCallum Esq S
Master Peter MacArthur, Lochgilphead M
Archie MacArthur, Esq., Lochgilphead J
Pipe Major Ronald Lawrie M
Professor Iain MacLeod M
Donald MacPherson Esq. M
Alex and Bridget Mackenzie J
Master Angus MacLennan, Govig, Harris R
Miss Catherine Hamilton, Braefield, Ardrishaig S
Lament for Peggy MacLennan M
Johnnie and Marie Hamilton M
Hughie Robertson, Esq., Ardrishaig M
George Bruce Esq., Ardrishaig M
Miss Ellis MacGregor of Erskine M
David MacLean's Farewell to the Scots Guards M
Baby Louise Sinclair, Dundee R
The Mountains of Harris M
Sandy and Chirsty, Amhuinnsuidh, Harris M
Mrs Iain Graham, Silvercraigs M
British Airways Club Pipe Band M
Ross and Ailsa MacFarlane, Ardrishaig M

Alex Moore Esq., Royal Hotel, Ardrishaig M
Mrs Patricia Wilson, Kilmichael, Lochgilphead M
Iain MacGregor Esq., Ardenlea, Ardrishaig M
Archie MacMillan Esq., Lochaline, Morvern M
Fred MacAllan Esq., (forester), Lochaline, Morvern M
Patricia Johnstone's Welcome to Ardrishaig M
Pipe Major Donald MacLeod R
Ronald MacDonald's Farewell to Ulva SA (this refers not to the isle of Ulva to the west of Mull, but to Ulva in Mid-Argyll, just south of Taynish and north of the island of Danna. Ronald, a piobaireachd devotee, farmed at Ulva before retiring to his native Ardnamurchan in 1980.)

The order of these compositions is as given to me by Duncan. They reflect many aspects of his life. Today (2003) he is 85, and not in the best of health, but he plays his chanter yet, and remembers the old days clearly.

DOUGIE FERGUSON from Islay is now living in Lochgilphead, where he is a respected authority on piping. At one time, living in Kirkintilloch, he worked in Grainger and Campbells, the pipemakers in Glasgow, when Donald MacLeod was the manager. Donald became Dougie's teacher, and taught him the art of circular breathing; it was Dougie who passed this on to Archie MacNeill from Gigha (Blind Archie), the composer of *Donald MacLean's Farewell to Oban*. Dougie was recently described on the BBC as one of the great characters of piping. Nowadays he does not care to talk about his piping; he says it stirs too many memories.

Today piping in the Ardrishaig / Lochgilphead area is in the hands of CRAIG and IAIN CAMPBELL of Baddan, a farm on the Oban road not far from Lochgilphead. Known universally as the Baddan twins, they used to play in the Power of Scotland pipe band. Now they are busy teaching youngsters and running the Glasgow-Skye Association pipe band. They put in a lot of effort to ensure that the traditions of local piping are passed on to the next generation. Pipers like them, who put into piping as much as they took from it, are the lifeblood of local tradition, all over the country.

Another member of the piping community is ARCHIE MCALISTER, Ardrishaig, who played in the Mid-Argyll band, and RODDY BUCHANAN is another local player. They, the Baddan twins, Dougie Ferguson and the MacLeans, Duncan and Allan, are keeping it all going.

SOURCES
Piping Times
Notices of Pipers
Duncan MacLean
Archie MacAlister
Local tradition

ARCHIE KENNETH

THE FOLLOWING ACCOUNT IS BASED on the tribute to Archie Kenneth by James Campbell, delivered at the Conference of the Piobaireachd Society in 1990. It is here a little condensed, and has been used with the kind permission of the author.

James Campbell said:

'If what I have to say leans towards the cheerful it's because he had a good span of life and shared in the taste of pipers for good company and he left a legacy of learning and enterprise for the benefit of this and future generations.

'Archie Kenneth was born in 1915 at Shirvan, Argyll. His mother was a Graham–Campbell. His father had been killed at Gallipoli before he was born. Thus it came about that his earliest years were spent in his grandparents' house at Shirvan [on the west side of Loch Fyne]. His uncle, Jock Graham–Campbell, was severely wounded in the War, and when he had recovered sufficiently to be able to return home his parents handed Shirvan over to him and moved some eleven miles to a house, built about 1910, on land which was Shirvan property. The land was called Stronachullin, and the house also became known as Stronachullin [north of Ardrishaig]. It was here that Archie fetched up at the age of four or five and it was here that, with two comparatively short interruptions, he remained for the rest of his life.

'The first interruption came when between the ages of eight and seventeen his schooling took place at two educational establishments in England. That was something of which he was heartily ashamed. At school he was remembered for his skill as a performer on the piano accordion and for his staunch championing of the cause of Scottish independence. I well remember an occasion when a visitor to Stronachullin, during a spell of particularly vile winter weather, ventured the conversational gambit that really one sometimes wished one lived in the South of England. Archie did not disguise his dissent. 'I would rather', he said, 'be a tinker on the roads of Argyll than live in the South of England'.

'The other interruption was War service in 1939/40. He had joined the Territorial Army before the War. His health was never consistently good [he suffered from epilepsy], and I reckon that a fully informed medical board would have ruled him out. But the medical vetting of the Territorials was cursory in the extreme. So the severe winter of 1939/40 found him an officer in the 8th Argylls in France. And when the fighting began in May he showed himself to be, as anyone who knew him would expect, a highly courageous and efficient platoon leader. Efficiency in accepted military understanding was not one of Archie's characteristics, but the 8th Argylls were adept in absorbing and exploiting to the common good, deviations from the military norm. There was an occasion in the early days at Aldershot when the officer with whom Archie shared a room had risen in sufficient time to prepare himself for an early morning parade. Nearing the end of his preparation he noticed that Archie was still in bed, and said 'Look, you'd better show a leg, we parade in ten minutes'. The next thing he saw was

Archie bolting out of the room in front of him. He had gone to bed in his clothes, and the business of washing and shaving had not been seen as a necessary preliminary to the day's work.

'There was another occasion at about the same time when Archie, smoking a pipe, encountered a company commander and executed a friendly salute. The company commander took me aside and said, 'James, do explain to Archie that he must never salute with his pipe in his mouth'. I dutifully discharged this instruction, only to be told that 'He was lucky to get any sort of salute'.

'After the unit's return from France in June 1940, and after an impressive spell of active service which saw him mentioned in dispatches, Archie was invalided out of the Army and he returned to Stronachullin and to service in the Home Guard. His interest in piping had developed in the years before the War and his training had been in the hands of his uncle. He also had the advantage of teaching by Pipe Major W. Ross during the latter's annual sojourn in Mid Argyll. This interest was further developed after his return from the War, side by side with a spell of research into the cultivation and hybridisation of rhododendrons. When the War was over, he subscribed to Frank Kingdon Ward's plant hunting expeditions in the Himalayas and in China. Kingdon Ward was the greatest plant collector of his time, and Archie became the recipient of rare seeds which enabled him to produce new and unique varieties of plants. From this hobby he later turned his attention to the botanical life of the West Highlands. Field botany became his principal natural history interest, and for many years his main efforts were directed to the flora in his particular area of Argyll – Knapdale and Kintyre. . . . As was recorded in an obituary notice in 'The Glasgow Naturalist', his work in this field made a very valuable contribution to the understanding of the taxonomy of a critical group of plants and led to the description of a number of new species. One such now bears his name in the records of the Botanical Society of the British Isles. This was just one instance of his talent for spotting and publicising the new and unusual – a talent which was freely displayed in his concern with his other great hobby, the music of the pipes.

'Apart from these two specialised subjects he maintained a wide inter-

Archie Kenneth in 1980, in typical headgear described by James Campbell as 'a knitted tea cosy'. (PHOTOGRAPH BY KIND PERMISSION OF THE COLLEGE OF PIPING)

est in affairs of the world and an amazing store of knowledge of literature and poetry. All this stemmed from an ability to read widely and to commit what he had read to abiding memory . . .

'He was a personality, an institution, almost a legend. Even his appearance was distinctive. Not for him the tie, the bonnet or the kilt. An open neck shirt, green trousers and a knitted tea cosy on his head were the order of the day. . . Some may remember, a few years back, his exposition on the subject of the discovery of the Walter MacFarlane Manuscript. He warmed to his work, and shed his jacket, and there were his green trousers sustained by red braces.

'Then there were his robust and forceful expressions of opinion in situations where others might be more hesitant. Instances of these were experienced with refreshing regularity when he spoke from the floor at Piobaireachd Society conferences. No one was left in doubt as to his belief and his meaning. This forthright trait is illustrated by a splendid story which I had from Kenneth MacKay. The occasion was the Tobermory Games, at which Archie was one of three judges. The entry for the piobaireachd competition was larger than usual, and the possibility occurred to the presiding judge that there might be difficulty in catching the last boat to Oban. So he suggested to his colleagues that indication should be given as soon as a competitor showed himself to be out of the running. Archie was quite uncooperative, and instead of humming and hawing and saying he did not quite fancy the idea, he gave it out that if the suggestion was adopted he would withdraw from the bench then and there.

'Such stories told to future generations might conjure up a picture of a certain grumpiness and intolerance, but of course we know such a picture to be false. Characteristic of Archie was his kindliness, his friendliness, his approachability. .

'What was and is the influence of Archie Kenneth? First of all there was his service on the Music Committee of the Piobaireachd Society for over forty years, of which the last twenty-five saw him as Editor of the Society's publications. Before he became Editor he was, so to speak, run in by his participation in the production of Book 10. The notion of Book 10 was conceived very late in my father's career, when he was over eighty and really beyond the unassisted labour which he had put into the production of the earlier books.

[Kilberry wrote to Archie outlining his idea of republishing tunes already printed in Angus MacKay's book, with editorial improvements] – 'Not something to be embarked on in your eighty fourth year without an assistant with a clear eye and with the knowledge and the tact and the sympathy to sustain you. This sustenance Archie provided. Simply as an example of his value was his discovery that the structure of the tune *War or Peace* as recorded by Angus MacKay made sense, albeit that the structure was unique. Previously the MacKay setting had been seen as more or less a hotchpot of random variations. The correspondence between them reveals Archie's increasing value as a spur and a prop, well appreciated by my father . . .

'And so when my father died in 1963 there was Archie to carry on. It was a stroke of great good fortune for the Society that he was available to preserve for another twenty-five years the momentum of publication and at the same time to retain the respect of a not uncritical piping public for what went out in the name of the Music Committee. He took over just about at the time that disability in his hands put an end to his playing of the pipes, but this misfortune seemed to serve to fuel his zest for the academic side of the business. His work was the more remarkable for the fact that much of the time he was exploring beyond the beaten track of tunes for which, either directly or by analogy, there was some traceable link with traditional teaching. Striking examples of his original scholarship are the number of tunes in the later books which were translations from the Campbell Canntaireachd. In less expert hands such expansion could have resulted at best in indifference and at worst in hostility. As it is, we and our successors are enriched by the production of Books 11, 12, 13, 14 and 15. The fact that the contents of these books are of less contemporary concern than those of earlier books is of small significance in the light of the declared aim of the Society to aid in the general advancement and diffusion of knowledge of the ancient Highland Piobaireachd. If all the Society had stood for was to enhance the popularity of tunes familiar to competition audiences it could with dignity have folded its wings years ago. In this connection there was no more rigid adherent to the set tunes principle than Archie. He was looking outward the whole time, being concerned to foster interest in unfamiliar tunes in the light of accepted principles relating to structure and timing.

'So there is one facet of Archie's influence – the record of his work as music editor plus, of course, his many contributions on all aspects of bagpipe music to various publications and in particular to the Piping Times. . . He left a mass of published compositions which will be available for the enjoyment of those following on. . . Archie himself used to say that there is always a tendency to cut a contemporary composer, or indeed author, down to size, and that a composer's chances of recognition improve after his death. It is then that his work can be assessed free from the constraint which politeness might impose in his lifetime . . .

'To a present assessment of the influence of Archie Kenneth there is no full stop. It extends not only to the past and the present but also into the future. . .'

In the discussion which followed, Seumas MacNeill said:

'I think we all enjoyed very much the reminiscence of Archie and the evocation of his spirit and soul and personality. There are just two small reminiscences I would like to add. One was when Archie was running around frantically moving papers from here to there at one meeting, and he suddenly stopped and turned to me and said 'You know, there's madness in my method'. It summed him up pretty well.

'The other thing I always remember about Archie – it was really Alec Haddow who pointed it out. He said 'Archie is the world's expert on canntaireachd but he is the world's worst singer of piobaireachd'. He never used canntaireachd when he sang. It was embarrassing when you were for example in the bar at Ardvasar and Archie would suddenly burst out singing in his own particular canntaireachd, particularly if it was a six-eight march. The other people at the bar used to look at us and wonder where we had escaped from. It was all part of the Archie picture.'

To this, Malcolm McRae added:

'One particular aspect of Archie that surprised me when I first got to know him was his enthusiasm for the folk type groups and the music they play. He knew all the tunes, he had a vast knowledge of accordion music and fiddle music, and he would enthusiastically listen to the groups that you hear on the radio, the likes of Whistlebinkies and so on. He got enormous pleasure and enjoyment from that type of music, and he was well known to ever so many people in the folk scene. He was a man of many, many parts, there's no doubt of that'.

For my own part, I owe Archie Kenneth a debt for his kindly encouragement when I was tentatively dipping a toe in the vast subject of the historical background to piping. His response to a small piece I sent him was typical: he gave it, however unworthy, his full attention, and his comments were penetrating and helpful. He finished with 'You definitely have something here – keep up the good work'. It meant a lot to a beginner. He then followed up by sending me references and quotations, snippets of music and other material, not strictly relevant to his own work, but immensely useful in mine. He did not know me at all at this time, but what mattered to him was the subject, not the person, and he was one of the most open-minded scholars I ever met, always ready to consider new ideas.

An interesting comment on Archie Kenneth was made by Allan Shaw, who was

Presentation of the Archie Kenneth Quaich to L/Cpl Limbu of the Ghurkas, the first winner, in 1993. James Burnett made the presentation on behalf of the Piobaireachd Society. (PHOTOGRAPH BY KIND PERMISSION OF THE COLLEGE OF PIPING)

a shepherd employed by Archie. He said that whenever they met, Archie shook his hand, and this was a gesture of respect which was much appreciated.

Archie Kenneth did not do much teaching, but a distinguished pupil of his, who certainly did justice to the reputation of his mentor, was Arthur Gillies (see below).

In 1993, in memory of Archie Kenneth, a new competition was introduced for amateur pipers, competing for the Archie Kenneth Quaich. Run by the Piobaireachd Society, it has become an annual event, held in Edinburgh. The first winner of the Quaich was L/Cpl Limbu of the Ghurkas.

Archie Kenneth was a prolific composer. His compositions include:

Alec Haddow's Welcome to Stronachullin 6/8 J 4
Alec's Milk Carton 6/8 J 4
Alistair Campsie! Alistair Campsie! 6/8 M 2
Alone on the Hill 7/4 SA 2
Arthur Gillies 6/8 M 4
The Back of the Moon R 4
The Banks of the Add 6/8 J 4
The Bicker R 2
Birdsong R 2
Breton Pipers' March 6/8 M 4
Bridge of Orchy S 4
Butterfly 6/8 J 2
The Ceilidh House 6/8 J 4
The Center Counter Reel R 6
The Clear Light of Morning 6/8 SA 2
Conal Crovi R 4
Dr Leslie Craig 2/4 M 4
Dunadd S 4
Durness S 2
Fannet 2/4 M 4
The Far North R 4
Flower(s) of the Hills S 4
The Flywheel S 2
The Gambit 3/4 M 2
General MacDonald's Reel (arr) R 2
Glen Grant 3/4 M 4
Go to the Hill R 2
Honeycomb R 4
Horseman's Wood R 2
Iain Kenneth's March 2/4 M 4
Iain MacLeod (Lochgilphead) = *Lochgilphead (Iain MacLeod)* 2/4 M 4
In Sight of Ireland 6/8 J 4
An Irish Song (arr.) 9/8 J 2
Island of Danna S 4

Loch Fyne

The Lady in the Bottle 6/8 J 2
A Lament P with 7 variations
Leaving Loch Fyne-side 4/4 SA 2
The Lights of Winter S 4
Loch Fyne by Moonlight S 4
Lochfyneside S 3
The Lochgilphead Pipers' March 6/8 M 4
The Lock Gate 2/4 HP 2
The Luckpenny 3/4 M 2
The Maids of Bute 3/4 M 4
Maty Kenneth 2/4 M 4? *Katy Kenneth*?
Meall Horn 2/4 M 4
Molly Brannigan (arr) 4/4 R 2
Mrs Arthur Gillies 6/8 M 4
Mull of Cara 6/8 M 4
My Payment for the Cast R 4
Neil Crawford 2/4 M 4
No I'll Not 9/8 J 4
On Tap 2/4 HP 4
Over to Islay 6/8 J 4
Perpetual Motion 6/8 J 4
The Price of a Bottle of Beer 6/8 M 4
The Ptarmigan's Reel 4/4 R 4
Rhiconich 6/8 M 4
A Ring at the Door 6/8 J 2
The Road to Kylescu 2/4 M 4
Salute to James Campbell P with 10 variations (see below)
The Shadows of Evening 6/8 SA 2
The Shiers' March 6/8 M 2
The Shining Light S 4
The Silver Chain of Water S 4
The Skaters' Strathspey S 4
Song of Rebirth 7/4 SA 2
A Song of Winter 6/8 SA 2
Spider's Web 3/4 M 4
Spring Water 2/4 M 4
Taken from the Top R 4
To Strike a Spark 4/4 R 4
Waiting on the Tide 2/4 HP 6
The Waves of Kintyre S 4
West Highland Hospital, Oban S 2
What I Would Do 6/8 SA 2
The Whistler R 4
(arr.) *Will You Go?* 9/8 J 4

Additions to this list will be welcomed. Archie wrote an interesting piece for the Piping Times in July 1980 (vol.32, issue 10) explaining the titles he had given his tunes.

A book of Archie Kenneth's piobaireachd compositions was published separately. Interestingly, when freed of the restraints of the Piobaireachd Society, Archie chose to write his compositions not in bars but in phrases, and felt no necessity for each phrase to contain the same number of beats. At first glance, these phrases look like bars, but closer examination reveals much more flexibility. He says in his brief introduction that such things are a subjective decision for each player.

The titles of the piobaireachd works in the book are:
Lament for the Years
Waves on the Shore
Land of the Shell
The New Lock
Stones of Kilmartin
Salute to the Spring
Oil on the Shore (Brittany 1978)
The Grumbling
Salute to James Campbell.

Jackie Pincet, the Breton piper, made a 6/8 March in four parts, called *Hello Archie Kenneth!*

MINARD

MINARD, NEAR FURNACE ON THE west shore of Loch Fyne, was the home of the Gayre family who in the 1970s made it a focal point of piping activity. They ran solo piping competitions, composing competitions and hosted the earliest Conference of the Piobaireachd Society. In addition, Lt Col. Gayre invited George MacIntyre to become his piper when he was 'fed up' with living in England. Among George's many compositions (see above) were two marches, *Lt Col Gayre, Baron of Lochore*, and *Madam Gayre, Baroness of Lochore*, as well as tunes named after local places, such as *Minard Castle* and *Minard Bay*. William Barrie made a four-part strathspey *Madam Gayre of Gayre and Nigg's Strathspey.*

The Piobaireachd Society Conferences were initiated by Seumas MacNeill and John MacFadyen in 1973, the first being held in the Minard Castle Hotel. The venue proved too far out-of-the-way for most members, and the Conference soon moved to Dunblane Hydro, before it settled for some years (1975-1984) at Middleton Hall, Gorebridge, in West Lothian. Since 1985, the Conference has been in the Royal Hotel, Bridge of Allan.

Colonel Gayre held composing competitions in the 1970s. There were two categories, 'a simple march' and 'a competition-type reel'. The prizes were £10

Loch Fyne

for the winner in each category, and £20 for the over-all best tune submitted. The winner in 1976 was George MacIntyre with a 2/4 march. That year the Minard competition for solo playing was divided into three events:
1. Two tunes selected from the new tunes submitted for the composing competition;
2. Two marches chosen from the works of John MacColl, John MacLellan (Dunoon) and Willie Lawrie, all Argyll composers;
3. A strathspey and a reel, piper's own choice

The playing competitions were held out in the grounds of the Castle, beside Loch Fyne, but if the weather was unkind, it moved into the Castle and was held in the Guise Gallery.

This photograph, taken at Minard in 1976, shows Iain MacFadyen, Murray Henderson, Iain MacLeod, Arthur Gillies, Angus J. MacLellan, John D. Burgess, John MacFadyen – and the sponsor himself, Colonel Gayre of Gayre and Nigg, the short bald gentleman with glasses. Seumas MacNeill is on the left.
(PHOTOGRAPH BY KIND PERMISSION OF THE COLLEGE OF PIPING)

TULLOCH GORM is a Strathspey in four parts possibly named for a hill, and a farm of the same name, just to the south of Minard; this is not certain, as there is a small village called Tullochgorm on the River Spey, near Grantown-on-Spey, and some of the family of the Cummings, pipers at Castle Grant, lived there in the 18th century. Without more evidence we cannot be sure for which Tulloch Gorm the tune was named, but the fact that the tune was one of the regimental duty tunes of the Gordon Highlanders, played after the 2nd Set, may indicate that it belongs, along with *The Haughs of Cromdale*, to Grant country rather than Argyll.

Mìd-Argyll

DUNTROON

The traditions about Duntroon Castle, near Crinan, sometimes spelled Duntrune, are entangled with those about Dunyveg, on the south coast of Islay – and to some extent with those of Dunaverty, a castle in the south of Kintyre.

In his essay on *The Piper's Warning to his Master*, Alec Haddow did brilliant work in bringing order to chaos, disentangling the strands and laying them before us. The piping world is in his debt.

He says there were 'few episodes more romantic, and few more tangled' than that lying behind the piobaireachd known as *The Piper's Warning to His Master*, whether it was in Islay or in Mid-Argyll, in the 17th century.

Some of the traditions grew out of shieling tales (the previous centuries' equivalent of soap opera, with wild, lurid and unlikely stories, but full of life and entertainment); some came from garbled versions of historic fact, and, as Professor Haddow remarked, some must even be close to the truth. They have been complicated further by having tales from other areas and other times grafted onto them, in the usual way of folk stories.

Professor Haddow distinguishes two main variants of the basic story:

1. The chief approaches the castle by sea, but is sailing into a trap as the castle has fallen to the enemy. His piper, a captive inside the castle, conveys a warning, the chief turns back, the piper is punished by having his hand/fingers cut off, and/or is put to death.
2. The piper is captured by the enemy approaching by sea, warns his chief in the castle that attack is imminent. The piper is then hanged from the mast of his ship.

The chief is usually a MacDonald, the enemy a Campbell (or Campbell's ally). The many versions of this story involve:

two MacDonald chiefs
two Campbell enemies
two (or three) castles
two wars
two main piobaireachd works 'inextricably entangled'.

The two MacDonald chiefs were:
i) Coll(a) Ciotach MacDonald (Coll MacGhilleasbuig), known sometimes as Colkitto, of Colonsay (see below);
ii) his son Alasdair MacColla, who was Montrose's lieutenant, and led a band of fighting Ulstermen in the Civil Wars of the 1640s.

Their two Campbell enemies were:
i) Archibald Campbell, 7th Earl of Argyll, who became a Roman Catholic and fled to Spain;
ii) his son Archibald, 8th Earl and 1st (and only) Marquis – for whom the Salute was composed (see below). Known as Gruamach ('Grim'), he was a rigid Calvinist.

These two Campbells had an ally, Campbell of Calder (= Cawdor).
The two castles were:
i) Dunyveg (or Dun Naomhaig) in the south of Islay, stronghold of the MacDonalds of Dunyveg and the Glens (of Antrim), who were descended from the Lords of the Isles;
ii) Duntroon (or Dun Trune), near Crinan, Mid-Argyll, 'a small but important castle' because it commanded an easy route from the western isles through to the central lowlands.

A third castle sometimes involved in these stories was Dunaverty, in Kintyre (see above, *Lament for MacDonald of Sanda*).

The two wars were:
i) the struggle between the MacDonalds and the Campbells, especially Campbell of Calder, for possession of Islay. The climax came in 1615 when the MacDonalds surrendered Dunyveg, but the war rumbled on for at least another half-century;
ii) the Civil War campaign of Montrose against the Covenanters in the 1640s, and a raid through Argyll made by Alasdair MacColla in 1645, opposed by the Campbells.

The two main piobaireachd works are:
i) *The Piper's Warning to his Master;*
ii) *The Sound of the Waves Against Duntroon Castle*, and three related works associated with Duntroon: a) *Duntroon's Warning*
b) *Duntroon's March*
c) *Duntroon's Salute* (also called *MacDonald's Salute*, but not the same as the other work of that name)

The grounds of all four of ii) have 'family resemblances' but their variations differ greatly. This suggests they may have been developed from the same basic air.

Pipe Major Willie Gray, in a letter, said that an elderly relative sang to him 'one or two fine piobaireachds, including *The Piper's Warning*' adding in parentheses the words '(Colle mo runn, sech-ainn an dun)', which mean 'Coll my love, keep away from the castle'. This is the title or first line of a Gaelic song, of which Fionn quotes the first verse in his Notes to Glen's Collection of Ancient Piobaireachd. This song may be the air lying behind the piobaireachd works – or, on the other hand, could be a piobaireachd song based on them, something which happened quite often. Note that the song seems to have Coll Ciotach, the father of Alasdair, as the hero of the story, and this might be an indication that the song was old.

Alec Haddow gives a few of the associated stories, songs and legends, involving i) Colkitto's attack on Dunyveg in Islay; ii) Colkitto's attack on the Campbells in Jura; iii) Alasdair MacColla's attack on Zachariah Malcolm of Duntrune in Mid-Argyll.

It seems that the story as recorded in historical records did not involve a piper or a warning at all, although there was a complicated power-struggle between Sir

James MacDonald and Campbell of Calder. As a result, Islay, and Dunyveg, were lost to the MacDonalds for good in 1647.

It was also in 1647, after the siege of Dunyveg, that Alasdair MacColla embroiled MacDonald of Sanda in the siege of Dunaverty, when 300 prisoners were treacherously massacred by the Covenanting army. Alasdair fled to Ireland where he died in battle, and around this time his old father, Colkitto, was hanged. (see *MacDonald of Sanda*, above)

Alec Haddow concludes that the Piper's Warning story probably has a kernel of historic truth in it: it happened at Duntroon, not Dunyveg, in spite of the story as told by Donald MacDonald and Angus MacKay. Montrose had been briefly in Argyll early in 1645, just before Alasdair MacColla's raid took place. Documentary evidence is sparse, but this was probably the time of the Piper's Warning.

Professor Ronald Black, in a paper to the Gaelic Society of Inverness, suggested that there may have been two incidents, two pipers and two tunes, the earlier being Colla at Dunyveg in 1615 and the second Alasdair MacColla at Duntrune in 1645, and the two have become merged together.

In the autumn of 1645, Alasdair landed in the south of Kintyre and marched north through Kintyre and into Knapdale, where he was met by hostile Campbells, Malcolms and MacNeills. He took Castle Sween, and burned it, before moving on. He then sailed his ships round the coast, while his men marched overland, to attack Duntroon.

Above: Duntrune Castle today (Duntrune is the modern spelling). The evening light emphasises its commanding position on the shores of Loch Crinan.

Right: Duntrune Castle in close-up.

An interesting variant of the tale reverses the roles: it has the piper being from the Duntroon district, and he was a Campbell, taken by Alasdair and forced to sail with Alasdair's fleet. He played a tune to warn Duntroon of the impending attack, and it was Alasdair who cut off his fingers. This is clearly a re-telling for a Campbell or Malcolm audience.

Another version which seems closer to the historic truth has Alasdair's men arriving to take the castle, while Alasdair sailed round to join them. But the Campbells then re-took Duntroon, and Alasdair's piper was a prisoner within, and played to warn the fleet. This story is supported by the discovery of a skeleton under the flagged floor of the kitchen, when alterations were being made to the castle early in the 20th century, by the Malcolm family of Poltalloch. The skeleton was lacking one hand. It was given Christian burial elsewhere, and the room where it was found was exorcised, as the piper's ghost was haunting it (but not, it seems, playing *The Piper's Warning*, which is a pity as it might have revealed exactly how the warning was expressed. The ghost seems to have just flitted about, unable to play because its hand was missing).

There may be an echo of another Campbell, George Campbell of Airds, who married the beautiful but ruthless Janet Campbell, known as 'the Black Bitch of Dunstaffnage'. She is said to have had a piper's fingers cut off, believed to have been a piper associated with Dunyveg. This was probably before 1642, but close enough in time to have influenced stories about the punishment of a piper.

Professor Haddow pointed out that the warning was the conspicuous lopping off of two bars of the music in line 3 of the Ground and all the variations; and in those days – or at any rate in Joseph MacDonald's time, 100 years later – a bar or phrase was known as a 'finger' . . .

Alec Haddow ends his excellent essay with the wish that we should remember that piper: 'no matter which castle, which master, which piobaireachd, may he rest in peace'.

The Lament for the Castle of Dunyveg is presumably to be dated soon after 1647. The work appears in the Campbell Canntaireachd MS, where its title is *A'Glas*, and only an Urlar and Doubling are given – and the Doubling does not resemble anything given in Angus MacKay's setting, which has Urlar, Dithis and Doubling, and the usual Taorluath and Crunluath variations. The Urlar in the Canntaireachd MS resembles that of Angus MacKay in its 1st and 3rd lines.

There has been argument about the *Piper's Warning*: to be effective as a warning, the tune would have to be one familiar to the chief, so that he would notice the deviation from the norm and recognize it as a cause for suspicion. As this work has been edited for publication, some editors, notably General Thomason, a tidy-minded engineer, wanted to 'restore' it to its (supposed) original form; but Kilberry pointed out that in that case the title would have to be abandoned – and he printed it with the truncated 3rd line, *hiharin dan, hiharin dan*. Its main interest to us is the way the warning was conveyed, so the Piobaireachd Society version, based on the settings of Donald MacDonald and Angus MacKay, remains in its notably defective, mutilated form.

Donald McPhedran is credited with the composition of the 4-part reel called *Duntroon*, based on the piobaireachd *The Sound of the Waves Against Duntroon Castle* – or on the air underlying the piobaireachd?.

Today the Castle of Duntrune (this seems to be the modern spelling) has been restored as a dwelling, and the owner, Mr Robert Malcolm of Poltalloch, lives there.

POLTALLOCH

THE MALCOLMS OF POLTALLOCH WERE descended from the Malcolms of Duntrune, who opposed Alasdair MacColla in 1645, of whom Zachariah Malcolm was the best known. Around 1850, Neil Malcolm of Poltalloch – the one who met Queen Victoria at the Crinan Canal

Top: Poltalloch still looks imposing from a distance, looking across the fields; but closer inspection reveals a depressing ruin of a once fine mansion house. Its roof was removed in 1957, and the family moved to Duntrune Castle.

Bottom: Poltalloch close up.

in 1847 (see below) – had John MacLachlan as his piper in the newly-built mansion house (see below). John won the Prize Pipe at Inverness in 1851.

A later Malcolm employed Alexander Cameron, son of Donald Cameron, as his piper. William MacLean of Creagorry was piper to Lord Malcolm of Poltalloch in the late 1800s, and William Lawrie shortly before the First World War. The Malcolms seem to have been able to afford the top pipers of their time.

They were a leading family on the social scene of London in late Victorian and Edwardian times, and played an important part in the running of the Argyllshire Gathering. Lt Col J. Wingfield Malcolm Yr. of Poltalloch was Senior Steward of the Gathering in 1875, a position held, over the years, by a number of figures familiar in the piping world: John Campbell of Kilberry in 1895, for example, H.L. MacDonald of Dunach in 1910, Brigadier Cheape of Tiroran in 1924 and two of the Campbells of Airds in the 1940s. J. Graham-Campbell of Shirvan, uncle of Archie Kenneth, was Senior Steward in 1955, and Lt Col George Malcolm of Poltalloch in 1960 and 1964, and so on. The Argyllshire Gathering has always, since its inception in 1871, been closely bound up with good piping, and many of the Argyll gentry used to sit as judges for the piping competitions.

Poltalloch House was a big and elaborate mansion house built in 1849, at a cost of £100,000, an enormous sum in those days, the equivalent of well over a million pounds today. The Poltalloch estate at that time stretched for forty miles around the house, or so it was said. The old house which was there before Poltalloch was built was called Calton Mor, but it is not known what kind of place it was. When the big mansion house was built, the grounds and nearby estate were cleared of many of the tenants, and these included several Gillies families, who moved to the Cowal peninsula. The family of John MacDougall Gillies was among them.

Poltalloch is situated in an excellent position overlooking the beautiful countryside of Mid-Argyll, and has extensive grounds and gardens, now sadly overgrown. The mansion has been abandoned, and its roof was removed in 1957, when the last of the Malcolms moved into Duntrune Castle, nearby. The ruins of the elaborate mansion are depressing, even on a fine sunny day: the contrast between the present decay and the past glory is too strong. From a distance, on the road below, and seen from about half a mile away, the house is still impressive, and gives an idea of what used to be, in its heyday.

As well as the piobaireachd works discussed above, these tunes are associated with Poltalloch and Duntroon:

Poltalloch House, by Robert Meldrum S 2
Poltalloch House, by John MacLachlan 6/8 M 2

DALNAHASSAIG

DALNAHASSAIG WAS A FARM NEAR Kilmartin, on the lands of Poltalloch. Here the wedding of D.R. MacLennan was held, when he married a daughter of the house. D.R.'s half-brother, G.S.MacLennan, made the tune, a strathspey called *Dalnahassaig*, to mark the occasion.

Dalnahassaig lies in the middle of the flat land beside the winding river Add, not far from the hill known as Dunadd, an ancient historical site where the Kings of Dalriada are said to have been crowned. Today Dalnahassaig is a sad ruin in the middle of a poorly drained bog. It can (just) be reached on foot from either Dunadd farm or from the Drimvore road, but it is a difficult and wet walk, even after weeks of dry weather. The name Dalnahassaig means 'Plain of the ford', but there is now a (dilapidated) footbridge crossing the river. The ford is still marked on the Ordnance Survey map.

It must have been a biggish farm at one time, with substantial steadings and houses for farm workers. It was part of the Poltalloch estate, and the tenants were MacCallums for several generations. It was a MacCallum daughter who married D.R.MacLennan, the wedding which gave rise to the tune by his elder half-brother, George S.

The farm eventually was in the hands of D.R.'s brother-in-law, a bachelor who remained there long after he was unfit to work the land, and as he grew older and less able, the farm and buildings fell into disrepair. When he had to be removed into care at Lochgilphead, the house was beyond saving, and the Poltalloch estate had the roofs removed from the buildings, before abandoning them. Today Dalnahassaig is a sad sight, but it is easy to imagine it ringing with pipe music and laughter as the wedding of the daughter of the house was celebrated.

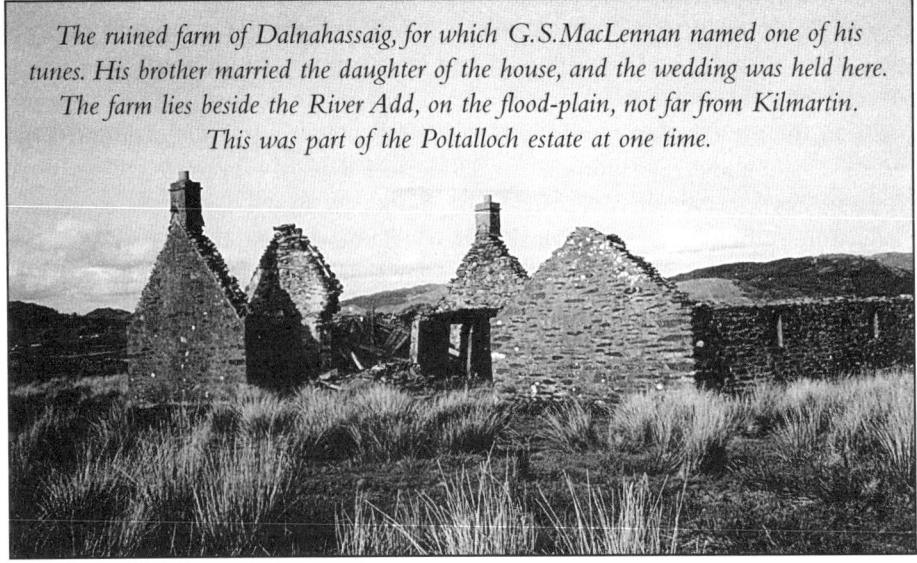

The ruined farm of Dalnahassaig, for which G.S.MacLennan named one of his tunes. His brother married the daughter of the house, and the wedding was held here. The farm lies beside the River Add, on the flood-plain, not far from Kilmartin. This was part of the Poltalloch estate at one time.

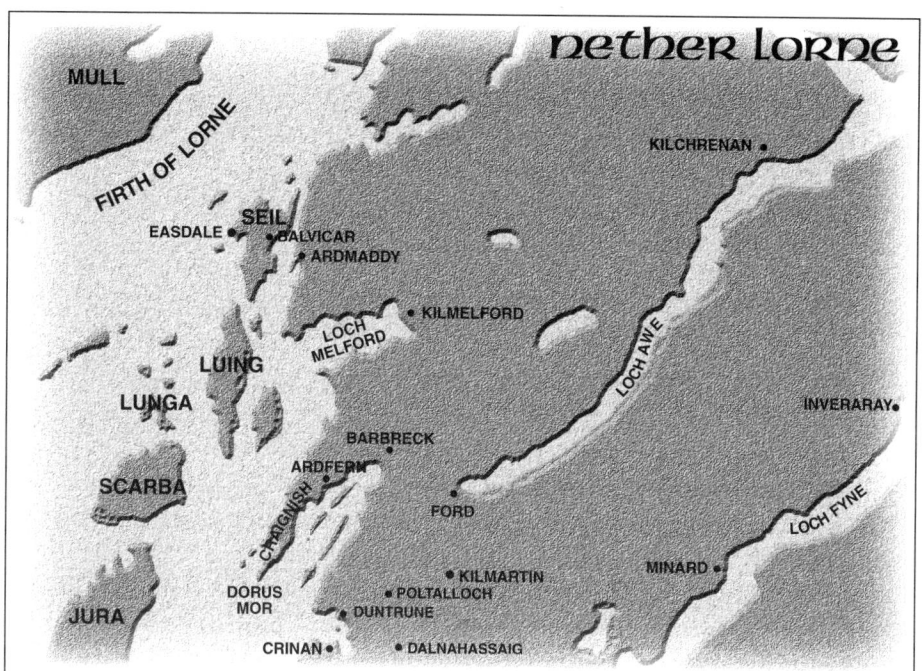

BARBRECK

THE REV. DUNCAN CAMPBELL, IN a talk in 1967 to the Gaelic Society of Inverness (see TGSI Vol XLV) on Gaelic Proverbs, quoted a saying: *Tha mi as ionnais, mar bha am Barra-bhreac gun piobaire* 'I lack it as Barbreck did a piper'. He told a story in explanation of this.

It seems that there was a man from Cladich called John MacArthur. This is the interesting bit – was it the Cladich on Loch Awe? If so, this could be evidence that the Loch Awe MacArthurs were indeed pipers (see below, John MacKenzie, Loch Fyne). No date is given for this story: is it possible that this piping John MacArthur was the same John MacArthur who fathered the piper John MacKenzie, born in 1807, at Ardmaddy?

Anyway, the John MacArthur of this story became piper to the Laird of Craignish. The neighbouring estate, further up the glen, was Barbreck, which belonged to a cousin, or possibly a brother, of the Laird of Craignish. Barbreck was too stingy to keep a piper of his own, but Craignish always had one in his household.

Barbreck was visiting Craignish, and as he was leaving, he met MacArthur the piper, and asked him if he would come over to Barbreck on New Year's Day, after he had played for Craignish, and MacArthur agreed.

He duly appeared on New Year's Day, and played and played until Barbreck was in raptures. By now, the piper was hungry, and even worse, thirsty, and said so, but Barbreck gave him only a morsel to eat and a drop to drink, and urged him to play one more tune before he left. So MacArthur played a tune called *Tigh*

Bhroinein, the House of the Stingy Man, and words were later put to it (which Rev. Duncan Campbell quotes). The final verse ends:
. . . Fagaidh mi'n nochd,
Gun bhiadh, gun deoch
Fagaidh mi'n nochd am Barra-breac;
'S cha till mi riu tuilladh
A sheinn do port-failte.

' . . . I will leave tonight,
Without food, without drink,
I will leave Barbreck tonight;
And I will never return
To play a salute for you'

We are reminded of the Sutherland story of Donald Mor MacCrimmon at a MacKay wedding where he was offered no refreshment. In protest, according to some traditions, he composed *Too Long In This Condition*.

In 1778 Colonel John Campbell of Barbreck raised the 74th Regiment, known as the Argyll Highlanders, and it was his piper, named MacCorquodale, who played for the recruiting and became the regimental piper. The regiment served in America from 1778 to 1783, and was disbanded on its return.

Hugh Cheape (Piper Press no. 6, May 1998) thinks that Campbell of Barbreck and his MacCorquodale piper may have served earlier in the 78th or Fraser Highlanders, fighting against the French in the Seven Years' War (1756-63). General Stewart of Garth said this regiment had thirty pipers and drummers. After the war, many of the regiment were offered land in Nova Scotia, and remained there, but Barbreck was one of those who came home.

A late 17th century source, quoted by Hugh Cheape, describes the relation between a laird and his personal piper: 'Pipers are held in great request so that they are train'd up at the Expence of Grandees and have a portion of land assign'd and are design'd such a man's Piper'. It is thought that MacCorquodale's pipe was bought for him by Barbreck, probably acquired in Edinburgh (see also Loch Awe).

PIPERS IN MID-ARGYLL

THE MACGLASRICHS WERE A FAMILY of MacIver Campbells from Glassary, near Lochgilphead. They moved to Lochaber and became pipers to the MacDonnells of Keppoch in the 17th century. The last of these hereditary pipers took part in the '45, and he emigrated to Prince Edward Island, Canada, a few years later, taking with him his pipes, played at Culloden.

JOHN MACDONALD, who served as a pipe major in the 73rd Regiment, was born in Craignish around 1755. His family were gardeners to the Campbells at

Craignish Castle, and he was the youngest of ten children. When he was fourteen he went to the island of Scarba as a tutor to a family called Livingstone, before moving to Killian, three miles west of Inveraray. He was teaching the children of the sixteen families employed on the one farm, but a Captain Campbell then took over the farm and dispersed all the workers. John went to Loch Awe for three years, 'during which time', he says in his *Autobiographical Journal,* 'I had the curiosity to learn to play on the bagpipes, an instrument very much used in that part of the country'. This was in the late 1760s. His next post was in Strathlachlan, near Strachur, on the east side of Loch Fyne, where he spent six happy years.

When this came to an end, he obtained employment in the north of Sutherland, and sending his chest to Tongue by boat, he set off in May 1776, to walk to Tongue, taking a month to reach it, in very hot weather. He must have been a good piper, because when in 1778 he joined the North Fencible Regiment, he was at once made Pipe Major, and was soon sent to the Duke of Gordon's house 'where I was detained for ten weeks to play the pipes'.

When the Colonel of the 73rd heard him play, he was head-hunted for the regiment, paid a bounty of twenty guineas cash and arrears of pay at one shilling and sixpence per day. It is interesting to read his journal and see how useful a training as a piper was to that young fellow from Craignish.

JOHN BUCHANAN from Lochgilphead, 1770-1845, was Pipe Major of the 42nd Highlanders in Flanders and Egypt in 1801, and also served in Portugal and Spain in the Peninsular Wars. In 1802 he won the prize pipe by coming first in the Edinburgh competition. In 1811, being unable to compete because he had already won, he was paid £1.11.6. for playing to entertain the audience while the judges were cogitating. He died at Lochgilphead in 1845, and was buried with full military honours at Kilmartin, where his widow put up a handsome headstone in his memory.

DONALD MACDOUGALL (was he one of the MacDougalls from Moleigh?) was a piper employed on the first steamship, Henry Bell's *Comet,* when she was plying valiantly, as one observer put it, between Fort William and Glasgow, by way of the newly opened Crinan Canal. Donald was employed by the owners for a wage of six shillings per week and his food, quite a handsome reward for the pleasant work of playing to entertain the passengers.

His job came to an abrupt end early in December of 1820; the *Comet* struggled out of Oban with all her pumps going, to try to cope with a leak, and in a snowstorm she struck a rock in the notorious Dorus Mor, to the south of Craignish. The Dorus Mor (Great Door or Entrance) is a narrow channel which has to be negotiated in order to reach the northern entrance to the canal. It has a dangerous submerged rock in the middle, just at the point where at certain states of the tide a strong and unpredictable tidal swirl can seize an unwary vessel and fling her onto the hazard.

Fortunately this happened in daylight and local small boats were available, so that everyone on board was rescued – but the company not only lost their ship but had to spend £5.18s.6d. on whisky for the rescuers. They consumed 'about thirteen gallons' of it, but doubtless earned every drop, the rescue work in wintry conditions being both cold and dangerous.

JOHN GILLIES

JOHN GILLIES (1873-1944), BORN in Kilmartin, became a piper in the Scots Guards for 21 years before he was Pipe Major of the 3rd Battalion from 1903 to 1906. He served in the South African War. On leaving the army he went out to Canada to be the P/M of the Seaforth Highlanders of Vancouver in 1911. With them he returned to serve in the 1914-18 War. He retired in 1933, and died in 1944 in Vancouver. (Notices of Pipers).

John Gillies' great-nephew, Neil Gillies from Barnton, Edinburgh, has most kindly sent me details of the Gillies family. They are distantly related to John MacDougall Gillies, whose Gillies ancestors went to the Cowal peninsula after Malcolm bought the Poltalloch estate (see above). The blood link is distant, but can be traced in every detail, going back to common ancestry in the 17th century: they had the same great-great-great-grandfather.

John Gillies was of a family which belonged to the Kilmartin area, near Lochgilphead, but John's

John Gillies was of a family whose roots were in Mid-Argyll. Born in 1873, he became Pipe Major of the 3rd Battalion Scots Guards, and later of the 1st Battalion. On leaving the army he emigrated to Vancouver, where he died in 1944.
(PHOTOGRAPH KINDLY LENT BY NEIL GILLIES)

DESCENT OF THE GILLIES OF GLENMORE FAMILY
kindly supplied by Neil Gillies, Edinburgh

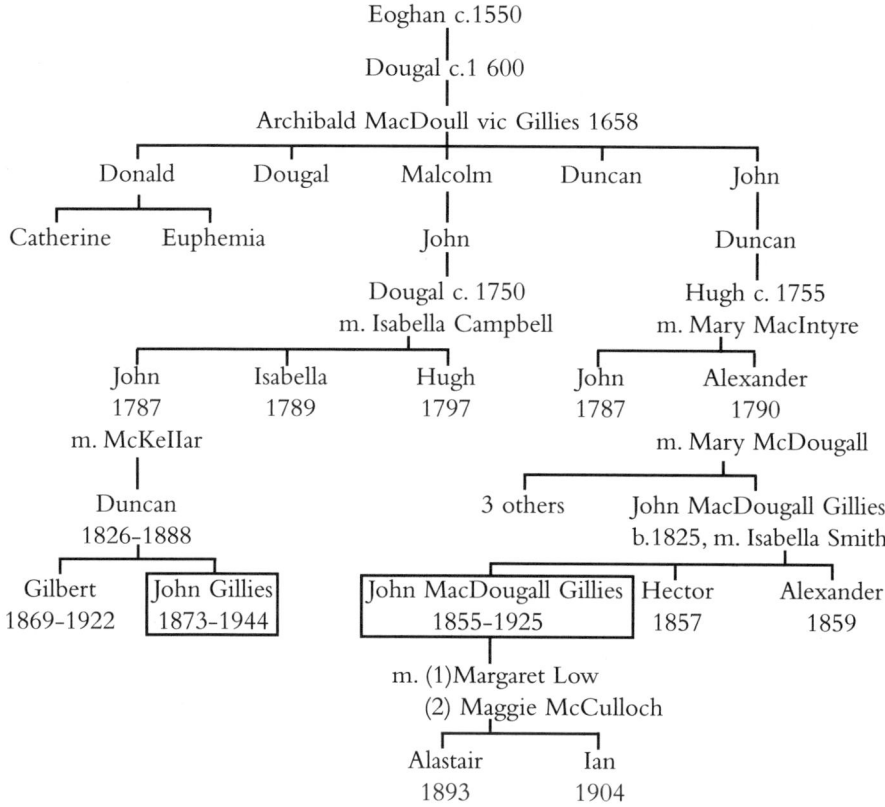

John MacDougall Gillies was related to John Gillies of the Scots Guards, but the link was generations back, in the 17th century

father was working in Baillieston, Glasgow, as gardener/caretaker to 'Mr Ward' when John was born in 1873. The family is not related to that of Arthur Gillies, nor that of Norman and Alasdair Gillies.

John's mother died when he was four, and the family returned to Lochgilphead, where John was brought up. He must have learned his piping in those years, between 1877 and 1890, though it is not known who taught him. Many excellent pipers were in the district at that time, including John MacLachlan and other pipers at Poltalloch, as well as Alex Cameron, Ronald MacKenzie, William Campbell and others.

At 17, John left home and returned to Glasgow to take up the grocery trade; but this was not to his liking, and two years later he joined the Scots Guards, giving his trade as 'Piper', which on his application form was crossed out and 'Grocer' substituted. His army papers give his description: five feet eight inches in height, weighing 127 lb, with a chest measurement of 34 inches (this was at 19 years old). His eyes were blue, complexion fresh, hair brown and religious denomination Presbyterian.

He did well as a piper in the army, his conduct being summed up as 'exemplary', see Notices of Pipers, above. He saw action in South Africa in the Boer War as a Pipe Sergeant, and in 1902 was promoted to Pipe Major. He served as P/M of the 3rd Battalion from December 1903 to September 1906, and when the 3rd Battalion was disbanded, John became Pipe Major of the 1st Battalion, until Janury 1911.

John Gillies when in the Scots Guards. He was a distant cousin of John MacDougall Gillies. (PHOTOGRAPH KINDLY LENT BY NEIL GILLIES).

He was given the honour of being Pipe Major of the massed bands of 1st, 2nd and 3rd Battalions of the Scots Guards, leading the procession at the funeral of King Edward VII, in 1910.

In 1911, the 72nd Battalion of the Seaforth Highlanders was organised in Vancouver, and John Gillies was persuaded to emigrate to Canada, in order to establish and lead their pipe band. He remained as their Pipe Major for the next 22 years.

Evidently his duties included some unusual engagements; his daughter Kate Gillies preserved a letter from the German Club of Vancouver (Deutscher Klub Vancouver). Dated June 17 1913, it reads:
'To the Major of Pipers,
Seaforth Highlanders Reg., Vancouver, B.C.
'Dear Major,
'We want to thank you herewith for your splendid performance at our

banquet in honour of Emperor William II, which has been to all of us a delightful surprise. Also for the Three Cheers, which you brought to the Emperor and which aroused such enthusiasm.

'We are sending you herewith a gallon of good Whiskey, which we hope you will enjoy and drink from time to time to the health of our Club and of your Regiment. We shall be pleased to have you with us on some further occasion and beg to remain ..'

This is an interesting variant of the Piper's Dram; luckily it did not catch on. The Emperor was of course Kaiser Wilhelm, and the outbreak of war only a year later put a stop to further meetings. The Seaforths were mobilized, and John Gillies led his men through the training in Canada and active service in France, fighting against the forces of the very Kaiser he had been cheering so recently. He was then in his forties.

In 1918, a competition was held at Tinques, France, with 28 military bands competing, including pipe bands, and the Vancouver Seaforths won 3rd place. He was awarded the Meritorious Service Medal at the end of the war.

On his return to Canada, he continued with the regiment, training his pipers into an excellent competition band, winning trophies all through the 1920s and 30s. He took an active part in the piping scene, much in demand as a judge, and helping to organize the British Columbia Piping Association. Three pipers from his band became Pipe Majors in World War II.

John did little solo competing in Canada, but in 1928 he won third place in the Open Piobaireachd competition at Banff, when he was in his fifties. He stood down as Pipe Major of the Seaforths in 1937, and the regiment presented him with a set of silver and ivory Henderson pipes. He was then working as a hospital clerk, a job he held for many years.

John Gillies' death in 1944 was on an occasion when the Lovat Scouts had just finished a training exercise in the Rockies, and the Scouts' Pipes and Drums were being entertained by the Vancouver Seaforths in the sergeants' mess. John Gillies gave an excellent brief speech, concluding with a blessing in Gaelic, and sat down to enjoy the entertainment, smoking his pipe. During the singing of *The Road to the Isles*, John's heart stopped, and he died, quietly and without fuss.

He was given a full military funeral, and buried in the Capilano Cemetery in North Vancouver, with two pipe bands in attendance.

The contribution made to piping in Vancouver by John Gillies, among many others, of course, laid the foundation for the high standard of playing in British Columbia today.

John's brother GILBERT DUNCAN GILLIES (1869-1922) was born in Kilmichael Glassary when his father was gardener to CAMPBELL of INVERNEILL – one of the many Campbell gentry who were passionately interested in piping, Inverneill judged at the Argyllshire Gathering on eighteen occasions. The father, DUNCAN GILLIES, may have been himself a piper, though no-one is certain of this. Duncan married Jessie Sinclair in 1867, and

Gilbert was born at Inverneill in 1869, before the family moved to Salen, in Mull. Duncan may have been working on the estates of MacLean of Duart, at either Duart or Aros. A daughter Jessie was born at Salen in 1871.

Duncan then moved to Glasgow, where he was gardener to Mr Ward in Baillieston, and John was born in 1873, Isabella in 1876.

On Christmas Day 1877, Jessie Gillies died, leaving four children aged eight or under. Duncan split up the family, sending Gilbert to Jessie's mother in Ardrishaig, and the other three to different aunts in Lochgilphead. In 1881, Duncan rejoined his children when he found work as a farm manager near Lochgilphead, but eight years later, he too died, and the children, all except Jessie, who was governess to the children of Malcolm of Poltalloch, went back to Glasgow.

Gilbert lived in the Townhead area, working for the Caledonian Railway Co. He came under the influence of a distant relative, John MacDougall Gillies (see below), and on his recommendation moved away from Glasgow into private service, as estate manager and piper to Campbell of Jura. He went to Jura in 1902, and married a Jura girl, Margaret MacGillivray – but she died two years later.

Gilbert remarried in 1906, and had a series of appointments in private service. He died in 1922 when he was a Ground Officer for the Marquis of Breadalbane at Taymouth, and is buried in Killin Churchyard.

Although Gilbert was definitely a piper, his niece said he was a better dancer than piper, and added that he used to dress his bag with white of egg and brown sugar, doubtless regarded as an extravagance for a man with eight children. It is thought that he may have learned his basic piping in Lochgilphead, and later may

Gilbert Gillies was the elder brother of Pipe Major John Gillies of the Scots Guards. Himself a piper and dancer, he did not pursue a competitive career in piping.
(PHOTOGRAPH KINDLY LENT BY NEIL GILLIES).

have had tuition from John MacDougall Gillies and possibly also from Alick Cameron.

JOHN MACLACHLAN was born in Glasgow but was of Argyll stock. He published a collection of 120 pieces of small music (marches, strathspeys, reels and jigs) in 1853, under the title *The Piper's Assistant*. He was piper to Neil Malcolm of Poltalloch, and one of his marches was called *Poltalloch House*. He first appeared in the prize lists of the Northern Meeting in 1843, when, as 'Piper to the late Sir Francis Mackenzie of Gairloch'(Sir Francis died earlier that year), he took third place in the Strathspey competition. By 1851 he was Piper to Neil Malcolm of Poltalloch, the first of many pipers employed at the mansion house, and that year he had the distinction of winning both the Prize Pipe for piobaireachd and also the Strathpeys and Marches competition (see also Donald McPhedran, below).

It is possible that John MacLachlan was the composer of *MacKenzie of Gairloch's Lament*. This has been associated with the death of Sir Hector MacKenzie in 1826, and it may have been composed for Sir Hector's son, Francis, in his father's memory, as Sir Hector is believed not to have had his own piper after John Roy MacKay went to Nova Scotia.

John MacLachlan was a versatile musician who was reckoned by pipers (quoted by General Thomason) to rank alongside Donald Cameron as a player of Ceol Beag. His sister Agnes was married to Donald MacPhedran (see below), in whose Collection of pipe music several of John MacLachlan's compositions appear. It is not known whether these MacLachlans were related to John MacLauchlan who was killed at Vittoria in Spain in 1808 (see above). Donald MacPhedran's aunt, Janet MacFarlane, was in 1823 married to Colin MacLachlan, ferryman at Crinan, who may have been of the same family as Agnes and John, possibly their father or uncle. Agnes was born in Crinan, and may have been Donald MacPhedran's cousin.

This John MacLachlan cannot be the same one who was piper at Ballindalloch, listed in the 1881 Census when he was in his thirties. His birthplace is given as Sutherland, but this may mean only that he had come to Ballindalloch from Sutherland.

WILLIAM CAMPBELL, nephew of James C. Campbell, piper to Queen Victoria and Edward VII, was 2nd piper to the Queen, under his uncle. He had previously been piper to Major Allanby, Ardrishaig. William won the Gold at Inverness in 1897, and was known for playing with his hands reversed on the chanter 'which looked most awkward'. He played, with his uncle, at the Queen's funeral in 1901. After his retirement, William went to Vancouver in 1910, and there taught piping; at that time, D.C. Mather and Donald MacIver were leading pipers in Vancouver, and John Gillies was soon to follow him.

JOHN GORDON was butler to Colonel MacDougall of Lunga from 1900 to 1908, a good player who often played for the reels at the Argyllshire Gathering

Ball. He was a pupil of John MacColl, and composed several tunes including the Slow Air *Bonnie Argyll*, and the 2/4 March in 4 parts, *Leaving Lunga*. After leaving Colonel MacDougall's employ he became caterer to the Officers' Mess of the Argyll and Sutherland Highlanders, at Stirling Castle.

COLONEL MACDOUGALL OF LUNGA employed a number of well known pipers in the latter years of the 19th century and early 20th. These included Ronald MacKenzie, Alick Cameron, D.C.Mather, John Gordon and William Lawrie.

Major Stewart MacDougall of Lunga was on the first Committee when the Piobaireachd Society was founded in 1903. When John and Angus Campbell of Kilberry objected to the method of transcription of piobaireachd music in the Society's early publications, MacDougall of Lunga was among those who rejected their proposal to abandon it and start again. He was then appointed to a sub-committee to deal with the set tunes for competitions.

Colonel MacDougall and his brother Captain MacDougall were both killed in the First World War in 1916, and their former piper, William Lawrie, died of his wounds in the same year.

MacDougall of Lunga is a 2/4 March in two parts. *Leaving Lunga* is a 2/4 March in four parts, composed by John Gordon (see also John MacColl).

Lunga is an island, now uninhabited, to the north of Scarba, in the Firth of Lorne. The name was given to an estate just north of Ardfern, Craignish.

WILLIAM MACPHAIL was the son of the Free Church minister at Kilmartin, and he became a doctor who specialized in the treatment of tuberculosis. After serving as a naval surgeon during the First World War, he lived near London, and was for many years President of the Scottish Piping Society of London, giving hospitality to many pipers, especially during World War II. He was a good player, taught by P/M James Sutherland when he was a medical student in Edinburgh. He composed a march called *Frimley*, the name of the place near Aldershot where he was a G.P.

He seems to have been a man of boundless energy and enthusiasm for piping, and his house was always open to any visiting piper. He kept a visitors' book which all were required to sign; it reads like a Who's Who of piping in the 1930s and 40s, when so many serving in the forces had to pass through London.

He ran the house as a kind of parody of army life, with daily orders being issued and morning parades held – the soldiers being told to parade in their pyjamas. A feature of this regime was that all ranks were reversed; orders were given by the privates to the officers, and colonels had to salute the lower ranks. He even formed his own pipe band, known as the Frimley Volunteers.

James Sutherland's daughter, Margaret Stoddart, tells of an occasion when Dr MacPhail and J.B.Robertson were travelling north by train, to visit her father in Edinburgh. During the war, trains were always greatly overcrowded, but the two of them secured a compartment of their own by travelling as Prisoner Under

Mid-Argyll

Frimley Volunteers Pipe Band was created by Dr William MacPhail when he was a GP in Surrey. He gave boundless hospitality to all pipers in the 1930s and 40s. Left to right: P/M James Sutherland, Dr MacPhail, Angus MacAulay, Major (later Colonel) Jock Campbell, Iain Grant (Rothiemurchus), Lewis Beaton, someone unknown.
(PHOTOGRAPH KINDLY LENT BY MARGARET STODDART).

A few Frimley band members

The band in full flow.

Escort. Presumably Dr MacPhail was the prisoner and J.B.Robertson, a soldier, was the escort. Apparently a prisoner could be conveyed with or without handcuffs, but if not handcuffed, the rule was that guard and prisoner must not travel with the general public. So the two of them had a comfortable night on their own. Margaret remembers the glee with which they told the tale on arrival at her father's house.

In the 1930s, Dr MacPhail was once on holiday at his family home in Kilmartin, and feeling like a blow, he was playing his pipes in the centre of the village, outside the local hostelry. A tourist bus drew in, and one of the passengers listened to his playing before handing him four shillings and a penny – for which he thanked her courteously. Later he said it was the easiest 4/1d he ever earned in his life.

Doctor MacPhail's Reel was composed by Andrew Bain.

ARCHIE MACNAB was born in Craignish in 1920, and was brought up there as a young boy, taught his piping by Angus MacLean, 'a winner of the Strathspeys and Reels at Oban in 1913, who was not only a good piper but a lifetime study of piobaireachd had made him an authority on the subject. The music which sang in his soul he carefully and unstintingly passed on to the young boy as they played together, master and pupil ... It is a great tribute to his ability that his pupil, after having as successive tutors James MacIver, John MacColl, Robert Reid, John MacDonald of the Glasgow Police and John MacDonald, Inverness, still referred to his first teacher when doubt arose.'. These are the words of Seumas MacNeill (Piping Times, Feb 1980), who said of Archie MacNab 'If ever there lived a man who was truly a legend in his own time, then this was he'.

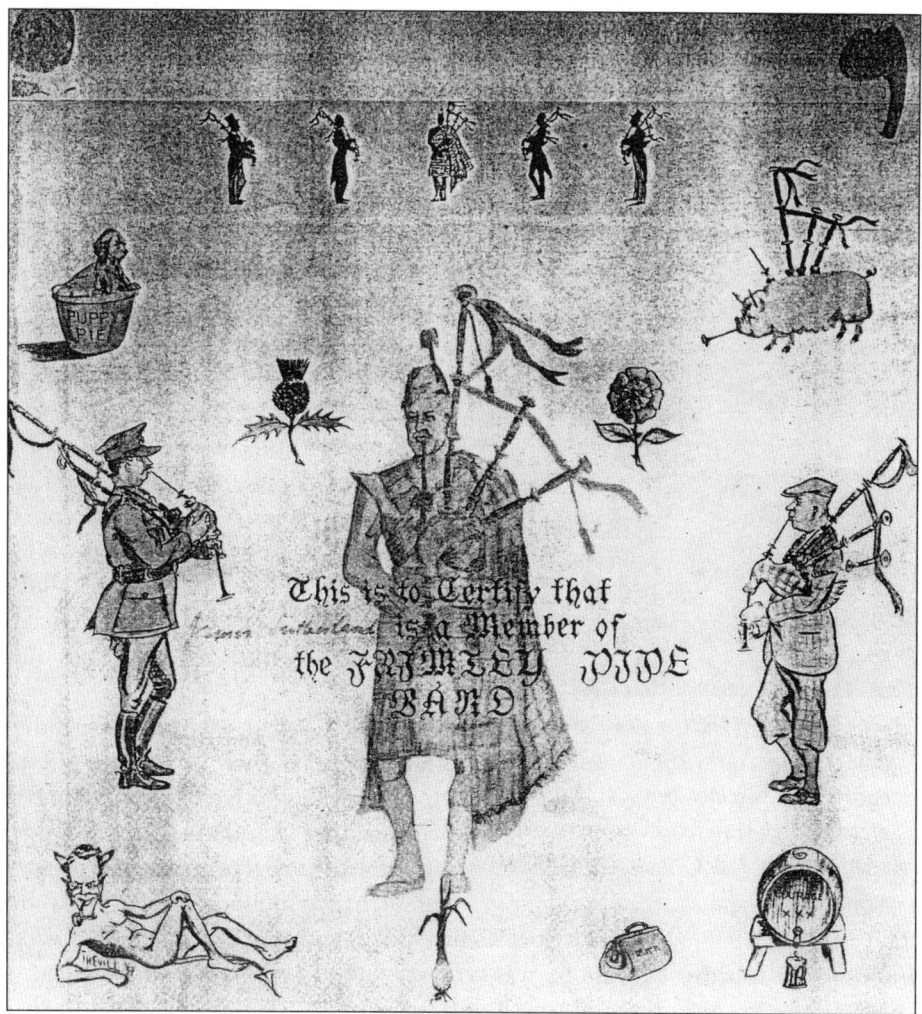

Dr MacPhail issued a Certificate to every piper who had played in his Frimley band. This was James Sutherland's, preserved by his daughter Margaret.
(KINDLY LENT BY MARGARET STODDART).

Major Archibald MacNab, of the Queen's Own Cameron Highlanders, occupied a unique position in the piping world. 'Outstanding even among a class of men which is famous for the diversity of its personalities, he was almost as good a raconteur as Willie Ross, a better maker of stories than Willie MacDonald of Lairg, and one of the greatest pipers of the [twentieth] century'.

In one of his letters, John MacDonald, Inverness, gave a list of players who in his opinion were likely to become the leading pipers of their generation, and he included Archie MacNab along with Robert Nicol and Robert Brown, Roderick MacDonald and Donald MacLeod. He added 'Another promising player is Victor MacLeod, Edinburgh Police', a name we seem to have heard no more. What happened to him?

Archie MacNab (1920-1980), who came from Craignish, though brought up in Partick. He is remembered as a superb march player. (PHOTOGRAPH BY KIND PERMISSION OF THE COLLEGE OF PIPING)

Archie MacNab came to live in the Partick district of Glasgow as a boy, but did not take much part in the competitions which other youngsters enjoyed. When he did compete, in the 1930s, he always won. Seumas MacNeill used to go past his house just to stand outside and listen to Archie's playing, which was 'clean and simple, expression was the dominant feature. It had a simplicity which denied the call for complex arrangements'.

With very little experience of amateur contests, Archie McNab entered in 1937 for the annual professional competition in Glasgow, and won a prize in every event, playing to great acclaim. He was only seventeen, inexperienced and up against the top players of his time.

At eighteen he was invited by the S.P.A. to judge their amateur contest, on his own, although he was younger than many of the players he was judging. Already his reputation as a player was such that nobody queried this. In the two years 1938 and 39 he won 37 first prizes and nine seconds — and very few thirds or fourths, 'because he was very, very good'.

Many remarked on the odd way he played, with his chanter far round to the left and his head turned slightly to the right 'as if he were listening critically to the sound of the chanter'. Seumas wrote 'I can still remember his distinctive tuning phrases, from a beautifully balanced instrument, bouncing back with sharpness and clarity from the corrugated iron fencing of the tuning field. It seemed at that moment as if all the other pipers in the ground had stopped to listen.'

That year, 1938, at the last Argyllshire Gathering before the war, Archie played *Kantara to El Arish*. To Seumas, 'his playing of that march was pure magic. Off and on for forty years I have practised to try and produce a little phrase in the fourth part the way he did it, but without success, so far'.

Archie McNab was one of a class taught by John MacDonald, Inverness, in 1938, in preparation for the Gold Medal. It was held in Glasgow for one week at the beginning of July, and the members of the class were:

John and Roddy MacDonald, Glasgow City Police (the Roideans, from South Uist)
Charlie Scott

John Johnstone
Hector MacLean
Hugh Kennedy
'Mr MacColl of the Scottish Pipers, Edinburgh', and Archie McNab.

At the end of the week the class asked for another week, and got it, and wanted yet another, as they said they were just beginning to see daylight in piobaireachd playing.

Later that year, 1938, the Northern Meeting was held in atrocious weather. 'Never did anyone play under worse conditions than Archie experienced that day. The lashing rain was so bad when he went out to the boards that the judges allowed him to shelter in their tent for ten minutes before deciding that it was not going to ease up and throwing him out. His performance in spite of the elements was faultless, and he became the youngest player ever to win the coveted medal (until John Burgess appeared).'

Archie MacNab made a widely-played setting of the 2/4 March *The 91st at Modder River*.

A 6/8 Jig in 4 parts called *Archie MacNab* was made by J. MacKinnon.

Archie MacNab (left) from Craignish and Owen MacNiven from Islay, in 1938. (PHOTOGRAPH BY KIND PERMISSION OF THE COLLEGE OF PIPING)

'By this time Archie had joined the famous Glasgow Police, but when war came along he found himself at Fort George learning the rudiments of soldiering under a mighty sergeant-major who turned out to be Donald R. MacLennan (D.R.). The stories of 'Archie in the Police' and 'Archie in the Army' deserve books to themselves. After a distinguished war service, he obtained a governing post in the international city of Trieste.'

Like so many excellent players, his competing career was broken off by war service, so that his name does not resound as it might have, in the records of the big competitions. After his army service, he went to Islay as a hotel manager for a while, before becoming Scottish representative for Shell, based first in Edinburgh, then in Oban. He lived for a time at Kilmelford.

Seumas concluded his article with the words: 'Archie MacNab was one of the world's greatest pipers, the finest march player I have ever heard. He was dark and handsome, kind and gentle (except to those who miscalled the bagpipe) and he had the priceless gift of inspiring young pipers. John MacFadyen remembered him, before the war, as "God in sky-blue plus-fours". Many – if not all – of the top pipers of my generation were inspired to seek perfection after hearing his immaculate playing. We will remember him as he was at his best, the king among pipers.'

Archie MacNab died suddenly at Epsom on January 4th 1980, at the age of 60.

NETHER LORNE

KILMELFORD

THE CUILFAIL HOTEL IN KILMELFORD, at the head of Loch Melfort, on the road from Lochgilphead to Oban, is of interest to pipers because at one time it belonged to John MacFadyen of Melfort, and the 2/4 March of that name, made in his honour by John MacColl, was first played publicly in the lounge of the hotel. It was said to be John MacColl's favourite, of all his own compositions. William Gray also made a 4-part Strathspey of the same name. A later owner was also a piper, Farlane MacKenzie.

Another tune is *Duncan MacNeil's Farewell to Melfort*, by Captain N.A.MacNeil, a 2/4 March in four parts; and John MacLellan made a 2/4 March in four parts, *The Pass of Melfort*.

Culfail Hotel, Kilmelfort, formerly owned by John MacFadyen of Melfort, subject of compositions by both John MacColl and Willie Gray.

ARDMADDY

Ardmaddy Castle, on the Seil Sound, to the south of Oban and east of Seil Island, belonged to the Campbells of Breadalbane. It should not be confused with another Ardmaddy, on Loch Etive, which appears in birth and marriage notices for the parish of Muckairn.

Ardmaddy Castle was re-built in the 17th century by the MacDougalls of Reray, who then lost it to the Campbells. The Breadalbane family, whose foremost seat was Taymouth Castle in Perthshire, held Ardmaddy from the mid -17th century until 1933. It is virtually the same as Carwhin and Mochaster, two of the designations formerly used by the Campbells of Ardmaddy.

Keith Sanger has drawn attention to a letter in the Breadalbane papers which was written in 1705: it says that McIntyre, that is JOHN MACINTYRE, who had been piper to Breadalbane at Glenorchy (see Glenorchy, below), and had been trained by the Rankins in Mull and the MacCrimmons in Skye, was 'now Mr Colins piper and to live in Nether Lorn however piper will answer Breadalbanes call from time to time if asked'. Mr Colin was a son of Campbell of Breadalbane and held the estate of Ardmaddy between 1679 and 1708.

It seems that John was needed only once, in 1709, when the factor sent him 'to attend your Lordship to Castle Kilchorn, his music being more for expeditions than for the house'. The factor was evidently not a fan of piping, belonging to the school that prefers its pipe music on a distant hill.

This was John MacIntyre who composed *The Prince's Salute* (see below).

The main claim of Ardmaddy to fame in the piping world is that it was the home of the piping Campbells of Nether Lorne, who produced the Campbell Canntaireachd manuscript in the 1790s (see below). Later, in the late 18th and early 19th centuries, Kenneth MacKenzie, uncle to John Ban, was piper there, and it was the birthplace in 1807 of Kenneth's nephew John MacKenzie, well known as a piper at Kenmore, Loch Fyne (see below). There seem to have been links, not yet fully explored, between MacKenzie pipers at Ardmaddy and at Taymouth, in the family of John Ban, suggesting that this was a line of MacKenzie hereditary pipers to the Breadalbane Campbells.

DONALD CAMPBELL from Nether Lorne was the father of Colin Mor Campbell, the piper who wrote the Campbell Canntaireachd manuscript in the 1790s (see below). The family were the hereditary pipers to the Campbells of Mochaster (which was known as Carwhin, or Corrohin, at the end of the 18th century), and 'were long known in the Highland musical world, and attained considerable eminence '.

Donald, born around 1726, was piper to Captain Colin Campbell of Carwhin. He fought at Culloden, but there are two traditions about this: some say he was a piper in the Argyll Militia, and as such would have been in the Hanoverian army; but Donald's great-granddaughter Ann Campbell (the lady who sold the two volumes of the Canntaireachd manuscript in 1909) said he fought on the

> **CAMPBELL PIPERS AT ARDMADDY AND ISLAY**
>
> DONALD CAMPBELL of Nether Lorne. Born c. 1726. Fought at Culloden. Piper to MacDonald of Glenaladale, then to Campbell of Carwhin (Mochaster) who 'settled' him at Ardmaddy, Nether Lorne.
>
> His Son, COLIN MOR CAMPBELL, wrote the Campbell Canntaireachd manuscript of piobaireachd music in the 1790's, probably at Ardmaddy. He became piper to the Earl of Breadalbane, but remained at Ardmaddy.
>
> Colin Mor had 12 children, including
> DONALD who was piper to Breadalbane in Taymouth in 1815
> and
> JOHN, born 1795 in Nether Lorne. He won the Prize Pipe in 1819 when piper to Breadalbane, and was engaged by Walter F. Campbell of Shawfield and Islay as his piper at Islay House, Bridgend. Looked after Walter F's young son, 1821-1831. Died in Bellshill, Lanarkshire, in 1831, aged 36.
>
> Although it was John who went to Islay in 1819, his father, Colin Mor, is often referred to as 'Colin Mor of Islay' or 'from Islay', which suggests the family may have had Islay roots.

Jacobite side while in the service of MacDonald of Glenaladale. She said he went into the service of Carwhin after that, and that Carwhin sent him to Patrick Og for tuition, but that cannot be right: Patrick Og died around 1730, long before Culloden. It was Carwhin who settled the Campbells at Ardmaddy (see above).

There is a story of the young Donald Campbell, at the age of seventeen, accompanying his laird, MacDonald of Glenaladale, in support of the Jacobite cause, his fee being three guineas (per year?). They took part in the Battle of

Culloden, during which Glenaladale fell, badly wounded. According to the story, the faithful Donald carried him from the field, and managed to get him home to Loch Shiel, more than a hundred miles away – but he had to leave his pipes on the battlefield.

Donald Campbell's son Colin Mor was the piper who wrote out the Campbell Canntaireachd manuscript in the 1790s, recording the piobaireachd works of his time in a written form of Canntaireachd, normally a system of sung vocables used solely for singing the music, rather than playing it or writing it down. It was a method of recording which probably pre-dated the writing of pipe music in staff notation, tentatively begun in the second half of the 18th century; there is evidence that the two forms of writing out pipe music developed side by side in some places.

Canntaireachd in written form was a new development, and the system used by Colin Mor Campbell in the 1790s, though undoubtedly based on oral Canntaireachd, seems to have been adapted for the new medium, and to differ from the sung form in some respects – though it is difficult to be sure, since every district seems to have had its own system, just as each had its own dialect of Gaelic.

It is thought that Colin Mor was recording the music as he got it from his father and other contemporary pipers. He included works not known in any other source (such as *Lochnell's Lament*), and he also gave to works we know from later sources different titles from those given in, for example, Angus MacKay's manuscripts.

Colin Mor seems to have been piper to Campbell of Carwhin, whose seat was Ardmaddy. Carwhin later became Earl of Breadalbane, but Colin was his piper only on a local level, so that he was resident at Ardmaddy rather than Taymouth, and was not the Earl's senior piper. He is sometimes referred to as 'Colin Mor of Islay', but there is no real evidence that he had lived there. Some say he wrote the Canntaireachd manuscript in Islay, but this may be because of confusion with Angus MacKay.

His son, Donald, won 5th place in the Prize Pipe competition in 1815, at the age of fifteen, when he was one of the pipers at Taymouth, to the 4th Earl of Breadalbane. Four years later, another son, John, won the Prize Pipe at Edinburgh, and was given a job by Walter F. Campbell of Shawfield and Islay; he went to live in Islay, at Islay House, Bridgend. Walter F. Campbell was the father of John F. Campbell, the folk-lorist and collector of Gaelic stories. It was Walter F. who, in the late 1830s, encouraged Angus MacKay to compile and publish a collection of piobaireachd works.

Archibald Campbell of Kilberry in his notes to Book 10 of the Piobaireachd Society collection, attributes family information to Miss Ann Campbell, who gave it to Sheriff John Bartholomew of Glenorchard in 1909. Kilberry says:

'Carwhin had commanded a company of the Argyll militia in 1745, and he settled Donald Campbell at Ardmaddy, near Easdale. Donald had a son, Colin, who was twice married and had twelve children, the eldest of whom was Donald, father of Ann; and the second son was John, afterwards piper to Campbell of Islay'.

John Gibson (1998, pp.139-140) calls John Campbell 'grandson of the Glenaladale piper who fled Moidart after Culloden', Glenaladale being near Loch Shiel, in Moidart district, but offers no explanation of this. Gibson explores this more fully in his second volume, 2002, and concludes that the piping Campbells at Ardmaddy may have originated in Keppoch.

There is a tune *Carwhin's Lament*, described by Archie Kenneth as 'not very good'; it may have been made by John Campbell (or Colin? Even Donald?) And in the Canntaireachd Manuscript is *Captain Campbell of Glenlyon's Lament*, which seems to have been composed by the same hand as *Lochend's March, Melfort's March*, and *Pipers Meeting*. Archie Kenneth's comment was that the composer, whoever he was, was not a composing genius. Was he one of the Ardmaddy Campbell pipers?

In the Preface to Angus MacKay's Collection, John Campbell was described in a footnote as being 'Late Piper to W. F. Campbell, Esq., of Islay, M.P.', when he competed at Edinburgh in 1815. This comment was added later, presumably after John's death in 1831, and has caused some confusion: Walter Campbell died in 1816, and was succeeded by his grandson Walter F. Campbell, at the age of eighteen.

In 1816, John Campbell was again in Edinburgh for the competitions – he had come 4th the previous year. He and Hector Johnston of Coll were each awarded £1.18s.0d., of which one guinea (£1.1s.) was for writing out pipe music in staff notation, and 17 shillings for travel expenses. John is described as being from Nether Lorne, but got the same travel allowance as the man from Coll; had he come from Islay?

John came 3rd at Edinburgh in 1816, and continued to compete, rising to 2nd in 1818 and winning the Prize Pipe in 1819. Clearly a good piper, he was an educated man. It is not known how he taught himself to transcribe pipe music in staff notation – presumably he did not learn this skill from his father, who used written Canntaireachd to write out the music.

While he was in Edinburgh in 1816 John produced a volume of his father's Canntaireachd manuscript, which he sold to Sir John MacGregor Murray. Dalyell in his *Musical Memoirs* (9-10) adds: 'but the contents merely resembling a written narrative in an unknown language, nor bearing any resemblance to Gaelic . . . nobody adventured so far as to guess at either airs or piobrachs'.

A piper and pipemaker from Glasgow, Murdo MacLean, offered to decipher the mystery, which presented no problem to him, but he received no encouragement – perhaps the gentry did not want to admit that a mere competitor knew more than they did – and the owner refused to part with the volume. The owner then lost it, and it seems to have been largely unlamented.

This manuscript was not seen again, but in 1909, Ann Campbell put an advertisement in the papers, offering old pipes for sale. Sheriff John Bartholomew of Glenorchard travelled to Oban to meet Miss Campbell and bought the pipes, and she asked if he would be interested in old volumes of manuscript. Fortunately he was an eminent Celticist, former secretary of the Scottish Pipers' Society and a well known piping judge, and recognized the significance of what he was seeing. He bought both volumes, and J.P. Grant made transcripts of the piobaireachd works in them. It is not known whether the volume lost by MacGregor Murray was a third volume of the collection, or merely a copy of one of the two.

Descriptions of the contents of the Campbell Canntaireachd manuscript appear in Volume 10 of the Piobaireachd Society's collection, pages v-vi, and in Donaldson, pages 449-454.

After winning the Prize Pipe in 1819, John Campbell became piper to Walter F. Campbell of Shawfield and Islay, whose son John Francis was born in 1821. The boy was brought up in Islay and seems to have been handed to the piper John Campbell for his early education, before he was sent to Eton. From John he learned to speak Gaelic, and to read and write in Gaelic, and he acquired a passion for Gaelic stories and traditions. John Gibson (315) says that John also taught the boy Celtic dance steps and traditions of Hebridean dance, and he saw to it that a lasting impression of Gaelic culture was left on the boy's mind, which survived even his Eton years.

John F. Campbell's own account of his Islay upbringing says: 'I was raised in the Highlands of Scotland, and as soon as I was out of the hands of nursemaids, I was handed over to the care of a piper. His name was the same as mine, John Campbell, and from him I learned a good many useful arts. I learned to be hardy and healthy, and I learned Gaelic. I learned to swim and to take care of myself and to talk to everybody who chose to talk to me. My kilted nurse and I were always walking about in foul weather or fair, and every man, woman and child in the place had something to say to us. Thus I made early acquaintance with a blind fiddler who could recite stories. I worked with the carpenters; I played shinty with all the boys about the farm; and so I got to know a good deal about the ways of Highlanders by growing up as a Highlander myself'.

It might seem curious that he describes himself as a Highlander, and not an Islander, and that he makes no mention of Islay, but this account was for the preface to his *Popular Tales of the West Highlands*, and he may have wanted to give the impression of a broadly based Gaelic education.

John Campbell must have taken his charge beyond the confines of Islay, as there is a story, told by John F. in later life, of their going to walk in Kensington Gardens, in London, and being asked to leave, as John (the piper) was wearing his kilt, which offended other walkers in the park. Kilts were regarded as indecent because nothing was worn beneath them; this made refined ladies nervous on windy days.

John had a brother, William Campbell, who was a tailor and kiltmaker in Glasgow, and it was to him that John F. Campbell went for his clothes. John F. always wore the tartan of the 42nd Regiment (Black Watch), and he commented that although he rather liked the two Sobieski brothers, he did not agree with their fanciful notions about the different tartans, and who was entitled to wear them.

John F. Campbell left us a description of the Gaelic Society of London in his day: 'the whole thing is a Celtic prance for wearing kilts and kicking up the heels and public dining to music tortured out of shape by a foreign professional. It is all my eye, so far. My few Gaelic words were the only Gaelic words spoken at the Gaelic Society meeting, and very few there understood them'. It is not clear what music was being played, nor on what instrument – possibly a harp?

John F. Campbell at that time was described by John Stuart Blackie as 'the finest fellow that I have seen here (in London), full of a free, frank, broad, vigorous and hilarious manhood. He is great in Celtic, and in geology; and can use a painter's brush to purpose besides . . '. But he was not musical. He did not learn to play the pipes, or any other musical instrument, and it seems he was no singer, either. He may have been tone-deaf; his booklet on Canntaireachd shows how little he understood.

He was only ten when his 'piper-nurse' died, but he had ample opportunity to become a piper if he had shown any inclination. His early years gave him an interest in piping, however, and he is known to have encouraged pipers, especially those from the islands.

He grew up to become one of the leading folk-lorists of the time, publishing his collection of Gaelic stories, *Popular Tales of the West Highlands*, in four volumes between 1860 and 1862. Volume I gives us a glimpse of John MacKenzie, Loch Fyne, a cousin of John Ban (see below), and we also have the occasional comment about pipes or pipers, such as his observation about local shinty matches: 'I have seen a parish shinny match in the Highlands become so hot and furious that the leaders were forced to get two pipers and march their troops out of the field in opposite directions, to prevent a civil war of parishes'. (Shinny was the old pronunciation and spelling of what we now call shinty).

This sketch of John F. Campbell was made by Lord Archibald Campbell, son of the Duke of Argyll, around 1870. Lord Archibald and John F. were cousins.

The piper John Campbell died in 1831, at the early age of 36. Gibson (p.139) twice refers to John as 'old', once calling him 'his old pocked piper-nurse', when he can only have been in his thirties. 'Pocked' suggests that he had survived an attack of smallpox in earlier life – or had he suffered from acne? Perhaps 'old' was a phrase used by John F. Campbell, remembering how the piper had seemed to him as a young lad, when everyone over 21 would have appeared old.

John was greatly esteemed by his laird,

Walter F. Campbell, who put up a fine headstone on his grave at Bellshill, in Lanarkshire, with an inscription calling him a 'faithful servant and piper'.

SOURCES
Piobaireachd Society Book 10
Angus MacKay
John F. Campbell
Notices of Pipers
John Gibson
William Donaldson
TGSI vol LIV, John F. Campbell by Frank Thomson
John Gibson 2002

Inveraray

Tunes associated with Inveraray (see also tunes associated with Loch Fyne, above):
Climbing Duniquaich, by D.C.Mather S 2
Lord Archibald Campbell's Salute, by John Grant P with 7 variations
Lord Colin Campbell's Salute, by Donald MacPhee P with 7 variations
MacPhedran's Dream 6/8 M 2
MacPhedran's Strathspey S 2
Major Campbell Graham MBE, by P/M A. MacDonald R 4
The Marchioness of Lorne, by J.C.Campbell 2/4 M 4
The Marchioness of Lorne's Strathspey S 2
The Marquis of Argyle's Salute P with 7 variations (see below)
The Marquis of Argyle's Strathspey S 2
The Marquis of Lorne's Salute, by Donald MacPhee P with 7 variations
The Marquis of Lorne's Strathspey (also known simply as *The Marquis of Lorne*) S 2
The Memorial Bells of Inveraray, by J. MacLellan 2/4 M 2
Miss Elspeth Campbell, by T. Douglas 2/4 M 4
O'er the Hills to Inveraray, by John MacLellan 6/8 M 4
Young George's Salute P with 11 variations (see below)

*T*HE MARQUIS OF ARGYLE'S SALUTE is a piobaireachd work with eight variations in the Campbell Canntaireachd manuscript, seven in Angus MacKay, five in Gesto, and four in Peter Reid. It seems to have been known simply as *The Marquis's Welcome* in some places. Argyll was spelled Argyle in those days.

As the Marquis of Argyle held that rank for only twenty years we can date the work, assuming that the title is correct, to the period between 1641 and 1661, when he was executed. Possibly we can narrow it down to between 1641 and 1645 (see below).

Gillesbig Gruamach, as he was known in Gaelic (Grim, or Dour, Archibald) was the 8th Earl. He was, to use a technical term, a Nasty Man. Considered to be the most powerful peer in Scotland, he was much flattered and fawned upon, but spurned these advances, being of a sour and gloomy disposition.

He had an unhappy childhood; his mother died when he was a baby, and his father re-married when Archibald was only three, and took no further interest in him. He went to St Andrews University, where he won a medal for archery, and even as an adolescent he began to take delight in acts of cruelty, assisting with glee in the savage suppression of the MacIans of Ardnamurchan. Throughout his life he enjoyed watching bloodshed so long as there was no risk to himself, and there is a description of him at the massacre of Dunaverty, walking ankle-deep in the blood of the victims – who had been promised mercy.

He grew up embittered, with a bad name for evicting his tenants and profiting financially from their removal. But his worst reputation was for abandoning his followers in times of strife. In 1643, he left Inveraray to the mercy of the invading Alasdair MacColla, slipping away by boat without standing to fight. At Inverlochy in 1645, he sat in his ship in Loch Linnhe waiting for the result of the battle, and at the first hint of defeat he was off, leaving his Covenanting followers to their fate. One of them, Campbell of Skipness, said he would have fought on the side of Montrose had he known what a coward the Marquis was. This defeat led to another devastation of Argyll by Alasdair MacColla, a disaster which the people again blamed on the Marquis.

In June 1646, Archibald took revenge on the Lamonts of Cowal, who had deserted him to join Montrose. The Campbells captured the Lamonts after the battle, and slaughtered 200 of them in cold blood, beside a mass grave already prepared. This atrocity was only the fore-runner of the killings at Dunaverty, and it is said that General Leslie carried out that massacre on the orders of the Marquis of Argyle (see above, *MacDonald of Sanda*).

The Marquis had been foremost in the crowning of Charles II at Scone in 1651, himself carrying the Crown into the church; then four years later he declared for Cromwell. In 1661, he went to London in an attempt to see the King and try to re-join his party, but he was arrested, and taken to Edinburgh, where he was tried and executed for treason. It was said that he faced his death with a courage he had not shown previously, but not many can have mourned him.

It is not known who made the Salute, but it seems likely that it was in celebration of the new title of Marquis, in or around 1641. It was probably part of the extravagant praise which his followers heaped on him in hope of preferment.

About the same time, a Gaelic praise poem was made in honour of the Marquis. Known in Gaelic as *Rug eadrain* from its opening words ('He hath made an intervention' in English), it seems to be the work of a member of the MacEwen family who were the bards to the Campbells at Inveraray Castle. As it praises the Marquis for his valour in battle, it was probably made before 1645 –

after Inverlochy the Marquis's courage would presumably not have been mentioned.

The poem is a typical Gaelic bardic praise poem, couched in extravagantly flattering terms, and to our modern tastes, a bit sickening. But this is what was expected of a bard, and if he had not laid it on thick, his praise would have been considered niggardly and insulting to its subject. A few verses will serve as examples; many of the verses are full of references to people from the classical world and Celtic heroes – this too was expected, and considered the mark of a well-trained bard.

The bard's purpose was to persuade his chief to restore to the bard's family a piece of land, at Kilchoan on Loch Melfort, which had previously belonged to them, and which they still considered rightfully theirs. The Marquis must have been constantly bothered with similar requests, but this one was worded in an unusual way.

Part of it goes:

(3) Madh sioth madh cogadh do chach,
     MacCailin is e ar n-ursgath;
     lamh leantar mar thuinn toruidh,
     Eachtair an fhuinn Albanuigh.

('Whether others be at peace or war, MacCailin (= Campbell) is our firm defence; his hand is followed as a wave of fruitfulness (prosperity); he is the Hector of the land of Scotland')

(6) Leomhan leimneach tar gach toigh,
     triath chothuighthe a creidimh;
     a n-iath Alban 'n phosda triath,
     go n-ardbhladh n-eaglasda.

('He is a lion who leaps over every house; he is a lord who defends the faith; in Scotland's land he is a pillar of lords, whose fame is high within the Church')

(7) Go bhfuil 'n a Mharcus ar med,
     tre itche cliar da choimhed;
     doigh le cach tuaith is theas
     gur'n thrath fuar gach flaitheas.

('He is a Marquis in degree, through the prayers of churchmen for his safe-keeping; all men, north and south, deem all his honours won when due')

(17) Leigidh dhamh duthchas m'athar,
     a n-onoir na h-ealadhan,
     a gheg tarla fa thoradh,
     do mhed th'anma is adhmholadh.

('Restore to me my father's heritage in honour of mine art (of poetry), thou branch laden with fruit, according to the greatness of thy name and of thy praises')

We do not know if the petition to restore the poet's land was successful; probably not, as the Marquis had other things on his mind.

The translation given here is by W.J. Watson, who used the high-flown poetic, almost biblical language of some formality, just as the poet did in the Gaelic. I would like to think that the Marquis was amused by the form of this request, but he was not a man easily amused at the best of times.

Thomas Pennant stayed at Inveraray Castle in 1772, as guest of a later Duke; and there he pondered on a portrait of the Marquis:

'. . . his hair short, his dress black, with a plain white turnover. A distinguished person during the reign of Charles I. . . a man, as his own father styled him, of craft and subtlety. . .'

Above: Inveraray Castle as Pennant saw it in 1772. This old building was pulled down to be replaced by the more modern edifice.

Right: The Castle in more modern times.

Walter Scott portrayed him in his novel *A Legend of the Wars of Montrose*, giving a detailed description of him, based on a contemporary portrait.

The novel *John Splendid* by Neil Munro also has an interesting depiction of Gillesbeg Gruamach, Marquis of Argyle, and the world in which he lived. Published in 1898, it was Munro's first novel, and has been described as 'arguably the first truly authentic Highland novel'. Its style is not unlike that of Robert Louis Stevenson, especially in *Kidnapped*, which had appeared only twelve years earlier.

Sour, dour, stern, grim, sinister, cruel are words which recur in accounts of the Marquis of Argyle, who might have evaded his tragic fate had he been a more likeable man.

Archibald Gruamach, Marquis of Argyle, painted by David Scougall. This portrait is now in the National Gallery of Scotland, Edinburgh.

YOUNG GEORGE'S SALUTE is included in the Inveraray section because of its connection with the Duke of Argyll. It may have been composed at Inveraray (see below).

The work has given rise to much dispute and speculation as to the identity of Young George. Early sources were confused. In 1785, the programme of the Edinburgh competition said George was the Laird of Callander – but none of the known Lairds of Callander was called George. The earliest published collections called the work simply *Young George's Salute* or *Welcome*: the Gaelic word Failte means Salute, Greeting or Welcome.

Angus MacKay, as so often, is more specific. He says it was *George Campbell Yr. Of Calder's Salute*. There was also a vague mention, made 'by a competitor', of the Campbells of Achallader, near Bridge of Orchy – but that family, too, had no sons called George.

Following Angus MacKay's lead, we are looking for Campbells of Calder, and there they are, at Cawdor Castle, near Nairn, on the south side of the Moray Firth. The Gaelic name for Cawdor is Caladair, and up to about 1800, Cawdor, when written in English or Scots, usually took the form Calder, which explains much of the confusion.

The Campbells had become the Thanes of Cawdor by marrying into the Calder family in the 1590s – the Calders were descendants of MacBeth, well-known Thane of Cawdor. And among these Campbells at Cawdor, we find several called George.

The most likely candidate for subject of the Salute seems to be George Campbell, fourth son of Sir Hugh Campbell, 14th Thane of Cawdor. George's exact birthdate is not known, but family expenses incurred in 1690 include the sum of £8.14s.0d. for a wig for son George, so he was probably born in the mid-1680s. In those days, boys of the gentlemanly classes were put into wigs as soon as their baby curls were cut off, around the age of five. They would wear a wig on formal occasions, much as our boys today might wear a kilt.

In April 1705, George's cousin Colin Campbell of Boghole (near Nairn) wrote from Edinburgh to his uncle, Sir Hugh: 'I hear young Mr George is very weell and will be hear in a few weeks in company with the Duke of Argyle'.

This suggests that young George was in attendance on the Duke of Argyll, and was in neither Edinburgh nor Cawdor, so he may well have been at Inveraray for at least part of this period. He was almost certainly depending on the Duke, who was his kinsman, to find him an army commission.

By May 11th 1705, George had been posted Ensign in the Foot Guards, and was on his way to his doom.

Another cousin, Sir Hugh's niece the Countess of Athole, wrote to him that year, saying: 'My young cousin George is made ensigne in the foot guards, and the commissioner has gott a promiss of the first Captain's commission that's vacant for him'.

The commissioner was an agent who secured promotion to different ranks at different prices, making a good living from his commission on these transactions. Promotion had generally to be bought for cash, unless someone of importance intervened, who had promotions in his gift. This ensigncy may have been gifted to George by the Duke.

Writing of this, the Countess goes on: 'This I hope his mother will not vex herself about, since the Guards never go out of this country . . .'

It seems that 'young' was the word associated with George throughout his short life, probably to distinguish him from his famous older relative, George Campbell of Airds (see below).

Before long, young George purchased, or was given, his captaincy, in Lord Mark Ker's Regiment, and he married a girl called Ruth Pollock, about whom we know nothing more. The Countess was proved wrong about his mother's need to be anxious, as the change of regiment was disastrous. Lord Mark Ker's was sent out to Spain to fight for Marlborough, in the Wars of the Spanish Succession.

Young George was killed in the Battle of Almanza on April 25th 1707. He died in his mid-twenties, leaving no children. His elder brother Colin also fell in the Spanish campaign. Their mother had every reason to vex herself with anxiety, after all.

The piobaireachd work is not called a Lament, but a Salute, which would suggest it was made in his lifetime, before his fate was known. It may have been made to greet him when he arrived in the Duke's household early in 1705, possibly on his first coming to Inveraray. If so, the composer may have been one of the Duke's pipers, but even if we could be certain of this, we would be none the wiser, as we do not know the names of Argyle's pipers at this time, although we know of one who was active during the '45.

Neil Munro wrote a story called *War*, set at the time of the '45, and in it the Duke's Second Piper appears, a man named Dol'(Donald) Dubh (= Black Donald), 'the same who learned the art of music right well from the Macruimens of Boreraig, and he had as sweet a finger on the chanter as Padruig himself'. This might suggest that Dol' Dubh had been in Skye before 1730, when Patrick Og died, but we cannot be sure of his dates. He is known to have been the Duke's second piper at the time of the '45, and was piper to the Argyll Militia when they were rounding up Jacobite fugitives on the west coast in 1746 (see above, Dugald Campbell). It would certainly be stretching surmise to breaking point to assume that it was Donald Dubh Campbell who composed *Young George's Salute* – but it is at least possible.

As a composition *Young George's Salute* is perhaps not the finest, lacking the inspiration needed by its length. It is competent work, but not brilliant, and seems to be an 18th century composition, to judge by its regular style, and its length. It may have been 'made over' later in the 18th century, with variations added by another hand.

The Cawdor papers make it clear that George's father, Sir Hugh, did not keep a piper, though he spent money on paying harpers for family occasions. The accounts give the impression that these harpers were hired rather than maintained in the household. It is most unlikely that the Salute was made at Cawdor.

The most we can say is that it was probably composed around 1705, probably by a Campbell piper, and possibly at Inveraray.

It has been suggested by Alistair Campbell of Airds that the subject of *Young George's Salute* may have been one of the Airds ancestors, George Campbell of Airds, who lived in the 17th century. This of course is possible, but probably unlikely, since this George Campbell became well-known in later life and would presumably not have continued to be known as Young George. We have evidence that George from Cawdor was called Young George by friends and family before he died young; and another Salute we have in honour of someone described as 'young' is the *Salute to the Young Laird of Dungallon*, who also died when barely in his twenties – so it does seem that the adjective was used of those who died young, or at least that it continued to be used about them when they failed to grow old. George Campbell of Airds did grow up and became famous, and I think it is unlikely that the title of a Salute to him would have still called him 'Young George'.

Probably the piobaireachd work *Lament for Airds* was made for George Campbell of Airds, but we cannot be sure of this. George Campbell who died in

1685 was the first Campbell of Airds, the third son of Sir John Campbell of Cawdor, and great-uncle of Young George (see below).

SOURCES
Wardlaw Manuscript, *Chronicles of the Frasers*
Piobaireachd Society Book 9
C. Innes: *The Book of the Thanes of Cawdor*
Alistair Campbell of Airds
Cassells' *History of the British People*, Volume V
Neil Munro: *The Lost Pibroch and Other Shieling Stories*
Cradle of the Scots, An Argyll Anthology

JOHN MACKENZIE, LOCH FYNE,
COUSIN OF JOHN BAN MACKENZIE

SOME OF THE DESCENDANTS OF John MacKenzie, fisherman, Loch Fyne, believe that they are direct linear descendants of the well-known piper John Ban MacKenzie, who was born in Ross-shire and was piper to the Marquis of Breadalbane at Taymouth Castle for more than 28 years (between 1832 and 1861). Most of them are not. The confusion is understandable, since there were two contemporary pipers, both called John MacKenzie, and both associated with the Campbells of Breadalbane. They were not the same person, however, but were probably first-cousins.

John Ban MacKenzie was born around 1796, probably at Altnabreac, in Achilty, Ross and Cromarty; his father was William MacKenzie, his mother Mary MacKay, said to be of a Raasay family. It is possible, though not proven, that this William MacKenzie was the piper in the 72nd Regiment who wrote home from New York in 1778. It is clear from his letter that this piper came from the Loch Tay area, and a family of MacKenzies appears in the records, living in Kenmore.

If this was the same family, which is by no means certain, we may surmise that the MacKenzies had been pipers to the Breadalbane Campbells for more than one generation, and that the position was heritable, as was often the case with piping families. The evidence is, however, inconclusive. In favour is the coinciding of the family names William, Kenneth, Duncan and John; against it is the reference in J.F.Campbell's *Popular Tales of the West Highlands*, telling us that John MacKenzie, Loch Fyne, used northern dialect words when telling Gaelic stories – this suggests that he had been taught the stories by Ross-shire relatives, his mother and his uncle Kenneth.

Be that as it may, in the early 1800s William's brother Kenneth and his sister Christian appear at Ardmaddy, the castle in west Argyll belonging to the Breadalbane Campbells. Kenneth was piper at Ardmaddy, and Christie seems to have been his housekeeper. In 1804, Kenneth married Ann MacLean, and while living at Ardmaddy, they had a son, Duncan, born there in February 1805. There may be some confusion with a Kenneth MacKenzie who married an Ann

MacLean in 1785, at Kenmore, Loch Tay, Perthshire. Their children were Donald 1791, Duncan 1793, Mary 1795, Catherine 1797 and Ann 1799. This does not seem to be the same Kenneth, but may have been related.

The link between Kenneth MacKenzie, his sister Christie and his brother William has no conclusive written proof, but it is a strong tradition in different branches of the family descendants in Scotland, England and Canada. It is to some extent borne out by birth and marriage records in the Old Parish Registers, but these are sparse.

On 7th April 1807, at Ardmaddy, Christie gave birth to a child described in the Register as a natural son (N.S.), the father being named as John MacArthur, Balvicar, a village a few miles from Ardmaddy, across Seil Sound. The boy was baptised John, and retained his mother's surname, MacKenzie.

John MacArthur was probably not one of the piping MacArthurs from Skye, Islay or Ulva (though he may have been), but is more likely to have belonged to the very old Argyll family of MacArthurs who originated near Loch Awe; a saying in Argyll was 'As old as the Devil, the mountains and the MacArthurs'. A number of that family is known to have lived on Seil Island, especially at Balvicar where work was available in the slate quarries. Some of these Loch Awe MacArthurs were pipers, but it is not known if John MacArthur was one (see also Barbreck, above). He could have been the John MacArthur who was piper to the Laird of Craignish, though the dates are not certain, for either of these John MacArthurs.

Whether the child grew up at Ardmaddy knowing his father, we do not know. In later life he said he had learned stories from his father, but he seems to have been brought up in the household of his uncle Kenneth, and he may have regarded Kenneth as his father; this is borne out by his death certificate, in which his grandson stated that John's father was Kenneth MacKenzie. Presumably this was to cover up the illegitimacy.

He grew up to be a piper, probably taught by his uncle Kenneth. As a young teenager, he was a piper to the Campbells at Ardmaddy, and we assume this was as assistant to his uncle. But in 1822 or 23, when he was about seventeen, he left Ardmaddy and went over to Loch Fyne, to join the herring fleet. He could expect to make a better living there than by remaining as an assistant piper at Ardmaddy (a contemporary Campbell described Loch Fyne at this time as being 'three parts fish to one part water').

He married Janet MacVicar, who was some six years older than himself, and they settled in the tiny isolated village of Kenmore, Loch Fyne, a few miles south of Inveraray. The Duke of Argyll had had the fisherfolk removed from Inveraray in 1777, ('forcibly banished', says a contemporary record), during the construction of the new village in the 1770s, as he objected to the smell of fish. The fisherfolk were re-settled at Kenmore, where two rows of cottages were built in 1770. Four families of MacVicars moved there in 1771, the rest of the houses were filled when families were forced out of Inveraray. The question arises: was Kenmore the original name of the site, or was the name introduced from

Kenmore, Loch Tay? Timothy Pont's map of the area, made in the 1590s, has a name which looks like Koungaur at the site of Kenmore, but the reading is doubtful.

We have a glimpse of John MacKenzie given to us by Hector Urquhart, one of J.F.Campbell's collectors of Gaelic stories. In *Popular Tales of the West Highlands*, Hector said that in April 1859, John recited for him ('recited' is his word) a long Gaelic story called *The Battle of the Birds (Cath nan Eun)*. J.F.Campbell wrote: 'The reciter is a fisherman, and has resided for the last thirty-four years at Ceanmore, near Inveraray, on the estate of the Duke of Argyll. He is a native of Lorn. He says he has known it (the story) from his youth, and he has been in the habit of repeating it to his friends on winter nights, as a pastime.' 'He can read English and play the bagpipes, and has a memory like Oliver and Boyd's Almanac'' (evidently these words were taken from Hector's own notes. Oliver and Boyd's Almanac was the equivalent of the Internet as a source of information). 'He got this and his other stories from his father and other old people in Lorn and elsewhere. He is about sixty years of age, and was employed, April 1859, in building dykes on the estate of Ardkinglas, where Hector Urquhart is gamekeeper. In reciting his stories he has all the manner of a practised narrator; people still frequent his house to hear his tales. I know the man, and I have heard him recite many. The Gaelic has some few north country words' (*Popular Tales*, pp.118-119). It is likely that J.F.Campbell was not aware that John had been brought up by his uncle.

Other stories were told by John MacKenzie and published in *Popular Tales*. One was *The Sea Maiden (A'Mhaighdean Mhara)*, published with the comment: 'Written, April 1850, by Hector Urquhart, from the dictation of John MacKenzie, fisherman, Kenmore, near Inveraray, who says that he learned it from an old man in Lorn many years ago. He has lived for thirty-six years at Kenmore. He told the story fluently at first, and then dictated it slowly. The Gaelic is given as nearly as possible in the words used by MacKenzie, but he thinks his story rather shortened' (p.156).

Another of John's stories was taken down by J.F.Campbell himself in August 1859 and 1860, at Inveraray. It is called *Bailie Lunain, the Baillie of London*. One recorded by Hector Urquhart in 1859 was *The Knight of the Riddles (Ridere nan Ceist)*. The notes repeat the information given earlier.

It is clear that John was literate, a man of high intelligence, musical and steeped in the traditions of his people. His cousin John Ban could neither read nor write, and depended on his wife for his correspondence. John Ban too was very much interested in his native language, and was knowledgeable about Gaelic and its dialects, but from the little information we have of the two men, it is clear that John the fisherman was exceptional. He probably had fewer opportunities than his cousin, but he made more of them.

John MacKenzie and his wife Janet MacVicar had six children, Duncan 1823, Kenneth 1825, Sarah 1828, Janet 1831, Isabella 1835, Anne (Nancy) 1837 or 38 (she married a crofter called Ferguson). John was only 17 when his eldest son was born, a few months after what was evidently a shot-gun wedding.

Presumably Duncan and Kenneth were named for John's cousin and uncle. Isabella, known as Bella Mhor (Big Bell), was the dominant character of the family. She was a big strong woman; one branch of the family says she was 6ft 2in in height, but the descendants of another branch insist that she was 6ft 7in. Anyway, she was prodigiously tall for a woman, and powerfully built, too. It was said she could lift a full barrel of herring when most men could not even push it along the ground unaided.

The story goes, and appeared in print at the time, that Bell behaved with extraordinary courage and compassion at the time of the cholera epidemic in Argyll, in 1848-9. She was only in her teens, but a big strapping lassie, even then.

The fishing boats had gone out as usual, with a supply of fresh water in small kegs, unaware that the water was contaminated. The crews fell ill at sea in their vessels, and the boats drifted back up the loch, full of dead and dying men. On reaching Kenmore, they lay off shore, and nobody wanted to go out to them for fear of the disease; but Bell waded out, towed the boats in, and carried the men ashore, where they were taken to an isolated place and laid in tents made of sailcloth. People brought food for them, and left it nearby, but did not want to risk infection by going too close. It was Bell who helped the elderly minister to feed and nurse the sick, and Bell who buried the dead – and was not struck down by the cholera herself. The family attributed this immunity to her love of a good dram, believed to kill all germs. Perhaps she never took water with it.

After her mother's death in the 1850s, Bell kept house for her father, and appears to have remained with him after her marriage, probably because her husband was a fisherman who was often away at sea for long periods. She married late, and her husband was the son of a fisher family called MacPhedran, who lived next-door-but-one to the MacKenzies at Kenmore. His name was John MacPhedran, and he was a piper, as was Bell herself. As is often said of piping families, the wife was a better player than the husband, and sometimes when he was playing at a wedding, he would take too much to drink. When he passed out, Bell would reach across and take the pipe from his hands and play for the dancing. She had been taught by her father, and inherited his pipe at his death in 1884.

Although she married late, in her thirties, Bell had seven sons in twelve years. She followed her parents' example in that her eldest son was born inconveniently soon after her wedding – but this was considered normal in country areas. Men preferred to know that their prospective wives were capable of child-bearing.

Bell's children were John 1865, Duncan 1866, Alexander 1867, Peter 1868, Donald 1870, Kenneth 1873, Neil 1877. It is generally said that Bell had six sons, so one of them probably died in infancy. Duncan and Donald were both pipers who played in the Inveraray band (see below).

Family tradition pictures John MacPhedran as a somewhat downtrodden husband, dominated by his remarkable wife. Opinions differ about his eventual fate: one version says he left home to join the Antarctic whaling fleet, and drowned in the Southern Ocean; others in the family say he died at home, of a chest complaint. He died between 1877 and 1881.

Stories preserved in the family tell of John MacKenzie's habit of picking up a fore-arm of whichever of his little grandsons was handy, and fingering piobaireachd on it. When sharing a bed with one of them, he inadvertently woke the child by playing pipe music on his arm in the middle of the night. The children were probably so skinny that their arms reminded him of a chanter. They were impatient with him, as they did not like having to stand still while he played.

When Bell was an old lady and no longer able to live alone, some of her sons were living at Inveraray. They decided to move her out of Kenmore, and loaded her belongings on a boat to take them round to Inveraray. Her father's silver-mounted pipe was put on top of the load, so that it would not be broken. But as they came in at the Inveraray pier, a sudden violent squall of wind capsized the overloaded boat, and the pipe fell off into deep water. It was never recovered: Loch Fyne is several hundred feet deep. Family tradition says this was John Ban's pipe, but it seems more likely it was her father's.

The family prospered at Kenmore while the herring stocks lasted, and the settlement there throve until well into the twentieth century. Today the lovely little village of Kenmore is derelict, reached only by sea or by a very dilapidated track from the main road, south of Inveraray. Some of the MacKenzie family were at the house a little to the north of Kenmore, called French Farland. John M. MacKenzie of the Victoria School, Dunblane, was a direct descendant in this line (see below).

SOURCES
OPR Kilbrandon, Inveraray, Weem, Crieff
Census Inveraray, Ardmaddy
John Gibson
J.F. Campbell
MacPhedran family tradition:
Duncan MacPhedran, Neil MacPhedran, Sarah Galbraith, Stewart MacKenzie, Kenneth MacTaggart
Sheila MacIntyre
Virginia van der Lande
History of Lochfyneside, Furnace, Crarae and Minard

THE QUEEN'S VISIT, 1847

A SCOTTISH ROYAL TOUR WAS made by Queen Victoria and Prince Albert in 1847. In August they sailed up through the Irish Sea to the west coast of Scotland. They called in at Inveraray, where J.F. Campbell of Islay and the Celtic Society met them, to great rejoicing, and they were entertained in Inveraray Castle by the Duke of Argyll.

The Inverness Courier carried an account of the occasion which in some details conflicts with that of the Queen's Journals. Neither names pipers such as

Hugh Lindsay and Dougald (or Donald) MacIndeor, and the presence of these two as individuals is part of piping tradition only; but it is the Queen's account which gives an idea of when and where they played for the royal party.

The edition of the Courier for August 24th 1847 describes the festive scenes in Inveraray on the morning that the Queen was due. The *Victoria and Albert*, being a paddle steamer, was not able to travel through the narrow locks of the Crinan Canal, so she was taken round the long way to Crinan, by the Mull of Kintyre. The steamer then waited in Crinan Bay for the Queen to re-join her.

Meanwhile, the royal family were on their smaller yacht, the *Fairy*, and were expected to reach Inveraray during the day. 'Inveraray was all in commotion, sweltering under a hot sun, the noise of bagpipes, the marches and counter-marches of well-appointed Highlanders, the waving of flaming colours and the press of crowding thousands. The herring boats were drawn up in the bay, their sails of reddish-brown full set, and each surmounted with a silk pendant'. (John MacKenzie, the Loch Fyne fisherman and piper, would have been aboard one of them).

On the Castle lawns were nine big white marquees, and a large tent covered with different tartans, 'which at a distance bore some resemblance to a gipsy encampment'. This was the tent of the Celtic Society from Edinburgh, high-born gentlemen who would not have enjoyed the newspaper's description. It goes on:

'Campbell of Islay had 150 men mustered for the occasion, dressed uniformly in his dark green tartan philabeg (kilt) and plaid, black jacket faced on the breast with red, and each bearing a Lochaber axe in his hand, and wearing a sprig of myrtle in his bonnet. Islay himself had arrayed his manly figure in the old costume, with his battle axe in his hand '.

The previous night, the Celtic Society had dined in style in their marquee, with many toasts 'which were drank in brimmers of champagne and greeted with tremendous cheering and succeeded by excellent pipe music, played by MacKenzie, the Marquis of Breadalbane's piper' (this was John Ban, first cousin of the Loch Fyne fisherman) 'and his young son who figured in our last year's Northern Meeting' (this was Donald, then aged 14. He is commemorated in *His Father's Lament for Donald MacKenzie*).

Next morning, our reporter remarked with some pain, the pipers struck up at six o'clock, and the crowds were gathering. When the royal squadron was sighted, after mid-day, sailing up Loch Fyne, the Highlanders lined the route between pier and castle. The Queen surprised everyone by climbing down into the landing barge backwards, 'sailor-fashion,' giving the crowd a fine view of her rear elevation, but Prince Albert walked down the steps 'in the ordinary down-stairs manner'.

The procession was headed by 'five determined pipers', and had to push its way through the crowd, 'the brilliant and happy assemblage'. One of the pipers may have been Donald MacPhedran (see below).

The Courier's correspondent implies that there was a lengthy luncheon in the Castle, from which the press was excluded, but Queen Victoria was more specific: the royal party immediately on arrival at two o'clock had lunch with the Duke and his family in the castle, then the procession re-formed, and according to the paper, 'the pipes were once more in requisition, and the vast mass of living beings were in noisy ecstasy'. The royal party re-embarked and had left Inveraray before three o'clock, a point on which the Queen is emphatic. It must have been a quick luncheon, with no time to relax. The yacht sailed down the loch to Lochgilphead, where they all disembarked.

Even the *Fairy* was too big for the canal, so the royal party had to go on board a horse-drawn decorated barge specially fitted out with a golden pavilion in the stern and adorned with long golden banners. The six horses and two postillions in charge of them were dressed in 'mediaeval crimson and gold'. The banks were lined with crowds for the entire ten miles of the canal, but this time they were eerily silent, as if awestruck.

Again the Queen's account differs: the newspaper said how much the royal family enjoyed their passage through to Crinan, but the Queen remarked how tedious the locks were – she was irked by the slow raising and lowering of the barge.

They went next day to Oban, and then up the Sound of Mull, where our corresponent reported that 'the bagpipe would have been lost amidst the surging of the ocean and the screaming of seabirds, and accordingly the national instrument was mute'. It is clear from later comments made at Fort William that the Queen's own piper (Angus MacKay) was with them, though he is never named. He may have joined the party at Oban.

From Tobermory they sailed for the islands, returning later to Oban and Fort William, where they disembarked. We are told that there was a Ball at the Mason Hall in Fort William. The Queen did not attend, but she sent fifteen officers from her party and her piper, 'placing his services at the disposal of the stewards. His playing was much appreciated, and many an excellent reel was danced to his strains during the evening'. Again, the Queen did not put this in her Journal, merely observing that Fort William was 'a very small place'.

The return journey through the canal was on September 18th, in steady rain. The royal party sailed into Crinan, and the Queen wrote that 'Mr Malcolm of Poltalloch, whose castle is just opposite' met them in Crinan and escorted them to the magnificent barge, which fortunately was roofed in. The Queen had probably complained of the tedium of the passage through the locks, because this time there was a piper at every lock, to entertain her as she rose or fell. Her only comment was: 'It rained almost the whole time'. They reached Lochgilphead at noon, and went on board the steamer *Black Eagle*, sailing immediately for Campbeltown ('a small and not pretty place').

From the descriptions, it is clear that J. F. Campbell had brought 150 men from Islay and Jura with him to Inveraray; he took such a large part in the Queen's welcome to Inveraray because he was a cousin of the Duke of Argyll. It seems likely that both Hugh Lindsay and Dougald (or Donald) MacIndeor were in his 'tail' of islanders, and this is confirmed by the gift of a new pipe for MacIndeor, from Campbell. Hugh Lindsay had won the Prize Pipe at Inverness only two years earlier, so he would have been welcomed into Campbell's 'tail', for this royal occasion.

The Highlanders were present throughout the luncheon at the castle, 'standing with halberds in the room', as the Queen remarked. Was this when the two pipers gave their performances, playing and dancing for her majesty? Probably not, as there was no time for entertainment at that point. It was certainly not at Ardrishaig, where she went straight to the royal barge, nor at Crinan, where she was immediately rowed out to her yacht. We do not know who were the pipers at the locks in September. Did any of the men from Islay and Jura remain on the mainland until the Queen's return? Could this have been when Hugh Lindsay and Donald MacIndeor showed off their skills, in the rain, beside the Crinan Canal? It seems the most likely possibility.

JOHN M. MACKENZIE

KENNETH MACKENZIE (1825-1879), SON OF John MacKenzie and Janet MacVicar in Kenmore, married Flora Galbraith, and from that marriage is descended the line of John M. MacKenzie (1922-1996). He was born in Campbeltown, and became well-known as the piping instructor at the Queen Victoria School, in Dunblane. Among his many distinguished pupils were Allan, Iain and Dr Angus MacDonald, the three brothers from Glenuig.

John himself was a pupil of Robert Reid, and he recorded the tunes he learned from Reid, played in the style he had acquired from the master. He accompanied the playing with spoken commentary on the tuition he received from Robert Reid. These tapes are now a valuable record of the so-called 'Cameron' tradition of piping.

On John's death on 12th June 1996, Hugh MacCallum wrote this tribute, which appeared with a photograph of John in the Piping Times for July 1996 (vol. 48, edition 10). It is reproduced here with the kind permission of Hugh MacCallum and the editor of the Piping Times:

'A native of Campbeltown, Kintyre, John joined the Argyll and Sutherland Highlanders as a young piper in 1938, and later became pipe-major of the 2nd Battalion and the 8th Battalion of that regiment. After leaving the Army, John returned to Campbeltown for a spell, and amongst many other activities, he became a founder member of the Kintyre Piping Society. He emigrated with his family to what was then Rhodesia in 1953, but returned to Scotland after several years there, and was appointed Piping Instructor to Queen Victoria School in Dunblane. He brought the band there to the very highest standard, and under his guidance they became World Juvenile Champions.' For years the band performed at Scotland's rugby matches at Murrayfield in Edinburgh, part of the great occasion of a rugby international. John's comment was 'I had 27 appearances at Murrayfield and never scored once'.

Hugh continues: 'John was no slouch on the competitive solo platform him-

This well-known photographic portrait of John M. MacKenzie appeared in the Piping Times with a tribute written by Hugh MacCallum.

self, and among his many successes included the winning of the March Strathspey and Reel for former winners at the Argyllshire Gathering. He excelled as a teacher, and some of his pupils themselves went on to become champion pipers. He produced his own book of pipe music, which proved very popular with pipers all over the world. His compositions were of the very highest quality, and became favourites not only with pipers, but other musicians as well. Later in life, he turned his talents to historical research and the composition of piobaireachd. He was much sought after as a judge, and was always prepared to give constructive comment and encouragement to younger players. John was a popular and well respected figure, and his piping stories became part of piping folklore. He was awarded the B.E.M. for his services to piping in the Army, and this was presented to him by Prince Philip at Queen Victoria School on his final parade before retirement.

'John was very much a family man, and received great support from his wife Margaret, and daughters Elizabeth and Catherine. He was also very proud of his five grandchildren. We extend our condolences to all the family at this time. On a personal note, I consider myself fortunate to have had him as a teacher and as a friend.'

To this tribute in the Piping Times, Ian K. Murray added:

'John MacKenzie was the most entertaining of companions. His stories, which were usually based in historical events (he was fascinated by history especially that of his own and other Highland regiments) were embellished with his own fanciful and humorous additions. One never knew however where historical fact ended and John's imagination began. His piping lore was equally amusing: he saw the funny side of most things and his humour was always good hearted.

'He took responsibility for the Stirling University Summer School for several years and there demonstrated his organisational flair, his ability to communicate ideas and a knack of persuading people (especially youngsters with whom he had an effortless rapport) to undertake responsibilities they would normally try to avoid. Those of us who attended the Summer School came away wiser and better pipers. This improvement was attributable, at least in part, to John's discerning choice of tunes – memorably melodic and written out in his clear hand.

'On one occasion I heard John express his disappointment that even some of the better pipers of today did not play marches, strathspeys and reels with the same full-bloodedness of his own contemporaries. Perhaps those of us who knew him could honour his memory by playing these tunes with bravura. Budding composers would do well to look again at the elegant simplicity of *Tug Argan Gap* – a tune that is a joy to play'.

One of John's stories is from his army days. It seems that when an officer went round the new recruits while they were eating, he would ask if there were any complaints, not expecting any response. But one young soldier said he had a complaint, the food was not good, and the stew they had been served that day was so tough it was uneatable. 'Nonsense' said the officer, and taking a piece of meat from the lad's plate, he put it into his mouth and tried to eat it. After several minutes of jaw-breaking effort, he managed to swallow it whole, and beamed at the boy. 'There you are, it's not uneatable at all, is it?' The lad replied ' But now try a piece I haven't chewed first'.

John MacKenzie was a direct descendant of John MacKenzie, Loch Fyne, who was a first cousin of John Ban MacKenzie, the famous Ross-shire piper. Jeannie Campbell has traced his exact line:

Christie MacKenzie, sister of Kenneth, the piper at Ardmaddy, and of William, the father of John Ban, had an illegitimate son John (see above). This John MacKenzie, born in 1807, married Janet MacVicar, Inveraray, and their son Kenneth, born in 1825, was, like his father, a fisherman at Kenmore.

Kenneth was the first of the family to live in Campbeltown, where he married Flora Galbraith, the daughter of Neil Galbraith, a quartermaster in the Royal Navy, and his wife Elizabeth Hamilton. Flora was born in 1836, and died in Glasgow in 1896. Was this Neil Galbraith the piper who played for Hallowe'en ceilidhs at Torrisdale and Whitestone in 1855 (see above), along with Donald Ferguson? It seems likely that he was.

Kenneth and Flora had a son Neil MacKenzie, who was John M.'s grandfather, born in 1866. He too was a fisherman, in Campbeltown, and in 1887 he married a rope factory worker, Catherine Lang, born 1867, daughter of a fisherman, Neil Lang, and his wife Agnes Mitchell. Neil and Catherine lived at 2 Lorne Street, Campbeltown.

Their son, Neil Lang MacKenzie, born Campbeltown in 1894, was a blacksmith. In 1920, he married a girl described as a 'bakeress', Marion MacLean, whose parents were a merchant seaman called John MacLean, and Isabella Docherty. Marion, who was John M.'s mother, was born in 1895.

Their son John MacLean MacKenzie, was born in 1922 in Campbeltown. He married Margaret, and they had two daughters, Elizabeth and Catherine.

The compositions of John M. MacKenzie include:
Alaster Hutcheon's March 4/4 M 2
Allan Dodd's Farewell to Scotland 2/4 M 4
Andrew MacNeill of Oransay 2/4 M 4
Birkhall R 2
The Bonnie Summer Days 4/4 M 2
The Cairn on the Hill 6/8 GA 2
Campbeltown Gaelic Choir 6/8 M 4 (1950)
Captain MacCallum (arr) 4/4 RM 2
Captain MacCallum's Reel (arr) R 2
Ceol na Mara, P with 7 variations
Corries (arr) R 2
Dr Jerry Colborne 2/4 M 2 (1978. Dr Colborne is a Canadian engineer)
Drum Major John Seton R 4
Fingal's Weeping (arr) HP 2
The Foxhunter's Jig 9/8 J 4
The Gypsy's Warning 3/4 RM 2

Iain Grant 6/8 J 4
Johnny and Jimmy 2/4 HP 4
The Laggan Pipers 2/4 M 2
The MacNeils (or MacNeals) of Ugadale 6/8 M 4
Mrs Margaret MacKenzie S 4
Neuve Chapelle 6/8 SM 2
Paddy's Green Isle 6/8 J 4
Pipe Major Peter Philliban 6/8 M 4
The Piper and the Dancer 6/8 J 4
The Raven's Rock R 2
The Road to Kintyre 6/8 J 4
Ronnie Lawrie's Rant 6/8 J 4
The Saffron Kilt (arr?) 6/8 SM 2
Samuel the Weaver (parts 3 and 4) 6/8 J 4
The Sandpiper R 4
Tug Argan Gap 6/8 M 4
The Wedding Waltz 6/8 Waltz 4
Willie Davey R 2
Note also:
John M. MacKenzie (SPA Glasgow), by Peter R. MacLeod 2/4 M 4
Any additions to this list will be welcomed.

SOURCES
Census records, Inveraray
Jeannie Campbell
Piping Times – Hugh MacCallum, Ian K. Murray

DONALD AND ARCHIE MACPHEDRAN

Although the Notices of Pipers state that Donald MacPhedran, noted as a piper and composer of light music, was the great-uncle of Archie MacPhedran, Pipe Major of the 5th H.L.I. (T.A.) Regiment, family genealogists have been unable to confirm this relationship. Both belonged to families of MacPhedrans who were fishermen and pipers on Loch Fyne, but the exact connection is not clear.

There is a widespread belief that both Donald and Archie were direct descendants of John MacKenzie and Janet MacVicar, Kenmore (see above), through the line of their daughter Bell, but this must be mistaken. They were connected to that line, but not part of it. The confusion probably arose because John MacPhedran and Bell MacKenzie, in Kenmore, near Inveraray, had a son Donald MacPhedran, who was a piper but was not the Glasgow pipemaker (see above, and below). Another source of confusion was a link with Kenmore, in Archie MacPhedran's family.

A letter written by Archie MacPhedran in 1947, with no designation, so that we do not know to whom it was addressed (but it was evidently someone in Canada), mentions his ancestry:

'There are quite a lot of MacPhedran's in Glasgow at present, in fact three different branches, but all from Lochfyne side. My Father was known as Archie 'Coll', my Grandmother was a sister of Evan MacColl, the Canadian Bard, and came from 'KENMORE' where they built a Memorial for him. One other family came from St Catherines and the head of the other family from Inveraray, died about three months ago, was Bailiff to the Duke of Argyll, aged 92.

'Most of his sons are in the Police Force and one of them is Superintendent and Fiscal of the Eastern Division of Glasgow with the same name as his Father.

'They are all very tall men, six feet and over. The Duncan one was Quartermaster and Captain of the K.O.S.B.'s and other three brothers were Pipers in the Scots Guards in the first World War.

'My own son joined the Engineers and finished up C.B.E. or Lieut.Col., retiring with the substantive rank of Major. I would like to ask you if your father is Dr.A.MacPhedran of Hamilton, Ontario, and if you had an Aunt Marion, I think that was her name.

'She [was] Matron of No.2 Canadian General Hospital at Le Tuport in France in 1917 [and] I met this Lady there when I was in a very bad way on my road to Blighty.

'I would advise you to claim the McAulay's instead of the Campbells when stating the Sept of our Clan.

' ... I was 40 years with the 5th Bn. H.L.I. (Territorials), 28 years as Pipe Major and I still have got the Glasgow Shepherds Pipe Band who as Juveniles won the Jr.World's Championship 10 times.

'Trusting you are all keeping well.

Your kinsman

(signed) Archie MacPhedran'

The meaning is not entirely clear in some parts of this letter, but it does confirm that Archie was not the son or grandson of Bell from Kenmore, though there was a Kenmore connection, through the MacColls. His grandfather, who died in 1870 at the age of 72, was Dugald MacPhedran, fisherman, married to Mary MacColl, of Kenmore. Dugald's father was John MacPhedran, farmer, married to Catherine MacKellar. This family of MacPhedrans in Kenmore must have been related to John MacPhedran who married Bell MacKenzie. It seems likely that Bell's husband and Archie's father were cousins.

In an article in the Piping Times in December 1991, Jeannie Campbell quotes the Oban Times for April 22nd 1939, which published a picture of Archie MacPhedran, with the comment:

'PM Archie MacPhedran who has retired after being Pipe Major of the 5th H.L.I.(T.A.) since 1915. He was officially known by the Government as senior pipe major in the British Army'.

This is followed by a report on the presentation to PM Archie MacPhedran on his retirement.

Archie was well known as P/M of the 5th HLI and as P/M of the Glasgow Shepherds Pipe Band, both top bands of their time. The Glasgow Shepherds included many young players who went on to great things in the piping world, boys such as John MacFadyen, Donald and Iain MacPherson, Tommy Pearston, Seumas MacNeill, John Weatherston and Bob MacFie. Archie retired from Henderson's in 1952 and died in 1962. He had been born in Glasgow in 1885, and Jeannie says his father Archie was from Inveraray.

Writing in 1992, Bob MacFie recalled competitions when he was a boy in 1939, held in Elmbank Street gym. He and his young friends were playing soccer in the basement, but were always careful to post sentries 'to warn of the approach of the club secretary, Malcolm Currie, or our 'pipey' Archie MacPhedran, either of whom would have frightened the devil himself'.

Donald McPhedran (1820-1888) has been traced by Jeannie Campbell, who gave the details in her book *Highland Bagpipe Makers*, originally published as a series in the Piping Times, and in book form in 2001. Her article is quoted here with her permission:

'Although a pipe maker in the later years of his life Donald McPhedran was

The 5th H.L.I. with their Pipe Major, Archie MacPhedran (1885-1962). The front rank of the band are (L. to R.) Archie McPhedran, Pipe Major, and pipers Robert MacPherson, Alex Cowie and George Clark. The location was Garrioch Drive, Maryhill, Glasgow. Archie served with the H.L.I. for 24 years before retiring in 1939, to become manager of Peter Henderson's pipe-making business.
(PHOTOGRAPH BY COURTESY OF THE COLLEGE OF PIPING)

better known as a player and composer. He was born on February 29th 1820 at Teigh-an-Ratha (sic) about one and a half miles from Inveraray, and christened on March 1st. His parents Colin McPhedran and Mary Macfarlane were married in 1819 and produced a large family. Donald was the eldest of seven. Colin himself was the son of Donald McPhedran and Flora McDiarmid who married in 1792 and had three sons.

'Donald's father Colin was married secondly to Janet Crawford and died on September 27th 1879 at Jamestown, Bonhill near Dumbarton.

'During his early youth Donald used to play and lead the procession through the town prior to the annual shinty matches held in Inveraray on New Year's Day, then play at the balls (dances) in the evening.

'He moved to Glasgow as a young man and worked as a joiner. He married on July 13th 1852 in Barony church, Glasgow, where the marriage is recorded as Donald McFedran to Ann McLachlan (see below). A son Colin was born to them on March 14th 1853, registered in Barony parish, but the baby did not survive long, his death being recorded in Blythswood parish, Glasgow, in 1855.

'Donald became Pipe Major of a Glasgow regiment of Volunteers and on October 14th 1859 played at the opening by Queen Victoria of Glasgow's new water supply, Loch Katrine Waterworks, composing the tune *Loch Katrine* for the occasion...

Donald MacPhedran. He was said by many to have been a great-uncle of Archie MacPhedran, but this must be mistaken. This portrait of Donald was published in the Piping Times in August 1997. It is a photograph which seems to have been coloured by hand, somewhat crudely with paint, and has now been restored by JeannieCampbell.
(PHOTOGRAPH BY COURTESY OF THE COLLEGE OF PIPING)

'In 1870 Donald was in Inveraray for the celebrations to mark the homecoming of the Duke of Argyll's son and heir the Marquess of Lorne and his bride Princess Louise, daughter of Queen Victoria. He played selections at the Castle for the Princess and played at the ball held in the Castle Pavilion for the County families.

'At the Argyllshire Gathering in 1873 the result of the Strathspey and Reel competition was 1. McPhedran, 2. R.MacKinnon, 3. D.McPhee. Robert

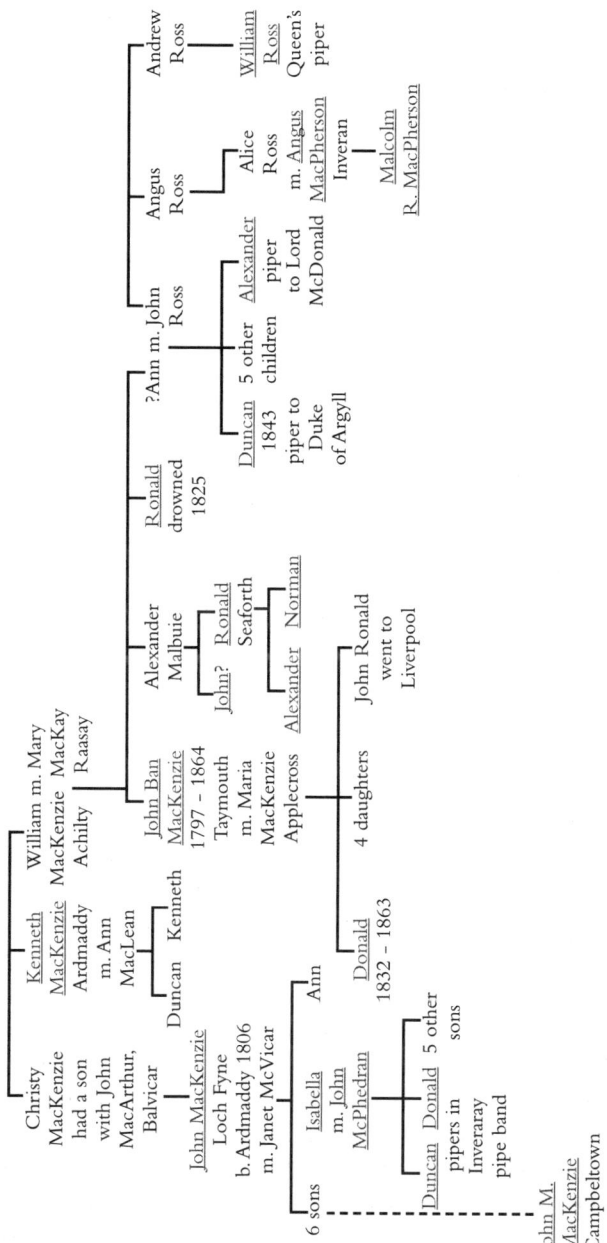

MacKinnon and Donald McPhee were both bagpipe makers in Glasgow and both published collections of light music including several tunes composed by Donald McPhedran. According to his obituary in the Oban Times Donald MacPhedran was the best player of dance music which this age had produced, had composed some excellent tunes and arranged and improved many others. He left an index of 900 tunes with the first bar of each written after the name of the tune. He is described as having finely chiselled features, and a face typically Celtic shaded by a broad Balmoral bonnet. From his photograph it can be seen that he played on the right shoulder' (as many of the MacPhedran pipers did).

Jeannie Campbell continues:

'In 1874 Donald was again at Inveraray Castle where he gave an exhibition of piping before Queen Victoria who was visiting the Duke and Duchess of Argyll'. (In the following year, the Duke appointed Duncan Ross as his resident piper – see below).

'By 1881 the McPhedrans were living at 776 Garscube Road in Glasgow, between Cowcaddens and Queen's Cross to the North-West of the City Centre. There were 10 households listed in the census at that address and the McPhedran family had two rooms.

'Donald McPhedran appears in the alphabetical section in the Glasgow directories between 1885 and 1887, listed as a bagpipe maker at 85 Doncaster Street. This is near Queen's Cross, between Garscube Road and Maryhill Road.

'Donald, unfortunately, was not in business very long as he died on December 8th 1888. On his death certificate he is described as a Joiner Journeyman, aged 65 and married to Agness MacLachlan.' (The names Ann and Agnes tend to be interchangeable, both giving the pet name Nan). 'His parents were Colin McPhedran, Dyer, and Sarah McPhedran, MS Macfarlane. The cause of death was Paralysis, the informant was his son John and the address was 68 Doncaster Street. An obituary appeared in the Glasgow Letter of the Oban Times on December 22nd 1888.

'In the 1891 census there are no McPhedrans at number 68, but at number 85, with 14 other households, we find Agnes McPhedran, widow, aged 71, born in Crinan, Kilmartin, and her daughter Mary McPhedran aged 25.

'Between 1903 and 1906 Donald McPhedran's Collection of Bagpipe Music was published. This was complied and arranged by his son, John McPhedran, violinist, flautist and piper, of 66 Lambhill Street, Glasgow. The reel *Duntroon*, probably Donald McPhedran's best known tune, is published in the collection where the composers are given as J.MacLachlan and D. McPhedran.

'Twenty-nine other tunes in the book are said to have been composed by Donald McPhedran. These include *Maggie Cameron, The Herring Wife, The Islay Ball, The Devil in the Kitchen, The Old Man's Address*, which is *The Sheepwife* under another name, *Inveraray Schoolhouse*, which is the *Caledonian Society of London*, and *The Prophet*, another name for the *Earl of Mansfield*. As the collection was published after Donald's death, it is probable that his son was confused as to which tunes were composed by Donald and which arranged by him. Also attributed to

Donald are a march arrangement of *Stumpie*, an arrangement of *Lady Madelina Sinclair* for the violin, and an enlarged version of the *Reel of Tulloch*.

'John McPhedran has three tunes in the collection, *Kelvingrove, Woodside* and *Burnbank*, all place names in the Kelvinbridge area of Glasgow. Twenty-one tunes are said to be composed by J. or John MacLachlan, including *Bonnie Anne, Abercairney Highlanders, The Bride's Jig, The Shepherd and the Goat, The Maid of Glendaruel* and *Poltalloch House*. Four tunes are by N.MacLachlan, and one by Mrs McPhedran.

'According to the Notices of Pipers John MacLachlan was a native of Glasgow but of Argyllshire stock. He was a first-class player of Ceol Beag, piper to Neil Malcolm of Poltalloch for some years and composer of the march *Poltalloch House* and many other tunes. In 1851 he won the prize pipe for piobaireachd at the Northern Meeting and in 1853 he compiled a book of 120 tunes which was entitled *The Piper's Assistant* and published by Alexander Glen in Edinburgh. Very few tunes in this book have the composers' names and only *Poltalloch House* is attributed to J.MacLachlan himself.

'John McPhedran wrote to the Oban Times in 1911 saying he had been asked many times for information on his father Donald McPhedran and was withholding it at present but might publish it in the future.'

William Donaldson (p.243) quotes General Thomason, writing about Sandy Cameron (brother of Donald) and his shop in the High Street, Edinburgh, 'where all pipers of note were accustomed to congregate when in Edinburgh ... I used to listen greedily to their conversation regarding the capabilities of the several pipers of the day. The opinion of the majority was certainly in favour of Donald [Cameron] as the best piper of the day, but he was close run by [John] McLachlan. As regards execution both were held to be equal, but McLachlan's style was characterised as 'light', whereas that of Donald was held to be 'the true MacCruimen style'.' This comment was published in the Oban Times in 1904.

William Donaldson adds, in a footnote, that John MacLachlan's sister Agnes 'was said to have been influential in forming her husband Donald MacPhedran's distinctive style'; he adds 'See MacPhedran's Pipe Tunes, from 'Cean-na-Drochaid', Oban Times, 8/9/1906, p.3'. This comment about Agnes MacLachlan seems to be borne out by the attribution of a tune to Mrs McPhedran, in the Collection.

An Edict of Executry in the records of the Commisary Court of Argyll, dated 1823, names WILLIAM MACFARLANE, piper on board the fishery cutter *Swift*, and six others named MacFarlane, 'the lawful children of John MacFarlane lately residing in Bravallich now in Inveraray and of the deceased Mary MacFederan his spouse and their husbands'; they were appointed executors of the will of John MacFederan, sometime merchant in North Carolina. Where was Bravallich? Was it Barmolloch, in the hills to the north of Inveraray?

The lawful children of John and Mary MacFarlane, listed in 1823, include Mary, the youngest of the family, married to Colin MacFederan, labourer in Inveraray. So the piper on board the fishery cutter *Swift*, William MacFarlane, was an uncle of Donald MacPhedran, the pipemaker in Glasgow, and Donald had piping on both sides of his family. He seems also to have been a first-cousin of his wife Agnes MacLachlan and her brother John (see above).

[I am indebted to Angus Martin for the exerpt from the Edicts of Executry in the records of the Commissary Court of Argyll, Bigwood p. 470].

SOURCES
Jeannie Campbell
Piping Times
Bigwood, Edicts of Executry

INVERARAY FUNERALS

ONE OF THE CAMPBELL CLAN histories has an account of the funeral of the 7th Duke of Argyll on 11 May 1847, only three months before the Queen's visit (see above). The coffin was borne by twelve Highlanders from Inveraray Castle to the pier, where all went on board the *Dolphin*, which took them across Loch Fyne to Kilmun, for the burial.

The procession from the boat to the burial ground consisted of the twelve Highlanders, walking two by two, followed by the Duke's piper (unnamed); then came seven pall-bearers drawn from the Campbell gentry, and then the coffin, with six more pall-bearers behind it.

The anonymous report goes on: 'The scene as the Procession moved on its winding way, slowly along the beautiful shore to the churchyard, was peculiarly interesting and full of solemnity; but we could not help thinking that, amidst such sublime scenery and upon such an occasion, that the wail of the pibroch amongst the mountains would not have been at all out of place; but, be that as it may, all was solemn and still, and perhaps the omission was dictated by good taste'.

We might wonder why the piper was in the procession if he was not playing – and we might wonder who he was. It is possible that this was the young Donald MacPhedran, just before he went to Glasgow. Often the death of a laird led to the departure of his piper (such as John Ban going from Taymouth in 1861). Had Donald gone before the Queen's visit to Inveraray in August 1847? Did he perhaps return for the occasion? We do not know.

Good taste seems to have played little part in the funeral of a later Duke, in 1914. He was the one who was married to Queen Victoria's daughter, Princess Louise. This time 'The Glasgow Highlanders, a hundred strong, with their pipe band, were lined along the pier at Kilmun, and between their ranks the gun carriage with the coffin was drawn by the officers, non-commissioned officers and men of the brigade', and the procession was lined up:

first came the Regular soldiers and the Territorials, with their two bands;
then the clergy of the different churches;
then the Inveraray Pipe Band under Pipe Major Charles Maitland;

then various Provosts, Chamberlains and Campbell gentry.

'The sad notes of the pipes told those along the roadside that the procession had started on its solemn journey ... the Duke's Pipe Band from Inveraray played the lament as they proceeded, to the accompaniment of the wailing of the pipes, muffled drums, the booming of the minute guns and the sound of the bell.' Perhaps there was something to be said in favour of good taste and the solemn stillness of the 1847 burial.

DUNCAN ROSS

ANOTHER LINK BETWEEN JOHN BAN MacKenzie and Loch Fyne may have been forged in 1875, when Duncan Ross was appointed piper to the Duke of Argyll at Inveraray Castle. He replaced Donald McPhedran who had been a visiting piper at Inveraray, called upon to play at important occasions at the Castle, but apparently not resident there, nor officially piper to the Duke (see above).

The Census for 1881 shows that Duncan's younger brother Alexander was butler (and presumably also piper) at Kilberry Castle. This must have been before he went to Skye as piper to Lord MacDonald.

The exact connection between the Ross brothers and John Ban MacKenzie is not clear. Although Duncan appears never to have claimed a blood relationship, he is reported to have said, in 1880, 'Many a story did old John MacKenzie tell me when I was turning his lathe and learning music with him. He was full four score when he died, and that is more than twenty years ago. It must be nearly a hundred years since he was in Raasay, learning Ceol Mor, Great Music, from MacKay'.

This is what J.F.Campbell wrote in his booklet on Canntaireachd, quoting the words of Duncan Ross, and it immediately rings alarm bells. It is usually assumed that 'old John MacKenzie' was John Ban, because of the reference to his learning Ceol Mor from MacKay in Raasay; but John Ban was not 'full four score' when he died, he was only 67, and he had died in 1864, not 'more than twenty years ago', but a mere sixteen, as Duncan Ross must surely have known. It was not 'nearly a hundred years' since John Ban was in Raasay, but only about sixty.

These discrepancies must make us wonder: was 'old John MacKenzie' not John Ban at all, but another John who went for tuition to John MacKay, Raasay?

Or was Duncan Ross simply mistaken, vague about the passage of time and inaccurate in his memory of John Ban's age when he died? Duncan had left home by the time of John Ban's death, and he was probably in England, or abroad with the army, when it happened; he might have been only vaguely aware of the deaths of young Donald MacKenzie and his father John Ban, within a year of each other, in 1863-4. Yet that definite statement that John was 'full four score' is puzzling.

Duncan is annoyingly imprecise about the lathe-turning – where was he doing this, and when? How old was Duncan at the time? Was it at Weem, where John Ban lived from 1832 to 1861, when piper at Taymouth? Or at John's brother's croft in the Mulbuie, in the Black Isle, where John Ban often visited in the winter months? Or at Greenhill Cottage, Munlochy, John's home in his retirement, between 1861 and 1864?

The reference to music is equally vague: 'when I was . . learning music with him'. Does this mean Duncan was a resident pupil having piping tuition? Or just picking up some tunes by singing them in Canntaireachd?

Why was he so vague? And if he was related to John Ban, why did he not say so? Does it mean there was no relationship? Or that there was a link but it had been suppressed for some family reason?

Throughout the lives of Duncan and Alexander Ross, their paths seem to cross with that of John Ban, and it is not clear exactly why.

Duncan Ross was born at Altnabreac, Achilty, Ross and Cromarty, in 1844, long after John Ban had established himself as piper to the Marquis of Breadalbane at Taymouth Castle, in Perthshire. Duncan's parents were John Ross, a gamekeeper who belonged to the parish of Contin, and Ann MacKenzie, said in the 1851 Census to have been born in the parish of Urquhart, in the Black Isle, Easter Ross, but in fact born at Killen, in Strathconon, in the parish of Contin, in 1812.

When, on April 4th 1834, John Ross married Ann MacKenzie, they were probably both employees on the estate of East Kinkell, in Urquhart. Ann's parents were Murdo MacKenzie, farmer, and his wife Ann MacLennan. Murdo's surname is given in the Old Parish Register as MacLennan or MacKenzie, which is odd, as neither can be a patronymic. He lived at Killen, near Scatwell, in Strathconon, a farm where there were several families of MacLennans and MacKenzies. The Scatwell piper at that time was Donald MacLennan, whose wife, a MacKenzie, gave birth to their son John, at Scatwell in 1817. This was Donald Mor MacLennan of Moy, who taught both Donald Cameron and John Ban MacKenzie, and was a great-uncle of G.S.MacLennan. It is likely that he was related to Murdo and Ann at Killen.

Ann's birth and baptism appears twice in the Register, the first time naming her father as Murdo MacLennan or MacKenzie, the second as Murdo MacLennan. In the notice of the birth of his later child, William, in 1815, Murdo's surname is MacKenzie, and that is the name which his daughter Ann used. Does the alternative surname suggest that Murdo's birth was illegitimate?

John Ross was born in 1807, an illegitimate son of Jane MacLennan and John Ross, waiter (this may mean a tide-waiter, a type of customs officer, rather than a table-waiter). The fact that the child took his father's surname, and that the father's name appears on the son's death certificate, means that he acknowledged paternity. Was Jane related to Ann MacLennan, i.e. did John marry his cousin? Was this illegitimate birth concealed in some way? It is hard to see how, when the child had his father's surname.

There seems to be a link with the John MacKenzie who became piping instructor at the Caledonian Schools in London, but this is another connection of which we cannot be certain. He was reputed to be a half-brother of Ronald MacKenzie, John Ban's nephew, but John was said not to be John Ban's nephew himself, which suggests he might have been a son of Ronald's mother before her marriage to John Ban's brother, Alexander. There was an Alexander MacKenzie at Altananbreck, married to Christian MacKenzie. If this Alexander was a brother of John Ban, he moved to the Mulbuie in the early 1840s. We may surmise that Christian had had a son John before her marriage; he would have been a MacKenzie, and the dates fit in reasonably well with a birth in the 1820s. While an instructor in London, John won the Prize Pipe at Inverness in 1874, and followed it up by winning the Gold Medal for Former Winners in 1876. He is said to have died in 1904, aged 77.

This is the John MacKenzie mentioned in his *Reminiscences* by Robert Meldrum: Meldrum says John was the composer of 'the excellent march *The Blue and Yellow Banner*, and was the first pipe-major of the Scots Guards'. Unfortunately this is not borne out by the records of the Scots Guards, which give Ewan Henderson as the first Pipe Major of the 1st Battalion, and Donald MacPherson, specially transferred from the 42nd, as first Pipe Major of the 2nd Battalion.

Meldrum says that John MacKenzie was afterwards instructor at the Royal Caledonian School, London, before he retired to Inverness. He was a prolific composer. 'It was from him that Pipe Major Alexander MacLennan, Inverness, got the pibroch *Barisdale's Salute*. He belonged to Ross-shire'. This is interesting, but it does not solve our problem: what was John's connection with John Ban and the Ross brothers?

John Ban's own birth/baptism was not registered, nor those of his brothers, Ronald and Alexander, nor of his sister(s). Later documents and inscriptions tell us that John Ban was born around 1796, at Achilty, west of Contin village, and his birthplace may well have been at Aultnabreac, on the north-western shore of Loch Achilty. Colin and Alexander MacKenzie, who were probably brothers, were living there in the 1820s, and an old man, William, in 1851. We know from John Ban's death certificate that his father's name was William.

In the 1851 Census, which records John Ross and his wife at Aultnabreac, their next-door neighbour was this impoverished old man of 80, William MacKenzie. He was married to a woman much younger than himself, who was probably his second wife, and there were two unmarried daughters, Isabella born 1815 and Elizabeth 1829. This William may have been a relative of John Ban, possibly even his father, if we assume that John's mother, Mary MacKay, was William's first wife. His wife in 1851 was called Janet, born 1784 in Urray, the parish adjoining Urquhart, in Easter Ross.

John Ban's sister, whose name has been lost, is said (in local oral tradition) to have married a Ross; could this have been a brother of John Ross the waiter, father of the illegitimate John who married Ann MacKenzie? Or even John Ross the waiter himself? Is it possible that this Ross had a brother, Donald, who was

Above: Altnabreac was a group of about four small houses beside Loch Achilty, to the west of Contin, Strathconon, Ross-shire. It is thought that the families of Duncan Ross, piper to the Duke of Argyll, Alexander Ross, piper to Lord MacDonald and of John Ban MacKenzie, piper to the Marquess of Breadalbane, may have lived here, and that this was the birthplace of all three pipers – who may have been related. The house depicted is the only habitable building there today.

Below: Ruined house at Altnabreac. There are the ruins of at least three small houses above the existing house at Altnabreac today. One of them could be the birthplace of John Ban Mackenzie.

Loch Achilty, seen from Altnabreac.

the father of Angus Ross, a piper in the Scots Guards?

While living in London, Angus married Annie Chapman, and their daughter was Alice Ross (who married Angus MacPherson, son of Calum Piobaire, and became Mrs MacPherson of Inveran). After leaving the army, Angus Ross was piper at Cluny, near Laggan, and died there in 1921, aged 77.

But his father, Donald, lived in Skye, and was probably born there, and it was Donald's first wife, Diana MacKenzie, who came from Easter Ross, being born at Conon Bridge in 1820. Was she related to Ann MacKenzie? Her father was Murdo MacKenzie, the same name as Ann's father, but they had different mothers. They may have been half-sisters. Diana's father was a piper.

Ann MacKenzie cannot have been the anonymous sister whose wedding John Ban celebrated with his composition, a march entitled *John Bain's Sister's Wedding* (this title is thought to have been added some time after the march was composed). But she may have been related.

There is some connection here with William Ross, who was Queen Victoria's piper from 1854 until his death in 1891. Born in 1823, William was the son of Andrew Ross and Margaret Young, but his mother died when William was only seven. The father at once re-married and emigrated to Canada, leaving his only son to be brought up by his Ross grandmother, at Greenhill Cottage, Kilcoy, in the Black Isle, Ross-shire, not far from Kinkell. It was not unknown for a father to leave his young son behind when he and his wife emigrated, and in most instances, the wife was not the mother of the child. One result was usually that the father's name was dropped from the family *sloinneadh*.

The only Andrew Ross who was baptised in the Parish of Knockbain, where

Kilcoy is situated, was the son of John Ross and Ann McPhail, born 1791. This Andrew may have been William's father, and Ann McPhail may have been John's first wife.

To reconcile all this we would have to assume that John Ross the waiter was born around 1770 and that he married Ann MacPhail, and their son Andrew was born in 1791. Ann died in the early 1800s, and John then had an illegitimate son John Ross by Jane MacLennan, in 1807. He may then have married John Ban's sister, but we do not know when.

Andrew Ross married Margaret Young, and their son was William, born 1823 – he became the Queen's piper. Andrew's half-brother, John Ross, the illegitimate son, married Ann MacKenzie, who may have been his cousin. Possibly another half-brother of John was Donald Ross, who lived in Skye, the father of Angus, piper in the Scots Guards. We are now knee-deep in conjecture, but this interpretation takes in the evidence we have, such as it is, and accounts for the family cover-up, with two or more illegitimacies to be concealed.

If this reconstruction, or part of it, is correct, then Duncan and Alexander Ross were first-cousins of Angus Ross, Scots Guards, and of William Ross, the Queen's piper. All four were step-relatives of John Ban, and there was piping in the family through both Murdo MacKenzie and the MacLennans. The link with John MacKenzie of the Caledonian Schools was through John Ban's brother Alexander, who married John's mother.

John Ross and Ann MacKenzie left Kinkell after their marriage in April 1834, and their eldest son was born in October of that year, in the village of Contin. They then moved to Aultnabreac (formerly Aultananbreac), a small cluster of houses beside Loch Achilty, to the west of Contin.

In 1841, two houses at Aultnabreac were inhabited, one by John Ross, aged 30, described as an agricultural labourer. Shortly before the Rosses moved in, there had been MacKenzies at Aultnabreac, and a family of Finlaysons; these MacKenzies may have been John Ban's family (and it may be coincidence that one of John Ban's daughters married a Finlayson). At the time of John Ban's birth in Achilty at the end of the 18th century, the families at Aultnabreac were MacRaes and MacKenzies. There may be a link with MacKenzies at Kenmore, Loch Tay, but the exact nature of the link, if any, has not been established (see above).

The birth of Duncan Ross in 1844, and the births of his brothers and sisters after that date, are not in the Old Parish Register, because the Disruption of the church in 1843 intervened: the minister of Contin parish was one of many in Ross-shire who seceded to the breakaway Free Church, leaving no minister of the Church of Scotland, the established church, to keep the register. The gap lasts for several years. Earlier siblings were registered, but we have to deduce the date of Duncan's birth from later references in the Census records. The birth of his piping brother, Alexander, born in 1849, is similarly to be deduced. The children of John Ross and Ann MacKenzie were: John 1834 (at Contin), Murdo 1836, William 1839, Ann 1841, Duncan 1844, Johann 1846, Alexander 1849, Mary

1850. All except John were born at Aultnabreac. A son Kenneth gave the information recorded on his father's death certificate. His birth-date is unknown.

By 1861, John Ross was a gamekeeper on the Scatwell estate to the west of Achilty, living at a house a few miles away, called Blackburn, near Little Scatwell. Five children were still at home, including Alexander who later became piper to Lord MacDonald in Skye – but Duncan, who was then 17, was not there. He may have gone south to live in England, or into the army. The Rosses were still at Blackburn in 1871. Blackburn was close to Killen, where John Ross's parents-in-law lived.

Duncan's mother Ann died in 1880, and his father two years later, when Duncan was piper in Inveraray. The family remained as crofters in Strathconon until well into the 20th century.

Another link between the Rosses and John Ban's family was the friendship between Alexander Ross and John Ban's nephew Ronald MacKenzie. Ronald was said to be Alexander's great-uncle. He was only about ten years older than Alexander, and as far as we can tell, Ronald's father and Alexander's step-grandmother were brother and sister. This is based on the theoretical reconstruction of the descent of the Ross family, with its illegitimate births, which may have prevented Duncan from claiming a family link with John Ban.

Duncan Ross's grandson, Roderick Ross, who lived in Brora, Sutherland, had a pipe which was made by John Ban at Taymouth in 1851. Ordered by the officers of the 78th Regiment as a present for Queen Victoria, the pipe was rejected on completion as the officers said John Ban was asking too high a price. John Ban kept the pipe, which was later bought by his nephew Ronald; it was a present for Alexander Ross, Duncan's brother, who was piper and valet to one of the officers in the Seaforth, Ronald's regiment, when they were in Canada in 1868. Alexander and Ronald used to give exhibitions with Ronald playing and Alexander dancing. In a letter about the provenance of the pipe, written by Roderick Ross after he inherited the instrument, no claim is made to any blood relationship with John Ban's family – yet the close connection between the Rosses and the MacKenzies seems to have been maintained for several generations.

It is not known for certain what happened to Duncan Ross after he grew up and left Loch Achilty, before he was appointed to be piper and valet at Inveraray Castle in 1875. He was probably in England, since his wife Anne was English, and their first child Annie was born in England in 1872. Was he in the army, or was he in London with John MacKenzie who was piping instructor at the Caledonian Schools? John was a distant step-relative, who may have been Duncan's piping teacher.

For the last quarter of the 19th century, Duncan was at Inveraray, living at Maltland in the village, travelling frequently from home with the Duke, and taking an active part in the development of the Inveraray Pipe Band.

In the 1881 census, Duncan was away as piper to the Duke in his London home, Argyll House, where he was one of 27 servants listed. His wife Anne Ross, then aged 31, 'wife of piper and valet', was in Inveraray, temporary head of household in her husband's absence. The children were Annie 9, born England, William Alexander 3, born Inveraray, and Violet 11 months, also born Inveraray.

In 1891, Duncan was at home, listed as a woodman, aged 47, born Contin parish, Ross-shire, speaking Gaelic and English, and living in a house with four rooms, in Maltland, Inveraray. There is no mention of his being a piper, but this is normal for some of the Census records. Even Calum Piobaire MacPherson was listed as a 'labourer', in Laggan.

Duncan's brother Alexander appears in 1891 in the census for the parish of Sleat, in Skye: Alexander Ross, 44, unmarried, butler, born Contin parish, Ross-shire, speaker of Gaelic and English. He was in the service of Lord MacDonald in Armadale Castle. In 1881 he was butler at Kilberry, so presumably took up his post with Lord MacDonald in the 1880s.

J.F.Campbell wanted to find out about the canntaireachd system of singing vocables to represent piobaireachd music, and especially about reading it in written form as presented in Gesto's manuscript. In March 1880, he was in Inveraray to consult Duncan Ross, 'the only interpreter known', but Duncan was abroad with the Duke and had no time to study the written words sent to him by Campbell. 'He had never seen his familiar ordinary Canntaireachd written or printed before ', wrote Campbell, later. It was familiar to Duncan only as an oral form.

On his return to Inveraray in May, Duncan read through Gesto's written canntaireachd version of *The End of the Great Bridge*, and at once played it on the chanter. His brother Alexander was there, too, and he 'aided with voice only' could both chant the music and play it on the pipe, without difficulty.

They set up an arrangement: a pianist played the melody with his left hand, following the music as sung and played by the brothers, and wrote it all down with his right hand. Presumably it was necessary to transpose the music into the equal-tempered scale before the conventional musician could write it in staff notation.

No mention is made of the difference in the scales, yet all present must have been aware of this problem. J.F.Campbell's resulting booklet *Canntaireachd* is virtually worthless, as he does not begin to understand the system or explore its possibilities; had he tackled the difference in scales, for example, his work would have had much more interest for modern pipers. He made no attempt to describe canntaireachd, and his theories about its origins were unacceptably wild. It does, however, give us a valuable glimpse of the Ross brothers and the extent of their expertise.

Gesto's canntaireachd transcriptions were in the 1880s regarded as pretty well unintelligible, totally baffling to the piping theorists, yet the two working pipers, Duncan and Alexander Ross, could not only decipher them without difficulty, but must have had a large repertoire of piobaireachd music to enable them to recognise the tunes as they read the written canntaireachd syllables. This also tells us that both Duncan and Alexander were fully literate, which was by no means common among 19th century pipers (neither Donald Cameron nor John Ban MacKenzie could read and write, nor even sign their own names). The brothers must both have had a working knowledge of a canntaireachd system as well, but where did they learn it? Indeed, brought up at Altnabreac, where did they learn to read and write?

Duncan played as a piper in the Inveraray Pipe Band, under their Pipe Major Charles Maitland. He was not himself Pipe Major, and may have been an occasional player as his duties at the Castle and elsewhere allowed.

It is not known when or where Duncan Ross died, but he and his family van-

Inveraray Pipe Band, around 1890. Pipe Major Charles Maitland is on the extreme left, Duncan Ross (with whiskers) 6th from the left, and the brothers Duncan and Donald MacPhedran on the extreme right.
(PHOTOGRAPH KINDLY LENT BY NEIL MACPHEDRAN, ONTARIO)

ished from the Inveraray Census some time in the 1890s. His death is not recorded in Inveraray. It seems likely that he retired from service at the Castle and that the family returned to England

His brother Alexander remained for many years with Lord MacDonald at Armadale. He had started as piper to Davidson of Tulloch, at Tulloch Castle in Dingwall – just as John Ban had been, before Alexander was born. Duncan Davidson sent him for tuition with the piper at Moy Hall, in Inverness-shire. He then became piper and valet to Captain Callander of the Seaforth Highlanders, at the time when John Ban's nephew Ronald was the regiment's pipe major. They saw service in Canada together, in 1868. Robert Meldrum's *Reminiscences*, published in 1951, refer to Alexander as Sandy Ross, and he says: 'Sandy was with the regiment as private servant to Captain Callendar . . . Not being a soldier, he could not get instruction with the members of the pipe band'. He had lessons from

Ronald as a private pupil.

On leaving the army, Alexander evidently went to Kilberry as butler to the Campbell family (when Archibald Campbell was a child of four). This must have been before he moved on, going to Lord MacDonald as butler and piper, living for many years at Armadale Castle in Sleat, and travelling widely with his lordship. He became a well-known figure in the piping world, and judged at the Skye Games in Portree until he was nearly eighty. A bachelor all his days, it was his proud boast that he had never worn trousers in his life.

In his very last years, in the late 1920s, he was piper at Allangrange on the Black Isle – an estate with a long record of employing good pipers, and again we come across John Ban, who had been piper there before going to Tulloch. It is curious how often the paths of John Ban and the two Ross brothers cross, from the time when they were born in Achilty. Alexander died at Allangrange in 1930, his great-nephew Roderick Ross beside him. He left his pipes, made by John Ban, to Roderick, his pupil.

SOURCES
J.F.Campbell: *Canntaireachd*, 1880
Census Inveraray, Urquhart, Contin
Letter written by Roderick Ross
OPR Contin, Urquhart
Jeannie Campbell
Neil MacPhedran
Notices of Pipers.

INVERARAY PIPE BAND

THE NOTICES OF PIPERS SAY that the Inveraray Pipe Band was organised and equipped in 1886 by Lord Archibald Campbell. Becoming well known, it performed several times at the Argyllshire Gathering in Oban, and played at the Glasgow Exhibition of 1901, to acclaim.

Some say that the band was formed as part of the celebrations on the marriage of the Marquis of Lorne, the Duke's heir, to Queen Victoria's daughter Louise, but the wedding was in 1870, and this seems a little early. Jeannie Campbell wrote about the band in the Piping Times in January 1999, and Neil MacPhedran in Canada also sent information (PT March 1999) and another photograph, undated, of members of the band, with identifications supplied by his grandfather, Donald MacPhedran (see above).

Jeannie wrote:

'Pipe bands in the Army date from around 1850, and non-army bands such as the Govan Police and Edinburgh Police first appeared in the 1880s. The Inveraray Pipe Band was in existence by 1890 and was probably one of the first civilian bands in the Highlands.

The band members were: Pipe Major Charles Maitland, Piper Peter Maitland, Piper Robert Stewart, Piper Duncan Ross (with moustache and beard), Piper Kenneth Dunn (a cousin of Duncan and Donald MacPhedran), Piper Robert MacNab, Piper Duncan MacPhedran (brother of Donald), and Donald MacPhedran (who supplied the list of names). Three drummers standing behind the pipers were John Patison, Harry MacIntyre and John McArthur (known as Jock Hope).

'The band was founded by Lord Archibald Campbell (1846-1913) who was the second son of the 8th Duke of Argyll, younger brother of the 9th Duke and father of the 10th Duke. The band's uniform was modelled on that of the Argyll Fencibles of 1745: Campbell tartan kilt and plaid with large shoulder brooch, dark green tunic with white facings and brass buttons, glengarry with boar's head crest, regulation sporran with six white tassels, red and white diced hose, white gaiters, white belts, claymore, dirk and sgian dubh.

'In 1896 Lord Archibald took the band, with eleven pipers and three drummers, on a four-day tour of Oban, Staffa and Iona, including appearances at the Argyllshire Gathering and other events. The entire band was taken by rowing boat into Fingal's Cave, Staffa, where they played, afterwards carving their names on the wall of the cave with their dirks and sgian dubhs.' This is thought to have been the first time a band had played in the cave – and perhaps the last? Are their names still there?

'At the Argyllshire Gathering the band headed the procession to the Games field. The band members in 1896 were Pipe Major Charles Maitland, pipers Peter C.Maitland, Kenneth Dunn, Malcolm Dunn, Daniel Kerr, John Kerr, Donald MacPhedran, Duncan MacPhedran, Duncan Ross, Ernest Smith, Robert Stewart, and drummers John MacArthur, Henry MacIntyre and Archibald MacNab.

'The Pipe Major, Charles Maitland (1862-1947) was a native of Inveraray and a master plumber by trade. Pipers Duncan and Donald MacPhedran were sons of John MacPhedran and Isabella (Bella or Bell) MacKenzie. Bella was a relative of John Ban MacKenzie and a well-known character in the district. She was said to have been a better piper than her husband. She had six sons, among them Duncan born 1866 and Donald born 1870' (see above).

'In 1897 the band again attended the Argyllshire Gathering when the customary procession was headed by Lord Archibald Campbell and preceded by the Inveraray Pipe Band. Also present was the band of the 1st Battalion Argyll and Sutherland Highlanders from Maryhill Barracks in Glasgow.

'The band was not at the 1898 Gathering when their absence was keenly felt, but they were back again in 1899. That year a grand Gaelic Concert was held on the evening preceding the Games, under the Presidency of Lord Archibald who was resplendent in full Highland garb. Each half of the concert began with a performance by the Inveraray Pipe Band, described as Lord Archibald's bodyguard, who made a brave show in full regimental Highland dress with handsome and highly decorative bannerettes bearing the Campbell device pendant from the pipes. The following day the procession to the Games field was led by the band with Lord Archibald at its head. At the Games Lord Archibald was accompanied by his wife Lady Archibald Campbell and his daughter Miss Elspeth Campbell' [she was herself a piper].

'The following year the band took part in an event of another kind when they led the procession at the funeral of Lord Archibald's father, the 8th Duke of Argyll. They were followed by the pipe band of the Argyll and Sutherland Highlanders and the bands of the Boys Brigade and the Volunteers.

'In 1901, the band were again in the news when they played at the Glasgow Exhibition where their performances were well received.'

CHARLES MAITLAND, born in 1862, was the first Pipe Major of the band. A master plumber in Inveraray, he was in the Argyllshire Volunteers for many years, and attended the Wet Review in Edinburgh in 1881. He died in 1947.

Archie MacNeill's *Memoirs* mention JOHN MACGREGOR, 'from a village on Loch Fyne', who came south to the Clyde area, and was a lodger staying in the MacNeills' house. Archie says: 'One night as I was playing the chanter he complimented me on the progress I had made. He also told me that he had often played to Lord Archibald Campbell of Inveraray Castle. He was what we sometimes call an ear player, but he played the orthodox doublings'. This must have been in the late 19th century.

PIPE MAJOR RONNIE MACCALLUM

Pipe Major Ronnie MacCallum, MBE is probably the piper who immediately springs to mind when Inveraray is mentioned.

Pipe Major Ronald MacCallum, who won the Gold Medal at Inverness in 1951, and the Gold at Oban the following year, was born in 1905, and began learning the pipes from his father Archibald MacCallum, of Macharioch, at the age of five. He was taught by William Wilson, a pupil of John MacColl, and by William Thomson, a pupil of John MacDonald, Inverness.

The Campbeltown Courier carried reports in 1922 of the teenaged Ronald winning prizes, including a 'handsome silver tea service' for his playing of Strathspeys, Reels and Marches, at a competition held in Rutherglen, at New Year. His brother Peter was winning awards for his dancing at the same Gathering. They went on to further triumphs at competitions in Glasgow, the same week. This habit of holding contests in the first week of January seems to have been dropped; perhaps a few hard winters made travel impractical at that time of year.

Pipe Major Ronnie MacCallum MBE (1905-1986), piper to the Duke of Argyll. Jeannie Campbell took this in 1976, on a Clan Campbell excursion to Inveraray (PHOTOGRAPH KINDLY LENT BY JEANNIE CAMPBELL)

In 1924 Ronald followed the family tradition of Territorial Army service, joining the 8th Battalion Argyll and Sutherland Highlanders. During World War II he was Pipe Major of the 11th Argylls, his band winning the Pipe Band Championship at Milngavie in 1945. After the war he became personal piper to the 11th Duke of Argyll, and head gardener at Inveraray Castle. He also returned to the Territorial Army, as Pipe Major of the 8th Argylls, until the battalion was disbanded in 1967, when he retired as senior Pipe Major of the 51st Highland Division.

Ronald MacCallum had a highly distinguished career as a competitor, which included winning both the Gold Medals in the early 1950s, playing as 'Pipe Major Ronald McCallum, Inveraray Castle'. His winning tune at Inverness was *MacFarlane's Gathering*. From the 1960s to the 1980s he taught piping in Inveraray and at a number of schools in Argyll. For services to piping he was awarded the MBE in 1964.

He composed *The Highland Brigade Depot*, a 6/8 March in 4 parts (1965). Ronald MacCallum MBE died in 1986.

Tunes composed for members of the family include:
Donald, Hugh and his Dog, by Donald Morrison J 4
Hugh A MacCallum, by Archie Duncan 9/8 RM 2
Pipe Major R. McCallum MBE, by George MacIntyre 2/4 HP 4
Ronald MacShannon, by Archie Duncan 9/8 RM 2

THE DUKE'S PIPER-GILLIE

A STORY, DATING PROBABLY FROM the early 20th century, is told about a piper/ gillie at Inveraray Castle. He was a young man, not long in the Duke's service. One summer's day, a party of important visitors was staying at the Castle, including such men as the Tsar of All The Russias, and an eminent cabinet minister.

The party that day was of two minds: one group wanted to go fishing, the

Left: The hill known as Duniquaich, Gaelic Dun na Cuaiche, seen from the war memorial in Inveraray. The hill was immortalised by D.C.Mather with his strathspey, Climbing Duniquaich, composed around 1900. (PHOTOGRAPH BY COURTESY OF THE COLLEGE OF PIPING)

Below: A drawing of Duniquaich and Inveraray in 1746.

other fancied a walk in the hills. So the chief gillie took the fishing party, and the walkers were entrusted to the care of the young piper. The older gillie impressed on him the need to be respectful at all times: these were great and important men, and the gillie must not eavesdrop on their conversations, must not speak to them unless spoken to, and he must defer to them in every possible way. The piper promised to do this, and the walking party set off.

As they came to the summit of the hill (perhaps they were climbing Duniquaich?), a magnificent view was spread out below them, mountains, lochs, the sea, Argyll at its very best.

'Ah' exclaimed the Tsar in delight, 'What wonderful scenery. . . If only we had brought the glasses. . .'

'Ach' said the young piper, 'We need no glasses, just pass the bottle round'.

PIPER'S KNOLL

ABOUT FIVE MILES NORTH OF the head of Loch Fyne, on the south-west ridge of Beinn Buidhe, high above Rob Roy's house in Glen Shira, there is a hill known as Tom a' Phiobaire, the Piper's Knoll. The piper's name has been lost, and with it the origin of the place-name. The piper may have been associated with Rob Roy MacGregor, who had a lifetime fondness for pipe music – it is recorded that his last words were 'It is all over. Put me to bed. Call the piper. Let him play *Cha till mi tulle* (I shall return no more)' . When at his house in Glen Shira, however, he was usually lying low while his enemies were seeking him, so perhaps would not have allowed a piper to advertise his presence – unless possibly the piper was his look-out sentry.

A SELECTION OF THE PIPERS ASSOCIATED WITH THE ARGYLL AND SUTHERLAND HIGHLANDERS

THE ARGYLL AND SUTHERLAND HIGHLANDERS, formerly the Argyll Highlanders (91st Regiment) which was amalgamated with the Sutherland Highlanders (93rd Regiment) in 1881, were for a time known as Princess Louise's, when Queen Victoria's daughter married the Duke of Argyll's heir, the Marquis of Lorne.

The regiment's history starts in 1794, but before that there were also Militia regiments and local defence volunteer regiments, known variously as the Western Defence Regiment, the Argyll Militia or Fencibles, and the Argyllshire Volunteers (see above, Dugald Campbell, Campbeltown).

The Notices of Pipers mention about 30 pipers associated with these regiments. There is much emphasis on the early years of the 20th century and on the First World War, as some of the Notices were written by Major Ian MacKay-Scobie, who had a detailed knowledge of army piping at that time.

Pipers mentioned elsewhere in the book, such as Donald Dubh Campbell and Colonel Duncan Campbell of Lochnell, are not included here.

Colonel BERTIE GORDON of Ellon Castle, Aberdeenshire, served with the 91st Argyllshire Regiment for many years. When he took over command in 1858, the regimental piping had been abolished eight years previously, by the orders of an inspecting general. The regiment under Col Gordon went to India where he revived the corps of pipers, with an old private, William W. Cameron, as Pipe Major, as he was the only one left of the previous corps of 1850. Colonel Gordon worked ceaselessly to have the 91st restored to its former position as a Highland regiment, and in 1864 had the satisfaction of having it made the 91st Argyllshire Highlanders.

ROBERT MACDUGALL was Pipe Major in the Argyllshire Regiment in 1864 when it was restored to the Highland Establishment as the 91st Argyll Highlanders. He was still P/M when it became Princess Louise's in 1871. 'On that occasion in Inveraray he was one of the party presented to Queen Victoria, who complimented him on his playing and that of his pipers'.

JOHN MACKAY, 1860 – 1925, was born in India, the son of a Pipe Major in the 25th (KOSB). He became a piper in the 91st Argyll Highlanders, and then in the 1st Battalion, after 1881. He later served under P/M Meldrum in the 2nd Battalion, and in 1903 moved to the Liverpool Seaforth, where he remained until his death in 1925. He was an excellent teacher, who won the Gold Medal at Oban in 1887 and at Inverness in 1889. He was the army piping champion and won many awards. He composed *The Badge of Scotland*, and his arrangement of *The Hawk that Swoops On High (Creag Ghuanach)* became the standard. He learned his piobaireachd from Alick Cameron, son of Donald.

JAMES LOUDON was a piper in the Argylls when the regiment, in South Africa in 1883, formed a mounted infantry company. He was their piper, playing on horseback. The horse's opinion was not sought.

WILLIAM ROBB was Pipe Major of the 2nd Argylls, 1887-91, and of the 1st Battalion, 1891-94. He won the Gold Medal at Oban in 1893. A composer of light music, he made the Slow Air *When the Battle Is Over* (also known as *The Battle Is O'er*). In 1895, when he was a piper in the 1st Battalion, he and piper James MacKay made a 35-mile march from Camberley to London, playing alternately all the way. In the Glasgow Exhibition of 1901 he was in the prize lists for both piobaireachd and light music, but was beaten by John MacColl and John MacDougall Gillies. He died in Glasgow in 1942.

HENRY FORSYTH was Pipe Major in the 2nd Scots Guards in 1895, and went on to become piper to the King from 1910 to 1941. During the Great War of 1914-18, he was Pipe Major of the 14th Battalion Argyll and Sutherland

Highlanders, and later was Sergeant-Major of a Base depot. He died in 1946.

COLIN THOMSON from Golspie, Sutherland, was Pipe Major of the 1st Argylls, 1894-1904, and served in the South African (Boer) War, 1899-1902. In 1904 he transferred to the Seaforth Highlanders. He was a composer of light music, and won the Gold Medal at Inverness in 1891. He died in 1931. There is some doubt about his origins, as there was no Thomson family living in Golspie at the relevant time, and it is not known where his parents belonged.

D. MACDONALD (the name is not certain, nor the date) is said to have been a piper in the old 93rd, later the 2nd Argylls. There is a tale of his getting drunk when due to play at an officers' dinner. He was playing beforehand when the Colonel asked him the name of his tune. 'Lochaber Nae Mair, sir' said the piper, swaying. 'Piper no more' said the Colonel, having him removed. It is not clear what is the authority for this story.

ROBERT MELDRUM in 1875 was the youngest pipe major in the British Army, when he was promoted in the 93rd Sutherland Highlanders. Six years later the 93rd was amalgamated with the 91st Argyllshire Highlanders and re-named the Ist and 2nd Battalion of the Argyll and Sutherland Highlanders, with which Robert Meldrum retained his rank, as Pipe Major of the 2nd Battalion. In his retirement, he lived in Inverness, and his *Reminiscences* were published in the Piping Times. He was the father of Ronald Meldrum, and had been a pupil of Calum Piobair MacPherson at Catlodge.

DR. ALEXANDER DUNCAN FRASER, 1849 – 1920, was born in Lochgilphead, but came of an Inverness-shire family. He became medical officer of the 4th Volunteer Battalion of the Argylls, and was later a Lt.Col. in the RAMC (Territorials). In the 1914-18 War he ran a military hospital. In 1906 he published a book *Some Reminiscences and the Bagpipe*. He had a fine collection of pipes.

CHARLES CAMERON was born in North Argyll, and served as a piper in the 1914-18 War. He became known as the Piper of Loos when there was a dangerously chaotic situation in the Battle of Loos. Men of different units were mixed up in the close hand to hand fighting, and unable to find their own units. Cameron stood out in the open under heavy fire playing the regimental assembly as a rallying point for his unit.

Lt.Col. ROBIN CAMPBELL served in the Camerons from 1899 to 1931, commanding the 1st Camerons from 1927. During World War I he commanded the 8th Battalion of the Argylls, and won the DSO and bar. He is commemorated in a Retreat March by John MacLellan, Dunoon, who served under him.

DUNCAN MACSPORRAN, born in Argyll, was a good piobaireachd player who became a piper in the 10th Battalion of the Argylls, and during World War I was promoted to Pipe Major. He left the army in 1919.

PETER MACCRIMMON, a descendant of Donald Donn MacCrimmon, son of Patrick Og, joined the Argylls in 1933, as a piper. He became a Corporal-Piper, serving with the 2nd Battalion in India, and during World War II. He was probably named after Patrick Og's third son, a brother of Malcolm and of Donald Ban.

NICOL MACCALLUM from Kilmartin was a piper in the 8th Argylls. He won the Gold Medal at Oban in 1935, having become Pipe Major of the 8th Battalion in 1930. After World War II he was a Superintendent in the Parks Department of the City of Glasgow.

Four McLACHLAN brothers from Allandale, Stirlingshire joined the Argylls at the outbreak of World War II. Their brother ARCHIE was a piper but he did not serve in the war. Of the other four, IAN and Pipe Major MALCOLM were also pipers, and their brothers KENNY and FINLAY joined them in the regiment. Malcolm was killed at El-Alamein by a sniper; Ian and Kenny died from wounds after an explosion. Finlay was a POW in the Far East, and was the only one to survive the war. Ian's pipes were sent home from Africa after Alamein.

JOHN KERR, born at Gifford, was a shepherd's son who joined the Black Watch but later transferred to the Argylls, serving in the North African campaign in World War II. He fought at Monte Cassino in Italy, and was twice wounded. Laurie Georgeson was his piping teacher, and after the war, John went into the Edinburgh City Police band. He was with them when they won the World Championship in 1950 and 1954, and remained with the band until 1964. He was a noted Highland dancer, a reedmaker and 'an admired composer'. A 6/8 March, *Rab's Wedding*, is his best known work. On his retirement from the police in 1976 he served as a Justiciary Macer in the High Court in Edinburgh until 1988. He died in 1995, aged 73.

WILLIAM MACCOMB was an Argyll who emigrated to Australia, where he became a piping teacher after the Second World War.

WILLIAM GRIEVE was Pipe Major in the Argylls, 1972-6, and emigrated to Canada, where he became P/M of the Calgary Highlanders, allied to the Argyll and Sutherland Highlanders.

ALEXANDER MACQUEEN YULE was a pupil at the Queen Victoria School, Dunblane before he joined the Argyll and Sutherland Highlanders. He gained his Pipe Major's certificate in 1954, and served 30 years with the regiment, finishing his army career at the Apprentice Training School in Harrogate. He was the composer of a march *Edinburgh's Royal Mile*.

ANDREW PITKEATHLY, who was born in Coupar Angus in 1929, joined the Argylls in 1946, and in the next four years won the Gold Medal at Inverness and the Open Piobaireachd in London. He became Pipe Major of the 1st Battalion of the Argylls in 1952, serving abroad all over the world. In 1966 he was appointed Piper to the Queen, until in 1973 he was commissioned. In '76 he became Director of the Army School of Piping, until his retirement in 1981. This gave him time to serve as a highly respected judge. He died in 1994.

This list of pipers associated with the Argyll and Sutherland Highlanders is merely a selection, and any additions will be welcomed.
Note also tunes:
The 91st at Modder River (Archie MacNab's setting) 2/4 M 4
The 93rd Highlanders Farewell to Edinburgh 2/4 M 4
The 93rd's Farewell to Parkhurst, by Robert Meldrum 6/8 M 2
The 93rd Highlanders Welcome to Parkhurst 1885 6/8 M 2 (attributed to 'the 93rd pipers')
Colonel Campbell of Inverneill's Farewell to the Argylls 2/4 M 2
Pipe Major James Jackson, A & S H, by William Lawrie 2/4 M 4
Major Byng M. Wright's Farewell to the 8th Argylls, by John MacColl 2/4 M 4
RSM Boyde, DCM, MBE, A & S H, by Andrew Pitkeathly 6/8 M 4
The Third Argylls, by P/M J. Smith 6/8 M 2

Loch Awe

IN JANUARY 1999, AN INTERESTING article by Hugh Cheape appeared in the Piper Press, about a late 18th century pipe belonging to the MacCorquodale family, who had an estate on the west side of Loch Awe, the estate of Phantelands (a name corrupted from Gaelic Fionn Eilean, White Island). Their stronghold was on a small island in Loch Tromlee. Hugh Shedden says : 'never powerful nor numerous, the MacCorquodales melted away in the sixteenth and seventeenth centuries' as a clan, leaving isolated families in the district.

It seems that their powerful neighbours, the Campbells of Barbreck, had had MacCorquodale pipers (in spite of the story of one of the lairds of Barbreck being too mean to keep a piper, see above), and the pipe has Campbell tartan ribbons. Hugh Cheape dates it to the second half of the 18th century, and adds that it has three drones.

The pipe is said to have been played for the recruiting of men into the 74th Regiment (Argyleshire Highlanders), raised in 1778 by Colonel John Campbell of Barbreck. This regiment served in America until it was disbanded in 1783. (See also Barbreck).

ARTHUR GILLIES (1934-2003) (See also cover-picture)

Iain MacInnes wrote an introduction to Volume III of the 1997 Recital Series of the Piping Centre in Glasgow, which gives us a flavour of Arthur Gillies:

'Arthur Gillies from Kilchrenan in Argyll has established a formidable reputation as one of our foremost exponents of piobaireachd. As a young man he had tuition from the Lawrie family in Oban, and later from 'big' Donald MacLean of Lewis. At the age of seventeen he won his first professional contest, and since then he has been a familiar and highly regarded figure on the piping circuit. Indeed he has the rare distinction of having won every prize at the Argyllshire Gathering in Oban, from the local events to the Gold Medal and senior Piobaireachd. In later years he was a regular visitor to the piping authority Archie Kenneth at Stronachullin, and this helped nurture a bold and rhythmic approach to the playing of Ceol Mor. Widely respected for his gentlemanly demeanour both on and

Arthur Gillies (right) with Angus MacColl, two stalwarts of Oban piping.
(Photograph by courtesy of the College of Piping)

off the boards, Arthur regards his recent win in the Tuagh Or Na Maighstirean (the Masters' Golden Axe, widely known as the Veterans' Prize) at the Lochaber Gathering as one of his greatest achievements.'

In 2001, the Piping Centre wrote of Arthur:

'Arthur Gillies is one of the world's most accomplished pipers. Amongst his peers he is considered a 'master' player and has demonstrated this by winning the Masters' Tuagh Or competition in Lochaber on two occasions.

'In fact, it is true to say that Arthur has won almost every major award in piping including the coveted Gold Medal and Senior Piobaireachd events at the Argyllshire Gathering, Oban.

'Arthur not only excels as a performer but is also an extremely fine teacher of vast experience. He is in demand throughout the world and recently has established links with many students in Germany where he has his own school.

'The Piping Centre was privileged to be able to employ him as an instructor at several summer schools where he proved to be an extremely effective and popular member of the team. Arthur demonstrated his ability to teach all ages and abilities in all styles of pipe music from Piobaireachd to Marches, Strathspeys, Reels, Hornpipes and Jigs. In addition to all of his piping skills, Arthur is an extremely fine gentleman.

'He has also proved that he is adept at working with pipe bands as well as solo players.

'The area of Argyll is richer for having his talent, experience and teaching ability resident it its locality'.

It is noticeable that these tributes stress the gentlemanly qualities of Arthur, on which everyone is agreed. He also proved himself to be a reliable employee, a quality brought to the fore in 1996, when he was presented with a banner for his pipes in recognition of 35 years' service with the Scottish Hydro Board. The banner was presented to him by Lord Wilson, the Hydro Chairman, himself a piper. When working as an engineer at the Nant Power Station, Ben Cruachan, Arthur used to practice his playing deep underground (no midges), and Lord Wilson commented that the underground chamber provided 'perfect acoustics for pipes'.

Some top-class pipers feel they should try to put back into piping all that they have received themselves, and Arthur was one of these. He recognised the lack of tuition in remote parts, particularly the western isles, and so far both Mull and South Uist have benefitted from his teaching. He also generously sponsored a practice room in the new College of Piping building in Otago St., Glasgow, the wall of which is adorned with a plaque in his memory.

He was born in Stirling in 1934, the son of Malcolm and Jessie Gillies. As far as he knew, there is no connection with Alasdair and Norman Gillies, nor with the piping Gillies families of Kilmartin and Cowal (see below). When he was very young, his parents separated and he was brought up by his father's family. He attended Oban High School, before becoming an apprentice joiner in Inveraray; in 1968 he went to the Hydro Board, for whom he worked for the rest of his career.

Arthur Gillies after winning the Senior Open Piobaireachd at Oban in 1993; he played the Lament for Pipe Major Robert Reid, composed by William Barrie.
(PHOTOGRAPH BY COURTESY OF THE COLLEGE OF PIPING)

Descended from Gillies families in Ardnamurchan, it was his grandfather who came to Loch Aweside: Arthur was not related to the Gillies branches established in Kilchrenan parish in the 18th and 19th centuries. But he was related to Big Angus MacDonald, late Pipe Major of the Scots Guards – they were fourth cousins, Arthur said, as well as good friends.

Arthur played Lawrie pipes, made around 1900. His piping teachers began with his uncle Allan, then with the Lawrie family in Oban, continued with 'Big Donald' MacLean from Lewis, and he went to Archie Kenneth for 25 years, for his piobaireachd.

Arthur was the composer of several tunes (see below). His best-known work is probably *Samantha's Lullaby*, which he wrote for the baby whom he and his wife were going to adopt; to their sorrow, the birth-mother changed her mind and would not sign the papers, so they lost the child they had had for only a few months.

Arthur was a competitor in all the big competitions from 1951, until his health compelled him to retire from the top echelons, after 51 years on the boards. He still made appearances at local Games, where his playing was greatly enjoyed. He was always renowned for the excellence of his pipe, with its rich harmonics, and for his crisp fingering. Not a man for acoustical theory, he always said 'I don't know how I set up my pipe, but I do know when it's going alright'. Sometimes his pipe produced a sound so rich and full, like an organ, that it was too much for the judges, who distressed Arthur's devoted fans by condemning it as 'unsteady', when it was spot on.

His musical playing won him the Gold Medal at Oban in 1975, playing *Farewell to the Laird of Islay*, the only piobaireachd work known to have been composed by Angus MacKay.

On one occasion he was playing the *Blue Ribbon* in the Clasp Competition at the Northern Meeting, and everyone was enjoying his performance. His pipe was perfect and singing beautifully, he was playing well, when he suddenly came to an abrupt halt. Nobody could understand it: his drones had not stopped, he was confident of the tune, so what had happened? He said later that he had new dentures, and his mouthpiece had suddenly become painfully jammed under them, so that he had no option but to stop playing.

When Big Angus MacDonald became ill, all his pipes were sold, and Arthur bought one of them. He had them with him at the Crieff Games that summer, and was in the beer tent talking to his friends, with the pipes, in their metal box, standing at his feet. To his horror, when he looked down, they had gone, and there was a slit in the wall of the tent just beside him. He was deeply upset, because these were Angus' pipes and he felt that people would think he had not looked after them properly. He suffered for a week, but did not know that the staff in the neighbouring tent of the Bank of Scotland had seen two men crouching beside the beer tent. They laid information with the police, who traced the thieves, and recovered the pipes, unharmed.

Too often, valuable pipes are left exposed (as Arthur's were not) at the Games, and it is only too easy for a thief to lift them. I have seen pipes worth over £3000 lying unattended in an open box: you might as well put a notice on them saying 'Here I am – steal me'.

Rosneath and Clynder Highland Games were started in the 1970s, but it was not until 1992 that solo piping was introduced. In 1996, Alex Ferguson, the manager of Manchester United Football Club (later Sir Alex), donated a handsome trophy for the winner of the piobaireachd competition. It was won (virtually) every year by Arthur Gillies, for the first years of the competition. Sir Alex has served as Chieftain and remains one of the sponsors of the games.

One day, on his way home from the Rosneath Games, Arthur was driving over the Rest-and-Be-Thankful, and pulled in at the car park on the summit of the pass. It was a warm evening, and he was thirsty, so he took out a bottle of mineral water and had a long swig. As he drove down towards Loch Fyne, a police car flagged him down, and he was asked if he had been drinking. Not alcohol, said Arthur. So where had he been, and where was he heading? He explained, and they asked if he could prove it. He produced the Alex Ferguson Cup for

Piobaireachd, which he had won that afternoon, and this was accepted as undeniable proof; relations suddenly became most cordial, and the police explained that he had been seen drinking before driving off, and the witnesses thought it was a whisky bottle, so they rang the police. Arthur showed them his bottle of water, and drove on, blessing the name of Alex Ferguson.

[Incidentally, the Pipe Major of the Milngavie and Strathendrick Pipe Bands, Archie Campbell, composed a tune for Alex Ferguson. Called *Sir Alex's Glorious Return to Govan*, it commemorated the occasion when Sir Alex received the Freedom of the City of Glasgow. Sir Alex and Archie Campbell had served their apprenticeship together in Glasgow. On the great day, the tune was played by one of the composer's pupils, Jim Semple of the Strathclyde Police.]

After his retirement from work, Arthur established the Nether Lorn Piping School at his home in Kilchrenan, with summer schools in Germany to supplement his tuition. Before this, he had held what amounted to open house for young pipers coming from Germany to compete at Oban, and the start of a slightly more formal school was a logical progression from this. Arthur was an excellent teacher, with the highest standards.

Though still competing locally because he enjoyed it, he came to the end of his major career. The obvious road from there was into judging, but he was reluctant to go on the bench, because he said he did not know enough, and his sympathies were too close to the pipers for him to be completely objective. But with his knowledge, experience and integrity, he was needed there at the top, his health permitting.

Since the above was written, we have had the sad news of the death of Arthur, in the summer of 2003, at the age of 69. He will be sorely missed, not least in Germany, where he did so much to encourage piping.

Tunes composed by Arthur include:
Ian Morrison, Stornoway 2/4 M 4
Samantha's Lullaby 6/8 SA 3
Lorna's Slipper J
Angus MacColl 6/8 M
Angus McInnes 6/8 M
John Patrick's Jig J
Martin Kessler 6/8 M

Four tunes were made for him:
Arthur Gillies, by Iain Morrison 1980 2/4 HP 4
Arthur Gillies, by Archie Kenneth 6/8 M 4
Arthur Gillies, by John Don MacKenzie J
Arthur Gillies, by Ronald Lawrie
And Archie Kenneth made *Mrs Barbara Gillies*, for Arthur's wife.

SOURCES
Hugh Cheape, Piping Times
Hugh Shedden
Arthur Gillies

A YOUNG PIPER'S PRAYER

O Lord, let me get to the contest
In good time to play my tune,
Let the judges be sober, and honest,
Let me reach the platform soon –
But don't let me be first on, I pray,
Not even in the first three,
And I don't fancy last, whatever they say,
The wait would be killing me.

Let me find out what everyone knows,
The best place to go for lunch;
And let me go where everyone goes –
But don't let me drink too much.
Don't let me find I've forgotten my hose
When I come to put on my gear;
Let my reeds be clean and the tape in place,
My High G strong and clear.

Lord, the right tuning place would assist,
Not too far from the Gents,
And could you help me remember my list
When I come in front of the Bench?
Remind me how the Urlar begins
When I'm thinking 'Oh, how does it go?',
And could you make sure that the tape still clings
When my chanter is in full flow?

O Lord, don't let me step on my lace
And trip when I'm walking round,
Fall over my feet flat on my face
Before I've finished the Ground.
Keep all my drones in tune, I pray,
Until the work is done,
Watch o'er my fingers as I play
And guide them, one by one.

Just give me the courage to begin,
With my trust in Providence —
And, Lord, preserve me from the sin
Of over-confidence.

OBAN AND DISTRICT

Pipe tunes associated with Oban and District
The Ball That Was In Oban R 2
The Bells of Appin, by Karl Walford 6/8 SA 2
Benderloch Bay, by Donald MacLean 2/4 M 4
Colonel MacDougall of Dunollie's Reel R 2
Donald MacLean's Farewell to Oban, by Archie MacNeill 2/4 M 4
Donolly Castle, by N. MacLeod 6/8 M 2
Dr Ross's 50th Welcome to the Argyllshire Gathering, by Donald MacLeod 6/8 M 4
Echoes of Oban, by Donald MacPherson 6/8 J 4
The Fair Maid of Oban R 2
Iain Ciar's Lament P with 8 variations
(possibly) *Iain Ciar's Salute* P
(possibly) *The King's Taxes* P with 7 variations
Lament for Airds P with 9 variations. The Campbells of Airds lived near Loch Creran, north of Oban.
Lament for Captain MacDougall P with 7 variations
Latha Dhunabharti (the Battle of Dunaverty) P, possibly = the Lament for MacDonald of Sanda (see above)
Lochnell's Lament P with 5 variations
MacDougalls' Gathering P with 5 variations
MacDougall's Jig 6/8 J 2
The Oban Strathspey, by Archie Munro S 2
(possibly) *The Old Woman's Lullaby* P with 3 variations
The Pass of Brander, by Dr Bruce E. Thomson 9/8 RM 2 (winning composition at Minard in 1978)
Rev. John MacLeod, Oban, by John W. Scott 2/4 HP 4
Salute to Captain MacDougall P
Scarce of Fishing P with 10 or 12 variations
See also lists of the compositions of John MacColl, the Lawries and Arthur Gillies.

TAYNUILT

Hugh Shedden's *Story of Lorn* tells us of a field known as Daileag, a little to the south of Taynuilt, near Oban, 'overlooked by the Piper's Hill'. This field was the site of a battle in the early 15th century, between seven MacDougall brothers and seven selected Campbells. In the first attack, incited by the piper (whose side was he on?), four Campbells were killed, but a counter-attack resulted in the death of all seven brothers. A general melee between supporters of both clans ensued, in which the MacDougalls got the worse of it. Cairns were raised to mark the burials of the dead.

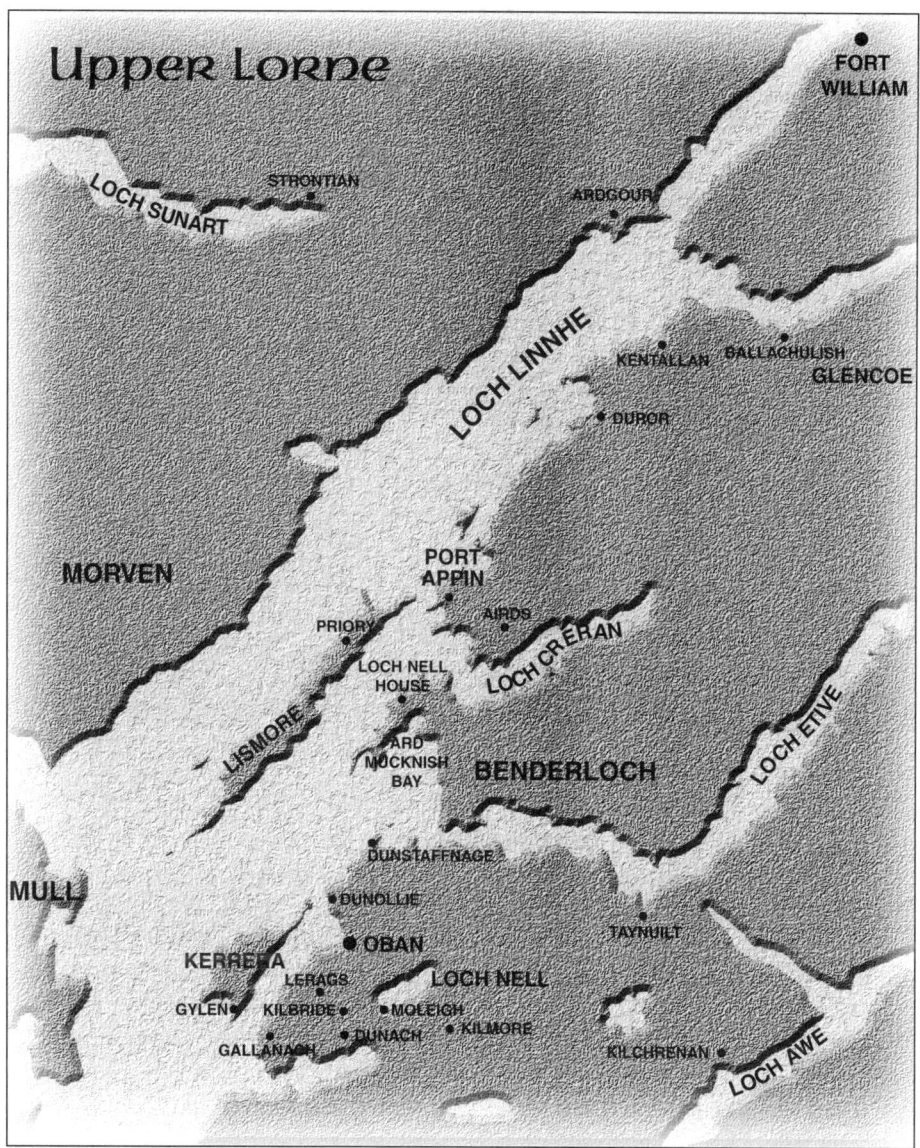

DUNSTAFFNAGE

DUNSTAFFNAGE HAS TWO MAIN POINTS of interest to pipers. One was Janet Campbell, 'the Black Bitch of Dunstaffnage', who married George Campbell of Airds; she was famed, among other grim exploits, for having had a piper's fingers cut off. This was in the mid-17th century, and the incident became bound up with the story of the mutilation of the Duntroon piper, a few years later (see above).

In July 1732, the master of a ship, the *Nathaniel and John*, of Londonderry, was seized in the harbour at Dunstaffnage and found to be illegally importing 20

Dunstaffnage Castle, to the north of Oban. It was built over a period of years between the 13th and 16th centuries, originally by the MacDougalls of Lorn, but taken over by the Campbells. It is a few miles from Dunollie, the later seat of the MacDougalls.

bushels of malt. For the subsequent legal proceedings, several local witnesses were listed (but never called), and they included 'Gavin Hunter in Dunstaffnage, and JOHN CAMPBELL, piper there'. Was he piper to the Black Bitch's father?

Another piping reference was in a novel by Tobias Smollet, published in the 18th century. In *Humphrey Clinker*, a castle identifiable as Dunstaffnage is described in some detail, and although the castle is not named, there is little doubt that it is Dunstaffnage.

In the book, a character called Jeremiah Melford visited the castle, where his host was a Mr Campbell, 'who performs well on the violin but has an invincible antipathy to the sound of the Highland bagpipe, which sings in the nose with a most alarming twang, and indeed is quite intolerable to ears of common sensibility, when aggravated by the echo of a vaulted hall. He therefore begged the piper would have some mercy upon him and dispense with this part of the morning service. A consultation of the clan being held on this occasion, it was unanimously agreed that the Laird's request could not be granted, with a dangerous encroachment upon the customs of the family. The piper declared, he could not give up for a moment the privilege he derived from his ancestors; nor would the Laird's relations forego an entertainment which they valued above all others. There was no remedy, Mr Campbell being obliged to acquiesce, is fain to stop his ears with cotton, to fortify his head with three or four night-caps, and every morning to retire into the penetralia of his habitation in order to avoid this diurnal annoyance. When the music ceases, he produces himself at an open window which looks into the courtyard which is by this time filled with a crowd of his vassals and appendants, who . . . bow to the earth with the most humble prostration.'

He would probably have applied the Black Bitch's remedy if he had dared.

The book has an interesting description of the piper, who always insisted on his privileges, and wore a kilt in the old Highland style, with purse, pistol and dirk, and 'a broad yellow ribbon fixed to the chanter (?) pipe is thrown over his shoulder and trails along the ground while he performs his minstrelsy... He plays before the Laird every Sunday on his way to the kirk which he circles three times, performing the family March, which implies defiance to all enemies of the clan; and every morning he plays a full hour by the clock, in the great hall, marching back and forth all the time with a solemn pace, attended by the laird's kinsmen, who seem much delighted with the music. In this exercise he indulges them with a number of pibrochs or airs, suited to the different passions which he would either excite or assuage...'

While at Dunstaffnage, Smollet (or his hero) attended the funeral of an old lady: he says that at the feast which preceded the interment, fifteen pipers played, and when the coffin was committed to the earth, the whole congregation stood bareheaded while the pipers played a pibroch right through. In the evening, a hundred gallons of whisky were drunk by fewer than a hundred people (we might wonder how he could recall the details).

This description was in a novel, dated 1771, and was of course fiction, but it is believed that Smollett based the character of the Laird on a real-life Campbell proprietor of Dunstaffnage, probably Dougal Campbell, or possibly his son Donald, 14th Captain of Dunstaffnage, and that is why he did not name the castle.

THE MACDOUGALL PIPERS TO MACDOUGALL OF DUNOLLIE

THE NOTICES OF PIPERS GIVE short accounts of the different MacDougall pipers. These seem to be based largely on family papers at Dunollie. The Notices tell us:

The MacDougall pipers lived at Moleigh, to the south of Oban, where they had a grant of land from the MacDougall chief, called Croit a'Phiobair, the Piper's Croft. They are known to have kept a piping school at Kilbride, designated Tigh nam Piobairean, House of the Pipers. A flat piece of ground behind it was called Iomaire na Spaidsearachd, the Marching Furrow, where the pupils practised their tunes on the full set.

ALASTAIR MOR MACDOUGALL was hereditary piper to the MacDougalls at Dunollie, and the first we know about. A notable player, said to have started the school for pipers at Kilbride which lasted until about 1745, he is believed to have been the composer of *Latha Dhunabharti (The Day of Dunaverty)*, in memory of the taking of Dunaverty Castle, Kintyre, by General Leslie in 1647, when many of the MacDougall clan perished (see above). Alasdair Mor lived from c.1635 to c.1708. (If so, he presumably composed *Latha Dhunabharti* some years after the massacre). He was succeeded by his son, Ranald Ban.

RANALD BAN MACDOUGALL is said in the family to have been the composer of *The King's Taxes*. He succeeded his father around 1709, and held his office for many years. He was the last to keep the piping school at Kilbride. Composed *Iain Ciar's Salute* and *Iain Ciar's Lament* for his chief who fought at Sheriffmuir; also said to have made the *MacDougall's Salute*.

RANALD MOR MACDOUGALL was Ranald Ban's grandson, the last of the hereditary pipers at Dunollie. Composer of a *Salute to Captain MacDougall* as well as a *Lament* for him (1812). After leaving Dunollie, he was Pipe Major to the local Argyllshire Militia from c.1806 to 1816. He died c.1835. It is sometimes said that this was 'Blind MacDougall', but this may be confusion with Blind Allan, father and son, in Glencoe. There is no evidence that Ranald Mor was blind.

ALLAN MACDOUGALL, a native of Argyll, was a Jacobite captured in the '45, described as in the Notices of Pipers as 'a blind Highland pyper in Lord Nairn's Regt'; the Muster Rolls of the Jacobite army have him as one of two pipers in the Atholl Brigade, of which Lord Nairn commanded the 1st Battalion. He was captured on January 17th 1746, a few months before Culloden, but was pardoned without trial, because of his blindness. His fellow piper, John Ballantine, was also captured, and taken to Carlisle for trial, where he was acquitted and released. Allan's son, also blind, was probably a piper, too (see also Glencoe, below).

DUGALD MacDUGALL, for many years piper to Dugald MacDugall Esq. of Gallanach, competed in Edinburgh in 1784, and came third. Two years later he improved his position to second. He was of the family of the hereditary pipers to the chief at Dunollie.

To a large extent the MacDougall pipers at Moleigh have been overshadowed by their descendants in Perthshire, about whom much more is known. Although the Aberfeldy branch was famed as players and pipemakers, it was the Moleigh MacDougalls who were the composers, and their works are still played today.

The Notices of Pipers list some of the MacDougalls descended from Donald, who left Moleigh for Taymouth in 1750. Jeannie Campbell gives an excellent account of them in her book *Highland Bagpipe Makers*.

The above Notices of Pipers, largely compiled by Lt John MacLennan in the late 1890s and early 1900s, present a few problems. What was the source of the

MacDougall pipers in Perthshire: P/M Duncan MacDougall on left, John MacDougall, second from left, rear row; Gavin MacDougall, third from left. This was around 1896 when they were serving with the 2nd Perthshire Highland Rifle Volunteers, some 150 years after their ancestor left the Oban district.
(PHOTOGRAPH BY COURTESY OF THE COLLEGE OF PIPING)

information, especially about the MacDougall pipers in Lorne before Donald left for Taymouth? Some at least of the information seems to have come from the papers of the MacDougalls of Dunnollie, but some of these papers may have been written in the 19th century and could be of doubtful authenticity.

Some problems arise: what is the evidence that Ranald Ban composed the *King's Taxes*? Is the *MacDougall's Salute* the work which we now call the *MacDougalls' Gathering*, which is nameless in most sources? And what is the *Salute to Captain MacDougall*? Finally, where does Blind Allan MacDougall of the '45 fit in? Was he one of the pipers at Molighe? Not enough is explained, but to some extent the information given in the Notices is borne out by that in the public records.

Alexander MacAulay in his article *The Art and History of the MacDougalls of Aberfeldy*, first published in Volume 16 of the Piping Times, and reprinted in Volume 32 in 1980, refers to the Records of Argyll by Lord Archibald Campbell, written in the late 19th century: this states that a MacDougall hereditary piper was with the Chief of Lorn at the Battle of Allt Dearg (Red Burn), fought between the Campbells and the MacDougalls in the 13th century. The tune played by the piper was called *Da laimh 'sa piob, laimh 'sa chlaidheamh* (*'Two hands on the pipe, and a hand on the sword'*). He says the music of this is preserved in South Uist.

Flat land between Lerags and Kilbride, south of Oban, which could be the Marching Furrow where pupils of the MacDougall piping school practised their playing. The school is thought to have flourished in the late 17th and early 18th centuries, though the dates are uncertain, as is the exact location of the school.

Alexander MacAulay also says that around 1500 there was more than one family of MacDougall pipers on the estate, and at that time they are mentioned as having a rent-free house with a croft called Monagh-leigh. 'They also had a piping school at Kilbride called Tigh-nam-piobairean (pipers' house) also maintained by the Dunolly estate with food and fuel. There was a house adjoining the school where the MacDougalls, reputed to be skilled woodturners, made their own bagpipes.'

Mr MacAulay refers to the Dunolly family papers to which he was given access by Madam MacDougall of MacDougall, and he says he found the above information in these papers.

To some extent this is borne out by the information of Miss Nancy Black, who also had access to information from the MacDougalls of Dunollie.

Mr MacAulay says that in Iain Ciar's time, after the upheaval following Sheriffmuir, the chief being away for some years, 'there was a drift of family employees from Dunolly. One of the piping families settled in Glencoe. A grandson of this line was Ailean Dall (Blind Allan), born at Glencoe in 1751. A travelling tailor by trade, he was also noted as a piobaireachd player, but it is his works in Gaelic poetry and literature that made him famous in his own time'. Obviously this cannot be the Blind Allan of the '45, who may have been his father. But was he the blind bard Allan MacDougall who was at Glengarry in the 1790s and made a poem about Glengarry's piper, John MacFarlane? It seems likely that he was (see below, Glencoe).

Looking down to the farm of Moleigh (centre, half hidden by trees) where the MacDougall pipers lived until the early 19th century. They held the farm from the MacDougall chiefs of Dunollie, as part of their payment as the chiefs' pipers. Moleigh was not far from Loch Nell, which lies in the glen to the left of this picture.

Mr MacAulay also says that in 1812 two pipers, Ronald Mor and his younger brother Ronald Og were at Dunolly (see below). Apart from this, the rest of the article is concerned with the pipe-making MacDougalls after they had gone to Perthshire.

The Old Parish Register for Kilmore and Kilbride, which includes Oban, starts in 1776, and the first entry which mentions Molighe (nowadays spelled Moleigh; the stress is on the second syllable, Mo-LEE) is dated 1786. Duncan MacCaog in Molighe, married to Margaret MacDougall, had his first child in that year. There was a family called MacCaog living at Molighe from 1786 to 1813, with brothers Duncan, Peter and Dugald. Peter also married one of the MacDougalls in Molighe.

The local historian, Charles K. Hunter, says that Molighe was a ten merkland farm, which was on land belonging to the MacDougalls of Dunollie (a merkland was the amount of land worth two-thirds of a pound Scots, and was usually equal to two pennylands; the acreage differed according to the fertility of the land concerned. It also differed at different times, so the exact amount of land is often difficult to estimate. Some define a pennyland as the amount of ground needed to support seven cows and two horses, along with arable land for oats, bere and potatoes. While not precisely definable, a ten merkland farm was pretty large).

The Notices of Pipers say that the piping school run by the MacDougalls was at Kilbride. There are two places called Kilbride in the district, the bigger one being a mile to the N.E. of Lerags, and about one and a half miles west of

The farm of Moleigh today. It belongs now to Donald Morrison from South Uist, a relative of the South Uist Morrison pipers.

Moleigh, as the crow flies; the smaller Kilbride is up Glenfeochan, about three miles S.E. of Moleigh. This latter was in the parish of Kilmore and on land belonging to Campbell of Glenfeochan, whereas Kilbride near Lerags was on the estate of the MacDougalls of Dunollie, whose chiefs were buried there after 1737. As the tradition says the piping school was given to the pipers by the Dunollie chiefs, it has been felt to be almost certain that it was at Kilbride, Lerags.

Charles Hunter has, however, cast doubt on the tradition of the piping school at Kilbride. He points out that Moleigh was in the parish of Kilbride, and considers it unlikely that the piping school would have been a two-mile walk away from the pipers' home. If the school was indeed on the croft at Moleigh, it is easy to see how the error could have crept in: it is only a short step from saying the school was in Kilbride (meaning the parish) to saying it was at Kilbride, which everyone took to mean the settlement near the church. There are extensive ruins of old farm buildings around the present farmstead of Moleigh. Any of these could have been the pipers' croft, and the farm is surrounded by flat land where the Marching Furrow could have been. The site overlooks Loch Nell, which is associated with *Lochnell's Lament* and *Scarce of Fishing*.

Nancy Black, however, who is a MacDougall descendant, disagrees with Charles Hunter: she was told by Miss Hope MacDougall, the last of the MacDougalls of Dunollie, that the Marching Furrow was below Kilbride, near the Lerags graveyard, and she accepts that the pipers walked from Moleigh to the school, a walk of a mere two miles being negligible in those days. It is not known what was Miss Hope's authority for her information, but family tradition has to be treated with respect.

Ruins of a chapel at Kilbride which lies beside the remains of a bigger church. This was formerly an important ecclesiastical centre, in late mediaeval times. The side-chapel has had memorial plaques attached to the walls in later times, to honour different members of the MacDougall chiefs' family, and these include both Iain Ciar, 22nd chief, and his grandson, Captain MacDougall, killed in Spain in 1812.

The church at Kilbride is now a roofless ruin, but enough remains to show that it was in its day an impressive building. Beside it are the remains of the chieftains' chapel, with memorial plaques fixed to the walls. Here is one to the memory of Captain Sandy MacDougall (see below). The first chief to be buried at Kilbride was Iain Ciar, for whom a lament was made by Ranald Ban MacDougall in 1737 (see below).

Before 1745, Kilmore was the centre of the community, and later amalgamated with Kilbride to form the parish to which Oban belongs. In the early 1700s, Oban itself was merely an anchorage, with a few hovels around the shore. Kilmore, a few miles to the south, over the hill, was the centre, both ecclesiastical and political, and before the Reformation the church at Kilmore was impressively large. Kilbride had been an important religious centre since the 13th century. Services were held there until 1877.

In 1757, the Reverend PATRICK MACDONALD from Durness, elder brother of Joseph, became the minister of both Kilmore and Kilbride, holding services for about 200 communicants in the two churches on alternate Sundays. He was an important figure in the district, where he remained until his death in 1824. He is buried at Kilmore, the inscription on his horizontal gravestone still legible.

There is a tradition that the grave of a certain Captain Campbell is also at

The ruined church at Kilmore, south of Oban. Kilmore and Kilbride combined to form the centre of the parish to which Oban belongs. At one time Kilmore was a large building. The minister here between 1757 and 1824 was the Rev. Patrick MacDonald, elder brother of Joseph, and author of Highland Vocal Airs.

Kilmore, though it has not been identified. He is said locally to have composed a 'famous pipe tune, a march about the Battle of Inverlochy'. I do not know what this would be – surely not *Black Donald's March*? It seems unlikely that this was made by a Campbell.

The Reverend Patrick's manse was on the south side of the Feochan river, near Cleigh, not far from the hump-backed bridge which takes the Musdale road over the river. A fine big stone house was built in 1830, but Patrick's older manse remained beside it until a few years ago (1990s), when it was demolished and a modern house built on the site.

The Reverend Patrick is remembered as a 'fierce but righteous' man, and he is mentioned by a young lady, Anne MacVicar (later Mrs Grant of Laggan) who was visiting Mary Campbell of Glenfeochan in 1773. She wrote that they set out for church: 'This was an odd, old church, almost ruinous. But when the preacher came in he roused all my attention . . . a superior musical genius, being a distinguished composer as well as a performer on the violin' (*The Clarion*, No.28, April 1962).

For us the main interest in Patrick MacDonald is his book *Highland Vocal Airs*, and the fact that he was the elder brother of Joseph MacDonald, author of the *Compleat Treatise* on Highland bagpipe music. While Patrick was at Kilmore, he compiled his collection of *Highland Vocal Airs*, published in 1784, with a Preface probably written by Sir John Ramsay. He made use of a collection put together by Joseph and presented to their sister Flora when Joseph left for India in 1760.

Above: Patrick is buried on the north side of the church.

Below: Patrick's gravestone is plain and unadorned.

Patrick's book became a 'musical landmark' in the next fifty years, an immensely important musical influence in Scotland.

William Donaldson says (p.49): 'It was typical of Patrick that if he did not know something, he would go and find out at first hand from somebody that did, and he was prepared to travel considerable distances to do this. Thus, when he decided he needed a section on piobaireachd, he used his family connections with Ronald MacDonald, the laird of Keppoch, to gain access to a notable piper'. The result was that he attempted the first printed transcription of piobaireachd in staff notation (Joseph's transcriptions were earlier, written in 1762, but were not printed until much later).

From the playing of that notable but unnamed MacDonald piper, Patrick 'wrote out four favourite pieces', which he annexed to the *Vocal Airs*. The Preface says: 'In performing [the quick variations] on the bagpipe, it is usual to introduce certain graces and flourishes, which are peculiar to that instrument, and to that species of music; and which can hardly be expressed in notes, or executed, at least, with the same effect, upon another instrument' (but this preface was not written by Patrick himself).

The four works he transcribed as for the violin were *MacIntosh's Lament, Cha till mi tuille (I will never return), The Finger Lock,* and *Cogadh no Sith (War or Peace).* We do not know his reasons for selecting these tunes.

Of his settings, faulty though they were, William Donaldson says (p.50) they are 'of the first interest, in that they are musically aware, and done by someone who was close to the tradition'. Although himself a very fine classical violinist – he once stood in for a famous Italian soloist at a concert in Edinburgh – Patrick maintained his vital interest in what Donaldson calls 'demotic music', and he seems to have been in close touch with his parishioners in Kilmore and Kilbride.

The question remains: when he was seeking information about piobaireachd, did he not go over to Molighe, barely a mile from his manse, and consult the MacDougalls? Was there a break in the MacDougall piping line around 1770? We have Ranald Ban who seems to have died around 1750, and we know his piping son Donald left for Taymouth soon after that. The MacDougall school was closed. The next notable pipers were Ranald Ban's grandsons Ranald Mor and Dougall, both probably born in the 1760s. But if there were no piobaireachd experts left at Moleigh, who then taught Ranald Mor and Dougall? Was it their uncle, Dougall, who was piper to Gallanach? Who, then, was piper at Dunollie from 1750 until Ranald Mor took over?

It is of course possible, indeed likely, that Patrick did consult the MacDougalls, but what he was seeking was not so much information about piobaireachd (of which he must himself have had considerable knowledge) as help with the transcription of this music, a very different thing. If, as seems probable, the MacDougall pipers were illiterate, their knowledge would be instinctive and transmitted by ear, and they may well have been resistant to the whole idea of transcription – as many pipers were. If they were unable, or unwilling, or both, to help the minister in his quest, he would then have turned to his own family connections. He was married to Barbara MacDonnell (his second wife), daughter of the 16th MacDonnell chief of Keppoch, so it was natural for him to go there on his quest. John Gibson says he 'collected these tunes in Lochaber', but it seems more likely that he already knew the tunes, but was seeking help in writing them down.

In those circumstances perhaps we may assume that a brother of Donald MacDougall, possibly called John, was himself a piper, perhaps not of the top flight but good enough to teach his boys, Ranald Mor and Dougall. This period in the development of the MacDougall family is clouded in mystery, which might in itself tell us that something had broken down. But the MacDougalls were still in Molighe, even though the school had been discontinued.

In 1789 John MacCulloch married Mary MacDougall in Molighe. Dougald MacDougall was the first male of the piping MacDougalls recorded in the Old Parish Register. Around 1789 he married Sarah Livingston, from a family who were living in Molighe.

Dougald and Sarah had seven children, Janet 1789, John 1790, Ann 1792, Mary 1794, Duncan 1797, John 1800, Alexander 1802. This Dougald or Dougall was probably the one referred to in the Notices of Pipers: he was piper to MacDougall of Gallanach, and competed in Edinburgh, coming 3rd in 1784 and 2nd in 1786. It is not known if his sons were pipers.

Hugh MacDougall, Molighe, was presumably Dougall's brother. He married Katherine Lamond or Lamont around 1794, she being from a family at Collagan, near Kilbride. Hugh and Katherine had three children, Janet, Flora and John. Again, we do not know if Hugh or John was a piper.

In 1796, the baptism of Alexander is recorded, the elder son of Ranald MacDougall and Elizabeth MacDougall. They had another son, Neil, in 1814. This Ranald was probably Ranald Mor, who was piper to the chief at Dunollie, and composed the *Lament for Captain MacDougall* in 1812 (and if the Notices of Pipers have it right, he also made a Salute to the young Captain). It is not known for certain where Elizabeth belonged, but her family was associated with the island of Kerrera, which, like Molighe, was part of the lands belonging to the Dunollie chiefs.

We do not know what became of Alexander and Neil. The long interval between their births, and the fact that only two were registered, may be significant. Were there health problems, or did Ranald just not have his children baptised? We must also remember that Alexander MacAulay mentioned Ranald Og as well as Ranald Mor, and we cannot be certain who Ranald Og was.

So it seems that at Molighe in the late 18th century, after the departure of Donald for Perthshire, there was still a family of MacDougalls, with Donald's nieces Margaret, Mary and Katherine, and nephews Dougall, Hugh and Ranald. Since both Dougall and Hugh named their eldest sons John, and their eldest daughters Janet, perhaps we may assume these were their parents' names.

There were MacDougalls at Moleigh up to 1861, when Mary MacDougall, nee Livingston, and her daughter Sarah, were listed. By 1871, there were no MacDougalls left there. The last one known to have been a piper was Ranald Mor, born 1775, who married Elizabeth MacDougall; he was the composer of the *Lament for Captain MacDougall* in 1812. It is not clear who Ronald Og was, named by Mr MacAcAulay as being at Moleigh at the same time as Ranald Mor. The by-name suggests he was the son of Ranald Mor, but tradition says they were brothers. Two brothers of the same name in the one family was not unusual in the Highlands.

We know for certain that by 1845 the MacDougalls of Dunollie had no piper. John, the 24th MacDougall chief who took the place of 'poor Sandy', his dead brother, was a navy man. When his father died, making him the new Chief, John came home for a long spell, but in 1845 he suddenly decided, at the age of 54, to return to the sea, and he went back into the navy, to the consternation of his family.

The family correspondence, published in *Highland Postbag* (pp.220-221), makes it clear that he wanted to take a piper with him, for some reason not explained (although many navy ships had pipers in the 19th century, perhaps to entertain the men on long voyages, and to encourage them take exercise). John asked his brother Allan to arrange this for him, and Allan asked John Ban MacKenzie's advice – John Ban was piper and butler to Lord Breadalbane at Taymouth Castle. John Ban recommended John MacKay, the brother of Angus, and Allan wrote to Dunollie:

'John McKay is son of the famous McKay [note that it was old John who was the famous MacKay, not Angus] and brother of Her Majesty's piper [this is Angus], and brother also to Donald who played to the Celts [Celtic Society] along with McKenzie during King George's visit to Auld Reekie in 1822.

'McKenzie says John is an excellent pibroch and reel player, he was lately Lord Ward's piper, who occasionally lives at Glengarry. McKay asks and McKenzie says a Gentleman's best plan is to give the piper a sum of money as pay and for clothes and that he will dress himself well in plain clothes to act as your body servant and in the McDougall Tartan for pipe playing, if you will give him £50 and his mess per annum. I see there are no pipers at all the thing out of places [unemployed], so I suspect if you want to give your sailors a reel to the Bagpipes you must give John McKay his own terms. McKenzie says McKay is a Pretty (underlined) man, and a first rate reel dancer as well as playing.'

Pretty meant fine-looking, handsome, well turned out. This John MacKay, the brother of Angus, had written a manuscript of piobaireachd music, containing many works he had learned from his father, and Angus may have drawn on this when compiling his own collection.

John MacDougall's reply to Allan's letter was:

'I have received yours of the 26th in reference to the Piper John McKay. I will give him £50 annually, that is to make his pay up to that sum, he being rated my Servant, on the following conditions: he is always to be well dressed in the Highland dress when required to play Pibroch and Reels, or when desired. Engage him and send him with a good dress of the McD. Tartan. He will mess with my Steward. I know nothing yet of my destination'.

MacKay was engaged, and on being told to report to the ship, the *Vulture*, a steam frigate, he asked for two days' grace as he was acting as Usher to the Lord High Commissioner of the General Assembly [of the Church of Scotland], which job he had had for the last three years. This was granted.

They sailed from Plymouth bound for Rio de Janeiro, and from there to St Helena, and then for Hong Kong. Nothing further is said about John MacKay, and we do not know if he gave satisfaction to his employer. How did the English sailors take to dancing reels to the pipes? Sailors had been made to dance for shipboard exercise and entertainment since at least the time of Nelson: he mentioned in a letter the step-dances practised by his men, though with no reference to an instrument accompanying them. John died within two years, on his return from China.

LAMENT FOR IAIN CIAR

THIS PIOBAIREACHD WORK, PUBLISHED IN General Thomason's collection, *Ceol Mor*, is said to have been composed by the MacDougall piper at Dunollie, Ranald Ban MacDougall, in 1737. It has close affinities with other works, notably *Chisholm's Salute*, reputedly made in 1836, and a setting of *The Glen Is Mine* in Donald MacDonald's collection. Both are said to have been based on *Iain Ciar's Lament*, according to Archibald Campbell of Kilberry, but *The Glen Is Mine* is older. Peter Reid called this work *MacDougall of Lorn's Lament*.

Iain Ciar was the 22nd Chief, a remarkable man. Some of his correspondence was published in 1984 by his descendant, Jean MacDougall, and it reveals a pleasantly civilised man, a loving husband and father, who led an adventurous life as a result of his supporting the Jacobite cause in 1715.

Iain Ciar's son was the last of the MacDougall chiefs to live at Dunollie Castle, which he abandoned in favour of a new mansion house built close by. Some of the stones from the old castle were used for the new house. The castle is now a picturesque ruin and a landmark at the entrance to the harbour at Oban.

Iain Ciar ('Swarthy') became the 22nd Chief of the MacDougalls of Dunollie in 1695. His date of birth is not known, but he must have been born around 1680, at Dunollie Castle.

In 1712 he married Mary MacDonald, who was only sixteen. She was the grand-

Dunollie Castle on its headland commanding the entrance to Oban Bay. Although a fortress is known to have existed on this site as far back as 698, the castle was probably built in the 15th century. It was replaced by Dunollie House in 1746.

The remains of Dunollie Castle today. Iain Ciar's wife Mary was told by her absent husband to fortify the doorway by lining the wooden door with peats, to absorb any gunfire, in case the castle was attacked in 1715. She was later forced to leave the castle, with her young children.

daughter of Sir Donald MacDonald of Sleat, a spirited girl, well educated and affectionate. The marriage was celebrated in some style, after the Dunollie chief had sent 14 galleys, manned by MacDougall clansmen, to fetch the bride from Duntulm, in the north of Skye. The couple were well matched and the marriage was happy.

The correspondence that has survived gives a glimpse of domestic life at the castle. By the time Mary was 19 she had three small children and another on the way, and the family was living peacefully at Dunollie, as we know from an order for seeds sent to Glasgow: they wanted to grow marigolds, parsley, watercress, thyme, carrots, parsnips, beets, radishes and white peas. Some of these would be grown to store for the winter months, and some were for medicinal purposes. A request for a spade and a shovel was included in the order.

This peaceful life was shattered when Iain Ciar sided with the Jacobite cause in 1715. He did not announce his intention to his Campbell friends at nearby Dunstaffnage, but had the nerve to ask the Campbells at Inveraray to send him arms. When these were not forthcoming, he kidnapped a Campbell blacksmith from Taynuilt and set him to work making and repairing weapons in a cave below the castle. This man was later released, and Iain equipped and trained a force of clansmen, before leaving to join the Jacobite army.

He left poor Mary, with her three small children and a new baby girl, to defend Dunollie, with a handful of loyal clansmen, but he took most of the able supporters, including his piper Ranald Ban MacDougall. Mary was understandably full of fear, and with reason, as the Campbells at once tried to seize Dunollie. Iain wrote to her:

'The base cowards why did they not attempt to meet myself . . . Keep the house and the cause, line the door with turf on the inside, my dearest keep good heartt, and the Lord give you strength and courage'

The next month he wrote: 'Dearest and only Comfortt, I'm hopeful you have not surrendered the house . . . keep it as long as you can'. He asked for more men, but told her to 'keep noe less in the house than twelve and for Gods sake keep courage for all things goes very well. Let my horse be sent and my cloak and all my clothes if you can see any savety for them if not it cannot be helped . . . Let me know of the children . . . once more I crave your stoutness in keeping the house. . . be noe ways concerned aboutt me for I am in noe danger . . . belive nothing you hear except what you hear to our advantage. You shall hear from me very shoone. Yours while I am, J.McDougall'

Iain Ciar sent home an interesting description of the Battle of Sheriffmuir, in which he was injured, being shot in the leg. It is curious that nobody who fought in the battle seems to have known who won; it was a messy and apparently indecisive engagement, and it was not until later that the government forces could claim the victory.

Iain wrote to Mary: 'I have the honour my dearest to be amongst the wounded for I received a slight one through the right thigh, my danger is already over. For the love of God be nayes concerned for me. I intreat you keep good heart for the fear I lay under about you keeps my mind still in grief. Manage everything, live to the best advantage you can. Let me know how the children are or if they are in life. I conclude with a kiss to yourself, heart and all I have , , ,'

With this letter he sent her '3 pairs of gloves, 1 pound of figgs, 1 pound raisins, 1 unce cinnamon, 4 unces white candy and 8 unces liqorice'

Iain's wound healed slowly 'for the ball in my leg was very big, but I can walk with all ease in my chamber'. He assured Mary that this was all the blood he would shed, but he was unable to travel to Dunollie to visit her in case the wound was re-opened. He sent his brother to recruit more men, but warned Mary not to part with the twelve she had in the house.

He kept up Mary's spirits with plenty of loving letters and sent her presents when he could: 2 silk napkins and a length of lace 'five ells and a quarter' long (an ell was 40 inches), and a piece of gold he had paid two guineas for 'and that is worth three or four. It is to tie about your neck with a ribbon', and he hoped she would wear it every day as long as she lived. He asked if she would like an ell or two of Holland (cloth), and the same of mussoling (muslin). He sent calico to make a frock for little Ketty, and later asked Mary's cousin in Perth to choose a dress for his wife. He even sent the baby's nurse a new apron.

In December 1715 Iain met the King (James III/VIII) and wrote enthusiastically, but by February next year his tone had changed. 'The misfortunatt relations of our undertaking is grievous to be reported, for we were most unhumanly betrayed by the Earle of Marr, the Marquis of Huntly and the Earle of Seaforth by whose doings we were obliged to fly and disperce, many of our Nobility have left the Kingdom so that I durst nott venture to go to my dearest . . I doubt nott butt your life and living will be very uneasy to you, as for your house if they please you are to give it up. I am hopefull they will use you more kind than to extend their severity'

His optimism was not justified, and the Campbells put Mary and her children out of Dunollie. Iain urged her to go to Inveraray and plead for peaceful possession of her own, but 'you are nott to make known what way I am gone'. He told her to go to her father in Skye if her petition failed.

Iain was now on the run, a hunted man, and his letters became sparse. Mary's plea was not granted. She did not go to Skye, but had to board out her older children with different families in the district, while she herself kept the two youngest and went into hiding on the island of Kerrera, near Oban. She lived in a hut at Gylen, in conditions of great poverty and discomfort, and for part of the time, Iain seems to have been hiding in a cave on the mainland opposite to Kerrera. There she took him food, visiting him under cover of darkness. One result was that when Iain had to move on, he left her pregnant.

To add to her difficulties, she became the prey of local gossip. Although loyal clansmen brought her a meagre supply of food and necessities of life, she could not explain her pregnancy openly, and of course the worst interpretation was put upon it. She wrote an agonised letter to her husband, complaining that any man who visited her was assumed to be her lover, and she found this hard to bear.

After some years of this misery and loneliness, she found a lump in her breast, and even in those times, the implications were only too clear. She reported it to her husband, who was so fearful for her that he could not bring himself to open a letter from a relative, as he was convinced it contained news of her death from cancer. In the end the growth must have been benign, as Mary outlived her husband by decades.

Before the birth of the baby, Iain had to go abroad into exile, for his own safety. Sailing from Stornoway, he had a bad voyage ('it blew most horribly, I did not know what fear was till then'), but eventually he reached France and settled there. His main dread was for Mary, and the impending birth. He sent letters to her but received none back, which 'gives me grounds to suspect my dearest is nott in life'. When a relative wrote to say the birth was safely over, he accused her of concealing Mary's death from him.

At last he heard from Mary herself that little Johnny had arrived and was thriving, 'he's as good a child as ever went on woman's knee'. But Mary was utterly wretched, still persecuted by malicious gossip, and now in ill health. She fully expected to be dead by the time Iain came home again. He said this would be soon, and he would bring her a new dress. She said it could serve as her shroud. Her husband begged her to seek advice from a doctor 'and do not dy in greef and despaire, . . . I know all your distemper proceeds from greef . . .' He could recognise depression even from that distance. Her inadequate diet probably contributed to it.

All this time, Campbell of Glenmacrie was living in Dunollie, and Mary remained in Kerrera. The daughter Ketty was happy enough in her foster home, but little Allan was 'not well kept where he was', so Mary took him to join herself and Johnny in their hut at Gylen.

She wanted to go to Iain in France, but he was against it as his own plans were uncertain, and the journey to Bordeaux would be too much for his wife. She was not pleased: 'You say I am your only concern you have, which I do not doubt, butt I am very sure if you were as fond of my company as I would be of yours, you would not be so long without me'.

In 1718 the Argyle managers met and decided to grant Mary 300 merks yearly out of her own confiscated money, because she had behaved herself 'very prudently both in words and actions, which some of your sisters in affliction has not done'. They wanted to make a condition, that she must go to live in Skye, but she ignored this.

The following year the Jacobites planned a last attempt to seize power. The Earl Marischal, plotting this, wrote to Iain Ciar: 'I long for the time when I shall see your claymores and bagpipes again', ending with 'burn this letter'.

In March 1719 Iain joined the Earl Marischal in Stornoway, where a troop of Spanish mercenaries had been brought in. The battle of Glenshiel was fought in June, when Rob Roy MacGregor led the Jacobite force, and the Munros and MacKays were in the opposing Hanoverian army (commemorated by Iain Dall MacKay in his piobaireachd work *The Battle of Glenshiel*). The Jacobites were routed, and Iain Ciar had once more to go on the run. This was probably the most dangerous period in his life, as the Jacobite officers were now hunted down with ferocity.

Once again he seems to have come to Argyll and hidden in the hills near Kerrera, and must have visited his wife and children. A cousin wrote to him 'As to your Lady, she is whiles tender which was her ordinar which was occasioned by your dooings . . .' This was a roundabout way of saying that Mary was pregnant again.

She appreciated that Iain's situation was serious, and in October wrote in alarm: 'As for your coming to see me for God's sake doe not propos itt', as the danger was too great.

In November, quite unexpectedly, Mary was granted a lease of Dunollie, under the Forfeited Estates Act, and was able to return home. There, early in 1720, her daughter Anne was born. Iain was in hiding in Mull at the time, under the assumed name of John Houston. Once the birth was safely over, he left for Lochearn – but in January of the following year, Mary was buying a new maternity gown and ordering christening clothes for yet another happy event.

From 1721 to 1725, the letters are few, and Iain was still a fugitive. He spent some of the time in Ireland, where he visited the Earl of Antrim (not the one commemorated in the piobaireachd lament of that name, but one of his descendants). There is a story of his being attacked by a bandit called the Red Robber, on his way to see the Earl; Iain fought the man in single combat, and killed him, cut off his head and his silver buttons, and took them as a gift for the Earl.

Sir Duncan Campbell of Lochnell, one of his neighbours in the Lorne district, and probably the man for whom *Lochnell's Lament* was composed, wrote cordially, offering to intercede for Iain, so that he could come home – even though Sir Duncan was a Hanoverian. This came to nothing, and the next we hear of Iain, he had evidently been captured, as he, Stewart of Appin and Rob Roy were in Newgate Prison in London. They were sentenced to be transported to Barbados, and on 24th January 1727 were taken to Gravesend to be put on a ship about to sail. At the last possible moment, a messenger arrived with the King's pardon. It was all over, and he could go home to Dunollie.

After a time the ancestral lands were restored to him, at least in part, and he and Mary resumed family life. Three more children were born to them, but Iain had only ten years at Dunollie before he died there, in 1737. His piper, Ranald Ban MacDougall, made the *Lament for Iain Ciar,* possibly based on the same air as *The Glen Is Mine.*

LAMENT FOR CAPTAIN MACDOUGALL

Iain Ciar's grandson was Alexander MacDougall, known to his family as Sandy, and to the piping world as Captain MacDougall, for whom the lament was made in 1812 – and probably also a salute, a little earlier.

From the family correspondence published in 1984, we know quite a lot about this admirable young man. Born in 1785, he was the eldest son of Alexander 23rd Chief, and heir to the title and the MacDougall estates in and around Oban. Their seat was Dunollie Castle, which dominated the entrance to the harbour at Oban, but the castle itself had been abandoned by Sandy's father as the family home, and a fine mansion house built, just below it. Sandy was the first son, after three daughters.

At eighteen he was sent to Edinburgh to study while his father was trying to buy him a commission in the Army, at a rate the family could afford. He boarded in Edinburgh with the family's man of business, John Young, who on April 6th 1803 wrote to Sandy's father:

'. . . I cannot resist congratulating you upon having such an excellent and superior young man for a son, superior to any I ever knew. He has a great portion of natural and useful sense, he has a prodigious stock of intelligence from observation, he is assiduous in his studies to acquire knowledge, he is obliging and sweet-tempered, he is funny, jocular and shrewd in conversation, he has no ill habits of any kind that I can discover, he wishes to appear like a Gentleman without any extravagant ideas, he is shocked by every kind of profligacy and idle folly, in short he does everything with a consideration and wisdom that would do credit to the most experienced, all of which is truth as god made me . . . No person could give less disturbance in a house than he does, nor could any body be easier to please'.

Clearly a well brought up young man, of whom any parent would be proud.

Soon after this, Sandy joined the Army as a lowly Ensign in the 69th Regiment, buying promotion to Lieutenant the following year (promotion for Army officers was largely a matter of what you could afford). He longed to be a Captain with a Company of his own, and wrote home to ask for the wherewithal for this; he needed £500, and he says disarmingly to his father 'Do you think the Cows look as if they would get me a Company?' In other words, are they worth £500? The answer was no, and a few months later in 1804, he was hoping for a Company costing £950. His father promised to try to borrow the money, but again the plan came to nothing.

The 69th was sent to Jersey, where Sandy was invited to dine with General Gordon, an acquaintance of his father. He wrote home:

'I was engaged to dine with General Gordon upon Wednesday, which day being very cold, he being much afflicted with the Gout, together with the dinner not being ready in time, and the house smoking, the old hero scarcely spoke a word to any person'. Hardly the social event of the year.

On Christmas Day there was excitement in Jersey when a 44-gun ship, with 260 souls on board, was blown onto rocks. Sandy describes how he volunteered to help to launch small boats into the storm, to try to save the endangered men, women and children, 'but I foolishly got a compleat ducking'. In the end, all were saved, but not by Sandy.

Late in 1805, he finally became a Captain, in circumstances which are not entirely clear. He wrote to his brother from Peterhead:

'On 19th December last I was thro' the interest of that worthy man, the Duke of Argyll, promoted to a company in the 72nd Regt by purchase, on account of this I left Jersey . . . I set out from Dunolly to join the 2nd Battalion 72nd Regt which are quartered here, a tollerable pleasant seaport town, in summer a great watering place'.

It seems likely that the composition by Ranald Mor MacDougall, the Dunollie piper, named in the Notices of Pipers as the *Salute for Captain MacDougall*, was made at this time, when the newly created young Captain was at home on leave at Dunollie, in 1805.

Sandy was five years with the 72nd, but in 1810 he transferred to the 2nd Battalion 5th Regiment, in order to serve under Lord Wellington in the Peninsular Wars. Active service in Portugal offered quicker promotion and a more exciting life. He wrote home frequently, and his letters begin to show a certain sober maturity when real fighting was in prospect.

In July 1810, he wrote:

'The Army here are at present on the frontiers of Spain . . . Lord Wellington with the Headquarters have been moving about very much of late. I went there the other day to see Colin Melford [a cousin] who is Commandant at headqurs . . . I remained to dine with Lord Wellington . . . The enemy are at present pouring an immense force into Spain and have a large body of infantry and Cavalry before Ciudad Rodrigo [a frontier fortress held by the British] which has made a most noble defence – but I am afraid it has fallen as no firing has been heard today from that quarter. We are only about 25 miles away. Lord Wellington would have attacked them but for their immense superiority of cavalry. But I am in hope they will be kept out of this Country [Portugal] owing to its Mountainous Rock Barrier where a small force can act against a greater. Because of the bravery of the Troops and the Confidence they have in their General, to make use of Boney's own words, should he come with the wings of an Eagle, we shall meet him with the Roars of a Lion'.

This was his last letter to reach home. Early in 1812, Wellington stormed Ciudad Rodrigo and took it back from the French, but in the action, Sandy was killed. He was 27 years old.

His father wrote to the second son, John, who was in the Royal Navy:

'His death is a severe loss to us all, but God's will be done'.

A few weeks later, his mother wrote to John:

'How you must regret not being better acquainted with your excellent brother whose death is not only regretted by his family and friends but I may say by the country at large, for he was most universally esteemed, respected and beloved by all who knew him and even those who heard of the uncommon good character he bore. His excellent dispositions and warmth of friendship gained him the love and esteem of all who knew him, and his abilities of late years appeared to be far above what we ever imagined. Perhaps in short there is no better test of a young man's character than that which he bears amongst his Brother Officers and by all accounts he stood Very High indeed with his former associates as well as

The pine tree planted near Dunollie house, behind the castle, has been there since 1812. Because young Sandy (Captain MacDougall) had been killed in Spain, there was no grave for his family to tend, and they planted the pine tree as a memorial. It is now showing its age, but should last a few years yet.

with those with whom he lately served'.

This seems a curiously impersonal way for a grieving mother to write, but it must be remembered that John had been away in the Navy for years, and his family barely knew him as an adult; many of the family letters never reached him, or were delayed for months or years, so that this one might have been read by anyone.

The family piper was Ranald Mor MacDougall, then living at Moleigh, near Kilbride, to the south of Oban. He is sometimes described as being an old man at this time, the family's ancient piper, but in fact he cannot have been much older than his forties. Some describe him as Blind Ranald or Ranald Dall, but there is no evidence that he was sightless. He had watched Sandy grow up at Dunollie, and had made a Salute to him. The *Lament for Captain MacDougall,* which he composed in 1812, must have come from the heart.

A feature of the work as recorded in Angus MacKay's manuscript is the five crotchet beats in the last-but-one bar of the Ground. Some regard this as a mistake, possibly a copying error, but there is a footnote in a copy of the tune given by Pipe Major Robert Meldrum to John MacDougall Gillies:

'Play this part exactly as written. It often happens in Ranald MacDougall's compositions that near the finish there is generally one crotchet more in the bar than in any of the others' – in other words, this five-beat bar was Ranald's signature to the work. Or was it a family trade-mark?

Pipe Major Meldrum could not remember where this information originated, but he believed it was sent to him from Taymouth; it may have come from one of the MacDougall pipers at Aberfeldy, although he mentioned John Ban MacKenzie as a possible source. The comment implies a knowledge of several other works by Ranald Mor; we know of the *Salute* as well as the *Lament for Captain MacDougall,* but even the titles of any others seem to have been lost.

Since poor Sandy was buried in Spain, the family planted a Scots pine tree in his memory, on a mound in a field known as the Gean Tree field, behind Dunollie House. This tree is still (2003) there, now big and ancient, but unmistakable. A memorial plaque is on the wall of the ruined MacDougall chapel beside the old church at Kilbride.

Four years after Sandy's death, his father wrote to John of 'my distress of mind', and 'the suffering I labour under at the loss of Sandy', evidently still in depression from the bereavement.

Walter Scott visited the Oban district, collecting atmosphere for his poem *The Lord of the Isles.* In a note in the published work, he wrote: 'The heir of Dunolly fell lately in Spain, fighting under the Duke of Wellington, a death well becoming his ancestry'. Sandy's elder sister, Bell, called this 'a pretty tribute to poor Sandy's memory'.

SOURCES
Notices of Pipers
OPR Kilmore and Kilbride

Jeannie Campbell
Margaret and Alasdair MacPherson
Mrs MacArthur, Glenfeochan
Nancy Black
Charles Hunter
Oban histories
William Donaldson
Patrick MacDonald
Jean MacDougall

LOCHNELL

IN 1714, ARCHIBALD CAMPBELL, 6TH of LOCHNELL, died, and his son, who was an ardent Jacobite in a strongly Hanoverian family, kept the corpse unburied for nearly three weeks, for political purposes. He wanted to make 'a masked demonstration in favour of the Stuarts', disguising it as his father's funeral. But his Hanoverian neighbours saw through this, and turned up in some numbers, 'to be a check upon the Jacobites', as a contemporary letter put it. So some 2,500 men, well armed and appointed, arrived for the funeral, 500 of them being Lochnell's own force, commanded by Rob Roy MacGregor, and they were 'carrying with them a pair of colours belonging to the Earl of Breadalbane, and accompanied by the screams of thirteen bagpipes. Such a subject for a picture'. Screams? We gather that the writer (who is not named) was not a piper, but enjoyed the spectacle of the two parties glaring at each other over the grave.

DUNCAN CAMPBELL, 8th OF LOCHNELL, raised and commanded the 91st Argyllshire Highlanders (which became the 1st Argyll and Sutherland Highlanders). He rose to the rank of Lieut.General.

Ruairidh H. MacLeod, in *Pipes and Drums in the Royal Army*, 1745, says that Colin Campbell of Ballimore was killed at Culloden, fighting for the Hanoverian side, and his company was given to James Campbell. 'His piper was nominally JOHN MacILRODICH who had gone recruiting and had been absent ever since. Sir Duncan Campbell of Lochnell had written to Lord Loudon asking him to allow John MacIlrodich pyper to return home to his family, since he had only been *lent* to Sir Duncan's nephew Captain Colin of Ballimore. 'As now there will be no difficulty of getting pypers' he asked for him to be returned 'as he is, after our former Highland Customs, my family pyper'.'

This was confirmed in another letter from Lt Donald MacDonald of MacLeod's Company stationed at Glenelg. He wrote in 1746: 'We have neither Drum nor pipes. Mr Bisset tells me that the piper of the Company went by a furlough from Col. Campbell from Fort Augustus to Argyllshire, where there he is detained by Sir Duncan Campbell being only given by him for a tyme to Ballimore, so Beggs your Ldp. may order a Drum or piper for the company here.'

Pipers now became increasingly hard to find. By May 1794, Lochnell was writing to Campbell of Knock: 'if you can meet with one or two good pipers, handsome fellows and steady, you might go as far as 30 guineas (as Bounty Money) for each'. A country schoolmaster's annual salary was about twelve pounds, so this Bounty was most generous.

The seat of the Campbells of Lochnell was not in the hills beside Lochnell. In Sir Duncan's time a spacious mansion, Lochnell Castle, was built in Benderloch, at the head of the bay known now as Ardmucknish Bay. It was enlarged by his successor at a cost of £15,000. In 1859 it caught fire and was burned to the ground, leaving only an old observatory tower standing on the site. This too had been burned, in 1850, but the remains of it are still a local landmark. After this, in the mid -19th century, the present mansion house was built further round the bay. It is no longer in Campbell hands. In early May each year the Highlands and Islands piping competition is held there.

SOURCES
Analecta Scotica I, 14, private letter, February 20 1714
Piping Times
Clan Campbell, The House of Argyle
Statistical Account for Argyll
Ordnance Gazetteer for Scotland vol. II

LOCHNELL'S LAMENT and SCARCE OF FISHING

From their association with Lochnell, near Oban, both of these works are to be linked with the Nether Lorne district of Argyll. Lochnell is a freshwater loch in the hills above Oban. The name is Gaelic, Loch nan Eala, and means Loch of the Swans. It is close to Moleigh, where the MacDougall pipers lived.

Of the two works, *Lochnell's Lament* is probably the older by some sixty years. It appears to be a genuine lament for one of the Campbell lairds of Lochnell, probably Sir Duncan Campbell of Lochnell, who was for some years the M.P. for Argyll, and was a dominant figure in the Lorne district. In 1729 he was an officer in the Black Watch Company, later to become part of the Black Watch or 42nd Regiment.

Sir Duncan's first wife was a daughter of the Earl of Seaforth, Lady Isabella MacKenzie. She had previously been married to one of the MacLeods of Dunvegan – the one who dismissed his pipers and replaced them with hunting dogs. When she died, Sir Duncan married Margaret, the daughter of Daniel Campbell of Shawfield, giving him a connection with the Campbells of Shawfield and Islay, the family who later had Colin Mor Campbell, John Campbell and Angus MacKay as their pipers.

Sir Duncan died in 1765. It is not known who his piper was, other than the

*A red-throated diver, or rain-goose,
a bird related to the American loon.*
(Photograph by kind permission of Laurie Campbell,
Photographer,
Paxton, Berwick-on-Tweed).

John MacIlrodich mentioned above; are we to assume the lament was composed by him? It is irregular in form, and appears only in the Campbell Canntaireachd manuscript of piobaireachd, compiled in the 1790s. None of the later published collections has this work. It was probably well known locally, and it should be remembered that Colin Campbell who wrote the Canntaireachd manuscript was himself a Nether Lorne man. The work is not widely known among pipers, probably because Angus MacKay did not include it in his collection.

The origins of *Scarce of Fishing* are more complex. All the early published collections except Angus MacKay's give it the title *Lochnell's Lament*, although it is not the tune alluded to above. To avoid confusion, Angus's title, *Scarce of Fishing*, has been adopted by the piping world, although this in itself creates a confusion all its own.

Most of the difficulty arises from Angus' use of an obsolete Gaelic word *geadhgaoban*, which he makes more difficult by mis-spelling it in his manuscript: there it appears, in Angus' own handwriting, as *geoghoeben*. This defeats most of us, including many Gaelic speakers.

The translation of geadhgaoban is given in (some) old Gaelic dictionaries as Raingeese, another obsolete word, old Scots this time (but I am told that the word Raingeese is still used in Orkney and Shetland). And at this point, if we reach it at all, we tend to give up, and assume that *Scarce of Fishing* means that the herring had failed and folk were starving and that this is a piobaireachd lament for their suffering. But this is far from the truth, and not what the title is about at all.

Loch Nell, in the district of Lorne, to the east of Oban. This loch is associated with two piobaireachd works, Lochnell's Lament and Scarce of Fishing.

Raingoose is the old word for a large bird now called the Red-throated Diver, related to the American Loon. It nests on remote lochs and is now quite a solitary bird. It had its name from its weird cry which is heard on calm summer evenings and makes the hair stand up on the back of the neck with its eeriness; this is said to be a sign that rain is coming, hence the name. It seems a safe enough prediction in the West Highlands. Nowadays you are lucky to see one at all, or at most a pair, but in the early 1800s they were plentiful. And they were subject to sudden population explosions, when hundreds of them might invade one loch.

Lochnell was one such, on the estate of Campbell of Lochnell, and the name itself suggests it was a haven for wildfowl of all kinds. Raingeese winter in coastal sea waters, and in the spring they invade inland lochs for nesting.

Bearing all that in mind, let us have a look at what Angus MacKay wrote. It is in Gaelic and English, and he put it in his manuscript as an explanatory note, in his own handwriting.

He wrote first 'Spiocaireachd Iasgaich, Scarse of Fishing' . This spelling Scarse was normal in the 18th century, so Angus was probably using a slightly archaic form. He may have meant it to indicate a noun, equivalent of our Scarcity. The usual Gaelic word for Scarce and for Scarcity is Gann, which is both a noun and an adjective – as some of our words, such as straight, good, round, bad, square and many others, can be used.

But the word he uses, Spiocaireachd, does not mean Scarcity so much as Being niggardly with something, Refusing to part with it, Preventing its being taken, Grudging it – and this, too, was one of the earlier meanings of Scarce in English; people used to say 'She's scarce with the vittles', meaning 'She's grudging with the food'.

So perhaps the title really means Prevention of Fishing.

And then Angus added a note in explanation of this title, this time in Gaelic: 'Tha Spiocaireachd Iasgaich am bliadhna an Geogheoben etc'. That 'etc' probably means there were ducks and swans there as well, and the rest of the sentence translates as 'There is prevention of fishing in the year of the raingeese'.

Does this present tense mean that this year the raingeese are wrecking the fishing, or does it mean every time the raingeese come, the fishing is ruined?

It was William Ross, the Queen's piper, who in 1869 gave the work the title *The Fishers of Geogh Brodinn*, which seems to be a garbled corruption of geadh-gaoban, clearly not understood by Ross – who was a Gaelic speaker. He must have had access to a tradition about the raingeese, but in the title he has confused geadh meaning some sort of goose with the Gaelic word geogh, meaning a rocky cleft in a sea-cliff, a word which you would not find in a placename on a freshwater loch. A later edition gives it as *George Brodin*.

Just in case his comment was still obscure, Angus added a note in pencil, in his own hand, saying 'Lochnell's Lament – Geoghoeben at Loch Nell'. So we take it that the fishing on Lochnell had been ruined by the greedy raingeese, and the title of this work, as Angus MacKay understood it, anyway, was really Campbell of Lochnell's complaint about those pesky birds taking over his loch – and we have to wonder why he did not take up wild-fowling instead. The estate at that time was one of those big sporting concerns where friends were invited to come up and shoot anything that moved. (But presumably nesting time was the close season for raingeese?)

So the title seems to be a mockery – but how did that come about?

There is the older, genuine lament from about 1765, and its title seems to have been transferred to the later work, presumably with ironic intent. But how? And why? Perhaps we can reconstruct a possible explanation.

A piping friend was out walking in atrocious weather, and the wind caught his waterproof cape and tore it. 'Oh dear' he said, '*MacKintosh's Lament* born again'. This may be a parallel: when Campbell of Lochnell complained bitterly about his fishing, was the name of the old lament resurrected, with irony? Is it possible that a local song had been made about Lochnell's discomfiture (perhaps made by the local poachers)? Was this song then given the old title, with comic intent?

And was that song then made into the Ground of a piobaireachd? Donald MacDonald may have got it at this stage, for he gives a Ground only, in his manuscript, and he gives no timing at all, just the notes in sequence as if it was just a tune he had heard sung or hummed – and that was in the 1820s.

Perhaps someone, we don't know who (could it have been Angus himself?), said 'That's a nice Ground, let's add some variations', and *Scarce of Fishing* as we know it today was composed. These variations are remarkably regular, as if composed by a computer, so closely do they follow the Ground. It has been said that a good composer always starts with a variation, usually the Siubhal, and works back to the Ground, but not in this case. It is obvious that the Ground is the basis for every one of those variations.

The above is of course pure speculation, a theoretical reconstruction of the way it might have happened. Perhaps it is a shame that the little Lochnell joke was killed stone dead when all those weighty variations were added.

Naturalists say that when red-throated divers congregated on a loch in large numbers, they would behave like other geese and murmur continually to each other, make a sort of low gobbling noise as they chatted quietly among themselves. Could it be that if *Scarce of Fishing* is played with this in mind, the same effect would be heard? I have never come across a player who did have that in mind, and this may explain why the variations often seem a bit shapeless. But when they are sung in Canntaireachd, that murmuring effect may sometimes be heard.

SOURCES
Piobaireachd Society books
Haddow
Dwelly's Dictionary
The Oxford English Dictionary (13 volume edition)
Scottish Natural Heritage scientists

VISITORS TO OBAN

IN 1784 THE FRENCHMAN BARTHOLEMY Faujas de St Fond, from the Rhone district of France, made a tour of the West Highlands by way of Inveraray and Dalmally, leading a party of four. His comments on a piobaireachd recital he had heard in Edinburgh are well-known, and he encountered the pipes again in Oban.

The party had come to grief not far from Oban the previous night, when one of their carriages stuck in the Glencruitten burn, and they had to be rescued by 'semi-nude natives' and escorted into Oban. There they found lodging in an inn of which the Frenchman had a low opinion.

Next day, he was feeling unwell, so stayed at the inn when the rest of the party went out for the day. He was hoping for peace and quiet, but a local piper arrived, to entertain him. St Fond said he himself 'could distinguish only one tune at all times on the pipes', and with his headache he found the noise unbearable. He begged the man to stop, but to no avail. In the end he took the piper by the hand, led him out of the house, gave him a generous amount of money to go away, and returned thankfully to the house. But the piper thought he was being paid for his lovely playing, and came back, and 'with a toss of his head, commenced to play again, louder and longer'.

The piping in Oban seems not to have appealed much to the tourist trade. In 1800, 'fine big Dr John Leyden', a geologist, wrote of 'the sounds and chatter of the inn's taproom, the bagpipe playing of a piper' which, he said, reminded him of 'that with which the ears of the damned are regaled' (how did he know that?).

Robert Buchanan published a book *The Land of Lorne* in 1871, in which he describes how he built himself a house in Oban. His local workmen, all Gaelic speakers, he considered to be lazy but interesting, 'fine natural bits of humanity, full of intelligence and quiet affection.'

Oban in the mid-19th century when it was beginning to develop as a centre of tourism.

'Noteworthy among them was old DUNCAN CAMPBELL who had in his younger days been piper in a Highland regiment, and who now advanced in years worked hard all day as a hodsman, and nightly – clean, washed and shaven – played to himself on the beloved pipes till overpowered by sleep. Duncan was simply delicious. More than once he brought up the pipes and played on the hillsides while the workmen danced. These pipes were more to him than bread and meat. As he played them, his face became glorified. His skill was not great, and his tunes had a strange monotony about them, but they gave to his soul a joy passing the glory of battle or the love of women. He was never too weary for them in the evening, though the day's work had been ever so hard and long. Great was his pride and joy that day when the house was finished, and with pipes playing and ribbons flying he headed the gleeful workmen as they marched away into the town'.

Could these tunes with a strange monotony about them have been piobaireachd? And who was this former piper in a Highland regiment? There are so many Duncan Campbells in army piping that it is not possible to identify this one – but I wonder how he reacted to being described as 'simply delicious'.

JOHN MACCOLL

THE PAPER GIVEN BY SEUMAS MacNeill to the conference of the Piobaireachd Society in 1991 has become the classic work on John MacColl, and was later reprinted in the Piping Times. I would not presume to try to improve on this, so with the permission of the Piobaireachd Society, Seumas' paper is here reproduced, very slightly shortened from the original:

'John MacColl was born at Kentallen in Duror on the 6th January 1860. For several centuries there have been MacColls in Duror of Appin, . . . and John's direct ancestors can be traced as far back as the seventeenth century . . . Three of his great-granduncles fought at Culloden. The eldest was severely wounded, and according to tradition, he begged his brothers to kill him – lest a worse fate overtake him and he fall into the hands of the English. This drastic deed was duly carried out, but with what anguish to the younger lads. When they eventually made their way back to Appin one arrived minus a hand. The inference is that grief, conscience and the fact that the Highland and the Biblical views of justice coincide, had combined to destroy the offending member.

'The youngest of the four brothers, John, was the great-grandfather of our John MacColl. He was too young to fight at Culloden, and was probably born about 1735. His son John was born in 1781 and died in 1866, having had six children. The fourth of these was Dugald, who had seven children, the youngest being John MacColl.

'Dugald MacColl was the tailor in Kentallen, but, as in all Highland communities, the struggle to earn a living was never allowed to encroach on the time set aside for the essential pleasures of life. Dugald was an enthusiastic piper and fid-

The birthplace of John MacColl in Kentallen, Appin. He was born here in 1860. The cottage is typical of most of the houses in Kentallen at that time.
(BY COURTESY OF THE COLLEGE OF PIPING)

dler, and no doubt his children were born to music and brought up on a diet of meal and marches, sgadan and strathspeys.' [meal is oatmeal, sgadan are herring].

'He was probably what used to be called a 'country piper' – one with little formal instruction, mainly self-taught but learning what he could from others like himself. Almost certainly he was one of the new breed of 19th century pipers, a player of the little music only, with no knowledge of piobaireachd.'

His wife, Elizabeth MacInnes, came of a musical family, too. She was related to Angus MacInnes, piper to Stewart of Fasnacloich (in Appin), and also to Paul MacInnes who had been a successful competitor at the Edinburgh competitions in the 1780s.

'Dugald MacColl taught all his sons to pipe. No doubt the four boys were all keen to make music – but young John had an entirely different approach to it from his brothers. While the others were happy that their home was a centre for music and song, John had within him the relentless attitude which afflicts all successful competitors – to do well is not enough, the only satisfaction is in being the best.

'He was not strategically placed to become a champion piper. He did not live near any expert, nor did he come from a line of great pipers. His lack of training in piobaireachd was something which was to diminish his status for ever in the eyes of those who had been fortunate enough to absorb ceol mor with their mother's milk.

'By the time he was seventeen he was looked on as the most promising piper in the district. He almost certainly had learned everything he could from the pipers round about, and he had read all that was available about pipers present and past.

'In the summer of 1877 then, with a good conceit of himself, he set off to play at his first piping competition, at Bonawe Highland Games. The way by road was long, so young John walked the 27 miles through Glen Sallach. By burnside and fragrant peaty pools, with summer flowers dancing before him, with joy and happy anticipation in his heart, John MacColl set out on his career of becoming one of piping's immortals.

'Coming home, it was a different story. Down the glen he trudged, sick at heart, the feet moving slowly. He had imagined he would conquer the world in a day, but the world hardly noticed him. Instead, he had heard piping such as he did not dream could exist – instruments that sang like organs, chanters ringing sweet and true, and pipers whose fingers rippled without effort. Beside them his efforts were puny. He was a country player who had been foolish enough to pit himself against the professionals.

'Many a young lad would have given up after such a disappointment, overcome by the shame of facing family and friends who had expected so much. But John MacColl was obsessed with the need to succeed, and before he arrived home he was planning how he would work and work until he could play even better than those who had barely noticed his presence.

'His first need was to find a real expert who could teach him properly. Taymouth Castle was the centre of the piping world at this time, but young John barely gave it a thought. In fact by the time he reached the watershed of Glen Sallach, he had decided that the place for him was Glasgow.

'. . . At Bonawe Games young John had heard a man from Glasgow play, a man called Donald MacPhee, who – according to Ronald Meldrum – was the best piper in Scotland at that time (1877). So Glasgow it was to be.

'First he had to earn enough money to get there, and to keep himself there. It so happened that his cousin Robert was manager at Bonawe quarries, so John became a quarryman, working long hard hours and saving every penny for the important move to the south.

'One year later, by the autumn of 1878, he had saved the sum of £17 – not a fortune, perhaps, but sufficient to take him to Glasgow and keep him in reasonable comfort for at least six months. So off he went for the second time.

'Donald MacPhee had a shop in the Union Arcade in Hope Street, a small bagpipe business which later became the firm of Peter Henderson Ltd. This was the centre of John MacColl's life for the next two years, for here, in Glasgow, he became a piper. MacPhee corrected his faults and taught him how to finger accurately and then how to express the popular marches, strathspeys and reels of the time. He was also introduced to piobaireachd, and received a great deal of instruction in the great music. MacPhee had published, in addition to his 'Tutor', a collection of piobaireachd consisting of eighteen tunes. No doubt, as is the way of masters with pupils, this was the textbook from which he taught John MacColl.

'John MacColl stayed two years in Glasgow, all of that time practising and learning. In 1880, however, Donald MacPhee died, at the early age of 39 years. There was nothing now to keep the young lad in Glasgow, so he decided to go home. His father had moved into Oban, and set up business at 17 High Street, but before John could begin to think of this as his home, he was offered the job of piper to MacDonald of Dunach, a small estate south of Oban.

'He was now twenty years of age, fresh from two years of constant tuition of the highest order. At Dunach he had time to let his playing mature, and the following summer – four years after his fruitless first attempt – he was ready to try the games once again.

'This time it was a different story. He was competing against the giants of piping – Ronald Meldrum, Angus MacRae, John MacDougall Gillies – so he could not expect to reach the top immediately, but he did let them know he was there, and he did win prizes. When in September of that year he won the Gold Medal at the Argyllshire Gathering in Oban, then he had really arrived.

'After winning the Gold Medal at Oban in 1881, he was awarded the Gold at Inverness in 1883, and the Former Winners in '84, '88 and 1900. He tied with John MacDougall Gillies in the Senior Open at Oban in 1901, won it outright in 1902, and added a Gold Medal for singing at the Mod.

'Also as piper at Dunach at that time was one Ronald MacKenzie from Ord, in Skye, who had been taught by Alexander MacLennan of Inverness. He was reputed to be an excellent player, and no doubt he did much to help young John, especially in his piobaireachd playing. This was the last formal instruction John MacColl received'.

H.L.(Harry) MacDONALD of Dunach, born in 1871 and educated at Harrow and Cambridge, was a fine athlete, and was said to be 'a proficient performer on the bagpipe'. He married a MacDonald cousin who was immortalised by Willie Lawrie in the march *Mrs H.L. MacDonald of Dunach* (see Jeannie Campbell, Patrons of Piping)

Seumas goes on: 'While at Dunach John MacColl began to compose. At first his efforts were tentative and simple, giving little hint of things to come. His strathspey *Mrs MacDonald of Dunach* is an exercise in composition rather than the free-flowing of real genius, but he soon found better sources of inspiration.

'The county families of Argyll have long been famous for encouraging piping, and none more so than the Campbells of Kilberry. John MacColl travelled to Kilberry many times with the MacDonalds of Dunach, and as a result of these visits he composed a slow march, *Archibald Campbell of Kilberry*. This is a much better tune, and it is rather surprising that it was not followed by more of the same type.

'While at Kilberry he met John Carruthers and his family, who had the home farm on the Kilberry Estate. One of the girls – Helen – was the real reason for his frequent visits, and she in time became Mrs John MacColl, later to be immortalised in the famous march.

Kilbowie Cottage, on the Gallanach road out of Oban. The MacColl family moved here in 1884. (PHOTOGRAPH BY COURTESY OF THE COLLEGE OF PIPING)

'Life at Dunach was very pleasant for a piper, but there must have been some irksome restrictions, too. John MacColl was now a regular competitor at the games, and soon after he was married he found that he could actually support his wife and family quite comfortably without the need for a regular job. He left Dunach therefore, moved into the High Street, Oban, and for the next 25 years lived entirely through teaching piping and competing at Highland games. Nobody in the history of piping has done this before, and nobody has done it since. He was the first truly professional piper since the MacCrimmons.

'With freedom to play bagpipes any time – all day every day if he wished – his standard of performance reached full maturity. In 1884 he won the Gold Medal at Inverness, and in 1888 he won the Centenary Medal at this meeting – while one of his pupils, William Boa, won the Gold Medal. In this same year he moved into the spacious Kilbowie Cottage, a mile from Oban on the Gallanach road. In 1900 he won the Clasp at Inverness, and in 1902 he won the first prize for piping at the Paris exhibition. Wherever there was a competition he had to be there, for this was his living.'

The Census for Oban in 1901 lists John MacColl at Kilbowie Cottage, and he is described as 'Professional Piper', a designation I have never seen elsewhere in the records.

Seumas continues:

'Nevertheless, throughout this period of his life, from about 1883 until 1908, John MacColl led what might have been a rather precarious existence financially, but for the fact that he was talented not only as a piper. His son, John

Carruthers MacColl, has recorded his memories of the stories of this time:

"He did tell me of finishing a dance, throwing off his kilt (having running shorts underneath) and competing in the hundred yards race. Then putting his kilt and things on ready for the next dance. This, of course, was just as a professional to augment his prize money for the day. Naturally his major earnings came from playing the pipes, dancing and teaching.

"Before the establishment of the Army School of Piping in Edinburgh under the late Pipe-Major William Ross there was an arrangement whereby my father taught individuals and groups of pipers attached to various Highland regiments, which meant travelling around Scotland in the winter months visiting Campbeltown, Inveraray, and even at times the Outer Hebrides.

"In the summer months, from June to the end of September, there were games in all sorts of places – villages and towns throughout Scotland, and even England and Ireland. He was away from home practically all summer travelling round the Games with only short breaks of a day or two back to Oban. My mother often told me of the excitement of these visits and the presents for the family – my sisters, brother and myself. It must have been lucrative in these days as he told me – and it is recorded – that he could earn £40 in an afternoon from piping, dancing and athletics – quite a lot of money in the eighties and nineties of last century !"

'The standard of living he provided for his family was far above the average for the period. An income of £40 in one day may have been the maximum for him, but it was not a unique occasion. At the time £40 was almost as much as a policeman, for example, could earn in a year. In addition to the normal comforts of life he had many of the luxuries, including a yacht which he raced with considerable success – naturally. The yacht was called *The Roe*, and William MacLennan (from whom John MacColl is believed to have derived much of his interest in march playing) used to call it "the dear boat".

'. . . Throughout all this time his ability to compose was improving, until he became widely recognised as of the very first rank, with claims to being the greatest composer of marches of all time – a claim which is no less valid today. A seemingly endless flow of original competition marches came from his fingers. *Jeannie Carruthers* was named after his wife's sister, who helped with the nursing of the children. Originally it was a lullaby, later made into the famous march. His own favourite was *John MacFadyen of Melfort*, called after a friend who was the proprietor of the Culfail Hotel. It was composed in 1905.

'Between the Boer War and the first World War John MacColl was employed by the Army on a part-time basis during the winter. His job was to go round the territorial regiments giving instruction and inspiration. His work in fact laid the foundation, in part at least, of the Army School of Piping.

'Two of these regiments had an even closer association for him – the Black Watch and the Scottish Horse, for he was a member of each of them in turn. The former apparently made no impact on him, but when he left the latter he composed the splendid 6/8 tune, *John MacColl's Farewell to the Scottish Horse*.

'Piping however did not occupy all of this time. He was a singer of note, winning a gold medal for Gaelic singing at the Luss Mod. He was a more than competent violinist, and even if he had never played pipes he would be remembered in other spheres – as John C. MacColl relates:

"In the games off-season he played shinty – his brothers and he excelled at the game – also football, and in later years, golf. As a youngster I was very proud of his Scotland jersey – he played shinty for Scotland against Ireland in 1887. At football he played for an Oban team (Glenmore) in local competitions and for the District of Lorne in district matches. Golf I suppose was a natural follow-on to shinty, and trophies now in my possession show that he was the Oban club champion in 1895 and 1896. His club handicap was plus two at the time.

"He was a member of the Renfrew Golf Club with me and I have a little token he received for holing out in one stroke at the fourth hole when he was 71".

'But in spite of his talents, piping was far and away his principal interest.

'His piobaireachd playing was a worry to many enthusiasts of his day – not because he was unsuccessful, but because he was not a strong link in the traditional line. One said of him, 'In ceol mor he lacked expression as compared with MacDougall Gillies, but played very correctly, and in consequence seldom failed to secure prizes'. John MacDonald, Inverness, however said 'In his playing of the *Kiss of the King's Hand* he once gave one of the most harmonious performances I ever listened to. On that occasion he seemed to be carried away by his playing. That was at Birnam'.

'Whatever his piobaireachd background he did manage to compose three pieces of ceol mor, two of which won first prizes in piobaireachd composing competitions.

'At last however the long, long summer had to end, and John MacColl left the life of a free piper and settled for something more mundane. In 1908 the Glasgow firm of R.G.Lawrie decided to start making bagpipes, and they asked John MacColl to take charge of this branch of their work. So ended the touring of the games. He was then 48 years of age and no doubt quite happy to settle down. (He lived at 34 Claddens Quadrant, as Jeannie Campbell tells us). Glasgow was now a thriving place for pipers, with John MacDougall Gillies in charge of Peter Henderson's – and the two used to meet and exchange ideas.

'In Glasgow he continued to take an active part in piping affairs, teaching many aspiring players and attending regularly the Saturday night meetings of the Scottish Pipers' Association.

'He retired from Lawrie's in 1925, but continued actively composing and teaching, for many years. In 1933 he produced *Captain Duncan MacGregor*, a modern bagpipe strathspey of considerable technical difficulty. His last great composition was *The Clan MacColl*, which he wrote for the clan in 1934.

'Perhaps his years in Glasgow were something of an anticlimax for him after the adventurous life of a free and independent piper, but they were valuable years, nonetheless. With MacDougall Gillies he built piping in Glasgow to a level from

John MacColl in his heyday, wearing some of the many medals he won for his piping.

which it is now unlikely to descend, and the magic of his music has been transmitted by pupils, so that now probably all of us have a little of it in our make-up.

'He died on the 8th of June, 1943. At his funeral John MacDonald of the Glasgow Police played the *Lament for the Children*.

'The tune however which professional pipers always associate with his name is not a lament, but a march, and personally *The Argyllshire Gathering* is the one for me. His best memorial is the playing of it every year in Oban on Games Day, by the cream of the pipers, as they parade through the town which was his home for so many years.'

Seumas then went on to speak of his own links with John MacColl. He remembered seeing him judging in the MacLellan Galleries in Glasgow, in the 1930s, 'a little round bald headed man', and later John MacFadyen said to Seumas 'Do you not remember the little well dressed gentleman first on the left inside the door of Room 7 in the Highlanders Institute on a Saturday night? That was John MacColl'.

Seumas spoke of Donald MacLean ('Wee Donald MacLean') who was a pupil of John MacColl for many years: Donald said that John taught the open C to pupils that he thought would never be any good, but if he thought they were going to be decent pipers he taught them to play the closed C right from the beginning.

Seumas's cousin, Alex MacNeill, was another pupil, and said his lesson was always due to end at the time the pubs closed in Glasgow – but John would cut it short and finish ten minutes early in order to get out quickly for a large one, 'in the normal fashion of lots of pipers'.

Speaking of John MacColl's family, Seumas said he had four children, two girls and two boys. DUGALD MacCOLL was the elder boy, but was a hopeless piper; Jeannie Campbell tells us that he was also employed at Lawries as a bagpipe maker.

His younger brother JOHN CARRUTHERS MacCOLL was a first-class player. He played in the City of Glasgow Pipe Band, and in the Territorial Band, and had competed on the circuit. He held three World Championship medals (1921, 1922, 1923). His mother put a stop to his piping; she had suffered enough while her husband had been competing, and she said firmly that one competing piper in the family was quite enough. He went to work for Babcock and Wilcox in Renfrew, as an engineer, and when he became a manager the firm gave him the use of the first car ever registered in Renfrewshire, and on his retirement he was allowed to keep it. He died in May 1990.

John MacColl's nephew, ARCHIBALD ROBERTSON MacCOLL (1873-1941) was born in Ballachulish, and became a stonemason. He won the Gold Medal at Inverness in 1892, and the MacCrimmon Shield at Cowal in 1912, as well as being an excellent march player. He emigrated to Queensland, Australia, in 1913, with his family, but served in the 1914-18 War with the Australian forces. He then went back to teaching piping in Australia, and was a successful band trainer He also taught Highland dancing. He died in Brisbane at the age of 68.

ANGUS MacCOLL from Oban is a grand-nephew of John MacColl, and ALLAN MacCOLL is also related.

John M. MacKenzie, in the discussion which followed Seumas's talk, said that one of John MacColl's closest friends was Willie Thomson, from Campbeltown, who taught Ronnie MacCallum; Thomson, a pupil of John MacDonald, Inverness, was piper to the MacNeills of Ugadale, and he used to meet John MacColl at the Argyllshire Gathering. The MacColl family and the Thomsons used to meet up for the Gathering, and take a house in Oban for a few days. The tune *Leaving Lunga* was composed jointly by Willie Thomson and John MacColl. Was this a different tune from the one of the same name composed by John Gordon, or did they make it over?

John MacColl's pupils included William Lawrie, and William Wilson. Wee Donald MacLean was his pupil for more than ten years (see below). There is a story that John MacColl was asked by one of his pupils, 'Mr MacColl, how old are the pipes?' to which he replied: 'Oh, very old, very old indeed. It says in the Bible that Moses was found among the reeds'.

The compositions of John MacColl:

Acha-Baba SM
Allan Gilmore Tom of Canna 2/4 M 4
Archibald Campbell of Kilberry 2/4 SM 2
The Argyllshire Gathering 2/4 M 4
The Argyll Squadron (Scottish Horse) 6/8 M (see PT Feb 1987)
Arthur Bignold of Lochrosque 2/4 M 4
The Braes of Kentallen M
Captain Duncan McGregor S 4
The Clan MacColl 2/4 M 4
Clan MacMillan M
(possibly) *The Cromarty Rangers March (71st Highlanders Quickstep)* 2/4 M. (This appears in the collection published by William Ross, the Queen's piper, with a note 'Copied from J.McColl', but it seems unlikely that it was a McColl composition).
Eobhan Ruadh MacFarlane M
Golfing at St Andrews M
H.L.MacDonald of Dunach SM. This is sometimes called *H.L. MacDonald's Favourite*
(Miss) Jeannie Carruthers 2/4 M 4
John MacColl's Farewell to the Scottish Horse 6/8 M 4
John MacFadyen of Melfort 2/4 M 4
Leaving Lunga 2/4 M 4 (attributed to J. Gordon, but John MacColl and William Wilson are said to have composed it jointly: did they arrange it?)
MacAlpine Downie of Appin M
Major Byng M. Wright 2/4 M 4
Major Byng M. Wright's Farewell to the 8th Argylls 2/4 M 4
Mrs John MacColl 2/4 M 4

Mrs MacDonald of Dunach S 2
The Piper's Excitement R 2
The Piper's Farewell to Paris M
The Scottish Horse 2/4 M (see PT June 1998)
    John MacColl made three piobaireachd works:
N.M. MacDonald's Lament P
Donald MacPhee's Lament P
Lament for Neil MacEachern of Conespie Islay 1933 P
    John MacColl also made a setting of *Lady Mackintosh's Reel* R 2
    A tune called *Coirechoille Blend* by John MacColl is named in a letter to the Piping Times in July 1973.
    And Willie Lawrie made *John MacColl's March to Kilbowie Cottage* 2/4 M 4 as well as *Mrs H.L. MacDonald of Dunach* 2/4 M 4.
    Some of the above works were unpublished and are found in manuscript form at the College of Piping, along with other, unnamed works by John MacColl, and an archive of his photographs and memorabilia.

SOURCES
Seumas MacNeill, Piobaireachd Society Conference Proceedings 1991 and Piping Times January-May 1998
Jeannie Campbell, Patrons of Piping, Piping Times, 1999
Pekaar

ARGYLLSHIRE GATHERING

THE NOTICES OF PIPERS, UNDER Argyllshire, have a photograph, taken in 1906, of worthies attending the Argyllshire Gathering.

    The Argyllshire Gathering is held every year, nowadays towards the end of August. It was inaugurated on 25 August 1871, and was a big social event, with balls, regatta and entertainments as well as the Games and the piping competitions. Today the social side is not to the fore, but the Gathering is still a two-day affair. This is probably because the Gathering was once two separate Games, held by the Lorn Ossianic Society on the first day, but the Argyllshire Gathering itself on the second day. The Oban Times commented that the Argyllshire Gathering was really for the gentry of Argyll, the County, who looked down their noses at the Lorn Ossianic, which was more for the common people. It was well into the 1880s before the two were combined into the Argyllshire Gathering as we know it.
    The Gold Medal for piobaireachd was presented by the Highland Society of London, and the first competition for it was in 1873 (see below). It was some time before the Senior competition for former Gold Medal winners was started, and meanwhile there was one instance of the Gold being won twice – by John MacBean. After 1879 first prize winners were excluded.

A Regatta in Oban Bay during the 19th century. Part of the Argyllshire Gathering, the Regatta continued until the early 1900s.

On the Wednesday nowadays all the piobaireachd events are held indoors simultaneously, in different hotels and halls throughout Oban. This is irritating for anyone who wishes to hear both the Gold and the Senior Piobaireachd (equivalent of the Clasp at Inverness), as they overlap almost completely. The Silver Medal and the MacGregor Memorial piobaireachd competition for players under 22 are also held on the Wednesday. On the Wednesday evening the Former Winners' March Strathspey and Reel competition is in the Corran Halls, but the rest of the Light Music is played at the Games on the Thursday, in the open air at Mossfield Park.

For some players the Wednesday is a severe test of stamina: it has been known for a piper to have to compete in the Gold Medal competition and, immediately before or after that, in the Senior, and then again in the evening, in the Former Winners MSR. It is too much, and players cannot give of their best when under such strain.

A feature of the Thursday is the march of the stewards from the centre of the town to the Games field, starting at 10 a.m. A band formed by the competing pipers, playing in unison, is followed by the stewards and any member of the public who enjoys marching to the pipes, usually a large crowd. There are no drums, and this parade gives the lie to the myth that it is impossible to march to a pipe band without drums.

The pipe major of the band is the winner of the Gold Medal the previous day, and if he (or she) has no experience as a pipe major, this can be a considerable ordeal. Before World War II the parade was always led by the senior serving Pipe Major of the British Army, but this convention was abandoned after the war.

1893 was the first time the piping competitions were held indoors, in the Drill Hall, because of atrocious weather, but after that the Gathering continued out of doors.

The first President was the Marquis of Lorne, eldest son of the Duke of Argyll and son-in-law of Queen Victoria – the Gathering was started to mark the occasion of his marriage to Princess Louise – but since 1901, the President has always been the Duke of Argyll (10th – 13th). A large force of stewards runs the piping events, and they are drawn from the landed gentry of Argyll and others of standing in the local community.

One of the stewards, ANGUS NICOL, has been for many years a staunch supporter of the Gathering, serving as Senior Steward in 1983 and 1998.

He also sponsors the prizes for the Silver Medal competition. As well as for this, the piping world owes him a longstanding debt for the excellent reports of piping competitions which he writes throughout the year for the Times newspaper, the only British daily paper which takes piping seriously. It does seem extraordinary that none of the Scottish papers can see beyond the facetiousness which we expect from the English on the subject of the pipes, yet the Times, the most English of them all, treats the subject with dignity.

At the Games in Oban, there are four platforms, one in each corner of the outdoor arena, and, again, four competitions are running simultaneously. Here the

Angus Nicol (on right), talking to Gordon Walker, with the Duke of Argyll looking on. Oban, 1993. (PHOTOGRAPH BY COURTESY OF THE COLLEGE OF PIPING)

problem is not that you cannot listen to the Marches as well as the Strathspeys and Reels, but that you can, all at the same time. But the organisation is excellent, and the usual traditional athletic and dancing events are going on as well. A popular spectacle is the shinty match between teams of very young boys, com-

An overview of the Oban Games in the Argyllshire Gathering Ground, some years ago.
(PHOTOGRAPH BY COURTESY OF THE COLLEGE OF PIPING)

Spectators at Oban Games in 1925. The weather looks none too warm.

peting for the Primary Schools Quaich.

There are few early eye-witness accounts of the Oban Games, apart from the reports in the Oban Times. In 1873, the first Games with a Gold Medal competition, the piping was heard by two English sisters, Gertrude and Constance Astley, remarkably silly girls who kept a joint diary. They were staying at Ardtornish, in Morvern, and came over to Oban in a yacht party, intent on attending the ball in the evening.

To pass the day, they went to the Games, five young ladies with their 'chap' (chaperone). They perched themselves 'like puffins on a slope above the arena . . a commanding situation & they see beautifully, but it has its disadvantages, the stones being very hard & insecure & the sun being very hot. The first performance is the competition for the prize for the best 'piobaireachd' playing. The first quarter of an hour of this is not unpleasant, but when it has lasted an hour and a 1/2 it becomes slightly monotonous & irritating. While this is going on with the players dressed with the utmost magnificence, others are putting the stone, throwing the caber, etc. . . All this time the pio-b-dchs have been going on, but at last even they come to an end . . .'

The sisters, who were 24 and 22 years old but seem to have been emotionally stuck at age 15, were mainly concerned as to whether their ball dresses had arrived safely. They spent the early evening sitting on the deck of their yacht listening to a band on the neighbouring steam vessel, 'occasionally assisted by the bagpipes on shore'. As they rowed ashore to go to the hotel to dress for the ball, fireworks ('not very remarkable') began.

The ball was in a large tent near the hotel, and started at 10.15 p.m., a feature being 'those delightful bagpipes which went on playing reels long after we were in bed', their chaperone having dragged them away 'in the wildest of spirits' at two o'clock.

Next day, having decided to call themselves Flotsam and Jetsam, they sailed back to Morvern to complete their holiday, before the 'horrid hateful steamer' called to pick them up and take them south.

They must have witnessed Donald Stewart MacDonald winning the first Oban Gold Medal, but clearly the experience meant very little to them.

Records of the winners at the Argyllshire Gathering are not complete, but the Oban Times has good accounts of the earlier meetings. In the official programme of the Gathering, the winners of the Gold Medal of the Highland Society of London are listed, from 1873 on. The winners include many illustrious names, among them Calum Piobair MacPherson, from Catlodge, near Laggan. Legend has it that in the 1870s he used to walk from his home, through the hills to Oban, a distance of about 50 miles, in order to compete. He won so often that in the end he arrived one day, only to be asked by the stewards not to enter the piobaireachd competition, so as to give the others a chance. He never competed at Oban again. It has to be added that the story is not borne out by the prize list for piobaireachd: Calum Piobair won just the once, in 1876.

Many pipers from the islands would come to Oban for the Gathering even if they were not competing. It was their one chance to hear the top players, and first-class piping, and to meet their friends and exchange piping talk. For a man like John Johnston from Coll, his annual visit to Oban was like a blood transfusion. Today we all have many more opportunities to hear good playing, and can travel across the country at will, but in the old days, Highlanders were dependant on these big meetings, for which special transport was usually laid on.

The winners of the Gold Medal at Oban since 1873 were:

1873 D.S MacDonald. This was Donald Stewart MacDonald from Carrbridge, piper to MacKintosh at Moy Hall and later to the Duke of Hamilton. He went to South Africa.
1874 Ronald MacKenzie, Piper to MacDonald of Dunach. He was from Ord in Skye.
1875 John MacBean, Piper to Lord Middleton, at Applecross.
1876 Malcolm MacPherson (Calum Piobaire), Piper to Cluny.
1877 John MacBean – this was before the Senior Piobaireachd for Gold Medal winners was inaugurated, and winners at Oban were allowed to take the Gold more than once.
1878 William MacLennan, Dundee Police, cousin of G.S.MacLennan.
1879 George MacDonald, South Morar.
1880 Robert MacKinnon (see above)
1881 John MacColl, Bonawe – he must have been newly back from Glasgow (see above). He won the Open 1901 (shared) and '02.
1882 Angus MacDonald, Piper to MacDonnell of South Morar.
1883 Angus MacRae, Piper to Mr H.E.Wood, Raasay.
1884 John MacDougall Gillies, Aberdeen. He won the Open 1901 (shared).
1885 P/M John Cameron, 2nd Bn. Queens Own Cameron Highlanders.
1886 P/M Robert Meldrum, 2nd Bn. Argyll and Sutherland Highlanders.
1887 P/M John MacKay, 4th Bn. Argyll and Sutherland Highlanders.
1888 Kenneth MacDonald.
1889 John MacPherson ('Jockan'), eldest son of Calum Piobaire.
1890 Norman MacPherson, son of Calum Piobaire.
1891 David C. Mather, Lochcarron.
1892 Archibald R. MacColl, nephew of John. He went to Australia.
1893 William Robb, army piper.
1894 George J. Ross, army piper who went to Australia.
1895 John MacKenzie, from Easter Ross, lived in Glasgow.
1896 Gavin Campbell MacDougall, of the pipe-making family.
1897 John MacDonald, later of Inverness. He won the Open 10 times.
1898 Farquhar MacRae, from Skye, lived in Glasgow.
1899 Murdo MacKenzie, piper to Mr A.E.Butter, Fascally. A Ross-shire man, later piper at Beaufort Castle, Beauly. He emigrated to New Zealand.
1900 No competition (Boer War).
1901 John Wallace, pupil of Robert Meldrum and John MacDougall Gillies, lived in Edinburgh. The Senior Open Piobaireachd began this year.
1902 P/M William Ross, 4th Highland Light Infantry.
1903 P/M Donald Mathieson, 3rd Bn. HLI, came from Sutherland.

1904 Pipe/Cpl George S. MacLennan, 1st Gordon Highlanders.
1905 George S. Allan, 2nd Scottish Horse. He won the Open 1906 and 1922.
1906 James A. Center, Edinburgh.
1907 P/M William Ross, 2nd Scots Guards. He won the Open the same year, and 1912 and '28.
1908 Roderick Campbell, Inverness. He won the Open 1910.
1909 William Gray, Govan Police. He won the Open 1913, 1919 and 1921.
1910 Pipe/Sgt William Lawrie, 8th Argyll and Sutherland Highlanders. He won the Gold Medal at Inverness in the same year.
1911 George Yardley, Cambuslang, went to South Africa, then New Zealand. He won the Gold Medal at Inverness in the same year.
1912 William MacLean, Glasgow.
1913 P/M James Taylor, H.L.I.
No Gathering was held during World War I
1919 P/M James O. Duff, Edinburgh.
1920 P/M William Taylor, Edinburgh.
1921 P/M James Mathieson.
1922 P/M Robert Reid, Glasgow. He won the Open 6 times.
1923 A.M.Calder, Edinburgh.
1924 P/M Chisholm, H.L.I.
1925 David Ross, Sutherland.
1926 John MacDonald, City of Glasgow Police ('Johnny Roidean'). He won the Gold Medal at Inverness in the same year.
1927 John Wilson, Edinburgh. He won the Open 1931.
1928 Hugh Kennedy, Tiree.
1929 P/M John D. MacDonald, 1st Scots Guards, from Melness, Sutherland.
1930 Robert B. Nicol, Crathie, the King's piper. He won the Gold Medal at Inverness in the same year, and the Open 1937.
1931 Robert U. Brown, Muir of Ord, later the King's piper. He won the Open 1935.
1932 Pipe/Sgt James B. Robertson, 2nd Scots Guards. He won the Open 1938 and '46.
1933 Malcolm R. MacPherson, Invershin, grandson of Calum Piobaire. He won the Open 1934.
1934 P/M C. Smith, 2nd Black Watch.
1935 L/Cpl Nicol MacCallum, 8th Argyll and Sutherland Highlanders.
1936 Donald Iain MacKenzie, Tongue.
1937 Donald F. Ross, Lochgilphead.
1938 Roderick MacDonald, City of Glasgow Police ('Roddy Roidean').
No Gathering was held during World War II
1946 P/M Peter Bain, Glasgow.
1947 Robert G. Hardie, Glasgow.
1948 Donald MacPherson, Glasgow. He also won the Open; and 14 more times
1949 Pipe/Sgt R.(Mickey) MacKay, Cameron Highlanders.
1950 John D. Burgess, Edinburgh. He won the Gold Medal at Inverness in the

same year, at the age of 16. His first Open win was in 1972.
1951 P/M Donald MacLean, Lewis.
1952 P/M Ronald MacCallum, Inveraray.
1953 James MacColl, Shotts.
1954 P/M Donald MacLeod, Seaforth Highlanders. He won the Open 3 times.
1955 William M. MacDonald, Inverness. He won the Gold Medal at Inverness in the same year, and the Open 1969.
1956 P/M Donald R. MacLennan, North Berwick. He won the Gold Medal at Inverness in the same year.
1957 R.S.M. John MacLellan, Seaforth Highlanders. He won the Open 3 times.
1958 Iain MacFadyen, Glasgow.
1959 Kenneth MacDonald, Glasgow.
1960 John MacFadyen, Glasgow. He won the Open 1967, '68 and '70.
1961 Ronald Lawrie, City of Glasgow Police.
1962 Seumas MacNeill, Bearsden.
1963 Sgt Angus MacDonald, 1st Scots Guards.
1964 Hector MacFadyen, Pennyghael, Mull. He won the Gold Medal at Inverness in the same year.
1965 Neil MacEachern, Islay.
1966 Duncan MacFadyen, Johnstone.
1967 William MacDonald, Benbecula. He won the Open 1973.
1968 Thomas Pearston, Glasgow.
1969 John MacDougall, Arbroath.
1970 Andrew Wright, Paisley. He won the Gold Medal at Inverness in the same year.
1971 Finlay MacNeill, Inverness.
1972 Hugh MacCallum, Bridge of Allan. He won his first Open 1960.
1973 Angus J. MacLellan, City of Glasgow Police.
1974 Kenneth MacLean, Glasgow.
1975 Arthur G. Gillies, Kilchrenan. He won the Open in 1993.
1976 Malcolm MacRae, Kirriemuir.
1977 Ian Clowe, Dumfries.
1978 James MacIntosh, Dundee.
1979 William Livingstone, Ontario.
1980 Murray Henderson, Eassie, Angus.
1981 Gavin Stoddart, Edinburgh.
1982 P/M Evan MacRae, Fort William.
1983 John Wilson, Strathclyde Police.
1984 Michael Cusack, Texas.
1985 Robert Wallace, Glasgow.
1986 Alfred Morrison, Bishopton.
1987 John Hanning, New Zealand.
1988 Roderick MacLeod, Cumbernauld.
1989 Cpl Alasdair Gillies, Queen's Own Highlanders.
1990 Sgt Brian Donaldson, Scots Guards.

1991 James MacGillivray, Ontario.
1992 Colin MacLellan, Ontario.
1993 Cpl Gordon Walker, Royal Highland Fusiliers.
1994 Dr Angus MacDonald, Skye.
1995 William MacCallum, Clydebank.
1996 Angus MacColl, Oban.
1997 James Murray, Cupar.
1998 Niall Matheson, Inverness.
1999 Major John Cairns, Ontario. He won the Gold Medal at Inverness in the same year.
2000 Michael Rogers, Maryland, USA.
2001 Jack Lee, Vancouver.
2002 Iain Spiers, Edinburgh.

The Oban Pipe Band also parades on Games Day, leaving the Square around noon to march to the Games field and to entertain at lunchtime. The band was formed in 1920, but lapsed for a time in the 1950s. Alister MacLennan became the Pipe Major when it was resurrected, and today it is thriving, with Iain Hurst as Pipe Major, and the support of fine players such as Angus MacColl. The official programme of the Argyllshire Gathering tells how the band raised money to build a new practice hall, the work of the actual building of the hall being undertaken by the bandsmen themselves, and their friends. The band also has a system of tuition for young pipers and drummers, which promises well for the future of piping in Oban.

In 1996, the Education Department of Argyll and Bute made an agreement with the Argyllshire Gathering Trust for joint funding for piping instruction in the primary and secondary schools of Oban. Ronald Lawrie was appointed instructor; he had already been teaching for 15 years in the secondary schools. On his falling ill in 2003, Angus MacColl has taken his place, until he recovers. In the past decade, both Ronnie Lawrie and Arthur Gillies have been across teaching piping to youngsters in Mull, and Arthur has been instructing in South Uist.

SOURCES
Notices of Pipers
Piping Times
Old Parish Register, Kilmore and Kilbride
Official Programme of the Argyllshire Gathering
Faichney, Alexander M.
Shedden, Hugh
Hunter, Charles
Mrs Grant of Laggan
Buchanan, Robert

From the poem *Close-Ups of Summer,* by Norman MacCaig (*Tree of Strings*, 1977):

Hens sloven. But the cock
struts by – one can almost see
the tiny set of bagpipes
he's sure he's playing.

The sun's the same – pipemajoring
across space, where the invisible judges
sit, wrapped in their knowledge,
taking terrible notes.

Lorne and Appin

AIRDS

THE CAMPBELLS OF CAWDOR WERE the Lairds of the estate known as Airds, near Loch Creran, Appin, to the north of Oban. The first laird was George Campbell, third son of Cawdor, who became Tutor (guardian) of his nephew the heir to Cawdor, managing the considerable estates for some years. He was much embroiled in the Cawdor family's struggle for possession of Islay, eventually ousting the MacDonalds. He married Janet, 'the Black Bitch of Dunstaffnage', beautiful but formidable, renowned for having cut off a piper's fingers, probably a MacDonald piper in Islay. George, who died in 1685, was probably the subject of the *Lament for Airds*. He was a great-uncle of Young George, for whom *Young George's Salute* may have been made some twenty years later (see above).

Although a third son, George became Sir George when his uncle, Sir Donald Campbell of Ardnamurchan, resigned his title in George's favour, in 1643, and gave him the lands of Airds.

The Lament is preserved only in the Campbell Canntaireachd manuscript of the 1790s. It was presumably composed around 1685, when Sir George died.

The 2/4 March in four parts, *Brigadier General Lorne Campbell VC of Akarit*, was made by Angus MacPherson, Inveran, to commemorate a more recent member of the Airds family.

PIPERS FROM THE LORNE DISTRICT

MANY OF THE STEWART FAMILY of pipers and singers, who became travelling folk probably in the 17th century, were based in Blair Atholl, but they originated in Appin. Some went to Lochaber and were involved with the Camerons of Lochiel, but most of them were in Perthshire. Many served in the Atholl Highlanders, some of them as Pipe Major. DONALD STEWART won the Prize Pipe in Edinburgh in 1825, JOHN STEWART was second in 1835. They were great army pipers, as is made clear in the Notices of Pipers, with a tradition of serving in the Gordon Highlanders. One was the Duke of Atholl's personal piper.

The family included Pipe Major JOHN STEWART of the Gordon Highlanders, whose sister married Lt John MacLennan, to become the mother of George Stewart MacLennan. G.S. commemorated his uncle in his 2/4 March *Pipe Major John Stewart*. Related to John and Elizabeth Stewart was Annie MacDiarmaid, who married Calum Piobair MacPherson.

In more recent times, a descendant of this family, GEORGE STEWART, is the Piping Instructor for East Sutherland Schools, based in Golspie. He was a pupil of Robert Nicol, to whom he went for tuition for 22 years, and of Bessie Brown, sister of R.U.Brown. George is related to the great folk singers, Jeannie Robertson and Lizzie Higgins. His distant cousin, JAMES STEWART from Banff, now living in England, is a competing piper, who holds the Oban Silver Medal.

The Stewart family has preserved an ancient form of Canntaireachd, handed down from generation to generation as a singing medium. Although it was written down in some places in the 18th century, canntaireachd evolved as a purely oral tradition, with the result that its finer points have been largely lost in modern times. The Stewarts still sing the canntaireachd they inherited, presumably evolved in Appin, and recently George Stewart and his wife Alex have recorded examples of it on CD.

DUGALD MACINTYRE from Lorne competed in Edinburgh in 1794, and was placed 2nd. In 1799 he came first and won the prize pipe. Was he related to John MacIntyre at Ardmaddy? (see below, Glenorchy)

ANGUS CAMERON belonged to Lochaber, where he was born in 1776. He became piper to Cameron of Lochiel, came second at Edinburgh in 1793, and won the Prize Pipe in 1794, when only 18. Later he had the inn at the north side of the Ballachulish Ferry, and seems to have immersed himself in the piping life on both sides of the loch. In 1841, Lord Cockburn described a visit to the inn, saying:

'Angus was the best piper in his day, but he had the misfortune to marry what was called 'a leddy' . . who thought pipes below her dignity, and so fiercely discouraged them that, at last, she has compelled her spouse totally to abandon the source of all his glory. On one occasion, when he was delighting a crowd of admirers and would not take a gentle hint, she stepped forward with a knife and stabbed the bag. . . . Though giving great praise to old rivals and young aspirants, he bemoaned the general decline of the art, for he said that there was not one single REAL piper – a man who made the pipe his business – in the whole of Appin. The reason for this, he thought was due to the decline of the chieftains and their gatherings'.

It is perhaps ironic that less than twenty years after Angus Cameron said this to Lord Cockburn, a boy was born a few miles away in Appin who became one of the great pipers of all time, and made the pipe his full-time business: John MacColl.

WILLIAM DUBH MACKENZIE was piper to Campbell of Barcaldine, near Loch Creran. The story goes that he was laying in stocks for the New Year, and was carrying two gallons of whisky home when he saw some people (wee folk) dancing. So he joined them, and they taught him the *Reel of Tulloch*, and he danced with them for a year. When he returned home he was the best dancer and player of reels in the country (see *Popular Tales of the West Highlands*).

NEIL MACLEAN, piper to Major Campbell of Airds, competed at Falkirk in 1783, and came first. A letter of 1783 published by William Donaldson reports on the competition of that year, and seems to be saying that there was something suspicious about Neil MacLean's win at Falkirk. The writer, David Trigge, said (Donaldson p.72): 'I discovered the preceding evening (before the competition) that . . . they (the Committee) determined that McGrigor Should not receive employment and that the Prize Pipes was to be given to Neil McLean all of which came out to be true. The Prizes were now adjudged 1st to Neil Macklean 2nd to Archd. McGrigor 3rd to John McGrigor – McLean the 1st Year of the Competition was Sett down as one of the four Bade Pipers 2nd. the Same and this Year in the Spring he went Six weeks to Young John McGrigor to receive further instruction and in that period he has made Such rapid Progress as to Beat all the Pipers in Scotland . . . the Young Lads were so much dashed that the Prizes were bestowed upon them when so many able performers were there that they were out of all Countenance the oldest of the three not 19 Years'.

Apparently there was much disquiet among the pipers about this result, as they thought 'Professor' John MacArthur was a clear winner; in order to 'redress the Grievances of the Pipers' and to redeem the good name of the Society, it was decided to hold another competition, this time in Edinburgh, with different judges, Trigge being given the task of inviting the pipers to take part. All agreed except the four McGregors, and Trigge goes on: 'McLean came to me too willing to go wt. me but he was Poisioned and went home. . .' As so often with Trigge, the meaning is not entirely clear. Poisioned? Presumably food poisoning – or alcoholic? – rather than skullduggery.

Neil then became piper to the Highland Society of London, who in 1784 had his portrait drawn and engraved. He looks a lot older than 20 in the picture, but this may be the effect of the engraving. He played on the right shoulder (which does not necessarily mean he was left-handed). His son was Allan MacLean (see under Ardgour).

Among his descendants were Hector MacLean, piper to the Clan MacLean in the 1890s, and another Hector, his son or grandson, who was a prominent player in the Scottish Pipers' Association and a member of John MacDonald's piobaireachd class in Glasgow in 1938 (see Archie McNab, above).

Neil NacLean in 1784 when he was 20. Piper to Airds, he had won the national competition at Falkirk the previous year, but there were suspicions that the result was rigged.

PAUL MACINNES from Fasnacloich, in North Argyll, in the Loch Creran district of Appin, competed at Edinburgh in 1783. Playing the *Park Piobaireachd*, he was placed joint third, with Donald Fisher, piper to Breadalbane, and each was awarded 'an elegant Highland dress with silver epaulettes, double silver loops and buttons, and feathers for their new bonnets', as well as money to defray their expenses. Paul and Neil MacLean must have been neighbours in Argyll. Paul was related to the mother of John MacColl, and to Angus MacInnes (see below).

On the same occasion, at Edinburgh in 1783, COLIN MACNAB, piper to the Laird of MacNab, played *Clanranald's March* and came second, winning an inscribed silver horseshoe with a coronet, to wear on his bonnet, and money for his expenses. In 1785, Colin MacNab competed as 'piper to Francis MacNab Esq. of MacNab', and was again placed second. Paul MacInnes, now piper to John Cameron Esq. of Callert, North Ballachulish, took third place.

DUNCAN MACNAB from Lorne came first in Edinburgh in 1789, and was awarded the Prize Pipe. Presumably he was related to Colin and Donald. Keith Sanger tells us that Duncan also competed in 1804, when he was described as 'formerly piper to the Laird of MacNabb, but now piper to the Inverness Militia'. Between these two competitions, Duncan was Pipe Major of the Caithness and Bute Volunteers, who went to serve in Ireland, based in Cork. One of the privates serving under him was Donald MacDonald, from Skye, who later published his collection of piobaireachd when he was a pipemaker in Edinburgh.

This Duncan MacNab was probably the piper named by Peter Reid in a note to the tune *The MacGregors' Salute*: Reid says it was played by JOHN MACNAB (some time in the 1820s, before 1826), that John was piper to the 92nd Regiment, and son of Duncan MacNab, piper to the Royal Scots.

DONALD MACNAB, probably related to Colin and Duncan (see above), competed at Edinburgh in 1797, as 'Pipe Major to the 4th or Breadalbane Fencibles', and came fourth. In 1805 he was piper to the Laird of MacNab, and was second, eventually winning the prize pipe in 1807.

Although the MacNab clan seems to have belonged mainly to the Tayside district, there was a family of them who were said to have been armourers and jewellers to the Campbells of Lochawe, at Kilchurn Castle, for 400 years.

ARCHIE MUNRO was described as being 'from Oban' when he competed at Edinburgh in 1837, and won the third prize, 'a superb dirk'. He is said to have been a brother of the second wife of Angus Cam MacPherson, father of Calum Piobair, and was piper to Glengarry, for whom he composed *Glengarry's Lament* in 1828. He was probably also the composer of the *Oban Strathspey*. He died in 1845, aged forty-five.

It is said of Archie Munro that he was sorry for the young Calum Piobair when his step-mother, Archie's sister, was giving him a hard time. She hated the pipes, and would not allow the boy to play, but Archie encouraged him and gave him instruction. This was presumably at Archie's home near Fort Augustus, and Calum used to walk there, over the Corrieairick Pass, a distance of some 20 miles of rugged country. Eventually Calum left home, and went south to find work in Greenock.

It has to be said that this story has been refuted by Jeannie Campbell, who found that Archie was of parentage different from that of Calum's step-mother.

ANGUS MACINNES was from Appin, and was piper to Stewart of Fasnacloich, near Loch Creran. Later he was piper to the Marquis of Huntly who sent him to compete in Edinburgh in 1838.

ALEXANDER MACARTHUR is listed by Jeannie Campbell as a pipe maker born in Lorne around 1830. He came from Lerags, south of Oban, the place where the MacDougall pipers are said to have had their piping school. His mother's name was Sarah Rankin.

He was a piper in the 93rd Highlanders for some years, and after his discharge around 1855 he settled in Glasgow as a pipe maker. He may have been related by marriage to Donald MacPhee, as his wife and Donald's had the same surname, Bell. The MacArthurs and the MacPhees both lived in Thistle Street, Glasgow.

Jeannie Campbell says that Alexander used to give piping lessons in Glasgow, charging 20 shillings for 21 lessons if three pupils were taught together. 'He was a careful teacher, a fluent Gaelic speaker, and a quiet man of pleasant manners'.

Alexander died from bronchitis in 1889.

DONALD MACFARLANE in 1911 was described as 'a young Oban piper and composer, son of Hugh MacFarlane'. The Oban Times in April 1911 had a letter listing his prizes and his compositions.

'WEE' DONALD MACLEAN

Donald MacLean of Oban and Glasgow was known as Wee Donald MacLean, to distinguish him from Big Donald MacLean from Lewis. He was small for a man, about 5 foot 4 inches.

He is remembered today by most people as the subject of the march *Donald MacLean's Farewell to Oban*. This was made in 1938 by Blind Archie MacNeill, after Donald had failed to win a place in any of the competitions at the Argyllshire Gathering, most unusual for him. Many considered he had been robbed, and that his MSR had been outstanding. His friend and teacher, Archie MacNeill, was laughing afterwards, and said he guessed that would be Donald's last appearance at Oban.

On the train on his way back to Glasgow, Archie gave the name to a tune he had composed earlier that summer; it became widely known and played, even though it was not Donald's last appearance at Oban. He is said not to have liked the tune very much; he was probably tired of hearing it, or perhaps he did not like having his disappointment that day underlined quite so publicly.

Donald MacLean was born in Ballachulish in 1912, but he told his pupil and friend, Finlay MacRae, that he was born in Glasgow, where his father was an engine-driver, and that his family was from Benderloch, to the north of Oban. He named his 2/4 March *Benderloch Bay* for his family's link with the district. His best composition is probably the 2/4 March *Mrs Donald McLean*, his mother with whom he lived in Otago Street. Whatever the birth-place, there is no doubt that he was brought up in Glasgow.

In the 1880s, a Duncan MacLean, who may have been Donald's grandfather, was living at Keil Farm, on the shores of Ardmucknish Bay, Benderloch, in a house called Jib. Duncan was born locally, in about 1818-20 (see below).

Benderloch Bay is probably another name for Ardmucknish Bay, but the name Benderloch Bay puzzles local people today, as they never call the bay that. It is possible that Donald MacLean gave his march this name to make its origins recognisable to those who would not know where Ardmucknish was – and maybe he thought Benderloch a more pleasant name than Ardmucknish. Or perhaps Donald's family, away in Glasgow, referred to it as Benderloch Bay, the bay at Benderloch, where their grandparents lived.

Duncan MacLean married a girl called Jane MacDougall, who was born in the parish of Kilbride in 1838. It would seem that she had been married before, and had been living in Glasgow in the 1860s. Her first husband was called Rodger, first name unknown, and their daughter Annie was born in Glasgow. There may have been other children of this marriage, giving the MacLeans a strong link with Glasgow. We presume that Mr Rodger died in the late 1860s.

By the 1870s Jane was married to Duncan MacLean and they were living in Benderloch, where Duncan was an agricultural labourer.

In 1901, the Census tells us that Duncan was dead, and his widow Jane was 'suffering from Creeping Paralysis'. Her son John was 29, 'cottar, platelayer, wilk merchant', born locally in 1872. (Whilks, or whelks, are edible shellfish).

Did Duncan and Jane have another son who went to Glasgow, to become an engine-driver, and the father of Wee Donald MacLean in 1912? We cannot be sure, but we know his father's name was Donald.

There was in Benderloch in the 19th century only one other family of MacLeans, and they too lived at Keil, on Ardmucknish Bay. They were John MacLean and his wife Anne MacLaren. In 1890 they were at Port Selma, very close to Duncan MacLean's home. But John came from Skye, born in Kilmuir, Trotternish, in 1854, and he spoke no English. The Register for Kilmuir lists the birth in 1854 of John MacLean to James MacLean and his wife Mary Martin, living in Kilmuir. The surname Martin is one associated with Kilmuir.

John and Anne appear first in Benderloch in the 1891 Census. Anne and their five children were all born locally, so we may deduce that John had left Skye soon after 1881, had come to Benderloch, married Anne, and settled there.

From the proximity of this family to the Duncan MacLeans at Keil, and the

A SUCCESSFUL YOUNG PIPER

PIPER DONALD MACLEAN, GLASGOW

Donald MacLean has taken his place among front rank performers on the Piob Mhor, and at many of the gatherings he has been conspicuously successful. He is regarded as one of the promising players in the younger school of pipers, and his career, it might be said, is only beginning. His latest success was at the Inverness Gathering in 1931, when he was awarded the Highland Society of London's Gold Medal.

'Wee Donald' MacLean as a young piper in the early 1930s. He won the Gold Medal at Inverness in 1931, when he was nineteen.
(Photograph kindly lent by Finlay MacRae)

absence of other MacLean families in Benderloch, it may perhaps be assumed that there was a link between the two families – was Duncan MacLean 1818 perhaps a brother or cousin of James in Kilmuir? Was it this link which brought James' son John to Benderloch when he left Skye?

The 1841 Census may have the answer: at Invercarnan, near Ballachulish, Duror, there was a farmer, Archie MacLean. He was born in 1796, and seems to have had a twin brother John. The 1841 Census gives very little detail, and no womenfolk are named here, but in the same household were Duncan and James, both born around 1820. It is possible that this James went to Skye, and his brother Duncan to Benderloch, where James' son John later joined him. This, of course, is conjecture, but it fits the facts as we have them, scanty though they are.

Wee Donald MacLean went for some ten years or more, during the 1930s, to John MacColl, the longest of his many distinguished pupils. Before going to John MacColl, Donald had learned from John Currie, a Mull man who was a pupil of Donald MacPhee. When Donald MacLean was 12, he met Blind Archie MacNeill, and joined the 139th Glasgow Company of the Boys' Brigade. He was strongly influenced by Archie for some years. He was in his late teens when he first went to John MacColl, an association which lasted until January 1940, when Donald joined the Lovat Scouts.

For some of the time in the 1930s, Wee Donald worked as a steward on board the liner *Letitia*, sailing between Glasgow and Montreal. The Donaldson line owned the *Letitia* and her sister ship, the *Athenia*, and in 1933 formed small pipe bands on board both ships. Donald and his friend, Duncan MacIntyre, were pipers and stewards. Two years later, Donald transferred to the *Athenia*, where Duncan, Peter MacLeod junior and Sandy Boyd from Largs were in the band. Donald said they had some grand piping nights together after work was over. Peter MacLeod composed a reel in four parts which he called *Donald MacLean (R.M.S.Athenia)*, and one called *Duncan MacIntyre (R.M.S.Athenia)*.

In the late 1930s, the Piobaireachd Society ran piping classes in the Drill Hall in Portree, starting with Willie MacDonald (Gruids) around 1935. He was followed by Willie Ross – he began with fourteen boys, who soon diminished to seven, as he told the rest they had no music in them and might as well quit. Peter Bain, himself a Portree man, was the next teacher, and then, in 1937, Donald MacLean taught the boys of Skye, including Finlay MacRae, one of a class of fifteen. The fee was 2/6 per week, but the Piobaireachd Society paid the teacher's salary, such as it was.

Donald was full of fun. On one occasion he was taking the class in Portree, and between tunes he was listening to the wireless broadcasting a commentary on the Scottish Cup Final, in which Clyde was playing. He was a lifelong Clyde supporter, and when they won the final that day, he sprang to his feet in exultation and threw his chanter high into the rafters of the hall, a considerable distance. Luckily it landed undamaged (don't try this at home; it could prove expensive).

On another occasion in Skye he had won a prize for his playing, and then played for the Jig dancing competition – he was a very fine player for dancing. At the award-giving he was in good form, and when Lady MacDonald of Sleat presented the prize to him, she said kindly 'You played very well for the dancing today, Donald', to which he replied, equally kindly, 'And you made no' a bad speech yourself, m'leddy'.

There was one day when all the stars of piping were tuning in a tent. Before the contest started, Donald, full of mischief, spoke to a local boy who was good-natured but a bit simple. 'See that big fellow? There's a message for him from the judges, will you go and tell him? They say there's no point in him entering for this, his playing just isn't up to the standard of the rest'. The big man was Willie Ross, who chased the poor boy.

Donald MacLean served in the Lovat Scouts during World War II, and was a piper in the Lovat Scouts Pipe Band, along with Ronald Morrison and Donald MacDonald, uncle of Willie MacDonald (Benbecula). The Pipe Major was Donald Riddell from Kiltarlity, succeeding Jim Johnstone, who had followed Angus MacAulay, South Uist. Donald's obituary in the Piping Times (February 1987) says that 'many of them remember vividly the days which Donald helped to make happier by the use of his bagpipes and his lively sense of humour'.

Wee Donald MacLean is described as 'of Oban and Glasgow'. In Glasgow he lived in Otago Street, close to the present home of the College of Piping. He was one of the first instructors at the College, in the days when it was in Pitt Street, in the late 1940s and 1950s. One of his most distinguished pupils was Duncan Johnstone, who later went also to Roddy MacDonald.

A controversial piper called Donald Main was to play a piobaireachd on the

The Lovat Scouts at Balmoral in 1941. The Pipe Major was Donald Riddell, and among the pipers was Donald MacLean (beside the P/M).
(PHOTOGRAPH BY COURTESY OF THE COLLEGE OF PIPING)

wireless. In those days, the piper making a broadcast had to have a helper present in the studio to keep his instrument in tune while he played, and on this occasion Donald MacLean had been roped in to do this. To his horror, Donald Main played *I Got A Kiss Of The King's Hand* very, very fast, making, in Wee Donald's view, a mockery of the work. ('Played it like a jig, he did'). Next day Donald was in Henderson's the pipemaker's, and the manager, Archie MacPhedran, asked him if he had heard that travesty of *I Got A Kiss* put out on the wireless. Donald said he had, and they discussed the performance, but Donald never let on he had had a hand in it – Archie would have said he should have let the pipe go out, if not actually stopping a drone.

In the late 1950s, he left the College to join a theatrical company, for what he called his 'Brigadoon years', touring with the musical show of that name, for which he was the piper. He met his wife, Jean Flockhart, at this time: she was a dancer with the company. She had links with Kincraig, in Badenoch, and they went there to live for a short time before emigrating to Tasmania.

They returned to Britain in the 1970s, to spend a short time in London. Then they went back to Scotland, and eventually settled in Beauly, near Inverness.

Finlay MacRae happened by chance to see Donald in the street, and resumed the lessons which had been interrupted by the war. For ten years Finlay visited Donald on Monday nights, and says that he learned a lot of pipe music and had a lot of piping fun.

One of many fine players whose competing career was cut short by the war, Donald had won his Inverness Gold Medal in 1931, at the age of 19, playing *The Blind Piper's Obstinacy*. When asked who was the best piobaireachd player he heard in his whole career, Donald said 'Donald MacPherson. His pipe was always perfect and his playing full of music'. He was less decisive about a favourite tune, but when Finlay asked him which he thought the most unusual of all the tunes, he spent a week playing through all the hundreds he knew, and eventually said 'I reckon *The Conundrum* by Peter MacLeod must be top of the list'. Few would disagree with that.

Finlay has a brown paper template of Donald's pipe bag, with all the dimensions for different bag sizes written on it.

Mrs Jean MacLean loved birds, and while living in Inverness used to take in injured birds and nurse them back to health. There was a pigeon which would fly round the room, calling while the pipes were playing and while Mrs MacLean was making tea for her husband's pupils. Finlay's tape of one of his lessons has pigeon calls as the background. The MacLeans, with their daughter Margaret,

Four prize winners at Cowal in the 1930s: (left to right) Robert Reid, Roderick MacDonald, Wee Donald MacLean, and Peter MacLeod junior.
(PHOTOGRAPH BY COURTESY OF THE COLLEGE OF PIPING)

lived latterly at 48 Springfield Gardens, Inverness.

Donald himself played a 'very mild' pipe, and said he had always done so. Presumably this means a very soft reed, and not a loud sound. As a teacher he was gentle and kind – 'too kind' says Finlay, 'we might have worked harder if he had pushed us more'. He never indulged in cracking his chanter on a boy's knuckles. He disliked the division of written piobaireachd into bars of equal length, and abhorred time signatures for the Great Music.

He was a regular attender at meetings of the Scottish Pipers Association (SPA), and Andrew MacNeill in 1994 recalled that they were held 'in the room at the right hand side ground floor of the old Highlanders' Institute (in Elmbank Street) and this was usually packed every Saturday night'. Wee Donald MacLean, Wee Donald MacLeod, the Peters MacLeod (as Andrew MacNeill put it) and Pook MacKenzie from Portree were a few of the worthies he could name.

Around 1950 the Professional Pipers' Association was formed, with a committee consisting of John MacLean, Wee Donald MacLean, Donald MacPherson, Thomas Pearston and Seumas MacNeill.

Donald judged at all levels, including the Gold Medal and Clasp competitions. His sympathies were always with the players. One of his beliefs was that a judge should not penalize a player for a wee choke, maintaining that a wee choke was not something a fellow did on purpose but merely something which happened to him regardless of his intentions ('he never tried it'). Not quite an Act of God, perhaps, but something which should not be allowed to spoil the tune. Whether this would apply to a series of chokes, or to a very bad and glaring choke, is not clear.

In November 1998, Dugald MacNeill wrote in his Piping Times 'Hints for Beginners':

'Wee Donald MacLean, Oban, Lovat Scouts, College of Piping, Brig o' Doon etc. was a beautiful player. Apart from his able playing, what made him good to listen to was his facility in tuning his bagpipe. He would not strive for perfection when he began but very quickly do an approximate tuning and then he would play a two-part tune, giving it good expression, correct timing and perfect execution. He would then adjust the drones, again very quickly, and play another tune and so on until the pipes were warmed up and steady. Initially he would play simple marches, but as the pipes improved he would play some slow pieces to listen more carefully to the chanter and drones. For the listener it was entertaining and for the player it was sensible. . . As a beginner, you should strive to follow Donald MacLean's example.'

In a letter from Queensland Australia in 1993, David Sinclair wrote, in discussing the individuality of different composers of Ceol Beag:

'. . . there have always been certain players who could interpret the work of a composer and bring out the genius and full beauty of the work. People used to say that John MacColl played in the 'round style' and that his pupil Donald MacLean played in the 'round style'.

'. . . a piping enthusiast of many years standing in Scotland wrote to me and said in his opinion no man in Scotland could get the lift into his playing of marches that Wee Donald (MacLean) could. So what did people mean when they said that John MacColl was a 'round player'? His march compositions are beautiful and the settings full of expression. So is it safe to say that Wee Donald was really a true interpreter of John MacColl's music? Donald, I believe, was also a true interpreter of Peter MacLeod's (senior and junior) music and yet the style of composition was different to John MacColl yet still very musical, beautiful material with the unmistakable stamp and characteristics of the MacLeod genius.'

It seems obvious that Donald was equally good in any style.

Donald spent his last years in Inverness, where he is remembered as an inspiring teacher, and as a gentle soul, devoid of jealousy or aggression, with no harm in him at all, but full of a playful mischievous humour, and of course brimful of music.

In 1986 he suffered a stroke, but for nearly a year appeared to be making a steady recovery, even managing to resume playing. He collapsed suddenly and died on November 12th, 1986, at the age of 73. Finlay played the Ground of the *Little Spree* at his funeral, and the Lovat Scouts' march *Morair Simi* at the graveside in Tomnahurich Burial Ground, Inverness.

SOURCES
Finlay MacRae
Piping Times
Proceedings of Piobaireachd Society Conferences

THE LAWRIE FAMILY

WILLIAM LAWRIE: see also below, Glencoe and Ballachulish

WILLIE LAWRIE, BALLACHULISH, WHO DIED of his wounds at Oxford in 1916, had a family connection with the piping Lawries in Oban. They can all be traced back to Ardnamurchan, where they probably went as lead-miners. 300 miners had been brought in by the Sunart estate in the 1720s, when the lead-mines at Strontian were started, many of them with experience at Leadhills in Lanarkshire and other Scottish mines. William Lawrie said his family had originated somewhere in the Borders, as far as he knew (see below).

The family of the piping Lawries in Oban first appears there as late as the Census of 1891, which lists James Laurie, 31, living at 17 High Street, Oban, with his wife Sarah MacInnes. James' birthplace is given as Ardnamurchan, his wife was born in Ardgour, and James' occupation was Seaman. Colin Lawrie has identified this James with one found in the 1881 Census, when he was a 21-year-old seaman on board a vessel, the *Ellen Brown*, berthed at Easdale.

By 1901, James had become a still-man at the distillery in Oban – but now his birthplace is given as Renfrew, a far cry from Ardnamurchan. His age is 41, and his wife Sarah is still from Ardgour. Their children are: Maggie 10, Angus 8 (who seems to have replaced an earlier Angus), James 7, Mary 4, Martin 2 and Kenneth 4 months. Sarah's unmarried sister, Rachel MacInnes, was acting as the children's nurse.

This Angus, born in 1893, was known as 'Old Toasty' when he grew up, and he was the father of Ronald Lawrie. Kenneth, born in 1901, was the father of the younger Angus, the bag-maker in Largs.

In 1851 there was a fatal accident in the lead-mine at Strontian, and in the subsequent enquiry, a miner named Alexander Lowrie gave evidence. He was probably related to both Lawrie families, in Ballachulish and in Oban.

The eldest son of Thomas and Christian Lourie, Strontian, was William; he went to Ballachulish, and founded the line which included Willie Lawrie, who died of his wounds in 1916. They also had a son James born around 1821 who lived in Appin, and their other sons were John 1808, another John 1817, Alexander 1819, Donald 1824 and Thomas 1829. The Oban branch seems to be descended not from Thomas in Ardnamurchan but from one of his brothers, James or John, both leadminers, born around 1780.

The link between the two branches was back in Ardnamurchan, the great-grandfather of Willie Lawrie being a brother of the great-grandfather of 'Old Toasty'. This means that Willie Lawrie was a third cousin once removed of Ronald Lawrie. The fact that the Oban family has different names is probably the result of a break in the family tradition: Old Toasty's father James was left as a child with a family of MacKenzies in Ardnamurchan, who brought him up after his father went to America.

William Lawrie married Ann Livingstone and they had a son John, born in Appin in 1849. He became a gamekeeper at Conaglen, in Ardgour, and may have been brought up by his Livingstone granny, the mother of Ann Livingstone, in Ardgour. There were strong links with Ardgour all through the Lawrie families, and a branch who lived in Renfrew were also from Ardgour – which is just over the hill from Strontian in Ardnamurchan.

KENNETH LAWRIE

In the Piping Times for October 1999, there appeared a letter from Hugh Major in Appin, telling of an incident when the Argylls were based at Dunoon at the beginning of the war in 1939.

'The duty piper played for reveille, but despite his playing there was no stirring of the Argylls, so he played *South of the Border, Down Mexico Way* – a popular hit of the time. This had the desired effect, with every window being thrown open amid much shouting and no doubt cursing. Questions were shouted out, 'Who's that idiot playing at this time of morning?', 'Who gave permission for that tune?'

'The piper was duly brought in front of his C.O. who by all accounts was bristling with rage. Rumours in the billet that he the piper was going to be court-martialled and thrown in the glass house. However, the piper's defence was that no one stirred when playing the normal duty reveille tune(s) so he decided to try another tune and *South Of The Border* was the first to come to mind. The C.O. decided that the piper be confined to barracks for a period of time and not to repeat his alternative tune.

'The piper was Kenny Lawrie, the brother of P/M Ronald Lawrie of Oban', and the writer adds that he had the story from Mr Dennis MacNeill who served with the Argylls and was captured at St Valery.

As a mere woman, I confess I find it hard to comprehend that grown men can make such a fuss about anything so trivial, especially in time of war.

ANGUS LAWRIE

Two members of the Lawrie family in Oban were called Angus: the elder was 'Old Toasty', born in 1893, the father of Ronald Lawrie; the younger is his nephew, son of his brother Kenneth, and is a prolific composer and a well-known pipebag maker.

The Piping Times for August 1980 has an account of Angus Lawrie winning 1st Prize in the Strathspey composing competition at Minard Castle, and coming second over all, for his strathspey *Lady Campbell of Longsdale*: 'Angus belongs to Oban and is cousin to Ronnie Lawrie of that fair town. He was taught piping first by his father, Kenneth, and then later in the Black Watch which he joined in 1949. He left the Army in 1950 and joined the Oban Pipe Band which had been founded by his father and his uncle Angus in 1925. The older Angus was affectionately known as 'Old Toasty' and this was the inspiration for the first hornpipe which young Angus composed and named for him. He (young Angus) was also in the 8th Argyll's Territorial Band with John M.MacKenzie and Neil MacEachern of Islay and Big Ronnie himself. In 1955 he joined the Glasgow Police and in 1957 joined their band with which he was still playing in 1980. It was around 1977 that he began to compose seriously high quality tunes.'

Another account says that Angus was in the Black Watch for two years, then joined the 8th Argylls in 1950, serving for seven years, until he joined the Pipe Band of the Strathclyde Police.

In the mid-1960s, Angus founded the Glasgow Police Shinty Team, of which Calum Finlayson was the first captain.

In July 2001, the Piping Times published a 2/4 march called *P/M Angus MacInnes Lawrie of Oban*, composed by Dr Ken Lawrie of Australia, Angus Lawrie's son. He sent the tune with a letter:

'I am writing to see if you would consider publishing a wee tune I've composed for my dad, Angus Lawrie. Formerly of the Glasgow/Strathclyde Police pipe bands and P/M of Britoil pipe band, my dad is well known in the piping world for his prolific and musical compositions as well as his famous hand-crafted pipe bags. My dad has been an inspiration to me across the miles. I have been fortunate that my career has taken me around the world, but the downside is being so far away from home and my folks. My chanter has followed me everywhere and it has been a real thrill to hear and play my dad's latest tunes as they pass through the phone lines, hot off the press ! Whether in the Highlands of New Guinea or remotest Australia, this has always given me that extra lift. So, while my music writing will never do him justice, I thought it worth a try composing a tune for him for a change'.

It is pleasing to find a son sincerely admiring his father, and not reluctant to say so.

The younger Angus Lawrie's compositions include:

The 1976 Police Tattoo 4/4 M 2 (Angus was playing in the Tattoo when news came that the band – Strathclyde Police- had won the world championship)
Alan Stuart and his Shadow 6/8 J 4 (a Canadian piper and his dog)
Alex and Hector 2/4 HP 2 (1974. MacDonald brothers in the Glasgow Police Pipe Band).
The Ballygawley Roundabout S 1 (1977. In County Tyrone, Northern Ireland)
Bob Kerr of Luss 2/4 M 4 (1976)
Brigadier P.W.Graham CBE 12/8 M 4 (1983)
British Caledonian Airways Pipe Band 12/8 M 4
Calum Finlayson MBE 6/8 M 4 (1976)
Davy Patrick's Ceilidh 6/8 J 4 (enlarged from 2 parts)
A Drop of Grouse 9/8 RM 2 (1980. Composed in appreciation of the Grouse Whisky company's sponsorship of solo piping).
Dugald Gillespie 12/8 M 3 (The officer in charge of the Strathclyde Police Band)
Farewell to the Highlands 18/8 SA 2 (1979. Made in memory of all Highland exiles)
G.Y.Slater 2/4 HP 4 (an Oban worthy)
Garry McAleer 2/4 HP 4 (1980)
George Sassoon of Benbuie Lodge 2/4 M 4
The Heroes of Oosterbreek 3 /4 RM 2 (1978. Made in memory of those who fell in the Arnhem raid)
Lady Campbell of Longsdale S 4 (Longsdale is a district of Oban. Lady Campbell was Angus Lawrie's nickname for his sister, Ina Campbell)
The MacDonalds of Baleshare S 4
Major Archie Addison 4/4 M 2
Martin Lawrie 9/8 RM 3 (1974. Martin was a cousin who died young)
Mrs Doreen Lawrie R 4 (Angus' wife)
Old Toasty 2/4 HP 4 (Old Toasty was Angus' uncle, also called Angus, who founded the Oban Pipe Band in 1925)
Paddy's Market 6/8 J 4 (a flea-market in Glasgow)
Pipe Major Ian McLellan BEM 2/4 M 4 or 6/8 M 4 (1982)
Ronan 2/4 M 4 (Ronan is the name of the house where Angus' cousin Ronald Lawrie lives)
Salute to Ian Ireland 6/8 SA 2 (Ian was a terminally ill child from Dunoon. He

died in 1980)
Wee Harry 6/8 J 4
Willie's Brogues 2/4 HP 2 (1977. Named after the large feet of Willie Sloan, President of the R.S.P.B.A.)
Any additions will be welcomed

IAIN LAWRIE was the only son of Willie Lawrie, and was born in 1913. In the Second World War he served with the 8th Argylls, but was captured at St Valery in France in 1940, and spent the rest of the war as a prisoner of war. He met George MacIntyre and John Wilson (see above) while in a prison camp.

Iain Lawrie's compositions include:
Mo Cailleag Fhein (My Own Lassie) 6/8 M 4
The Everlasting Hills 6/8 SA 2
The Three Sisters of Glencoe 6/8 J 4

The origins of JAMES ('Jack') MCINTOSH LAWRIE are obscure. He was a Pipe Major in the Gordon Highlanders around 1900, and by 1908 was Pipe Major of the 2nd Argyll and Sutherland Highlanders, a post he held until 1922. He was the first Pipe Major of the Argylls to land in France in 1914, and served throughout the war.

A pupil of G.S. MacLennan, he won the Gold Medal at Inverness in 1913, the last of the Northern Meetings until 1919. Presumably he had Argyll connections, as he seems to have been the composer of *Torosay Castle*, a 3/4 Retreat March in four parts, which suggests that he had been piper at Torosay, in S.E. Mull, before he went into the army. But his link, if any, with the Oban Lawries or the Ballachulish branch, has not been established.

In 1909, G.S. MacLennan made a 6/8 March in four parts, and after his death, his son George gave it the name *Pipe Major J. Lawrie*, as he knew his father 'thought highly of Jack Lawrie's playing and compositions'. Jack had been Pipe Corporal to G.S. when he was in the Gordons.

RONALD LAWRIE

RONALD LAWRIE IS THE SON of Angus 'Old Toasty' Lawrie, and was born and brought up in Oban. Of his own career, he remembered that when Willie Ross went to Oban to teach the Oban Pipe Band and start a piping class for the young people, he himself was one of them. It was a tremendous thrill for the boy to meet the famous Willie Ross, who he knew was a marvellous piper.

Later he had the great experience of listening to Robert Reid (who had been taught by John MacDougall Gillies) once a week at the Glasgow Pipers Club and he used to go to his shop and to his home for tuition.

He felt he was very fortunate in joining the Glasgow Police Pipe Band while the famous Glasgow pipers were still there, such as Pipe Major John MacDonald and his brother Roddy, John Garroway, and Major Archie McNab.

Ronnie Lawrie's own distinguished pupils included Hector MacFadyen, 'Big' Angus MacDonald of the Scots Guards and Angus MacColl.

He commented that it can be very satisfying to bring a pupil through to a high standard. He favours traditional teaching methods, the way he was taught himself: 'by the finger'. His teachers sang the tunes over, a lot of the time. The pupils used books too, but learned tunes from the finger, a method he said was very accurate, provided the tutor was skilful. When the learners could read a little music, they began to pick out the tunes themselves, but soon got to the stage where, if they heard a pipe tune being played, they could memorise it very quickly without the book.

He would give his pupils books to learn from, but always sressed that true expression comes from singing the music to them, and making them learn to sing it themselves before they put it on the chanter.

Ronald Lawrie, with his cousin Angus, was in the 8th Argylls T.A. Band in the 1950s, along with John M. MacKenzie from Campbeltown and Neil MacEachern from Islay.

It was Ronald Lawrie who as Pipe Major of the City of Glasgow Police Pipe Band took them to their first Champion of Champions victory. He had to step down as Pipe Major in 1972, because of ill health, and was succeeded by Iain MacLellan.

When Ronnie Lawrie was a pupil at the College of Piping in Glasgow, Tommy Pearston once said to him 'You want to chuck it, you'll never be a piper'. After Ronnie won the Gold Medal at Oban in 1961 the first thing he did was seek out Tommy and say 'Remember you told me to chuck it?' Tommy said 'Aye, but that was just to get you to practise – and it worked, didn't it?'.

John MacLellan, at the Piobaireachd Society Conference in 1989, said that when Ronald Lawrie and Hector MacFadyen were coming into the piping world in the early 1960s, Hector had a set of Lawrie drones and Ronnie had a set of Henderson drones; they both got small brass tubes and a tool, and they inserted the tubes into the drones. Anyone who was about at the time will remember that both of them had fairly full-sounding drones, but when they put in those tubes, the difference was fantastic – how much the sound mellowed was amazing. Certainly recordings of Hector's drones have preserved a sound which still makes pipers sit up.

Ronnie Lawrie, judge at the Silver Chanter competition at Dunvegan in 1999. (PHOTOGRAPH BY COURTESY OF THE COLLEGE OF PIPING)

Lorne & Appin

On pipe band playing, Ronnie Lawrie said it was important to have a good grounding in the rudiments of piping before going into a pipe band, because it was too easy to learn bad habits from the players of different standards in a band.

He is of the opinion that bands should get back to the simple way of playing pipes. He thinks the bands are over-reaching themselves with their arrangements of their medley programmes. 'There's melodies I just don't understand. They're composing and playing too much stuff that isn't up to quality ... the musical content is too often not there. They throw in counter-point and seconds and harmony and it's just too much colouration all over. At least, that's how I see it.'

He would also like to see the pitch of the pipe bands come down a bit; 'they're getting too high, too shrill. It doesn't sound like a bagpipe any more. And, of course, this is happening in the solo side of things, too. But to alter that, the pipers and the pipe bands will have to want it themselves.'

[Quotations based on an interview with Ronnie Lawrie in the Notes from the Piping Centre, Autumn 1999]

Ronald Lawrie composed:
Anne Edgar 2/4 M 4
Arthur Gillies
The Banjo Breakdown, setting R 5
Doctor Herb Dedo's March 12/8 M 4. (Dr Dedo was a specialist in San Francisco who operated successfully on Ronald's hearing in 1980).
George E. Schell's March through Caithness 2/4 M 4. (Mr Schell is a Director of Arts in the Community College, San Francisco. This piece commemorates a sight-seeing tour in the north).
Glenfinnan Highland Gathering 2/4 M 4
Ina MacKenzie 2/4 HP 4
Mrs Betty Hardie 2/4 HP 4
Also note: *Ronnie Lawrie's Rant,* by John M. MacKenzie 6/8 J 4
Ronnie Lawrie (Oban), by William M. MacDonald S 4

I KNEW AN OLD PIPER

I knew an old piper who swallowed a reed —
Did he succeed
In swallowing a reed?
He did indeed.

He swallowed the reed to play high G,
Aiming for ghost-tones on his D —
He got high G in a sad lament
But it came out higher than he meant —
He played the lament with his bass drone out,
The one judge who noticed was full of doubt —
He adjusted his bass in the third variation,
Ignoring a certain wah-wah-wah sensation —
Then his middle drone stopped in the final line,
Just when he thought it was going fine —
And his teeth fell out in the Urlar repeat,
He said it was something to do with the heat.

I knew this old piper who thought he had won,
He felt he'd played well and was second to none,
His fingers as supple as ever they were,
His Crunluaths crispy and ever so clear —
The secret, he said, lay in good preparation,
And went off to start on a wee celebration.

I knew an old piper who swallowed a reed —
Some will try anything to give them the lead,
But it's not recommended for anyone, nor
Did HIS name appear among the first four —
And the rest of his life, to sing a true note,
He had to put plenty of tape on his throat.

I knew this old piper, he swallowed a reed —
He had no need
To swallow a reed,
And now he's deid.

Glencoe, Ballachulish and Glenorchy

Tunes associated with Glencoe, Ballachulish and Glenorchy district include:
The Ballad of Glencoe, arranged by Jim Hamilton 6/8 SA 2
The Bonawe Highlanders, by D.Bowman 6/8 M 4
Glencoe Mountain Rescue Team, by Major Eric Moss 2/4 M 4
The Glen of Sorrow, by William M. MacDonald 9/8 SM 4
John MacDonald of Glencoe, by William Lawrie 2/4 M 4
Lament for Glencoe (Great Is The Cause Of My Sorrow) 6/8 SA 1
Lament for the Dead (The Rout of Bendoeg) P with 8 or 9 variations. Bendoeg is probably Beinn Doaig or Toaig, not far from Glenorchy, and was presumably the scene of a local battle or skirmish, involving the Breadalbane Campbells and invading cattle reivers.
Leaving Glencoe, by P/M MacDonald (Sydney) 2/4 M 4
Loch Etive Side, by J.Cameron, arr. Ross 2/4 SM 2
The Massacre of Glencoe P with 6 or 7 variations (see below)
The Pap of Glencoe, by William Lawrie 2/4 M 4
People of This Glen (Mhuinntir A'Ghlinne) 6/8 SM 2 (see below)
Pipe Major William Lawrie's Favourite, by George Grant 2/4 M 4
The Portsonachan Cook, by Dr Bruce E Thomson 2/4 HP 4
The Three Sisters of Glencoe, by Iain Lawrie 6/8 J 4
Tommy MacDonald of Barguillean, by Dr Bruce E.Thomson 2/4 M 4

MacKENDRICKS OR HENDERSONS

THIS FAMILY, SPELLED MACEANDRAIG OR MacEandric in Gaelic but often called Henderson in English, were pipers to the MacDonalds (MacIains) of Glencoe. There is a possibility that the name MacEandric is a corruption of MacIainruig, that is, a branch of the MacIain family. One of them was IAIN BREAC MACEANDRIC, who is said to have composed the Gaelic words to the tune *We Will Take The High Road*, in 1644. He was an ancestor of Donald and Archie who fought in the '45.

In 1689 when the Glencoe MacDonalds were gathering at the south end of Loch Lochy before the battle of Killiecrankie, their piper was said to be a Henderson, known as 'Big Henderson of the Chanters' (his first name has been lost). He was the MacIain chief's piper, and was still with him at the time of the massacre in 1692, escaping to Ardnamurchan, where he settled.

In the Muster Rolls of the Jacobite army of 1745, two pipers DONALD and his nephew ARCHIE are listed. Their surname is given as MACERICH, but this is probably a way of writing (or possibly a misreading of) MacEnrich, with the e strongly nasal. They were the regimental pipers to Alexander MacDonald of

Glencoe's Company, and served throughout the campaign.

The Rolls mostly list the fates met by the men (Tried, Transported, Killed, Pardoned and so on), but there is no entry of this for the uncle and nephew. The Roll has Archie simply as the Piper's Nephew, and it is not stated whether he was himself a piper, but tradition says that he was. He was probably his uncle's apprentice-pupil and gillie.

The MacEandrics were said to be descended from the Lords of the Isles, by a marriage between Iain Og, 1st of Glencoe and a daughter of Dougall MacHenry, in the 11th century. But a glance at the Old Parish Registers of the 18th century shows that most of the Henderson families of the district (and they were not numerous) came from the Glenorchy district, which is adjacent to the lands of Glencoe and includes Kingshouse. There was a nest of them at Arivean, which lies in Glenlochy, about five miles west of Tyndrum and ten miles east of Dalmally.

This was the home of Duncan Henderson and his brother Peter or Pat, both of whom were the fathers of several 'natural' (illegitimate) children, as well as having large families with their wives. The rate of natural children among the Hendersons in the parish was far higher than average – but we do not know if these Hendersons were pipers. It seems likely that Glenorchy Hendersons went to Glencoe as pipers to MacIain before the Massacre, but we cannot prove it.

In 1998, a large stone known as the Henderson Stone was dedicated in remembrance of the victims of the Massacre. It is said that the stone was used by the MacEandric pipers of Glencoe for transmitting messages to the nearby townships when their usual signal rock, at a greater height, was not suitable because of adverse weather. A ceremony was held, at which piper and latterly judge, Joe Henderson played *People of This Glen*, and ministers and priests from the Catholic, Episcopalian and Presbyterian churches officiated at an outdoor service. The Henderson Stone is now on a plinth not far from the Glencoe Visitor Centre.

GLENORCHY

A HOUSEHOLD BOOK KEPT BY Lady Glenorchy, wife of Sir John Campbell of Glenorchy, has an entry for the week September 6-13th 1662 which says: 'The pyper and his man being here some part of the week, Glenlyons fidler and his man some part of the week.' Alas, she gives no detail – she was simply counting bednights and meals. Her husband was away in Edinburgh, and Campbell of Glenlyon had visited during his absence. Glenlyon seems to have brought his own fiddler, but the piper was probably Glenorchy's own.

In September 1669, she records that 'two pypers and their men' spent three nights at Glenorchy, and Keith Sanger thinks this may have been part of the preparation for an excursion to Caithness, which resulted in the battle between the Breadalbane men and the Sinclairs in Caithness, commemorated in the piobaireachd work *The Carles Wi' the Breeks*. (It is so called because the Caithness men or carles, being of Norse origin, wore trousers rather than kilts).

The Clan MacIver has a tradition that the Earl of Breadalbane's piper at the Battle of Altimarlach (Wick) in 1680 was Finlay MacIver, who was afterwards appointed personal piper to the Earl. The MacIvers were related to the Campbells of Cawdor. Finlay may have been one of the two at Glenorchy in 1669 – the Earl of 1680 was then Sir John Campbell of Glenorchy.

It is interesting that Lady Glenorchy makes mention of each individual musician having his own man. This seems to indicate a status above that of mere servant or estate employee, as we assume the piper's man was a gillie who carried and looked after the pipe. Stories about early pipers often make reference to such an arrangement, which is sometimes assumed to be fictional; here is documentary evidence that pipers did have gillies, at least at Glenorchy at the end of the 17th century. Possibly the gillie was a pupil learning the care of the pipe and its music.

DONALD ROY (RUADH) MACINTYRE was a young piper to Lady Glenorchy's husband, Sir John Campbell of Glenorchy, later to become the Earl of Breadalbane. In October 1675 Sir John sent word to John Campbell of Innergeldie, telling him to 'give Donald Roy pyper fortie pund Scotts to learn his trade and give him four pund Scotts to buy him cloaths'. It is not made clear who was teaching Donald.

We know his surname from another item from 1675 when a plaid was bought for Donald Roy MacIntyre pyper, and in 1674 £24 had been outlaid in Edinburgh for pypes for Donald Roy. His son, or possibly his nephew or grandson, JOHN MACINTYRE, was in 1697 sent by the Earl of Breadalbane first to the Rankin school in Mull and then to the MacCrimmons in Skye. Keith Sanger gave the details of these items in his interesting article in the Piping Times in March 1992. This John MacIntyre is believed to be the composer of *The Prince's Salute, Menzies' Salute, My King Has Landed In Moidart, MacIntyres' Salute*, and the *Battle of Sheriffmuir* – though some say this last was the work of Finlay Dubh MacRae, who composed the *Earl of Seaforth's Salute*.

JOHN MACFARLANE

JOHN MACFARLANE WAS A PIPER who belonged to the Dalmally district, near Glenorchy. His home was Edendonich, close to Dalmally. He is described in the Notices of Pipers as 'a fine specimen of a man and an excellent player'. He was the eldest of the ten children of William MacFarlane and Catherine Morison, born in 1764 at Stronmilchan, not far from Edendonich, both near Dalmally. The first four children were born at Stronmilchan, the remaining six in Edendonich before 1787.

There were about a dozen MacFarlanes of William senior's generation living in Glenorchy in the 1760s and 70s, but we cannot tell if they were William's siblings or cousins, or possibly not related at all.

William MacFarlane, father of John the piper, was himself described as a piper in the birth notice of his son George, in 1776. In John's entry in 1764, the father was 'William Macffarlan weaver in Stronmilchan', but later entries make it clear that he was known as Will. The Parish Register does not go far enough back for us to find out who Will's father was, nor whether he too was a piper. The fact that Will called his first son John may indicate that Will was the son of John MacFarlane who was piper at Inverioch (see below).

MacFARLANES IN GLENORCHY

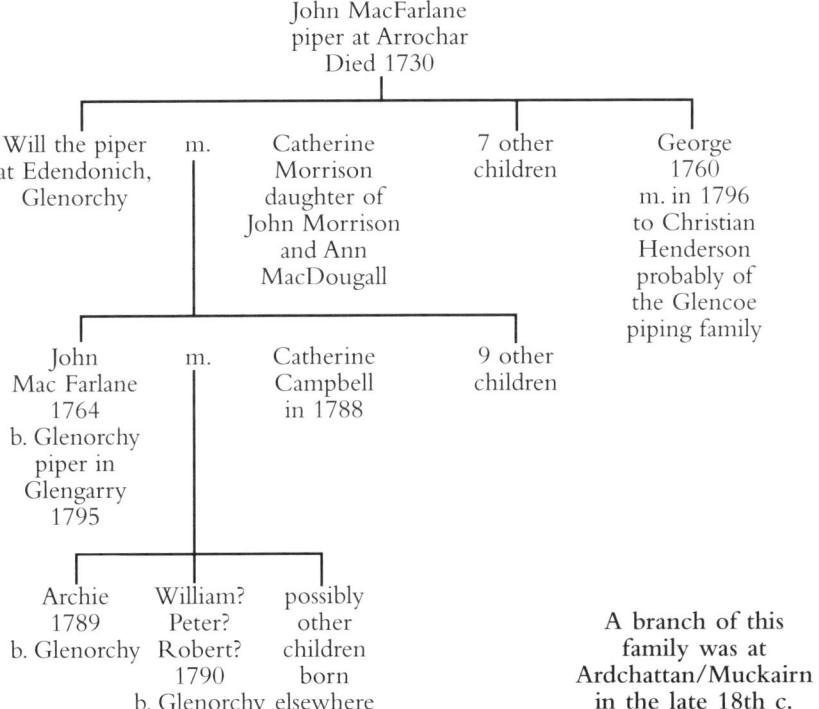

A branch of this family was at Ardchattan/Muckairn in the late 18th c.

We do not know if other members of the family were pipers, but it seems likely enough. George, born 1776, married Christian Henderson when he was twenty, and she was probably one of the piping Hendersons or MacEandrics of Glenorchy and Glencoe, who lived at Arivean, not far from Dalmally.

John, in 1788, registered as John MacFarlan Piper, married Catherine Campbell, from Dalmally, and two of their children were born at Edendonich, Archie in 1789, and another son, possibly called William, in 1790. The name was written in the register, re-written and crossed out several times, and the name which was finally inscribed on the top of this mess could be almost anything, but has been read as William, probably because John's father was William. We forgive the registrar for this when we read the note he added to the dry notice of this baptism:

'N.B. The baptism of the above child to John MacFarlan Piper was in the presence of the child's father and mother, the Grandfather and Grandmother and the Great Grandfather and Great Grandmother, the Two Last strong and vigorous, viz. John Morrison and Ann MacDougall, Edendonich'

This christening must have been unique, and the minister felt it worthy of a special note. It tells us that one side of the family had been at Dalmally for at least three generations, and that there was MacDougall blood in it; possibly Ann MacDougall was related to the Glencoe pipers (see below), and they in turn were kin to the MacDougalls who had the piping school near Oban (see above). She may also have been related to the blind poet at Glengarry who made a poem about her grandson (see below).

There was another John MacFarlane who was piper in Arrochar and died in 1730. He may have been the father of Will and the other grandfather of John MacFarlane, Glenorchy. This older John was piper at Inverioch House, Arrochar, and his grave is at Ballyhennan, near Tarbet, Loch Lomond. Was he the father of Will, the weaver and piper in Glenorchy? We cannot be certain. The Morrison grandfather who attended the baptism of John's son was his maternal grandfather, who lived in Glenorchy. There is no proof that the older John MacFarlane was related, but there are not many MacFarlane pipers on record, and these things, the talent and the careers as professional players in big houses, tend to run in families.

In the 1790s, John MacFarlane from Glenorchy was in Glengarry as piper to Alasdair Ranaldson MacDonnell, the laird of Glengarry and descendant of both Donald of Laggan and Alasdair Dearg, both commemorated in beautiful piobaireachd laments composed in the 17th century. Whether John went to Glengarry direct from Dalmally we do not know, but it seems that he may have had a few years in the army before this (see below).

John Prebble in his book *Mutiny* gives a scathing portrait of young Glengarry, depicting him as a man of 'monstrous absurdity, . . . with grand and eccentric manners'. He seems to have striven all his life to be larger than life, full of a ridiculous romanticism, and Prebble says he 'rarely stepped abroad without a chief's ancient tail of henchman, bard, piper and gillies'- playing at being a mediaeval clan chief.

As a military leader young Glengarry was dangerously volatile and unpredictable, and this may be the reason why his piper, John MacFarlane, was said to be careful of his manners, as watchful as a helmsman studying the weather.

While John was at Glengarry, the laird's bard, Blind Allan MacDougall, who may have been related to him, composed some verses about him, which probably date from around 1795.

The poem is called *Oran do Mhac-Pharlain, Piobaire Mhic-ic-Alastair (Song for MacFarlane, Piper to Glengarry)*, and it is headed 'Air fonn An Comunn Rioghail Runach' (To the tune of *The Royal Secret Society*). The earliest edition of his poems, published in 1798, describes Allan as filidh, not bard, to Glengarry – a filidh was the very top rank of poet, superior in every way to a mere bard.

The poem goes like this:
Mo shoruidh gu Mac-Pharlain,
A's dh'innsinn da gu luath,
Nam b'fhear a dheanadh facail mi,
Gun d'thugainn ionnsuidh sgairteil air,
A dh'innse roinn ga chleachduinnean
'Ghruaidh mar chaoran, 'shlios mar fhaoilinn,
'S i ri taobh a chuain.

'My compliments to MacFarlane,
And I will tell you quickly,
Preferring to make my words
Without putting too vigorous a rush on it,
To tell you partly about his habits
And partly about his aspect and appearance,
His cheek red as a berry, his side white as a seagull
Beside the ocean'.

Suil chorrach ghorm, 's i liontaidh,
Fo d'mhalaidh ghrinn gun ghruaim;
Do dheud mar chailc no iobhracdh,
Cho snaighte ris na disnean,
'S a bheul a labhradh siobhalta
Le firinn anns a gach uair,
Iomaigh mhaiseach, 's lionmhor tlachd,
Cha laidh ort gart an fhuachd.

'A rolling blue eye, full and rounded,
And fine eyebrows without a frown;
Your teeth like chalk or ivory,
Hewn into cubes like dice;
And your mouth speaking courteously
To everyone all the time,
With truth always of much appeal,
The threat of coldness is not upon you'.

Gur maith thig feileadh breachdain dhuit,
Am pleatadh ann an cuaich,
Paidhir dhag fo t-achlaisean,
Biodag air chrios acfuinneach,
Lann thana ghorm chinn aisnich,
'S i le faobhar sgaiteach, cruaidh;
'S mairg a choisneadh ort am buille,
'S urrainn thu 'thoirt uait.

Glencoe, Ballachulish, Glenorchy

'The kilted plaid becomes you well.
Folded into pleats,
A pair of pistols under your arm,
A dirk fastened to your belt,
A slender blue sword with a ribbed point
With a sharp edge made of steel;
Pity him who earned the blow
That you can deliver with it.'

Nuair theid am feadan riobhach
Fo d'mheoir is dionaich fuaim,
A'roinn ciuil bho'n t-shiunnsair iongadach,
Gu siubhlach, luthmhor, ioraltach,
Gu pongail, fonnmhor, innealta,
Bho d'riobhaid ga chur suas,
'S tearc ri fhaicinn fear do choltais
'S toirm nan dos ri d'chluais.

'When the reeded chanter is going well
Under your fingers with an air-tight sound,
The notes of the music from the instrument are marvellous,
Swift, nimble, well executed,
Accurately pointed, melodious, in tune,
With your reed putting it forth,
And rarely do we see a man of your like
With the sound of the drone beside your ear'.

'S cuis sholais bhi ga t-eisdeachd,
'S tu's binne gleus na chach,
Gun stri no spairn fo t-aodach ort,
A cumail deo ri gaothairibh,
Le seideagaibh neo-shaoithreachail,
Gur blasda caoin do chluain;
'S eibhinn t-iolach, seinn le grinneas,
Bileach, milis, cruaidh.

'And a source of pleasure it is to hear you,
And you tuning more harmoniously than the rest,
Smooth and effortless under the bag
Which keeps the wind in your instrument,
With diligent steady blowing,
Agreeable and smooth is your interpretation
And delightful the sound, elegant music,
Well-reeded, sweet, incisive (hard-edged)'.

Nuair ghluaiseas tu gu h-aigeannach
Air mhadainn gu parad,
Le d'cheum eutrom, bearraideach,
Do chruit ga speiceadh, farumach,
Toirt failt do'n Choirneal Gharrannach
Gu caithreamach fo d'laimh;
'S glan do thorman, ceolmhor, stoirmeil,
'S tu cuir foirm fo chach.

'When you march in sprightly fashion
In the morning on parade,
With your step light and nimble,
Your instrument played resoundingly,
You give a salute to Colonel Glengarry
With a joyful sound under your hands,
And clear are your drones, harmonious and ringing,
Encouraging them all to best display'

Do phearsa chumbach, mhileanta
Bho chrun do chinn gu d'bhomm;
A chleachd a bhi 'm beachd inntinneach,
Gu reachdmhor, neartmhor, rioghalach,
Comh-thional feachd a piobaireachd
Le d'phuirt is lionmhor fonn;
'S fada chluinnte fuaim do chaismeachd,
Sgairt nam feadan toll.

'Your well-shaped form, soldierly
From the crown of your head to your soles;
Always in lively posture,
Energetic, vigorous, dignified;
Assembling a host through your piping
With your tunes of many melodies,
The sound of your marches, heard from afar,
The loud cry of your chanter's finger-holes.'

Thig boineid agus fabhor air
Fear ard is aillidh gruag,
Cul-dualach nan cuach sar-mhaiseach,
Gu cam-lubach, cas-fainneagach,
Le sioda 's riobhaich caramh air,
Bho bhunn gu bharr a nuas;
'S deas fo sgarloid deagh Mhac-Pharlain,
Dol an lathair sluaigh.

'Your bonnet with its favours on it
Well becomes the tall man with the handsome head of hair,
Locks of magnificent curls,
Thick with ringlets,
With silk ribbon beautifully interwoven,
From the base to the top;
And elegant in scarlet is the worthy MacFarlane
Going in the sight of people'.

Sar cheannchadair na dibhe thu,
Nuair a shuidh tu s'tigh-osd;
Air bord cha stop a thaitneadh riut,
Bidh fion ga ol gun airceas leat,
Gun ghoinn' air or ga sgapadh ris,
Nuair thachras da bhi d'choir;
O lamh ga riachaid, 's cridhe fialuidh,
'S do mhiann bhi mor !

'The king of spenders
When you visit the inn,
Not for you the stoup of ale
But wine unstinting
And gold unsparing spent on it
When you have it,
From a ministering hand and a generous heart,
With the wish to give'.

Tha do bheusan giulanta,
Cu d'chliu a chur an liad,
Ro cheart an cleachdadh ionnsuichte,
A gluasad 's gach ceum curamach,
Co faicleach ris a stiuradair,
'S e 'g amharc dlu nan nial;
Eolach, fiosrach, le sar-mhisnich,
Measail anns gach gniomh.

'Your manners are civilized,
And as a result your fame has spread,
So correct in educated manners,
Every movement studied,
As careful as the helmsman
Closely studying the clouds,
Expert, knowledgeable, with great courage,
You are respected in your every action'.

'S eibhinn an tir abhachdach
An d'fhuair thu t-arach og,
Mu Urchaidh nam breachd tarr-gheala,
'S a ghleann 'm bi feidh a's earbeinnen,
Am faicte fleasgaich mhearr-chasach
A dheanadh sealg gu leoir.
Am beinn 's an amhuinn spurt ga ghabhail,
Aidhearach le spors.

'The pleasant country is delightful
Where you were nurtured in your youth,
In Orchy of the white-bellied trout,
And in the glen of red and roe deer
The fleet-footed young man was seen
Doing plenty of hunting.
On mountain and river was sport for your taking,
You delighted in the chase'.

'Sguiream anns an uair so dhiot,
A's druidean suas mo ghloir;
Is saighdear ri uchd cruadail thu -
'S comh-lionmhor euchdan fuaighte riut ,
'S nach urrain mise a luaidh
A liughad buaidh a th'ort 's cha bhosd;
Dhiult a Sas'nnach dol a d'bhualadh,
Ge bu chruaidh a dhorn.

'But now I must stop
Talking about you;
You are a real soldier in the face of hardship,
And with so many brave deeds credited to you
That I cannot enumerate your many qualities,
Your virtues cannot be counted.
The English have pulled back from engaging
Hard though their fist may be.'

(I am indebted to Fred MacAulay and Duncan MacLean, who both kindly checked my translation of this poem).

We are obliged to Allan MacDougall, for giving us this word-picture of John MacFarlane. So often these figures from the 18th century or earlier are shadowy and colourless, as is the other John MacFarlane in Arrochar – but Allan has kindly told us what John looked like: a tall man, with a red face, pale skin, protuberant blue eyes, white teeth, a fine head of hair, and an affable manner: and we hear of his kilt and plaid, his dirk and sword, and his hair dressed for army service, and his scarlet tunic.

This last was a military uniform, and may well have been the scarlet tunic with green facings introduced by Sir James Grant (who was young Glengarry's guardian) for his Highland Fencible regiment: a number of men transferred from that company to the newly formed Glengarry regiment.

We also learn that John loved wine when he could afford it, and was generous in treating his friends. But he knew how to behave in company, and seems to have been quite the gentleman. The end of the poem tells us he had already been involved in fighting, but was at home because of a cessation in hostilities.

This helps us to date the poem to the mid-1790s: the British had withdrawn from the Netherlands in 1795, after defeat by the French. From the position of the poem in the published works of Allan MacDougall, issued in 1798, the date of his song for John MacFarlane would be around 1795-6, as poems before it in the book can be dated 1793-4, and those immediately after it belong to 1796-7. Do we then assume that John had seen military service overseas?

Allan makes no reference to John's wife and children, and there is no trace of him or them in the Old Parish Register for the Glengarry district in the 1790s – but this may be because the OPR for Glengarry was not kept systematically during that period. It is possible that John and Catherine did have more children after they went to Glengarry.

We do not know what became of John MacFarlane's wife or family, but there may be a link with a piper William MacFarlane, son of John MacFarlane and Mary MacFederan, who in 1823 was piper on the fishery cutter *Swift*. This cannot be William born to John MacFarlane in 1790, as he has the wrong mother, but he may have been related. Did John perhaps lose his wife Catherine and the child born in 1790, and did he marry Mary MacFederan as his second wife? William the piper was probably born around 1800, but we do not know where. Mary was an aunt of the piper Donald MacPhedran (see above).

In 1794, the year after war broke out against the French, it had been agreed that Glengarry's son, the wild Alexander MacDonell, should raise a Company, to be known as the Glengarry Fencible Regiment. Alexander had previously been second-in-command of Breadalbane's Company, but was now given sole command of his own. Presumably he was the 'Colonel Glengarry' to whom Allan MacDougall refers in his poem about John MacFarlane. Some men transferred to Glengarry's from Grant's Strathspey or 1st Highland Fencible Regiment, especially those who were Roman Catholics; these included an eighteen-year old piper from Kilmonivaig, Duncan MacDonnell.

Service in a Fencible Regiment is not really compatible with army duty overseas, to which the poet made that veiled reference. The Fencible Companies were supposed to be for the defence of the realm, remaining in the country when the regular army was abroad. Perhaps John had been in the regular army, had returned home, joined Grant's Fencibles and was now part of Glengarry's Regiment. This seems the simplest explanation.

John MacFarlane does not appear to have competed in the Edinburgh competitions; this may have been because he was temperamentally unsuited to competitions, as many fine players are, or, perhaps more likely, it may have been because Glengarry had as his first piper Pipe Major John MacDonald of the 42nd, veteran of Ticanderoga. He, according to the Preface to Angus MacKay's Collection, 'had been Piper to the Glengarry family for some generations', and in 1801 he was 'a veteran of near four-score', still competing, and the judges awarded him 'a suitable premium'.

It seems clear that John MacDonald was first piper at Glengarry, and John MacFarlane was possibly brought in as second piper when John MacDonald was beginning to feel his age. John MacDonald would have been piper to the Laird's

Donald MacDonald junior, son of the pipe maker and collector of piobaireachd. This drawing was made by David Dighton in 1822, when Donald junior was piper to Glengarry and had accompanied his Laird to Edinburgh for the King's visit.

father, of course, and perhaps John MacFarlane was regarded as the son's piper. It was of John MacDonald that the story is told in a footnote to Angus MacKay's (Logan's) Preface: 'The lady of Glengarry observed one day to John that it was a matter of surprise he did not employ his leisure hours in doing something. 'Indeed, madam,' said John, 'it is a poor estate that cannot keep the Laird and the Piper without working.'

We do not know what became of John MacFarlane, but, by 1822, Glengarry's piper was the young Donald MacDonald, son of Donald MacDonald from Skye, the pipemaker and piobaireachd collector. David Dighton made a drawing of him on the occasion of the Royal Visit to Edinburgh, when Glengarry took his 'tail' of Highlanders, including his piper, to join the festivities. Young Donald seems to have been followed as Glengarry's piper in the 1820s by Archie Munro, from Oban.

Although we have this likeness of Donald, the poem by Allan MacDougall tells us more about John MacFarlane than a drawing would have.

SOURCES
Notices of Pipers
Old Parish Register; Census Records
Collected Works of Allan MacDougall, 1798

The MASSACRE OF GLENCOE
The *MASSACRE OF GLENCOE* – the piobaireachd – commemorates the killing of MacIain of Glencoe and 37 of his MacDonald clan at Glencoe on 13th February 1692. Soldiers of the Earl of Argyll's Regiment commanded by Captain Robert Campbell of Glenlyon were quartered on the Glencoe people. When at a given signal they turned on their hosts and slaughtered them, there was throughout the Highlands a feeling of horror, not only at the killing itself but at the violation of the unwritten laws of Highland hospitality. It was felt to be the end of civilised living.

Because some of the killers were Campbells it is often assumed that the massacre was part of the ancient feud between Campbells and MacDonalds, but the Campbell involvement, however willing, was driven by the government of the day, seeking to subdue Highland chiefs who did not support the new king, William. The chief mover behind the massacre was the Scottish Secretary, Sir John Dalrymple. Among his less creditable remarks was his observation to the military governor of Inverlochy that 'the winter is the only season in which we are sure the Highlanders cannot escape. This is the proper season to maul them, in the long cold nights'.

The chiefs were required to sign an agreement of loyalty to the king before the deadline of January 1st 1692. The weather was very bad at that time, with deep drifting snow, and MacIan, the Glencoe MacDonalds' chief, was an elderly man. He made it to Fort William in time, only to be told he had to sign the agreement in Inveraray. He failed to reach there by the required date, although

Glencoe, scene of the massacre of the MacIains (Clan MacDonald) in 1692.

he arrived and duly signed the agreement a few days later, and certainly could not be accused of not making the effort. The Secretary of State, however, seized on the chance to be rid of a small but troublesome clan, and to make an example to other rebellious chiefs. He ordered troops to be sent into Glencoe, to carry out the killing.

The manner in which it was carried out was part of the outrage: to quarter men on families they would be required to murder gave the massacre a cruelly ironic twist. When the killing began, many MacDonalds fled into the night in wintery storms, and some, including the Chief's wife, died of exposure in the hills, as Dalrymple had hoped they would.

Although the Chief's sons eventually returned to Glencoe, many of their clansmen left the district, and some, fearful of Campbell vengeance, changed their names. There are traditions of families called MacPhail in Islay who were originally MacDonalds from Glencoe (some later reverted to MacDonald), and another branch who moved north-east up the Great Glen called themselves Collie. Others who settled in Glenurquhart and other districts around Loch Ness kept both their MacDonald name and traditions of their origins in Glencoe, although there is evidence that there had been MacDonalds in the district for centuries before the Massacre: the fugitives were merely seeking out their own kin, for safety. There are today in many parts of the Highlands – Strath Halladale, Caithness, for example, and Sleat in Skye – MacDonalds who are descended from the Glencoe MacDonalds.

Another tradition, preserved in Skye, says that when the three sons of MacIan fled, one went to Fort William, one to Sleat in South Skye, and one to the Uists. This tradition has no mention of their returning to Glencoe, which is historically documented.

Pipe Major William Ross of Edinburgh Castle was a descendant – his mother's name was Collie – and there is a strong possibility that John MacDonald, Inverness, was from the Glenurquhart branch of the Glencoe MacDonalds. William M. MacDonald, Inverness, was also probably related to these MacDonalds from Glencoe. His family came from Kinmylies (near Inverness), where some of the Glencoe descendants are believed to have settled, and they too retained the tradition of their origin. Willie named his published collection of pipe music *The Glencoe Collection*.

A slow march, *People of this Glen*, which appears in piobaireachd form as *Breadalbane's March*, is based on a Gaelic song *(Mhuinntir a' Ghlinne seo)* commemorating the massacre (see above). There is a tradition that the tune was played in Glencoe the night before the massacre, by Hugh MacKenzie (or possibly MacKinnon), piper to Glenlyon, in an attempt to warn the MacDonalds of their danger; but there are many fanciful and romantic traditions about that night, most of them invented later. Much of the literature dealing with the massacre is emotionally slanted, and the facts, chilling enough by themselves, lose their impact when sunk in a sludge of sentiment and romance.

People of this Glen was played in Brussels in 1815, to rouse the men for their march to Quatre Bras, for the final stand against Napoleon. It is said that the song on which the pipe tune is based was made to encourage the people of Strathspey to rise in opposition to an outlaw who was terrorising the district, around 1630. (See also above: the tune was said to have been played in Antrim to warn the women that the Kintyre men were about to lift their cattle).

The piobaireachd work, *The Massacre of Glencoe*, seems to have been made some time after the massacre. The name of the composer is not known. The work was a favourite of the mother of Willie Ross, Mary Collie, whose father, William Collie, left a volume of his memoirs in which he tells of the family tradition about the change of name. His account is borne out by evidence in the Old Parish Registers, Census records and in local oral tradition around Loch Ness.

BLIND ALLAN MACDOUGALL

A MACDOUGALL PIPER WHO WAS probably related to the MacDougalls of Moleigh, near Oban, was ALLAN MACDOUGALL, born in Glencoe in 1751. He may have been the son of the blind piper of the same name, captured in the '45 (see above). Allan senior was captured as a result of his blindness: at the Battle of Falkirk he lost his bearings and wandered accidentally into the Hanoverian lines, and was taken prisoner. He was kept in Leith Jail until he was released in 1747, under the terms of the General Pardon.

His son Allan too was blind, and Nancy Black (p.110) says he 'was a travelling tailor carrying on his trade in the crofts of the poor and the houses of the well to do. It is written in the [MacDougall] chief's family papers that one of Blind Allan's compositions was the beautiful *Cronan nan Cailleach – The old woman's lullaby*' (but it is also linked to Jura, below) . There seems to have been some confusion about the two blind pipers of the same name.

Barbara Fairweather in her booklet *Living in Old Glencoe* makes it clear that Allan MacDougall, born around 1750, was the same man as the bard who composed the poem to John MacFarlane (see above). She writes:

'Allan MacDougall or Ailian Dall (Blind Allan) was born about 1750, and was apprenticed to a tailor. In this period, tailors travelled from house to house, thus Allan heard, and learnt, many old songs and tales. He was quick witted, and once, when sitting cross-legged at his work, he roused the anger of a fellow apprentice, who put a needle in Allan's eye. He lost the sight of the first eye, and soon that of the second.

'Unable to work at tailoring he tried earning a living by fiddling at country weddings and fairs, but made little money. His family moved from Glencoe to Inverlochy (near Fort William), to farm, and Allan's music became popular. Here he composed his songs and poems which were published and also became very popular. Colonel Ronaldson MacDonald of Glengarry gave Allan a cottage and croft and made him his Bard. Allan died about 1826 and is buried on the Burial Island (in Loch Leven)'.

This account of Blind Allan makes no reference to his being a piper as well as a fiddler and bard, and to that extent conflicts with Nancy Black's, and the evidence found in the MacDougall papers. But it may be that the two Blind Allans have become merged as the traditions were handed down. Note that Barbara Fairweather is specific about the cause of the second Allan's blindness, which she implies was not inherited.

Sometimes the composer Ronald Mor MacDougall, who made the *Lament for Captain MacDougall* in 1812, is described as Blind Ranald, and the same name has been used of his grandfather Ranald Ban MacDougall, composer of the *Lament for Iain Ciar*. There is no evidence that any of the MacDougall pipers at Moleigh was blind, and this tradition has probably been mistakenly transferred from the two blind MacDougall pipers in Glencoe – who were probably related to the Moleigh family.

DUNCAN BAN MACINTYRE

DUNCAN BAN MACINTYRE (1724-1812), THE bard known in Gaelic as Donnchadh Ban Mac-an-t-Saoir, is the name always associated with Glenorchy. He has two links with the piping world: he was the official bard to the Highland Society of London who ran the national piping competitions in Falkirk and Edinburgh in the 1780s, and as such he had to produce appropriate poetic effusions every year, in praise of Gaelic or the Prize Pipe or the Committee, whatever he could think of. And before that, he had made an excellent Gaelic poem, *In Praise of Ben Dorain (Moladh Beinn Dobhrain)*, regarded by many as his masterpiece, and he cast it in the form of a piobaireachd poem, made in the 1760s.

These piobaireachd poems, attempting to imitate the structure of a piobaireachd composition, were a feature of 18th century Gaelic literature, probably going back to the time of Iain Dall MacKay in the late 1690s (see also below, Alasdair Mac Mhaighstir Alasdair, under Ardnamurchan).

Duncan was born at Druim Liaghart, Glenorchy in 1724. His family had links with MacIntyres in Skipness, Kintyre, to which the piper and pipemaker Robert MacKinnon belonged (see above). Duncan served in the Argyll Militia Regiment in the '45, and 'made a brief appearance at the Battle of Falkirk in 1746, fighting without enthusiasm on the Hanoverian side', as Derick Thomson puts it (*Introduction*, p.190). On his return he became a forester – that is, not tending trees but acting as a gamekeeper/stalker in a deer-forest – in the Glenorchy district.

In 1767 he went to Edinburgh where he joined the police, then called the City Guard. He served with them for 26 years, and then, at the age of 69, he went into the Breadalbane Fencibles in 1793 as a form of national service, and stayed with them for six years. Professor Thomson says (*Companion*, p.159): 'He seems to have settled well in Edinburgh, playing up to his reputation as poet; being of a cheerful and convivial disposition, he was ready to compose occasional songs (i.e. to mark an occasion) to suit any company. That he made six songs in praise of Gaelic and the bagpipes (1781-9) for the London Highland Society competitions may suggest some lack of originality at this stage, and the truth is probably that his true inspiration, and perhaps his source of guidance, lay in the past, before he moved from the country'.

For us, the interest of his official poems is his subject matter and what they can tell us about the competitions, which is very little. We knew from the Highland Society Minutes that the Prize Pipes were made (by Hugh Robertson) from cocos wood, and Duncan tells us that it came from the West Indies. But much in the poems is mere formal poetic rhetoric, and gives us little in the way of detail.

William Donaldson (p.70) quotes the Society's Minutes for 1783: 'the bard Ma can T'sior was introduced, and pronounced his annual Gaelic poem, in praise of the martial music and prowess of the Caledonians'. A contemporary letter from the same year (Donaldson p.74) describes an impromptu ceilidh in the Tea Room, at which the pipers played for dancing of Strathspeys and Reels, and 'the Old Bard I taught to Clap below his leg which afforded high fune'.

The spelling of Duncan's name in the Minutes gives us a hint that not many understood his poetry, which he declaimed during the interval at the competitions, and probably few of the audience were listening. It is no surprise that the post of Bard to the Society was abolished in 1803, as 'totally unnecessary and a misapplication of the funds' (Donaldson,p.66).

Unlike Alasdair Mac Mhaighstir Alasdair, Duncan was illiterate, and composed all his poetry in his head. He was (or we are) fortunate in that his parish minister, the Rev. Donald MacNicol, wrote down his poems for him, so that the transcriptions, being contemporary, are likely to be reasonably accurate. It may have been the minister who read Alasdair's poems to him. Certainly he knew them, and his own work shows the influence of the earlier poet, some thirty years his senior. Alasdair's poems were published in 1751.

Duncan Ban MacIntyre died in Edinburgh in 1812, and is buried in the old Greyfriars Kirkyard.

Duncan made a rich variety of poems – about his Campbell lairds, about both the Hanoverian cause and the Jacobite, and about the piping competitions. He made three love-songs, including a long one to his wife, and a number of drinking songs and a waulking song. Several of his works have been set to music and are still sung today, especially by Gaelic choirs. But his best work is his nature poetry, composed when he was at Glenorchy, and Professor Thomson says: 'There is reason to think that his poetry died when he left the countryside he belonged to'.

He shows his intimate knowledge of the Glenorchy hills, and in particular of the deer living on them. Professor Thomson reckons that *In Praise of Ben Dorain* is really a work in praise of deer, 'and there can be no doubt that this poem was Duncan Ban's greatest achievement, and it must rank very high in Gaelic literature as a whole.'

There is a story, probably not true, about two men who were looking for Duncan. When they met him, they asked him 'Are you Duncan Ban MacIntyre who made *Ben Dorain*?', to which Duncan replied ' The Good Lord made Ben Dorain; I merely praised His work'.

Like Alasdair's *Moladh Moraig*, Duncan's *In Praise of Ben Dorain* is cast as a piobaireachd poem, and Duncan may have been using Alasdair's work as his model. Professor Thomson thinks that *Moladh Moraig* was the prototype of 'this complicated poem structure', but, in my opinion, Iain Dall MacKay was using it some thirty years earlier in his *Corrienessan's Lament*. In this context, perhaps Rob Donn's two efforts in the genre should also be considered: *Piobaireachd Bean MacAoidh* and *Iseabail Nic Aoidh* are both piobaireachd poems, with varying success. They date from the 1740s (see below).

This is not the place for detailed analysis of *Moladh Beinn Dobhrain* as a piobaireachd poem. It is sufficient here merely to observe that Duncan's efforts to reproduce piobaireachd form in poetry are not entirely successful, and we have to ask ourselves why he bothered.

The best of piobaireachd is of course not regular, but it has patterns of its own which are not here in the poetry. We have nothing in the music (as known today) of Duncan's construction, and it would seem that not only was he following Alasdair's lead here, but he was not at all slavish in his imitation – nor really interested in piobaireachd form. So why, we ask ourselves, did he carve up his work in this way? His poem is a great work of art in its own right without that added complication; it adds nothing, it is irrelevant to the subject, and as an imitation of piobaireachd form it seems to be a failure. In *Moladh Moraig* there was some point, as the poem is about a girl playing the chanter, but pipe music has no place among the deer of Glenorchy. Duncan must presumably have simply been following Alasdair, to see if he could do it too. It was not entirely successful with Alasdair, either, and less so in Duncan's hands.

Marion Campbell has suggested that Duncan might just as well have used the terminology of classical music, and labelled his movements Largo, Andante Cantabile, Allegro pastorale, Alla marcia and so on – though she adds 'but this hides something of the achievement'. The achievement, however, was in the poetry itself, and I cannot feel that the so-called piobaireachd form adds anything to it.

From these two poems perhaps we might deduce that in the 18th century there were piobaireachd works (music, that is) with a structure of three lines of equal length, and no repeat of the first line. There have been suggestions that this was once an accepted form, but it was 'made over' in later times, and transformed into a four-line construction by that repeat of the first line in all variations. This changes the patterns, but the three-line form had equally acceptable patterns of its own, and this may well have been a type of piobaireachd played then.

We know that there were piobaireachd compositions in the 18th century which had Crunluath variations but not Taorluath, and several are found in the MacArthur-MacGregor manuscript. They are mainly works which have a Crunluath Fosgailte, and a tripling of the previous variation rather than a Taorluath. The Crunluath variations represented in the literary piobaireachd works seem closer to the Fosgailte form, and may be intended as such.

There are, however, no musical works where Urlar and Siubhal alternate, with the variations of a length different from that of the Urlar; nor do we find a Crunluath stuck on the end, with a different pattern. These are aberrations, unacceptable and alien to piobaireachd form. We have to conclude that Duncan Ban MacIntyre, wonderful poet though he was, either did not fully understand piobaireachd form or did not care about it; he was probably using it on the pattern of his predecessor, Alasdair, and because it was a fad of the time, however irrelevant to his own work.

See also piobaireachd poems by Alasdair Mac Mhaighstir Alasdair and Norman MacLean, below, Ardnamurchan.

SOURCES
Prebble: *The Massacre of Glencoe*
Glenurquhart records
Katherine Stewart, Abriachan
William MacKay: *Urquhart and Glenmoriston*
John Prebble: *Mutiny*
Keith Sanger
Alexander McDonald
Christian Aikman and Betty Stuart Hart

Derick Thomson: *A Companion to Gaelic Scotland*
Derick Thomson: *An Introduction to Gaelic Poetry*
A' Choisir-chiuil, The St Columba Collection of Gaelic Songs
Marion Campbell

WILLIAM LAWRIE

(I am indebted to Gordon Lawrie, Dunbarton, for much information about the Lawrie family)

WILLIAM LAWRIE (1882-1916) WAS THE son of Hugh Laurie or Lourie, a slate quarrier who lived at East Laroch, the designation for Ballachulish, on the south side of Loch Leven. Ballachulish was famed for its slate quarries, the slate being used for roofing, all over the world.

The spelling of the name Lawrie varies with each record of the family, and the differences have no significance whatsoever, being at the whim of whoever was writing down the information, often not a family member at all. The differing spellings may appear side by side in the same document (e.g. the 1891 Census) for brothers and sisters of the same family. Colin Lawrie tells me that Willie Lawrie signed his name with the Lawrie spelling, so that is used here.

William's father Hugh was born in 1847, in Glengarry, Inverness-shire, and his mother was Agnes Falconer, two years older. She was born in Haddingtonshire, the old name for East Lothian, near Edinburgh.

Glengarry used to be part of the parish of Kilmonivaig, and the Old Parish Register for Kilmonivaig has no Hugh Laurie or Lawrie born in the 1840s. Registration was not then compulsory, so the omission does not necessarily mean he was not born there; it means he was not baptised there, if indeed anywhere.

The earliest Lawries or Louries that we can trace in this family were in Ardnamurchan in the 1770s, so far as we can tell from the inadequate records. Three brothers, John, James and Thomas, were lead-miners at Strontian, Ardnamurchan (the place where the mineral Strontium 90 was first found: it is named after Strontian, which means 'Point of Houses').

Three hundred lead-miners were brought to Strontian when the mines were started in the 1720s, 'from outwith the area', and many were from other lead-mining places, such as Leadhills in Lanarkshire, and leadmining districts in Dumfries-shire. It seems likely that the father or grandfather of John, James and Thomas was among them. In 1851 there was a fatal accident in the mine, and one of the witnesses in the subsequent Enquiry was a blaster and pickman called Alexander Lowrie, probably a descendant of John, James or Thomas.

Thomas was born at Strontian around 1780, and he married a local girl, Christian MacPherson. By 1841 they were living at Achaneilt, and ten years later had moved to a twelve-acre croft in Appin, at Rubh Garbh. Presumably they both died in the 1850s, as they do not appear in the next Census. The family continued in the same croft for several generations.

Glencoe, Ballachulish, Glenorchy

Thomas and Christian had about eleven children that we know of, including James, born around 1821, who married a Skye girl, Isabel Ferguson, and remained in Appin, where their descendants still live.

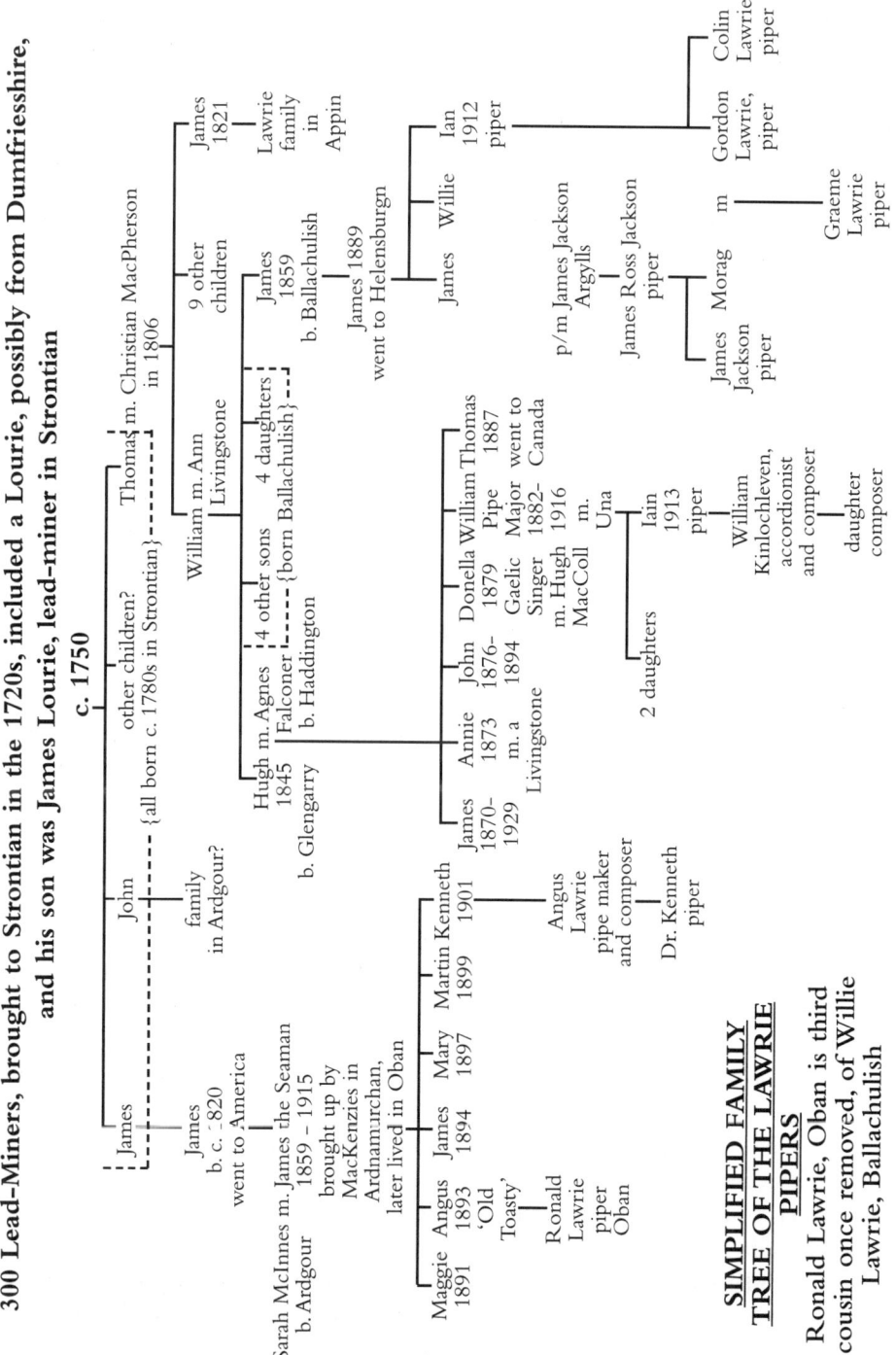

300 Lead-Miners, brought to Strontian in the 1720s, included a Lourie, possibly from Dumfriesshire, and his son was James Lourie, lead-miner in Strontian

SIMPLIFIED FAMILY TREE OF THE LAWRIE PIPERS

Ronald Lawrie, Oban is third cousin once removed, of Willie Lawrie, Ballachulish

The eldest son of Thomas and Christian was William, born in Strontian in 1807. His wife was Agnes or Ann Livingstone, whose birthplace seems to differ with different documents – she may have come from the south side of Loch Eil. William and Ann were the grandparents of Willie Lawrie. They married in 1844, and they had at least nine children, of whom the eldest was Hugh, born in 1847, the father of Willie Lawrie.

Hugh's birthplace is given consistently as Glengarry, Parish of Kilmonivaig, presumably, as they say, because his mother happened to be there at the time. But why was she in Glengarry? Were William and Ann living there, or just visiting? Was William working there? Lord Ward had recently bought the bankrupt Glengarry estates, and Angus MacKay had been his piper in 1841-3; by 1845, Angus was the Queen's piper, and his place at Glengarry had been taken by his brother John, but John was lured away by MacDougall of Dunollie in 1845, to be his piper in the Royal Navy (see above). From the wording in the correspondence about this, it seems that John MacKay in 1845 had already left Glengarry, as he is described as being 'lately' piper to Lord Ward. Was William Lawrie perhaps a piper, who was taken on to replace John MacKay? If so, he did not last long there, as his next son, William, was born in Appin, and the succeeding children were all born in Ballachulish.

Another puzzle about Hugh is his name: there are no other Lawries in this family named Hugh, and the name was not used again among his descendants. Why was he called Hugh? It is most unusual for an eldest son to be given a name outwith his family *sloinneadh*, and indeed we might expect him to be named for his father or his paternal grandfather, that is, William or Thomas. There may have been unusual circumstances around the birth of Hugh in Glengarry, and we do not know the names within Ann Livingstone's family, which may have included a Hugh. Sometimes estate employees named their sons after the Laird or the Factor, people with power over their lives, in the hope of currying favour, but this would be unusual with an eldest son. There are instances of a child being given the name of the doctor or midwife who delivered the baby, especially if it had been a difficult labour. Is it significant that the second son, born in Appin, was named William? Had there been a son who died, born before Hugh and named Thomas after his grandfather? The three-year gap between the marriage of William and Ann and the birth of Hugh may be significant.

Clearly William and Ann were in Glengarry after their marriage, then went to the family home in Appin, before William found work as a slate quarrier and they settled in the slate quarrying village of Ballachulish, also known as Laroch. This must have been just before 1850. The slate-quarrying ties in with the occupation of William's family in Ardnamurchan as lead-miners.

Their children, all born in Ballachulish after the births of Hugh and William, were Christina 1853, Dugald 1855, Donald 1856, Flora 1857, James 1859, and Ann 1864. Christina and her younger sister Ann were both domestic servants in local big houses. Ann had a son, William, in 1893.

It is with James 1859 that our troubles begin. There were three James Lawries born around 1860 who appear to have been related but must have been three separate people, although their parentage is not clear.

James 1859, son of William Lawrie and Ann Livingstone, went to Luss on Loch Lomondside, where he married Catherine Johnson, then living in Luss, but originally from Jura. She may have been related to the piping Johns(t)ons in Islay, and so to the piping MacEacherns of Conisby, in Islay . There was one son, William, from this marriage, but Catherine died young, in childbirth.

James then moved over the hill to Helensburgh, on the Clyde, where he married his second wife, Catherine MacLauchlan. Their children included Ian Lawrie, born 1912, who was a piper, the father of Colin and Gordon. This Helensburgh branch of the Lawries includes Pipe Major James Jackson, and his nephew Graeme Lawrie, both pipers. There is a strong link with the Boys' Brigade in the family, over the generations, and with the 8th Argylls. Colin Lawrie ran the Fruin Memorial Pipe Band for many years and Gordon ran the Dumbarton Pipe Band.

Another James Lawrie born around 1860 appears in the Oban records in the Census for 1891, married to Sarah MacInnes from Ardgour, living in the High Street, Oban. This James is described as a Seaman, and Colin Lawrie has found a James Lawrie, born in the parish of Lismore and Appin in 1860, who was a seaman on board a boat, the *Ellen Brown*, berthed at Easdale when the Census for 1881 was taken. Easdale was the centre of the slate quarrying trade. It seems likely that the *Ellen Brown* was one of many vessels putting in to Easdale to take slate away, possibly bound for Glasgow or Oban.

This James, seaman, born 1860, was the grandfather of Ronald Lawrie, and founder of the Oban branch of the piping Lawries. His birthplace is given variously as Parish of Lismore, and Ardnamurchan, and even Renfrew – where there were Lawries from Ardgour, Gordon tells me.

It is tempting to identify this James with James 1859, son of William and Ann, but this cannot be so. An added complication is a third James, also born around 1860, in Strontian, who must have been related: he went to live in Morvern, where he married Elizabeth Empster (she was connected to the family of James Hunter, Chairman of the Crofters' Commission and author of many books on Highland history). This James Lawrie, too, cannot be the Oban James, so we have three related men called James Lawrie, all born around the same time.

The Oban Lawries are themselves uncertain of the background of James the Seaman, and the reason for this seems to be that James' parents emigrated to America, leaving the child to be brought up by a family in Ardnamurchan, possibly called MacKenzie. He may have been an illegitimate child of his father, and retained the name of Lawrie. His father was said to be called James, too, and the older James was believed to be a son of one of the miners in Strontian, James or John Lowrie, brother of William. The combination of a possible illegitimacy and the fostering outside the family would account for the apparent break in family tradition, and the different first names of the Oban Lawries.

The 1891 Census gives us Hugh Lowrie at Ballachulish Road, in a four-room house; he is now 44, born Glengarry, his wife Agnes from Haddington, and their children are James 21, Annie 18, John 15, Donella 12, William 9 and Thomas 4.

All the children were born in Ballachulish, and Hugh, James and John were all slate quarriers. Annie was a pupil teacher; she taught in the church school of St John's, Ballachulish. This William, 9, was Willie Lawrie, piper and composer, born Ballachulish in 1882, who died of his wounds in 1916.

Also living on the Ballachulish Road, i.e. in the village, were Dugald Lowrie, 36, and his wife Jane, who was from Glasgow. They had two small sons, James H., 3, and Duncan F., 2. This was Hugh's brother, and nearby was his sister Christina, 38, general servant, born parish of Appin. She lived in Ballachulish, and brought up her nephew James, son of the James who went to Luss.

In 1901, Hugh and Agnes appear again, and we learn more about Agnes. She was born in St Lourence, Haddingtonshire, and she did not speak Gaelic, although all her children and her husband spoke Gaelic and English. Now only two sons were at home, William 19, a slate quarrier, and Thomas 14, a slate dresser, and there was a little grandchild Agnes Livingstone, 4, born in Ballachulish, who had no Gaelic. The eldest daughter Annie had married Archie Livingstone. Note that Hugh's mother Ann was also a Livingstone.

Donella, second daughter of Hugh and Agnes, married Hugh MacColl. She was a fine Gaelic singer, and is believed to have won the Gold Medal for singing at the National Gaelic Mod. She died in 1941.

The eldest son of Hugh and Agnes was James, born 1870, died 1929, unmarried. The second son was John, 1876, who died young in 1894. The youngest son was Thomas, 1887, presumably named for his great-grandfather the leadminer in Strontian. Thomas was a slate-quarrier like most of his male relations, and is believed to have gone to Canada to join the Mounties. He dropped out of the picture and it is not known when or where he died. Most of the family graves are at St John's Church, Ballachulish, but there is no stone to Thomas.

William Lawrie was the third son of Hugh and Agnes, born in 1882 at Ballachulish. He joined the local volunteer regiment (the Argyll Volunteers) as a lad, and worked as a slate quarrier, with his father and brothers, until in his mid-twenties.

It is not known where the piping talent lay in the generations before his, but his uncle James 1859, who went to Helensburgh, is known to have been an excellent dancer, who taught Highland dancing in Helensburgh, and it is thought he may also have been a piper. His sons were friends of Andrew MacNeill in Helensburgh, in their boyhood. Willie's father Hugh is not thought to have been a piper, but various uncles and cousins may have been, as may his grandfather William.

Willie studied piping under John MacColl and was one of his most promising pupils. In 1912 he was appointed Pipe Major of his volunteer battalion. He was for some time piper to the Earl of Dunmore, who was the Colonel of the 4th Camerons, and then to Colonel Stewart MacDougall of Lunga. He may have been piper to the MacDonalds of Dunach for a time, and composed a 2/4 march, *Mrs (H.L.) MacDonald of Dunach* (not to be confused with John MacColl's strathspey *Mrs MacDonald of Dunach*).

Willie Lawrie won numerous first prizes at all the principal Gatherings, including the Gold at Inverness in 1910 and the Clasp in 1911; also the Gold at Oban in the same year, 1910. At Inverness he created a record by winning on the same day, not only the Gold Medal, but also the march, and the strathspey and reel. 1910 was definitely his year.

As a composer he was in the first rank, many of his tunes being still played, most notably *John MacDonald of Glencoe, Inveraray Castle* and *John MacColl's March to Kilbowie Cottage*.

On the outbreak of war in 1914, he accompanied his battalion (8th Argylls) and went to France in 1915. He was badly wounded in the trenches, and invalided home in 1916. He died in a military hospital in Oxford on 28 November 1916. The loss is still felt in the piping world, an anguish at the pointless tragedy of his death when he had still so much to offer. He was only 35, at the height of his piping career.

While in France he composed the *Battle of the Somme*, a favourite marching tune among units there. This attribution does not seem entirely certain; Lt.Col. David Murray says the tune is 'usually attrubuted to Pipe Major William Lawrie', though G.S.MacLennan sometimes gets the credit.

Willie Lawrie was a fine looking man, a notable piper, and a good instructor. Speaking of him in 1989, D.R.MacLennan said: 'A very nice, sweet player he was, an extremely amiable chap, and of course a great composer. He and my brother [G.S.MacLennan] were great buddies; he was a couple of years older than my brother. A terrible loss'

In the Piping Times for May 1998, a 6/8 jig was published for the first time. It was found pasted inside the back cover of a book which had belonged to John MacColl. It was written in pencil by William Lawrie, and had been folded up and kept for some time, probably in a pay book. The title was *The Ghurkas' Joy*. The tune was composed while Willie Lawrie was on active service, and is headed '1st 8th Argylls Lacon France 2nd June 1915'.

Willie was married and had two daughters and a son, Iain Lawrie, born in 1913, who served with the 8th Argylls and was captured at St Valery (see above). Iain's son, another Willie Lawrie, lives at Kinlochleven, and is a noted accordionist and composer, who won the Scottish Accordion Championship. His tunes are apt to be confused with those of his grand-

William Lawrie (1882-1916). (PHOTOGRAPH BY COURTESY OF THE COLLEGE OF PIPING)

father, whose talent he inherited and passed on to his own daughter.

The Ballachulish branch of the Lawries is rich in artistic talent, producing pipers, composers, singers and dancers – and two Lawrie cousins of Willie Lawrie were in the Ballachulish shinty team which won the Camanachd Cup n 1911 and 1912.

Willie Lawrie's compositions include:
The 8th Argylls' Farewell to Basincourt 4/4 M 2 , or 2/4 M 2
The 8th Argylls' Farewell to the 116th Regiment de Ligne 2/4 M 2
(possibly) *The Battle of the Somme* 9/8 RM 2 (There seems to be some confusion with a work by G.S.MacLennan, but that may be his Retreat March *Sunset on the Somme*. The Gordon Highlanders Collection gives the tune *The Battle of the Somme*, but it is unattributed, being called 'Traditional').
The Braes of Brecklett 2/4 M 4
Captain Carswell 2/4 M 4
Clacheanruaig (or Clachenrick) S 4. This sometimes appears as *Clachlarrick*.
Duncan Johnston 2/4 M 4
The Gurkhas' Joy 6/8 J 4
Inveraray Castle S 4
John MacColl's March to Kilbowie Cottage 2/4 M 4
John MacDonald of Glencoe 2/4 M 4
Lament for Lord Archibald Campbell
Mrs (H.L.) MacDonald of Dunach 2/4 M 4
The Pap of Glencoe 2/4 M 4
Pipe Major George Ross' Farewell to the Black Watch 2/4 M 4
Pipe Major James Jackson, Argyll and Sutherland Highlanders 2/4 M 4 (This was the grandfather of James Jackson, Alness)
Willie MacColl 2/4 M 4
Note also *P/M William Lawrie's Favourite*, by George Grant 2/4 M 4
Any additions will be welcomed

SOURCES:
Census records
Report on the Sunart Oakwoods
OPR for Kilmonivaig, Ballachulish, Haddington
Stuart MacDonald
Col. David Murray
Piping Times

glenoaruel

STRACHUR DISTRICT (east of Loch Fyne)

Tunes associated with the Glendaruel district include:
Captain Campbell of Glendaruel's March 2/4 M 4
The Dream Valley of Glendaruel 3/4 RM 2
The Glendaruel Gun Club, by J.R.C.Peterson 2/4 M 4
The Glendaruel Highlanders, by Alexander Fettes 6/8 M 4
John MacVicar of Glendaruel, by J.R.C.Peterson 6/8 J 4
The MacFarlanes' Gathering (Togail nam Bo) P with 6 variations
The MacFarlanes' Reel R 2
Miss Campbell of Glendaruel's Reel R 2
Sweet Maid of Glendaruel 2/4 M 2 or 6/8 M 2

JOHN MACDOUGALL GILLIES

Jeannie Campbell, in her book *Highland Bagpipe Makers*, says that John MacDougall Gillies' parents were John Gillies, a granite worker, and Isabella Smith, who married in Aberdeen in 1854. John was born in Aberdeen on 20th May 1855. The Gillies family came from Glendaruel in Argyll, his father being born at Kilmodan, Argyll – his parents were Alexander Gillies and Mary MacDougall, who belonged to the Strachur district, to the east of Loch Fyne. P/M Fettes of the Aberdeen Volunteers composed *The Glendaruel Highlanders* for the Gillies family.

Colonel Campbell of Glendaruel was the Commanding Officer of the Argyll Volunteers in the early years of the 20th century, and he made *The Glendaruel Highlanders* his battalion's March Past, when they were part of the 8th Argylls. Much later, the tune was taken up by Andy Stewart, who wrote foolish words to it as *Campbeltown Loch, I Wish You Were Whisky*. This at least had the merit of making the tune well-known, but Pipe Major Fettes gets little credit for his work.

A distant connection of John MacDougall Gillies, Neil Gillies from

John MacDougall Gillies (1855-1925)

Barnton in Edinburgh, is a great-nephew of John Gillies, Pipe Major in the Scots Guards. Neil has traced the exact nature of the link between John MacDougall Gillies and John Gillies, and has shown that they had the same Gillies great-great-great-grandfather – so the connection is indeed remote, but it is there, and can be proved. Neil also found that the Gillies families who were in Cowal in the middle of the nineteenth century had gone there from the Kilmartin area of Argyll, probably displaced when Malcolm of Poltalloch built his great mansion (see above).

John MacDougall Gillies was the eldest of three sons, and Jeannie Campbell says his first teacher was P/M Fettes. He was also taught by Pipe Major William Murray, and by Alick Cameron, piper to the Marquis of Huntly and son of the great Donald, when John was in Aberdeen, working as a house-painter (Seumas MacNeill said this ruined his fingering and was the reason he did not excel at

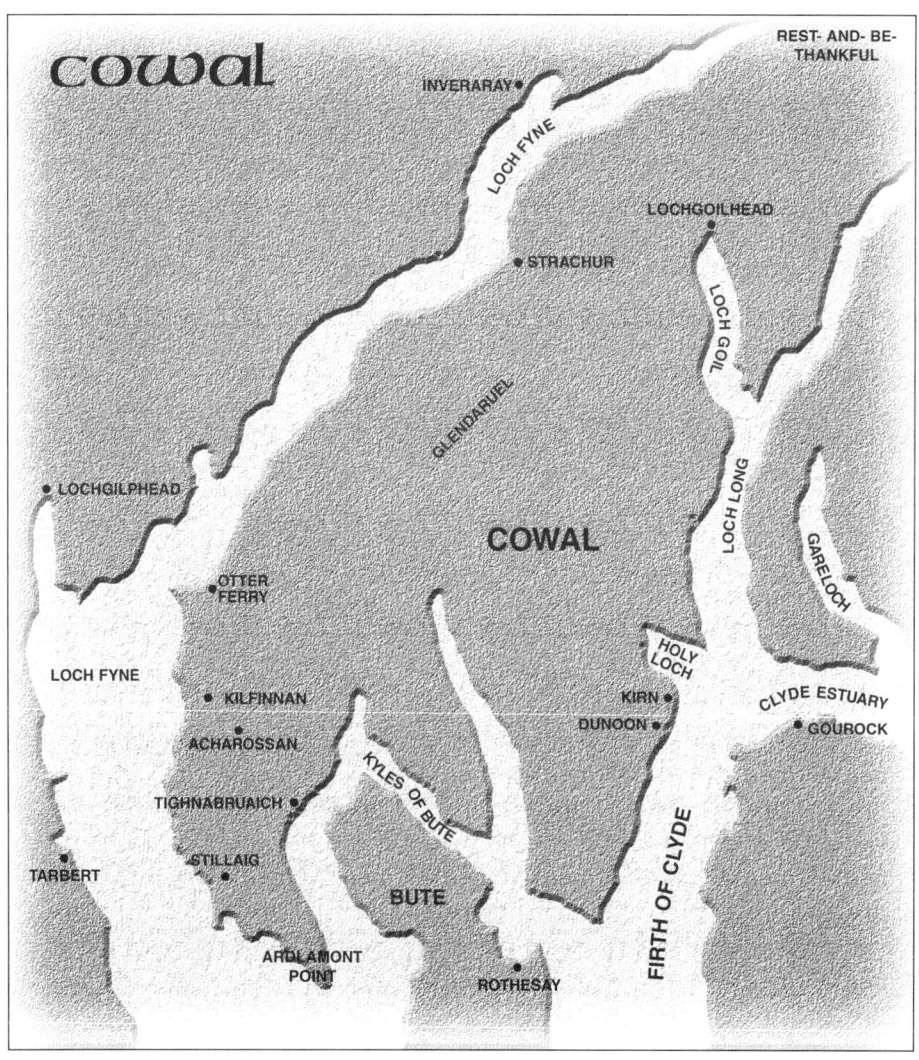

marches and tunes needing fast fingers, but many would dispute this). John joined the Aberdeen Volunteers as a piper under P/M Alexander Fettes.

When under tuition from Alick Cameron John won the Prize Pipe (equivalent of the Gold Medal) at Inverness in 1882 and the medal at Oban in 1884. He had married Margaret Grieve Low, a dressmaker, in 1881, and they made their home in Aberdeen until in 1886 John took up an appointment as piper to the Earl of Breadalbane, at Taymouth Castle, in Perthshire. He stayed there for only two years, disliking the position of servant – tradition says he took umbrage when ordered by the Countess to put down his pipe and sweep up leaves from the castle drive. Whatever the reason, he left for Aberdeen, where he resumed his work as a house-painter. His wife died there in 1890, aged only 31.

After his wife's death he moved to Glasgow, to share his digs with his tutor and friend Alick Cameron. Late in 1891 he married again, his second wife being Maggie MacCulloch from Cardross in Dunbartonshire. They had two sons, Alistair and Ian, and until 1905 John was still working as a house painter.

He became a piper in the 5th HLI (militia regiment) and was their Pipe Major for many years, during which time the band won many prizes. In Glasgow he lived latterly at 409 Great Western Road, just on the city-centre side of Kelvin Bridge.

In 1876 he had won the piobaireachd competition at Braemar, and this was the start of twenty years of winning prizes for his piobaireachd, though his light music was less successful. He was a thoughtful student of piobaireachd, steeped in the Cameron traditions. He won the Gold Medal for Former Winners at Inverness in 1885, now replaced by the Gold Clasp; and in 1896 he was the first winner of the Gold Clasp on its inauguration.

On the death of Peter Henderson in 1905, John took over Henderson's pipemaking firm as manager, a post he held for twenty years. His successor was Archie MacPhedran. Jeannie Campbell suggests that it may have been on the recommendation of Alick Cameron that John was appointed as manager, as Alick had been testing chanters for Peter Henderson.

D.R.MacLennan, in his entertaining talk in 1989 to the Piobaireachd Society, recalled John MacDougall Gillies as being a great player, especially memorable with the *Earl of Seaforth's Salute*, and said that when John was manager of Peter Henderson's around 1918, they used to get together quite often in the daytime, to talk piping (what else?), when D.R. was playing in pantomime at the Theatre Royal in Hope Street, Glasgow, not far from Henderson's.

Piping legend also has a story of John MacDougall Gillies in his Henderson's days. Pipers used to gather in the back shop on Saturday afternoons for gossip and a tune, and when pub opening time was getting near, John MacDougall Gillies would drop a hint by picking up the pipe and launching into *The Men Went To Drink*. Those who went to him for lessons in the evening said he used to draw the lesson to a slightly early finish, to give himself time for a quick one before the pubs closed.

As a teacher MacDougall Gillies was said to be patient but crusty, and very

The 5th H.L.I. with their Pipe Major John MacDougall Gillies (centre), probably around 1920. (Photograph kindly lent by Neil Gillies)

exacting. He kept his pupil Robert Reid on one composition for a full year – and it was *Too Long In This Condition*, appropriately enough. Dr Colin Caird was one of his pupils, too, and described him as a little meek old gentleman with a small pointed beard, very quiet. 'He came into the room where the pupil was waiting, said 'good afternoon' and solemnly laid a chanter down in the middle of the table. And there the chanter stayed, he never played it but it was a symbol of office and after the lesson he picked it up and went out with it. Gillies did all his teaching by means of singing his own canntaireachd'.

Archibald Campbell of Kilberry, as a Gillies pupil, was full of praise for his teacher, but did venture to give the opinion that Gillies was 'apt to allow his pupils not to make sufficient difference' in the pacing of Singlings and Doublings. He said he regarded John MacDonald as the model to copy in pacing his Doublings.

Kilberry's notes on the *Vaunting* suggest that what Gillies had taught him in 1900 was not what appeared in the Piobaireachd Society Book in 1910, for which Gillies had been partly responsible – Kilberry reckoned that Gillies had forgotten teaching him differently.

In *Side Lights*, p.14, Kilberry said that in his view, John MacDonald was apt to cut his semi-quavers as in Ceol Beag, something which was anathema to Alec Cameron – and Kilberry had noticed 'a tendency in this direction in Gillies's playing nowadays. In fact', he adds, 'there are one or two points in which Gillies has altered during the 13 years that I have known him. But Gillies still tells one not to cut short notes too short. According to Cameron, one of the arts of

Glendaruel

piobaireachd is to play notes short without cutting them: in other words, to play 'round' and at the same time with expression'.

In his notes to *The End of the Great Bridge*, Kilberry wrote: 'I remember once hearing Gillies play this tune in the workshop at the back of Henderson's shop with the first variation doubling distinctly slower than the way taught to me by Sandy Cameron. Afterwards I played the tune as taught to me and said to him 'I suppose that you would say that the doubling of the first variation was too fast.' He replied, 'Oh, no, just about right'.

Kilberry said he believed that *Donald Ban* was Gillies' favourite tune. He referred to *Patrick Og* as 'one of Gillies' masterpieces'. John MacDonald cast doubt on the veracity of Kilberry in recording Gillies' views on the playing of *The Wee Spree* (see above).

John MacDougall Gillies was involved in the writing down and hence the preservation of the piobaireachd work *Togail nam Bo, the Lifting of the Cattle*, or *MacFarlanes' Gathering*. Two brothers from Cowal, Donald and John Leitch, both good pipers, had in 1895 played the tune for the Provost of Dunbarton, Robert MacFarlan, who commissioned it to be written down, with the help of John MacDougall Gillies, from the brothers' playing. It was said to be a tune current

'THOGAIL NAM BÒ THEID SINN.

The song and music of Togail nam Bo. Which came first,
the song or the piobaireachd MacFarlanes' Gathering?

in that part of Argyll. Its resemblance to *Too Long In This Condition* suggests that it was a work that was probably known in different forms all over the country, and that its basic melody was probably a song. *The History of Clan MacFarlane* gives a Gaelic song to the tune of the piobaireachd work (see above).

Sir Walter Scott gave a rendering in English of what he called the sense of the music:

> 'We are bound to drive the bullocks
> All by hollows, hirsts and hillocks,
> Through the sleet and through the rain,
> When the moon is beaming low
> On frozen lake and hills of snow,
> Bold and heartily we go;
> And all for little gain'.

Probably not one of his better efforts. The reference to the moon is an echo of the term 'MacFarlane's Lantern' for the moon, since cattle raids were usually expected on moonlit nights.

Kilberry records that Gillies claimed that *MacFarlanes' Gathering* was a 'genuine separate piobaireachd known in Glendaruel and other parts of Cowal for years'. The setting played now is Gillies', evolved from what he picked up in Glendaruel. The tradition is that 'it was composed by Andrew MacFarlane, who fell at Flodden, while *Too Long In This Condition* is ascribed to a MacCrimmon maltreated as a prisoner after Sheriffmuir. The question is really whether *Togail nam Bo* is this or whether it is a 'lost pibroch', for it seems to have existed undoubtedly one ' (What does this mean?). It was a lady, Mrs Leitch, who gave him, Gillies, the tune. Was she the mother of Donald and John, from Cowal?

Although the *MacFarlane's Gathering* appears from its title to be a clan gathering tune or *brosnacha* (incitement), the fact that it is qualified by the words *Togail nam Bo*, *Lifting of the Cattle*, indicates that this is gathering in another sense. The MacFarlanes, and indeed all the clans in that district, bordering on the Lowlands, were notorious for their activities as rustlers of other clans' cattle, in the sixteenth and seventeenth centuries. The music itself seems to confirm this background: it has none of the ding-dong, sometimes unmusical, battle variations of many gathering tunes, but is more melodic and musically pleasing.

In 1920, Gillies and eleven others formed the Scottish Pipers' Association (SPA) in Glasgow, and he became the first President. The Association's MacDougall Gillies Trophy, which was the top amateur piobaireachd prize for many years, is the figure of Gillies himself, playing the pipes.

John's brother Alexander was also a good piper.

[The above account owes much to Jeannie Campbell, to whom I am, as ever, indebted]

Robert Meldrum, in his *Reminiscences* published in 1951, said that the name of John MacDougall Gillies was one 'that will live in the history of piping. . . We [Meldrum and MacDougall Gillies] were about the same age. I was getting taught at the barracks by Willie Murray, Pipe Major of the depot, and I used to pass on my knowledge to John. He had a brother, Alick, who was a better player. John was afterwards taught by Alick Cameron, Donald Cameron's son, who was with the Marquis of Huntly at Aboyne Castle. He was for about two years piper to Breadalbane, and then went to Glasgow in the railway service. When Peter Henderson, the pipe maker, died, Gillies was made manager of the business and remained there until his death. He had much of the tradition of the Camerons, studied pibroch most assiduously and did a great deal of teaching '.

Robert Meldrum also mentions John MacDougall Gillies in connection with the pipers' 'strike' in 1885: 'I had gone to this gathering' (the Northern Meeting) 'knowing nothing of an unfortunate, though perhaps amusing, difference between the pipers and the management. On my arrival, Willie MacLennan met me and asked me what the devil I was doing there. I replied that I was not afraid of any of them, and I asked why I should not be there. He explained that they had protested against the smallness of the prizes and that they were not going to play. I replied that I paid for my return ticket to Inverness and was going to play. Eventually Angus MacRae and Gillies played, though they had protested, but MacColl and MacLennan did not. They got into some trouble for 'booing' some of those who played. Gillies got the pibroch' [the Clasp] 'and I was second. The judges praised my playing but for my reed. Someone had removed my own reed and substituted another.' (This is a suspicion often voiced by pipers. It is on a par with the feeling that someone was in your garden planting weeds while you were away on holiday).

George S. MacLennan (1883-1929), one of the many pupils of John MacDougall Gillies. Although universally known as 'G.S.', he was baptised George Charles Stewart MacLennan, but seems to have dropped the Charles.

John MacDougall Gillies' pupils included Robert Reid, who in 1912 was in the HLI with John as his Pipe Major. Reid served in Palestine and France in the 1914-18 War, and himself became Pipe Major in the HLI. He won the Gold at Inverness in 1921, at Oban in 1922, and the Clasp six times, the Open six times.

John also taught G.S.MacLennan, Willie Gray, Archie MacNeill and Iain MacPherson (father of Donald and Iain). Angus MacLeod, of a Skye family of pipers, went in 1896 to live in Glasgow where he could get tuition from John MacDougall Gillies. Angus became Pipe Major of Maryhill Pipe Band, and later when he moved to Grangemouth he continued to go to John MacDougall Gillies.

Pipe Major Robert Reid, possibly the most distinguished of the many pupils of John MacDougall Gillies.

Other pupils were Pipe Majors Smith and Ferguson of the Argylls, Pipe Major Yardley of Cambuslang, Pipe Major Lynch of the 93rd Regiment , and George MacDonald, Pipe Major of the Millhall Band when it won the world championship at Cowal. He was later Pipe Major of the Dunoon Ballochyle Band.

One of John's amateur pupils was James MacKillop, 1874-1946. He was a friend of General Thomason, and was the Hon. Pipe Major to the Scottish Pipers Society from 1900 to 1911, and the first Hon.Secy. to the Piobaireachd Society. After the First World War he became an estate factor in Islay. He died in Edinburgh in 1946.

Another amateur pupil was Sir James Douglas Ramsay, Bt, of Banff. He was one of Gillies' earliest pupils, a fine player who became Pipe Major of the Royal Scottish Pipers' Society from 1939 to 1947.

Archie MacPhedran (see above) was another pupil, and Lewis Beaton, Skye and London (1890-1944). A.K.Cameron, Montana, also said he was taught by Gillies.

Archibald Campbell, Kilberry, makes much mention of Gillies in his notes on his teaching, *Side Lights on the Kilberry Book of Ceol Mor* (1984) and *Further Side Lights* (1986), edited by his son James Campbell. In Kilberry's hierarchy of the best players of his day, he puts Alick Cameron, son of Donald, at the top, with Gillies second, and John MacDonald, Inverness, third.

Kilberry says categorically that although John MacDonald was a 'most beauti-

The funeral cortege of John MacDougall Gillies in 1925, passing across Kelvin Bridge in Glasgow, led by the Pipes and Drums of the 5th H.L.I.
(PHOTOGRAPH BY COURTESY OF THE COLLEGE OF PIPING)

ful piobaireachd player, MacDougall Gillies is nevertheless his superior, incomparably so in knowledge and also as a player in everything but mere technique. There is far more feeling and expression in Gillies's rendering of a tune than in anything that MacDonald can produce. . .'

He adds: 'There is just this, however, to be remembered about Gillies. He and Keith Cameron, the youngest of the family, were boys together and Gillies was taught principally by Keith. Keith being the youngest is said to have been more with his father (Donald) than the two elder brothers. Keith is said to have been a player of exceedingly fine taste . . . He died young.'

As stated, Dr Colin Caird, a gifted amateur, was also taught by John, as was Willie Barrie, who came from Bute and eventually emigrated to British Columbia.

There is a story that John MacDougall Gillies was known as Jack Gillies until, at the start of his competing career, he was told he would win nothing without a Mac- in his name, so he took his grandmother's surname, MacDougall, and added it to Gillies. There is, however, evidence that his father sometimes used the name MacDougall Gillies, too.

A strathspey in four parts called *John MacDougall Gillies* was composed by William Gray.

John died on December 17th 1925. He was given an impressive funeral with the pipes and drums of the 5th HLI leading the cortege through the streets of Glasgow.

JOHN GILLIES was Pipe Major in the Scots Guards, in the 3rd Battalion from 1903 to 1906, until the 3rd was disbanded. He was then transferred to become Pipe Major of the 1st Battalion until 1911, when he was succeeded by Alec Ross, brother of Willie Ross. John Gillies' great-nephew, Neil Gillies, now living in Edinburgh, has traced the family back to Argyll, and linked this Gillies line to that of John MacDougall Gillies (see above).

SOURCES
Notices of Pipers
Neil Gillies
Jeannie Campbell
Archibald Campbell of Kilberry
Piping Times October 1996

Dunoon and Cowal District

Tunes associated with Dunoon and Cowal district include:
Dunoon Castle, arranged by Donald MacLeod 2/4 M 4
Glen Caladh Castle, by John MacLellan 2/4 M 4
The Hills of Cowal, by John MacLellan 2/4 M 4
The Kyles of Bute, by Captain Charles Smith 2/4 M 4
Lochanside, by John MacLellan 3/4 RM 3
Major Roger Rowley's Welcome to Toward Castle, by Samuel Scott 6/8 M 4
The Taking of Beaumont Hamel, by John MacLellan 2/4 M 4

DUNCAN LAMONT (Donnachadh Beag) was piper to Lamont of Lamont at the end of the 17th century. His chief was so pleased with him that he gave him the farm of Stiallag, on Loch Fyne, near Ardlamont, and in thanks, Duncan composed 'the piobaireachd known as *Stiallag*, to which he added verses in praise of his new possession, each verse ending 'Sleam fhein Stiallag (Stiallag is my own)'. The piobaireachd known as *Stiallag* is no longer current under that title. It may have been re-named, or could have dropped out of circulation. Or it may have been a song rather than a piobaireachd work, possibly words composed to a Ground of a piobaireachd. Who knows? Perhaps it was a form of the *MacFarlane's Gathering*.

Stiallag, now Stillaig, is on the east coast of Loch Fyne, opposite to Tarbert, between Portavadie and Asgog Bay, not far from Achrossan, the family home of Dugald Campbell of Kintarbert (see above).

ALEXANDER LAMONT from Ardlamont, Argyll, competed in Edinburgh in 1785, as piper to John Lamont Esq. of Lamont. He played the *Prince's Salute* and *In Praise of Mary*, which in the official programme is given the alternative title *The Laird of McLachlan's March*. In 1788 he competed again, and was placed third. He may have been a descendant of Duncan, above.

DONALD and JOHN LEITCH were pipers, brothers born in Cowal, who were good players. Around 1895 the Provost of Dunbarton, Robert MacFarlan, heard them playing *Togail nam Bo (MacFarlane's Gathering)*, and had it written down, with the help of John MacDougall Gillies. They may have had the tune from the singing of their mother (see above).

THOMAS DOUGLAS, a native of Cowal, was a piper and composer in the late 19th and early 20th centuries. His work was immensely popular in the early 20th century. He published several works in David Glen's collections, including *General Thomason's March* and *Miss Elspeth Campbell's March*.

DAVID B. MATHIESON (1883-1960) was born at Kirn, near Dunoon, but came of a Sutherland family. He went into the 9th HLI, then moved to the

Seaforth Highlanders in 1900. He was in the 1st Battalion in 1901, where he was taught by Pipe Major William Taylor, became an acting piper (?) in 1902 and full piper in 1905. He transferred to the Reserve in 1908, and became piper to Mr Gregson of Tilliefourie, Aberdeenshire. When Willie Taylor was posted to the Depot in 1909, Mathieson became Pipe Major to the 1st Seaforth in India. From there he went to France in September 1914, and was severely wounded two months later, having his pipes smashed by a shell as he was playing. The middle joint of his bass drone is preserved in the Museum in Edinburgh Castle. He was given the job of Mess Sergeant in the 3rd (Special Reserve) Battalion in Cromarty from 1915 to 1918, before becoming its Pipe Major until 1924, when he was appointed Pipe Major of the 6th (Morayshire) Battalion. He won the Gold Medal at Oban in 1921, and was known as a good composer and teacher.

He retired in 1934, and died in 1960.

SOURCES
Notices of Pipers
Proceedings of the Piobaireachd Society Conference
Piping Times

JOHN MACLELLAN, DUNOON

THE MAIN AUTHORITY FOR THE life of John MacLellan is an article written by his great-nephew Pipe Major Jim Henderson. This was published in the Box and Fiddle Magazine, whose editor allowed it to be re-printed in the Piping Times in September and December 1999, since it was clearly of great interest to the piping world. The following account is drawn partly from that article and partly from public records.

John MacLellan, Dunoon, was born there on 5 August 1875, fourth of the six children of Neil MacLellan and Mary Darroch. (There is a small discrepancy in the dates: Jim Henderson says it was August 8th, the records say the 5th. There may be confusion with a baptism date).

The article says that Neil and Mary came to Greenock in 1869, and they were married there in June. Their eldest child was born a month after the wedding.

Mary was the daughter of John Darroch and his wife Marion Shaw, who were both born in Jura. They were married in Jura on 12 December 1833. In 1851 they were living at Keills, a township of 21 houses, and they had seven children, of whom Mary was the second, born in September 1838, at Keills.

Ten years later all of John and Marion's children except two had left home, and Mary may have been in Islay, which may be where she met Neil MacLellan.

Neil was born in Islay in 1843, and was five years younger than his wife, which probably explains why she was inclined to edge her birth date forward. Neil appears to have been born in the parish of Kilchoman, at either Braigo or Toranduch. Two MacLellan families living close to each other near Kilchoman

John MacLellan, DCM, known as John MacLellan, Dunoon (1875-1949).
(PHOTOGRAPH BY COURTESY OF THE COLLEGE OF PIPING)

had sons of the right age named Neil:
1. An agricultural labourer, living at Braigo, was Neil MacLellan who was 34 in 1851, listed in the Census as having a wife Margaret aged 31, and four sons Archie, 10, Neil, 7, John, 5, and Donald, 1. There was also a daughter Marion, 3.
2. And at the same time there was a family at Toranduch, that of Archie MacLellan, 34, who was a farmer with 10 acres of land. He and his wife Christy, 32, had two sons, Neil, 8, and Hugh, 6 months, and two daughters Ann, 6, and Flory, 3.

All members of both families were born in Islay, with the exception of Neil 8, son of Archie, who was born in Greenock.

Either of these two children called Neil could be Neil MacLellan who later married Mary Darroch and was the father of John MacLellan, Dunoon. The names of Neil Braigo's children are reflected in those of Neil in Dunoon: Archie, John and Neil, Margaret and Marion, and this may be an indication that Neil Dunoon's grandfather was Neil MacLellan at Braigo. Neil Dunoon was born in Islay, so was probably the son of Neil Braigo. It is very likely that Neil Braigo and Archie Toranduch were either twin brothers or cousins.

After the wedding of Neil Dunoon and Mary Darroch, their first home seems to have been at Harkness Cottage, Dunoon, where they had part of a house belonging to a widow from Jura, Mrs Isabella Harkness, 60.

There had been Harkness families in Dunoon since at least 1785, and Isabella had been married to John Currie Harkness, in 1838. Her maiden name was MacLean, and she was born in 1810, to Lauchlan MacLean and Marion Buie, in Lagg, Jura. Her family were neighbours of the Lindsays, at the Post Office in Lagg, where the piper Hugh Lindsay was born in 1820. The MacLeans in Jura were related to the Darrochs.

The MacLellans' eldest child, Sarah, was born at Edward Street, Dunoon, on 11 July 1869. Perhaps she was named after Isabella's daughter, Sarah Harkness, since there were no Sarahs in either Neil's or Mary's family. Archie followed in 1871, Margaret in 1873, and John in 1875. He was born in St Andrew Street, Dunoon. Then came Neil in 1878, and Ann (Annie) in 1882. In the Census of 1881, the father, Neil, is described as a Carter.

In 1882, Neil died, at the age of forty. Jim Henderson says that 'there is evidence that Mary Darroch MacLellan took her young family back to her native Jura for a time. . . It is not known how long they stayed on Jura, but eventually they returned to Dunoon'. By 1891, the widowed Mary was living in Craignish Place, Dunoon, in two rooms, with four of her children, and earning her living as a washer-woman. Her son Archie had taken over his father's work as a carter, and young John, now aged 16, is listed as a grocer. He later became a house-painter.

It is clear that the family was not well-off, and that Mary had a struggle to support her children. To bring up four children in two rooms while trying to wash, dry and iron other people's washing must have been a nightmare, especially in the wet climate of Dunoon, but she was helped by her family being hard-working and steady.

Jim Henderson says that it is not known who taught John his piping. Some suggest his teacher was Willie Lawrie, but he was eight years junior to John, so this seems unlikely. Others suggest it was John MacDougall Gillies, but again the timing is wrong. It has been suggested that he might have been taught as a boy in Jura after his father's death, and Hugh Lindsay springs to mind as a possible tutor. He would have been 62 in 1882 when the MacLellans moved back, and he was an excellent player who had been taught by Angus MacKay (see below). It is not known when Hugh Lindsay died – but the concensus of opinion is that it was probably in the 1850s, only a few years after his triumph at the Northern Meetings. This was long before John MacLellan was in Jura.

There is the possibility that, when a boy in Jura, the young John had lessons from Neil Lindsay, nephew of Hugh, before Neil emigrated to California – but who taught Neil?

John was brought up latterly in Dunoon, but in 1892, at the age of 17 he enlisted as a piper in the Highland Light Infantry, and in 1894 went with the 1st Battalion to Malta, and later to Crete. He served in the South African War of 1899-1902, where he won the D.C.M. for gallantry on the field. His great-nephew says he refused to talk about this in later life, saying it was a long time ago. He seems to have been a modest, reticent man, unwilling to talk about himself and his own achievements.

Jim Henderson says that John left the army in 1903, and played in the Govan Police Pipe Band, along with his brother Neil, for some years. But by the end of 1905, he was back in Dunoon. Here he started to teach, and his pupils included James Wilson, George MacDonald and brothers Charles and William Jeffrey. He also taught his nephew Neil Henderson (Jim's father) and Neil's brothers Alasdair and John Henderson. Jim himself had lessons from John as a boy. It was around this time that John compiled and arranged the Cowal Collection (see below).

In 1912 John joined the 8th Argylls (TA), and two years later when he was 39, the regiment was mobilised and sent to France. He served in the pipe band inder P/M George Ross, until Willie Lawrie took over in 1915, about the time that John was wounded at Laventie in N.W. France. He seems to have been away from the band for some time after this, and served with the rifle section. He left a number of poems he wrote while in France, and one of them is inscribed on the memorial at Buzancy, in France.

He was an extraordinarily talented man. Besides his skill at poetry, he had gifts as a musician, playing not only the pipes but also the piano, the fiddle and the penny whistle. He wrote songs as well as poetry, and set them to his own music. He was a house painter by trade, but was also gifted as a painter of pictures in many media, including oils, watercolours – and army blanco.

After the War, from 1919 to 1933, he was Pipe Major of the 8th Argylls, after becoming a house-painter in Dunoon in the post-war years. He went to live with his sister Maggie in the town.

In the 30s and 40s he helped to teach the Dunoon Grammar School Cadet

Pipe Band, and also gave a hand with the local Boys' Brigade. During the second World War he composed a tune called *Dunoon Home Guard*.

He became known in the piping world as John MacLellan, Dunoon, partly to distinguish him from John A. MacLellan of the Army School of Piping in Edinburgh Castle, in later years (they were not related), but also because he came to be identified with the Cowal Games, which started as the Dunoon Games in 1871, before John was born.

John MacLellan died suddenly on 31st July 1949 at Dunoon Cottage Hospital, after a short illness. He was 73. He was buried, with full military honours, in Dunoon Cemetery, and George MacDonald, his pupil and Pipe Major of the Dunoon Ballochyle Band, was the piper. In 1972 a memorial plaque was erected in the Castle Gardens, Dunoon. This plaque refers to his most famous work as *The Bens of Jura*, the name he always used himself for the tune known outwith the piping world as *The Road To The Isles* (see below).

Today John is remembered principally as a composer. He made a number of memorable tunes, including the beautiful 3/4 Retreat in three parts, *Lochanside*. He also made the 2/4 March in four parts, *The Taking of Beaumont Hamel*. His 12/8 Waltz in two parts was named *Mary Darroch* after his mother. As the Notices of Pipers put it, 'most of his tunes appeared in the Cowal Collection of Bagpipe Music, and some in other collections, but without being acknowledged to him always.' This seems to be the price of modesty.

While serving in Malta he made a 2/4 march, *The Bells of Malta*, and while in South Africa he made the retreat air *The Highland Brigade at Magersfontein*, and 'a nice little two part strathspey' called *Chasing De Wet*, to commemorate an unsuccessful pursuit of a Boer general who was an expert in hit-and-run tactics. Two attractive 6/8 marches in two parts were *The Surrender of Cronje* and *The Fall of Port Arthur*, also made during the Boer War.

The Heroes of Vittoria and *Cowal Society* were two more of his compositions. And he made *The Bloody Fields of Flanders* when serving in France.

After the war, his compositions included *South Hall, Bonnie Dunoon, Glen Caladh Castle, Colonel MacLean of Ardgour* and many others.

As stated, John MacLellan's most famous work was the tune now known as *The Road To The Isles*, which he made around 1890 or '91. He gave it the title *The Bens of Jura*, clearly from his mother's birthplace. But during the South African War it was played under the name *The Highland Brigade's March to Heilbron*, and later, still in army hands, it was changed to *The 71st's Farewell to Dover*. In time, it acquired the title *The Burning Sands of Egypt*, though the Scots Guards always called it *The Sands of Cairo*.

D.R. MacLennan told the Piobaireachd Society Conference what happened next:

'Malcolm Johnstone from Barra was going north on the train and playing this tune in the railway carriage' (as you do, or, at least, used to), and Mrs Marjorie Kennedy Fraser and the Rev. MacLeod heard it. 'Ah,' they thought, 'This is an old, old Gaelic tune. We must get this brought forward'. And the Rev. MacLeod wrote the words 'A far crooning is a-pulling me away'. I think they are the most atrocious words that ever I heard, I mean, they've no euphony in them or anything else. Just atrocious. However, the thing became popular, and the Glasgow Orpheus Choir sang it and they made a great fuss about it. And then of course it was translated into Gaelic and back again into English, and poor old Jock never got a damned halfpenny out of it. No royalties in those days – and nobody wanted to know it wasn't an ancient Gaelic tune at all'.

Perhaps the final insult came when the tune was published in Logan's Book 8, with the comment that as a pipe tune it was based on the song *The Road To The Isles*.

THE COWAL GATHERING

IN 1997, THERE WAS CORRESPONDENCE in the Piping Times about condition of the public toilets at the Cowal Games. This gave rise to a piece by Iain K. Murray, which is reproduced here with the permission of the author:

'The Cowal Gathering seems to be one of those events in the piping calendar that participants and spectators love to hate. An example of that ambivalence appeared in the Piping Times of October 1996. Your anonymous reporter found the ladies lavatories to be a faithful replica of the facilities in a Rwandan refugee camp. I am assuming your columnist is a lady. If the assumption is wrong no doubt his case will be coming up shortly. The report reminded me that I had a copy of the history of the Cowal Gathering written in the mid 1950s by William Laidlaw Inglis. I read the history again in order to discover whether the sanitary provision at the Gathering was based on some time-honoured tradition.

'The precursor of the Cowal Gathering was the Dunoon Highland Games of 1871 held at Achamore Farm where 'everything passed off well'. The impression one gets of the County of Argyll in those days is that there were more pipers and composers of bagpipe music per square mile than in any other county. However, the organisers of the games seemingly failed in their search for a piper and were forced to import a Mr Eunson of Leith. The Leithal Orcadian, who provided the music for the 'athletic sports', contributed to a financial surplus which was distributed among the deserving poor.

'There is evidence of a march, strathspey and reel competition having been held in 1883 amidst the athletic and cycling events. The following year, the games became a 'gathering' and an entrance fee of one shilling was charged. The cost was evidently regarded by the general public as exorbitant – the overcharging referred to in the report of October 1996 appears to have a long tradition – and they stayed away. The organisers were so alarmed that they reduced the entrance fee to six old pence on the day of the Gathering and announced their capitulation by means of the town crier.

'In 1900, after the Boer War, the games were resumed. The entrance fee remained at six pence and 5,000 attended. The winners of the piping competitions all came from Dunoon and district, and included that composer of unique melodies, John MacLellan. At later games the attendance reached 10,000. Undaunted the Ladies Guild of the local church set up a tea tent to provide a temperance alternative to the attractions of the beer tent.

'In 1906, the Games, re-constituted as 'The Cowal Highland Gathering' included a band competition, the first winner of which was the 1st Volunteer Brigade of the HLI under its pipe major John MacDougall Gillies, a native of Glendaruel. Four years later that cringe-making music hall artist Harry Lauder with the aid of a promised trophy persuaded the committee to extend the competition to include civilian bands.

'Although some time between 1901 and 1905 a book of tunes was published by Joseph Quigley under the title 'The Cowal Collection of Modern Highland Bagpipe Music', this book was not written under the auspices of the Games Committee. It was edited by John MacLellan and included very few tunes played today – *Lieutenant Macguire's Jig, The Skyeman's Jig* and *The Heroes of Vittoria* are some of the better known tunes. In 1912 the Gathering Committee published the Dunoon Collection of Highland Bagpipe Music, following a competition for the best tunes to commemorate the 1911 Gathering. It contained sixty-one tunes including evergreens with well known names – *Portree Bay, The Atholl and Breadalbane Gathering, South Hall* (which did not win the first prize – it went to the march *The Raasay Highlanders*), *The Fiddler's Joy, Inveraray Castle, Bessie MacIntyre, The Blackbird,* and *Dovecote Park.*

'The Cowal Collection was again published in 1920 with for example *Farewell to the Creeks, The Brolum, The Taking of Beaumont Hamel* and *Dugald MacColl's Farewell to France.* The 1932 Collection is a disappointment with only twenty tunes published out of an entry of two hundred and thirty five including *Ballochyle* and *Bencorrum.* The 1958 Collection (known as Book 5) is a compilation from the previous four books.

'In 1912 the Gathering was extended to two days and was revived after the war in 1919 when the Town Council succeeded in relocating a goatherd and goats from the park just ten days before the opening day when Pathe Gazette filmed the event for showing in cinemas countrywide.

'It has to be said that without Cowal, piping would have been the poorer. Not only did the competitions for tunes result in some excellent compositions, but the piping competitions, which the top players and bands entered, can only have raised standards.

'The promoters of the Wembley Exhibition of 1924 invited the committee to hold the Gathering in London, but that mad idea came to nothing presumably because the committee concluded that the lavatories at Wembley would not reach the standard of those in Dunoon.

'The biggest crowd to attend the Gathering – 30,000 – made the journey to Dunoon in 1950 when the Prime Minister Clement Attlee was present. Apart from the 1932 Cowal Collection referred to, and the quaintly titled Stave-Flourishing Competition introduced in 1928, the history of the Gathering otherwise discloses no earth-shaking event and a careful reading fails to provide any information about the sanitary arrangements. How did they cope with 30,000 spectators, a Prime Minister and occasional visits of the Duke of Argyll?

'And just in case you ask ... The Piper of Loos on page seven of the third book of tunes relates solely to an act of bravery in the Great War.'

In 1994, Jeannie Campbell wrote an account of the Cowal Games in 1906, with a photograph of a band marching along Argyll Street, Dunoon, on their way to the Games. This turned out to be the Dunoon Ballochyle Pipe Band, under their Pipe Major George MacDonald, who was a reed-maker. A piper in the band was John MacLellan's pupil, James Wilson, who became P/M of the 8th Argylls in succession to Willie Lawrie after he died of his wounds in 1916. Following James Wilson the next P/M was John MacLellan, who had taught Wilson and other pipers in the band. George MacDonald was a pupil of John MacDougall Gillies.

The 1906 Gathering was the first to have a pipe band competition, and a shield was to be awarded for the best of the Grade 1 bands. Money was raised by public subscription – £43.18.6. in all, a substantial sum for those times – and the Duchess of Argyll, Princess Louise, a daughter of Queen Victoria, designed the shield with her own hand – or, as Jeannie cautiously says, helped to design it. It is known as the Argyll Shield. There was considerable correspondence about the appointment of the judges.

Today the Dunoon Argyle Pipe Band is active in the district and in the winter runs recitals in the drill hall. Dunoon Grammar School also has its own band, which bodes well for the future of piping in Cowal.

The piping tutor in Cowal is Annie Grant, who has done sterling work in keeping the traditions going in the district. A respected judge and member of the Piobaireachd Society, she has recently taken on the considerable task of Convener of solo piping at the Cowal Games.

SOURCES
Piping Times: Jim Henderson
Iain K. Murray
IGI Argyll, Renfrewshire
OPR Jura, Dunoon
Piobaireachd Society Conference Proceedings

MORVEN, ARDGOUR AND ARDNAMURCHAN

THE PARISH OF ARDNAMURCHAN, TO the west of Fort William, belongs to the presbytery of Mull, in Argyll, but part of the parish is in what used to be Inverness-shire, and so is outwith the area covered by this book. Acharacle is on the boundary and has been included with the rest of Argyll.

Tunes associated with Morvern and Ardnamurchan include:
Ardnamurchan Point by Captain J. Peterson 4/4 M 2
Kaid Sir Harry MacLean's Moorish Salute, by H. Forsyth 2/4 M 1
The Kilchoan Occasionals, by Captain J. Peterson 6/8 J 4
Kinlochaline Castle 2/4 M 4
Leaving Ardtornish, by William Ross 1935 4/4 SA 2
The Linn of Lorn, by T.P. McGloan 2/4 M 4
Lovely Loch Sunart, by Captain J.R.C.Peterson 6/8 M 4
The Maid of Morvern 6/8 SA 2
Mingary Castle, by Captain J.R.C.Peterson 9/8 RM 6
Moladh Moraig (In Praise of Morag) P with 8 variations (see below)
Salute to the Young Laird of Dungallon P with 7 variations
Sanna Bay, by Captain J.R.C.Peterson 4/4 M 4

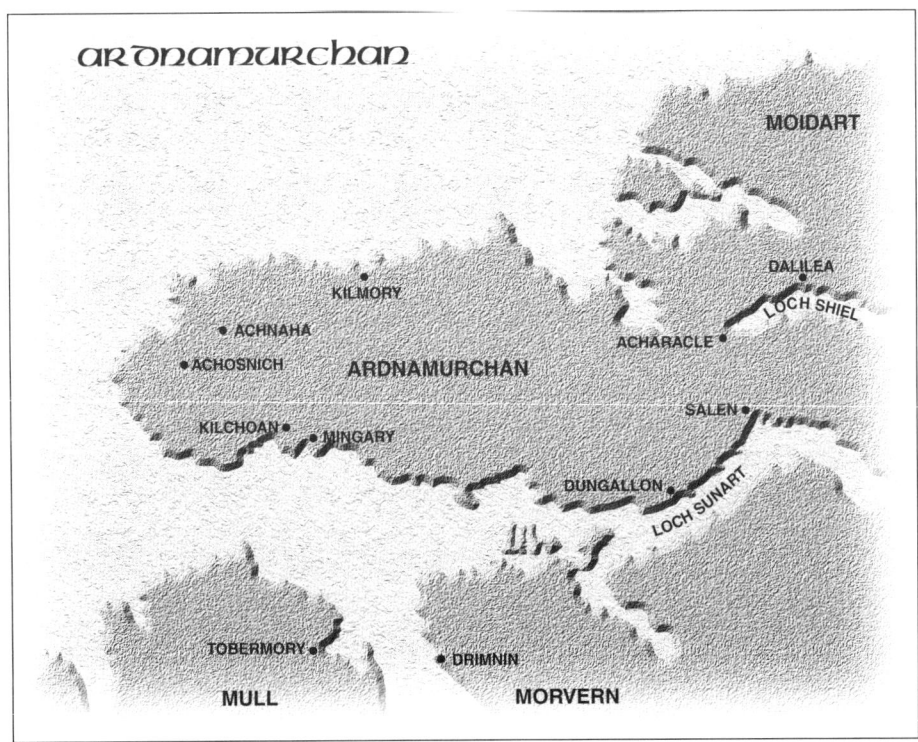

KILCHOAN

Kilchoan in Ardnamurchan is named in the story of the Irish lord who visited MacLean of Duart; the Irishman's piper beat MacLean's Rankin piper in competition. After Rankin cut off his own little finger in chagrin, the Irish lord and his piper fled. They had reached Kilchoan when MacLean caught up with them, and killed them both. They are said to be buried at Kilchoan. Neither the Irish lord nor his piper are named, but if the piper was a better player than Rankin, he must have been good. This must have happened (if at all) in the 16th century. John Johnston, Coll, said he had heard his uncle in Canada play a *Lament for the Lord of Connaught*, made in memory of this Irish nobleman (made by whom? Presumably by Rankin).

The Maid of Morvern is a Gaelic song which has been made into a Slow March for the pipes. The song is lamenting the loss of the maiden's true love who was drowned off Ardnamurchan. The date is unknown.

ALLAN MACLEAN who probably came from Mull, was piper to Alexander MacLean Esq. of Ardgower (Ardgour) in 1806. Competing at Edinburgh he was given second place after a MacArthur player (called John in the Preface to Angus MacKay's piobaireachd collection but more probably Archie MacArthur, piper to Staffa) had angrily refused to accept second, declaring that he should have been placed first. Four years later, Allan MacLean won first place in his own right, described in 1810 simply as 'from Mull'. According to the Notices of Pipers, Allan was the son of Neil MacLean, first prize winner in 1783 (see above, Appin)

MURDOCH MACLEAN may have been a brother of Allan (above). He was piper to MacLean of Ardgour, but later, before 1814, he went to Glasgow where he was a pipe-maker. After 1820 he was in Inverness. He began competing in Edinburgh in 1807, and came fourth in 1814, and second in 1815. He never achieved first place, although he continued to compete until 1829.

He was able to read Canntaireachd in written form, and play the tunes thus written, and offered to interpret the Campbell Canntaireachd manuscript in 1816. His offer was rejected by the Edinburgh authorities, who may have been reluctant to advertise their own ignorance. The Notices of Pipers say 'His name should be remembered among the pioneers of writing piobaireachd music on the stave', and he was rewarded in 1814 and 1818 for producing such written music. It is not clear how he learned this skill, but presumably he had some training in it while in Glasgow.

Jeannie Campbell has an account of Murdoch MacLean in her book *Highland Bagpipe Makers* (2001).

The YOUNG LAIRD OF DUNGALLON, for whom a Salute was made, was probably a Cameron, and the Dungallon of the title seems to be the place on Loch Sunart, Ardnamurchan, rather than the Dungalan in Colonsay. The Gaelic spelling of both place-names is Dungalan, and the spelling with ll seems to have come in by analogy with English 'gallon'.

Allan Cameron, 16th of Lochiel, sent 300 men to support Montrose in 1645, although he himself was too old and infirm to join the campaign. He was a nephew of Donald Dubh Cameron, from whom he inherited the title of Lochiel.

Allan had two sons, and a daughter called Jean who married Alasdair Dearg of Glengarry (the subject of the piobaireachd *Lament for Alasdair Dearg*), the son of Donald of Laggan (subject of another piobaireachd lament). Allan Cameron's second son, Donald, was given the lands of Glendessary, and Donald's eldest son, John of Glendessary, was an uncle of Allan Cameron of Erracht, who raised the Cameron Highlanders.

John of Glendessary married twice, and his son Archibald, by his second wife, was given the tack (long lease) of the lands of Dungallon. This estate was named after a ruined and ancient stronghold on the tiny tidal island in Loch Sunart, between Borrodale and Salen, on the south coast of Ardnamurchan. The family seat of Dungallon was at Glenahurrich, in Sunart, between Loch Sunart and Loch Shiel.

Archibald Cameron, first laird of Dungallon, married a daughter of Sir Ewen Cameron of Lochiel, who was a distant cousin. Archibald died in 1719, and was succeeded by his eldest son, John Cameron, second of Dungallon. John inherited as a young child, and was barely twenty when he died in 1739, unmarried, and his younger brother Alexander Cameron became the third (and last) Laird of Dungallon.

Alexander had a colourful career. He joined his chief in support of Prince Charles Edward in 1745, and became the Prince's standard bearer. After Culloden he was eventually captured and imprisoned, after some months in the heather. His lands were attaindered in 1747, and ten years later he became a Captain in the 1st Fraser Highlanders. He died in 1759, and left what was remaining of his inheritance to a cousin, Captain Allan Cameron of Glendessary – who was married to a sister of (the first) Mrs MacLeod of Talisker, both being daughters of the 13th Laird of Coll.

This was the end of the short line of the Camerons of Dungallon. Angus MacKay quotes a Gaelic verse, said to be the words to the Urlar of the piobaireachd salute:

Tha oighre og air fear Dhungalain
Is fhacainn fallain togail mail;
Tha oighre og air fear Dhungalain
'S fhaicinn fallain's fhaicinn slan.

'The laird of Dungallon has a young heir,
May we see him in health round collecting the rent;
The laird of Dungallon has a young heir,
May we see him sound, may we see him in health'

If this verse is genuine, i.e. made at the time of the Dungallon family, and there is no reason to suppose it is not, then it may provide a clue to the identity of the Young Laird of the title of the salute. Neither Archibald, 1st of Dungallon, nor Alexander, 3rd Laird, was born as the expected heir to Dungallon, both inheriting or being given the title and lands in adulthood, after the death of the expected heir. This leaves John Cameron, the short-lived 2nd Laird of Dungallon, as the heir referred to in the song. Perhaps the preoccupation of the song with the heir's state of health is significant; he may have been an ailing youth, possibly consumptive.

In the Campbell Canntaireachd manuscript the work is called *Dungalan's Lament*, a title which suggests it was made to commemorate the untimely death of Young Dungallon at the age of just on twenty. (Gesto links the work with the MacLeods by calling it *Mac Mhic Thormoid 'Son of the son of Norman'*, possibly a reference to the Harris branch of the clan. And Gesto adds to this title the words 'alias *MacLeod Gesto's Lamentation*'. It is not known what was his authority for this).

Tommy Pearston, in the Piping Times for January 1996, observes that the work seems to have been very popular at one time, since it appears in so many of the older printed sources.

It should perhaps be noted that both the works entitled for someone designated as 'Young' refer to men who died young, in their twenties: Young George of Cawdor (see above) and the Young Dungallon never became other than young, and this could be evidence for identifying exactly who they were.

It is not known who composed the work. It was probably one of Lochiel's pipers, but we do not know who they were. The muster roll of Lochiel's regiment in 1745-6 names Alexander of Dungallon as a Major on Lochiel's staff, but no regimental piper is listed. Many of the other regiments and companies had named pipers on the roll, but not Lochiel's.

SOURCES
Alexander MacKenzie
John Stewart of Ardvorlich
Memoirs of Lochiel
Fionn (Henry Whyte)

ELDERLY LADY

I belong to the generation that makes jam,
An endangered species, right enough.
We knit thistle hose for pipers,
And run the W.R.I.;
We know what to do with rhubarb,
And after sixty years of dedicated listening
We've learned nearly as much about piobaireachd
As the players know themselves.
Well, nearly.

Not for us the joys of the Internet,
We don't send text messages saying I Hart U
Or get into debt;
We are old, or should I say mature,
Or even boring – but comfortable with it.
We listen, and little boys ask questions:
'Did pipes have two drones
When you were young, Granny?'
(Maybe I'm not as old as I thought I was
Even though I can't remember
What I came through here for,
Or the name of the fellow
Who won the Gold last year).

No, son, they had three drones,
And Donald Duaghal was already dead,
And so was Calum Piobair, and John Ban.
Don't tell me – you never heard
Of any one of them,
And really do not care.

But not only am I old enough
To make chocolate cake
And clootie dumpling,
Dying arts, along with the Gaelic,
But I can remember when the Glenfiddich was started
And the hall was kept unheated
For the sake of the instruments,
And we sat on hard benches
With no backs to them,
Suffering agonies of backache,
For shivering hours,

Rigid with the cold,
For the sake of our art.
You youngsters just don't know –
(Oh here she goes again,
We just don't know we're born . . .)

And I recall the post-war days
– Which war? Well, dear child,
Not the Crimean -
The days when the MacFadyens
Had a promising future,
And Donald MacPherson might
Turn out to be a rising star,
And Seumas was on 'Chanter'
Every Wednesday night
At half-past six – or was it seven?-
And we never missed a minute -
Those were indeed the days.

Pipes did have three drones, of course,
And Donald Duaghal long dead,
The MacCrimmons had given up their college -
But another had just been started
In Otago Street -
Things were looking up.

It won't be all that long
(Though he doesn't think it now)
Before that same wee grandson
Is deaving his own family
With memories of how he spoke once
To Niall Matheson, and went to hear
Chris Armstrong win the Knock-Out,
And how he suffered in the gales
At Helmsdale that day in August,
And I doubt if he will be eating
Blackcurrant jam on his bagel.

And my great-great-grandson,
Living in his bijou bungalow
On the moon,
Commuting twice a week by rocket
To Scotland for tuition,
Will no doubt be thinking

(Though I hope too kind to say so)
'Silly old fart of a Grandpa,
You canna live on memories' -
And he'll be right.

But memory is the rocket fuel of old age,
As he will find out in his turn.

IN PRAISE OF MORAG

ALASDAIR MAC MHAIGHSTIR ALASDAIR (ALEXANDER MAC-DONALD) was a well known Gaelic poet in the 18th century, who belonged to Ardnamurchan. He clearly had a lifelong interest in the pipes, and often mentioned them in his poetry, although probably not himself a piper.

One of his best known poems was *Moladh Moraig, In Praise of Morag*, a title familiar to pipers as the name of a piobaireachd work. Alasdair made the poem in the 1730s, in praise of a young lassie with whom he was infatuated. It angered his wife Jane (who was a MacDonald, related to the MacIains of Glencoe), and according to tradition she withdrew all marital services; he had to compose a *Dispraise* of poor Morag, retracting all he had said and attacking the girl in shamefully scurrilous terms, before Jane would relent. This vicious attack on an innocent girl's reputation did Alasdair no good, except that it made his two poems famous among the more salacious readers of his time.

He was probably living in the Argyll (western) part of Ardnamurchan when he made *Moladh Moraig*. Born in about 1695 at Dalilea, near Loch Shiel, in the Inverness-shire half of the parish, he went to Kilmory as a catechist in 1729, and was able to put pressure on the local landlord to start a school there, of which he became the teacher in 1732, with an annual salary of £18. Late in 1736, the school was moved across the boundary to Islandfinnan, in Loch Shiel, but two years later was back in Argyll, at Kilchoan, on the south coast of Ardnamurchan. Only one year later, in 1739, it was moved yet again, this time to Corryvullin, near Mingary, where Alasdair remained until he retired from teaching in 1745. So the young Morag could have been from any of the places in Ardnamurchan where Alasdair was teaching, and we have no way of knowing which.

Moladh Moraig is a piobaireachd poem, that is, it is composed with some attempt to represent the metrical structure of a musical piobaireachd work composed for the pipe. The words 'Air fonn piobaireachd' appear beside the title, apparently meaning 'To a piobaireachd tune', but probably 'Following pipe music' would be closer, and I do not think we can interpret this phrase as an indication that the word piobaireachd was then used as pipers use it today.

The piece is divided into 21 stanzas, with eight long lines (16 short lines) to each stanza. These stanzas are headed Urlar, Siubhal or An Crun-luath, but the names are not used as pipers would use them. There are 7 different Urlar stanzas, and 12 Siubhals, and 2 Crun-luath stanzas at the end.

What the names amount to is simple changes in the rhythm of the poem: the Siubhal variations increase in complexity as the poem develops, and the Crunluath has many more lightly stressed syllables, to try to imitate complex gracenoting. It is not very successful in its attempt to represent a piobaireachd work, and seems to show only a superficial knowledge of the form – at least the form as we know it today.

The first 16 stanzas describe the poet's feeling for the young girl Morag, and he gives lustful images of her, and laments that she is unattainable because he is a married man. Then come two verses about pipe music, 32 lines, in two stanzas, both headed Siubhal. Then comes another Urlar, the seventh, concerned with good living in high society, and the final two verses, the Crun-luath, have a change in subject matter, when the poet awakes from his dream of Morag and turns to his wife Jane.

For comparison with the piobaireachd work, we have to bear in mind that each 16-line verse of the poem represents one LINE of the music: it is the equivalent of a 16-phrase line. This means that the variations were of three lines of equal length, with no indication that the first line (verse) might be repeated. Is this an aberration, or an indication of a piobaireachd form no longer used?

As observed with the piobaireachd poem of Duncan Ban MacIntyre (see above), the omission of Taorluath variations may be a reflection of a known 18th century form of piobaireachd with only the Crunluath, usually a Crunluath fosgailte. Most of the known examples of piobaireachd poems have this in common. Possibly, though, the omission of a Taorluath is no more than habit or imitation: once it had been done in verse, the other poets followed the model, and so the literary form was established.

The two piping stanzas go like this (lines 469-500 of the poem):

        Nuair chuala mi ceol leadanach
        An fheadain a bh'aig Moraig
        Rinn m'aignidh dannsa beadarach
        'S e freagra dha le solas:
        Seimh urlar socair, leadarra
        A puirt, 's a meoir a'breabadaich,
        B'e siud an oirfeid eagarra
        Do'n bheus na creaga mora.
        Ochoin ! a feadan bailleagach
        Cruaidh, sgailleagach, glan, ceolmhor,
        Nam binn-phort stuirteil, trileanta,
        Reidh, mion-dhionach, bog, ro-chaoin;
        Am marsal comhnard, staideil sin,
        'S e luthmhor, grasmhor, caismeachdach,
        Fior chruinn-luth brisg, spalparra
        F'a cliath-luth bras-chaoin, sporsail.

'When I heard the melodious music
Of the chanter that Morag has
My spirit did a merry dance
A most joyful response
Hearing the well-balanced harmonious Ground
Of the tune, jumping from note to note; (or:with breabach movements)
It was that accurate melody
To which the great rocks provide a bass.
Ah, the chanter with its grace-notes
Hard, sharp-cut, clean music
With the steady quick-moving melodious tune,
Even, controlled, soft and smooth;
That regular, rhythmic march
So nimble, graceful, rousing,
The fresh brisk crunluath strutting along
Under her musical fingering,
Quick, gentle and sportive'.

Chinn prois, is stuirt, is sprachdalachd
Am ghnuis nuair bheachdaich guamag
A'seinn an fheadain ioraltaich,
B'ard iolach ann am chluasaibh;
A suain-cheol sithe, mireineach,
Mear-stoirmeil, pongail, mionaideach,
Na b'fhoirmeile nach sireamaid
Air mhireid ri h-uchd tuasaid.
O ! 'm buille meoir bu lomarra
Gu pronnadh a'phuirt uaibhrich,
'S na h-uilt bu luthmhoir cromaidhean
Air thollaibh a'chrainn bhuadhaich;
Gun slaoidmheoirich, gun ronnaireachd,
Brisg, tioram, socair, collaideach;
Geal-ludag nan gearr-chollainnean
'Na crap-luth loinneil, guanach.

'There was no pride, no haughtiness, no strength
When I was watching the girl playing the chanter so cleverly,
Its high sound in my ears;
Her intricate, fairylike, merry music
Brisk-moving, accurate, precise,
A music than which we would not seek
Anything more stirring when roused by the prospect of battle.
O, the finger strokes on the chanter, so closely defined,
Beating out the spirited tune,
Her fingers curving so nimbly

On the holes of her excellent chanter.
No lazy fingering, no wet blowing,
But brisk, crisp, balanced, clamorous playing,
Her white little-finger with short sharp strokes
Making the elegant vibrating curl (birl).'

The poem, *Corrienessan's Lament*, made by Iain Dall MacKay in 1697, is, in the MacLagan manuscript reading of the text, clearly a piobaireachd poem, and a much better attempt than *Moladh Moraig* in that it shows a deeper understanding of the piobaireachd form.

Although the variations are not named, *Corrienessan's Lament* has Urlar, 1st Variation with Doubling, and a Dithis variation and Doubling (but no Taorluath or Crunluath variations) – and they are in the sequence we would expect in a piobaireachd composition. It is hard to imagine Iain Dall putting seven differing Urlar lines in one work.

The man who made that earlier piobaireachd poem, Iain Dall, was not only a piper himself but a very fine composer, and it is obvious that Alasdair was not. While he clearly enjoyed the music, his appreciative descriptions are rapturous rather than technical, the sort of comment you might hear in the bar at the Northern Meeting. It is not enough to use such phrases as 'a well-balanced Ground', 'a quick-moving crun-luath', 'lazy fingering' and 'wet blowing'. They show that he knew pipers and piping, but it is clear that he was not a piper and did not fully understand piobaireachd form.

Professor Thomson directed the reader to the further development of 'this metrical scheme' by Duncan Ban MacIntyre in his *Praise of Ben Doran*, later in the 18th century. But this too is not deeply rooted in piobaireachd form, and owes a lot to Alasdair's work (see above).

It is probably no coincidence that three of the four piobaireachd poems that we have bear titles which are also the names of piobaireachd compositions: *Corrienessan's Lament* seems to have come down to us as an old Ground and one variation, which were developed (alas) by Dr Bannatyne in the 20th century; *Moladh Moraig*, both poem and piobaireachd work, seems to have links with Jacobite politics; and *Isabel MacKay* is the name of both song and piobaireachd, though the two are not, at first sight (hearing?) related directly. The song *Isabel MacKay*, however, is sung to the Ground of the *Prince's Salute*, and Allan MacDonald has shown that the *Prince's Salute* and the piobaireachd *Isabel MacKay* are based on the same basic theme notes. The relation between the song *Isabel MacKay* and the Ground of the *Prince's Salute* is very close, so much so that if we knew only that the poem was based on a piobaireachd work, we would be able to identify which one, as the unique structural patterns are faithfully reproduced.

Rhythmic change in the variations of piobaireachd is represented more cleverly in *Isabel MacKay* (the poem) than in either *Moladh Moraig* or *In Praise of Ben Doran*. In both of the latter, the poet has triumphed over the imitator: both are far better as poetic works, but less successful as piobaireachd poems. *Corrienessan's*

Lament (the poem), however, seems to me the best of the genre, as well as the oldest. It is the only one where the piobaireachd characteristics are integral to the poem and not just superimposed on it as a curiosity. Indeed, it is done so subtly that later editors missed it entirely, failed to recognise the piobaireachd structure, and inadvertently destroyed it by changing the order of the verses.

Whether the piobaireachd work came before the poem is not always certain. There can be little doubt that the *Prince's Salute* was the model for the poem *Isabel MacKay*, but the relation between the two *Corrienessan's Laments*, poem and piobaireachd, is not clear, although the poem does refer to a lament, played by the poet between the two sections of his poem.

Moladh Moraig is more of a puzzle, but the triple metre of the poetry seems more likely to be an echo of the triplets in the music than vice versa – because the former is just that, an echo. Duncan Ban MacIntyre's work, as a form of piobaireachd, seems to be more a vague reproduction of Alasdair's than based on a specific piobaireachd composition.

So it looks as if the poetic piobaireachd works were probably based on the musical, rather than vice versa, though this is not entirely certain.

Some say that the title of the piobaireachd work *Moladh Moraig* refers to the name Morag used as a codename for Prince Charles Edward Stuart, in political correspondence and in poetry – and presumably in conversation – in the 1740s; it is possible that the striking use of triple phrases in variations two and three represents the Prince's disguise as a spinning-woman, when Flora MacDonald brought him across from Uist to Skye, after Culloden.

Alasdair Mac Mhaighstir Alasdair, who was Flora's first cousin, used this name Morag for the Prince in his poem *Oran Luadhaidh no fucaidh (A Mhorag chiatach a'chuil dualaich)*. This is a political poem addressed to the Prince, and it was written probably in 1747, after the Prince's return to France.

I will not burden the reader with detailed analysis of *Moladh Moraig* as a piobaireachd poem, nor an examination of its relation to the music. Suffice it to say that there is no correspondence between the (very intricate) patterns of rhyme and alliteration in the poem and the (equally intricate, but unusual) structural patterns formed by the phrases in the piobaireachd; nothing that is the equivalent of the dependence of the poem *Isabel MacKay* on the patterns of the *Prince's Salute*. Both the poem *Moladh Moraig* and the piobaireachd have complex patterns, but they are not the same.

The patterns of rhyme and alliteration within the poem are elaborate and skilfully wrought. As Gaelic literature it is a supremely fine piece of work; as a piobaireachd poem it falls short, and leaves us wondering why it was cast in this form at all. Was it merely because Morag played the chanter?

Alasdair took a keen interest in politics, and being ardently pro-Jacobite was active both before and during the Rising of 1745. He was reported to the Presbytery for 'wandering through the country composing Galick songs, stuffed with obscene Language'. One of the poems he made during the campaign was his *Moladh air Piob-mhoir MhicCruimein, In Praise of MacCrimmon's Great Pipe*, which seems to have been the pipe of Donald Ban MacCrimmon, killed at Moy in 1746.

The poem is mainly about the importance of the pipes in battle, and he calls this pipe the king of music, seeing it as presiding over the fighting while men hacked each other to pieces.

It is the last stanza which appears to speak of Donald Ban, referring to him, in a piping context, as 'the excellent fair-haired man from Skye' (a' bhan-Sgitheanach ghlormhor). Professor Thomson comments that 'it seems remarkable that the pipes being celebrated were being played that day on the Hanoverian side' (when Donald Ban was killed). Perhaps we should remember that Donald had little choice about which side he supported, and he was killed accidentally by his own side at Moy, which must have angered his Jacobite friends – and also that, a little earlier, when Donald's brother Malcolm had been captured and imprisoned by the Jacobites, their own pipers refused to play unless he was released. Clearly, the bond between pipers is stronger than mere politics.

Another of Alasdair's poems was called *Oran Nuadh*, A New Song, another political work, made before the Rising started. It has a description of a military piper:

> 'S fuirbidh tailceant, 's cumpa pearsa
> Treun-laoch spraiceil, doid-gheal,
> Piob da spalpadh suas 'na achlais
> Mhosglas lasan gleois duinn;
> Caismeachd bhras-bhinn, bhrodadh aigne
> Gu dian-chasgairt sloigh leis;
> Chuireadh torman a phort baisgeil
> Spioraid bhras nar poraibh.

> 'He is a strongly built warror, well-shaped in form,
> A powerful man and vigorous, with white hands,
> His pipe jutting proudly from beneath his arm,
> Rousing our fighting anger with his tune;
> His march pours forth, stirring the enthusiasm
> For the slaughter of armies;
> The music of his sparkling tune would put
> Good keen spirit into the clan'.

After the '45 Alasdair remained bitterly opposed to the Hanoverians and to the Campbells. In 1750 he went to live in the island of Canna, but for only a year or so. He seemed unable to settle, and wherever he went, in Glenuig, Knoydart, Arisaig or Morar, he quarrelled with the local priest or the landlord, or both, and moved on. Eventually in about 1770 he died at Sanntaig, in Arisaig. He must have been in his mid-70s.

NORMAN MACLEAN

THE NEAREST, POSSIBLY THE ONLY, modern equivalent of *Moladh Moraig* is the Gaelic poem published in 1967 by Norman MacLean, entitled *Maol Donn* in Gaelic, *MacCrimmon's Sweetheart* in English. This appears in both languages in an anthology of 20th century Gaelic poetry, *An Tuil*, edited by Ronald Black, published in 1999. Norman's poem was the work which won the Bardic Crown at the National Mod in Glasgow in 1967.

Norman MacLean, brilliant in so many fields as Gaelic singer, composer, poet, writer, humorist, raconteur, comedian and piper, made his poem on a slightly different pattern from that of the 18th century piobaireachd poems, dividing it into Urlar, Taorluath and Crunluath, the sections differing mainly in their rhythms, but also with a change of thought in each.

It is cleverly set in a piping competition where the poet is watching and listening to a competitor playing *Maol Donn*; while he is listening, his thoughts wander (as they do), and he reflects on the likeness between a piper struggling to finish his performance without an error and his own struggle to get through life.

If we did not already know that the poet is a piper, it would be clear from the wording of his poem, equally pleasing in both Gaelic and English; he handles the terminology of piping deftly and with an understanding not immediately obvious in the work of Duncan Ban MacIntyre (see above).

Norman MacLean divides his poem into three movements only, movements rather than variations, the Urlar, Taorluath and Crunluath, a form found in some existing piobaireachd works. The only composer of piobaireachd poems who attempted a more subtle approach was Iain Dall MacKay in 1697; his representation of piobaireachd form was, however, too subtle for his later editors who failed to recognise what he was about, and they destroyed the patterns by changing the order of the verses. Later attempts, in the 18th century, are duly labelled, more obvious, but less close to the music.

As in the 18th century poems, the length of the different movements is not constant. Norman's Urlar has ten stanzas, his Taorludh (so spelled) has nine, his Crunludh only seven, and his Urlar repeat only three. Again, we have to look to Iain Dall for consistency in this regard. Norman's second Urlar is not so much a repeat, apart from one line, as a winding up, and the poet uses to good effect his image of the piper sailing his boat through the tune, to bind the sections together, and link the beginning to the end in Celtic style. Only the first verse of the final section is really the Urlar repeat, as he goes on to mention the applause and the after-effect of the music on the audience and on himself.

The main echo of the music is in the rhythms, and pipers might not agree with the metres that Norman uses. Perhaps the number of beats in a phrase should not differ so markedly between the Taorluath and Crunluath sections, though the embellishments change in the music to give a slight difference. But I know of no piobaireachd work (and certainly not *Maol Donn*), which has shorter phrases in the Crunluath than in the previous variations, and this could be regarded as a flaw in the work as a piobaireachd poem. But perhaps that is mere pedantry. The change is pleasing to the ear, poetically.

Norman's poem is of course in the idiom of modern Gaelic, and it does not have the same intricate patterns of internal rhyme which in some of the 18th century works echoed the phrase-patterns of the pipe-music. But the more modern work does have its own patterns, of end-rhyme and of internal rhyme, more half-rhyme than full rhyme, and of alliteration, holding the structure of the poem together as it did in the old days. Though different from the older works, this is a beautifully crafted piece, fully worthy of the bardic crown.

Norman's poem is reproduced here with his kind permission and that of his translator and his publisher. The Gaelic is given first, and the translation, made by the editor, Ronald Black, follows separately, since the translation is an enjoyable poem in its own right. We owe Dr Black a debt for making it available to those who cannot read Gaelic.

MAOL DONN, by Norman MacLean

An t-Urlar

Bu tu a'chraobh leatha fhein an lios nan sul
 'S tu 'gleusadh dhos na piob' le meoirean grinn;
Bha 'n comhlan balbh gun deo an talla dhluth
 Nuair chuir thu bat' do chiuil le uaill bho tir.

Shuigh do lamhan pongan direach geur
 On Spainnteach chruaidh a cheannsaich thu le baidh,
'S mar dh'fhalbhas ceo air beinn roimh theas na grein'
 Theich draghannan an t-saoghail o m'inntinn chraidht'.

Dhearc suil mo chuimhn' air laithean geala cian,
 Mo shaoghal socair 's rathad nan dul mo dhan -
Co-ionnan leam an t-urlar direach dian
 Ri tus mo chuairt neo-chaochlaidich don bhas.

Gu cinnteach dana lub thu 'm port gu d'dheoin
 Is dh'fhuadaich thu 'n teagamh grod o d'chridh,
Mar sin air slighe reidh roi-ordaicht' m'oig'
 Ghluais mi troimhn latha 's shluig mo chiall am brigh.

An Srathan liath nam fang air Braigh Loch Iall
 Bha'r dachaigh seasgair blath, fo chuip na gaoith',
Gun sgiths le furtachd leugh mi leabhar na bliadhn'
 Is fhuair mi firinn lom nach diobradh 'chaidh.

Cha robh ar teachd-an-tir san am ach truagh -
 B'e beachd nan uasal Galld' gur mor ar feum -
Ach fhuair sinn lon, is dh'fhuadaich sinn am fuachd
 Mun chagailt choir le gniomhan ghaisgeach treun'.

Chan fhaicinn iarmailt dhearg aig ceann an la
 'S cha chluinninn sgriach na comhachaig anns a' choill
Gun smaoineachadh air fuil chaidh dhortadh trath
 'S air blaraibh aost' 's cinn-chinnidh meallt' le foill.

Sa gheamhradh dhileach, talamh is speur 'na cheo,
 B'e m'annsachd riamh mun tein' a'Ghaidhlig chaomh;
Bhiodh 'Fear na h-Eabaid' 's orain nuadh 'tighinn beo,
 'S an cill mo chuimhn' bha 'n-diugh 's an-de mar aon.

Uair eile dh'aithnich m'aigne cumhachd Dhe,
 Bha 'n fheadag 'tuiteam sios on iarmailt fhann;
Bha samhchair 'snamh gu ciuin air loch 's air sleibh
 Os iochdar-druim mo chridh aig fois sa ghleann.

Le curam dh'fhag do mheur an grunnd 'na dheidh
 Is leig thu t'eich gu aonach saor gun srian -
B'ionnan leam an taorludh gaireach treun
 Ri laithean m'shaors' san d'fhuair mi fios air pian.

An Taorludh

Bu phroiseil do shiunnsair nuair ghreasaich thu'n cronan,
Bras-mheoirean ceol-sturtail gloir-ghleust' ga phogadh -
Taorludh air taorludh gu caithreamach ceolmhor,
 Thilg thu 'chuing's leig thu t'sheoltachd fa sgaoil.

Mar dhireas am fireun gu h-aotrom thar mhointich
Dh'eirich do spiorad air buillean geur sroiceach,
Bha t'inntinn 'na lasair is t'earbsa 'nad roidean,
 Dhearc do shuil sgaoilte air deireadh 's air tus.

De'n smuain bha 'nad inntinn air 'n turas ro-shiubhlach
Do lamhan glan innleachdach carach ga giulan?
De'n dealbh o chian chuir do chuimhne roimh t'shuilean
 Nuair ghluais thu le misneachd an taorludh gu crich?

Rugadh mo naire ann an luthchleas is ard-agal,
Gleadhraich is upraid a'bhaile gam thaladh -
Bu ghionach an t-acras is miann rinn mo chradhlot,
 Dh'ol mi mo shath de dh'fhion taitneach an t-saoghail.

Le iuchair ur-dheanta ar leam mar an ceudna
Gum feuchainn ri fuasgladh gach ceist rinn mo leireadh,
Bu ghniomhach mac-meanmain 's mo smuaintean air speiceadh
 An athbhliadhn 's an-uiridh mo steidh, seach am-bliadhn'.

Mar dhamh ann an ceo ghluais m'aigne san fhasach,
Le bhith sireadh na firinn' bha mo chre air sarach';
Ged a theann mi air bardachd cha robh cairdeas mar b'abhaist
 Eadar mise 's na sraidean am baile na stri.

Bu tric air an oidhche bhiodh m'inntinn am bruillean,
Ann an dorchadas uaigneach bhiodh an t-eagal gam bhuireadh,
Mo chorp air a leonadh le faobhar nan cruaidh-lann,
 Glaiste 'na phriosan bha mo chridhe fo bhroin.

Cha robh tlachd ann an leabhar 's an ceol-phiob' cha robh tamhachd,
Ghabhainn uidh ann an uiread, ach b'e 'n uine mo namhaid;
Ged bhiodh smuaintean a'sruthhadh, chan fhaighinn an sas annt',
 Bu ghuirme leamsa na beanntan fad as.

Nuair theann thu air 'chrunludh bha 'm bonn oir 'na do leirsinn,
Le meoirean troma bhuail thu 'm feadan gu gleusta;
Bha thu 'g ainich gu luath mar each saraicht' cur reise
 Nuair thog thu an crun air ceann-deiridh do phuirt.

An Crunludh

Nuair thug thu ionnsaigh dheineasach
Bha airtneal agus eislean ort;
Ach dh'ainneoin sgiths gun d'eirich thu
 'S thainig luths gu d'mheoirean.

Bu bhinn do phiob mhor acainneach
'S tu 'n luib a'chrunluidh thartaraich,
Do mheoir mar eich dian astarach
 A'gearradh leum le solas.

Bha dranndan aig duis lionmharra
'S bha ribheid gheur gam miadachadh –
'S i phiob nach leig air diochuimhn thu
  Ged's urramach do sheoltachd.

O's tu an laoch a chliuthaichinn
'Nam dhan le inntinn dhurachdaich –
Mar chluich thu 'm port gu fiughantach
  'S mar bhuail thu balbh an comhlan.

B'ionnan do cheol faramach
'S mo bheatha luaineach caithriseach,
Nuair bha gach crioch sior tharraing uam
  'S an namhaid air mo thorach.

B' i 'chrioch bha riamh air m'aire-sa
'S bha mo cheum ro chabhagach,
'S mo leirsinn air a dalladh orm
  Chan fhaicinn feum san lo seo.

Ach theirig smuaintean siubhlacha
Fo bhuaidh nam ponga luthmhora
Nuair shin thu ris an urlar dhuinn
  'S tu criochnachadh gu doigheil.

An t-Urlar

Bu tu a'chraobh leatha fhein an lios nan sul,
  Bha 'ghloir dhuit dluth 's bha 'phrois ag at do chleibh,
'S nochd thu tiamhaidheachd 'nad anam ruisgt'
  Nuair sheol thu bat' do chiuil gu cala reidh.

'M measg sloisreadh chomhradh 's molaidh 's beucaich aird
  Is sailtean air an lar a'bualadh cruaidh,
Thug siol do theisteis rabhadh dhomh air fas
  Is thuig mi, sann san la seo fhein tha'n duais.

Ma mhealas sinn an la seo mar as coir
  'S ma chuireas sinn ar beoil air blath a'chiuil
Bidh 'n-de 's an-uiridh dhuinn mar bhruadar gloir
  'S bidh h-uile maireach sinte ri ar duil.

English translation, made by Ronald Black:

MACCRIMMON'S SWEETHEART

The Ground

You were the only tree in the garden of eyes
 As your nimble fingers tuned the drones of the pipe;
The hall was packed and the silent crowd held their breath
 When you pushed the boat of your music from land with pride.

Your hands extracted notes that were straight and sharp
 From your Spanish hardwood so affectionately tamed,
And as mountain mist dissolves in the heat of the sun
 The cares of the world departed from my anguished mind.

My memory's eye beheld bright far-off days,
 My tranquil world and the hopeful road my theme -
Synonymous to me the straight and vehement ground
 With the start of my unaltering race to death.

With bold assurance you bent the tune to your will
 And gnawing doubt you banished from your heart,
And so on the smooth predestined path of my youth
 I moved through each day and my sense imbibed their sap.

In the grey old Strathan of fanks in the Braes of Lochiel
 Was our warm sequestered home, lashed by the gale,
With ease unexhausted I read the book of the year
 And learned the starkness of truth that would never fail.

Our livelihood was wretched for the time -
 Lowland officials felt that great were our needs -
But we found nourishment, and ways to beat the cold,
 Around the kindly hearth with brave heroes' deeds.

I couldn't see red sky at the end of the day
 And couldn't hear the screech of the owl in the wood
Without thinking of blood spilt early in life
 And of ancient battles and chiefs treacherously betrayed.

In the rainy winter, with earth and sky a mist,
  What I always loved around the fire was mellifluous Gaelic;
'The Man of Habit' and new songs would come alive,
  And in the cell of my memory today and yesterday were one.

At another time my spirit recognised the power of God,
  With the plover falling down from the languid sky;
Silence floating gently on loch and hill
  While the very bottom of my heart was at rest in the glen.

With care your finger left the ground behind it
  And you let your horses free to go unbridled to the heights -
Identical to me the brave rumbustious taorludh
  And my days of freedom when I came to experience pain.

The Taorludh (Free Movement)

Proud was your chanter when you quickened the melody,
Swift music-smart glory-trimmed fingers were kissing it -
Taorludh on taorludh triumphantly musical,
  You threw off the yoke and unleashed your skilfulness.

As the eagle soars over moorland so lightly
Your spirit rose upon sharp cutting strokes,
Your mind was aflame and you trusted your paths,
Your eye looked divided at end and beginning.

What thought were you pondering on the speediest of journeys,
Borne along by your fresh clever dexterous hands?
What film from afar did your memory show you
  As your taorludh was confidently drawn to a close?

My shame was born in agility and eloquence,
For the city's uproar and bustle attracted me -
Intense were the hunger and ambition that drove me,
  And I drank my fill of the world's pleasant wine.

With a modern key I thought in addition
That I'd try to unlock every question that vexed me,
Imagination was active but my thoughts were confined -
  My basis the future and past, not the present.

Like a stag in the mist moved my mind in the wilderness,
Through searching for truth my body was tired;
Though I turned to verse the old friendship was gone
　Between me and the streets and the city of strife.

Often at night with my mind in a torment,
In lonely darkness fear would embrace me,
My body was torn by the edge of the swordblades,
　Locked in its prison was my sorrowing heart.

With no pleasure in book nor repose in pipe music,
In so much I'd be interested, but my enemy was time;
Though thoughts would rush by, I couldn't get hold of them,
　The hills farther off were to me always greener.

When you turned to the crunludh the gold medal seemed close,
As your powerful fingers struck the chanter with skill;
Breathing fast like a hard-pressed horse in a race
　You picked up the crown at the end of your tune.

The Crunludh (Crown Movement)

When you made a brave effort
You were faint with exhaustion;
Despite tiredness you rose
　And strength came to your fingers.

Sweet was your great accoutred pipe
As you rattled out the crunludh,
Your fingers like horses strong and swift
　Leaping high with pleasure.

Copious drones humming
With crisp reed augmenting them –
It's the pipe unforgettable
　Though noble's your skill.

You're the warrior I'd celebrate
In my song with earnest mind –
How you played the tune heroically
　And struck the audience dumb.

Synonymous your echoing music
With my restless sleepless life,
Each aim forever eluding me
 And the devil in pursuit.

The end was always in my thoughts
And my step was too hasty,
And since my eyes had been blinded
 I'd see no point in today.

But fleeting thoughts were driven off
By the power of the music
When you brought us back to the ground
 To finish as is proper.

The Ground

You were the only tree in the garden of eyes,
Glory was close and pride puffed out your chest,
And you revealed the gloom in your naked soul
As you sailed the boat of your music safe into port.

Midst rumbling conversations, clapping, shouting loud,
And heels being beaten hard upon the ground,
Your testimony's seed brought me a warning about growth
And I realised how each day brings its own reward.

If we enjoy the present as we should
And place our mouths upon the music's bloom
Each yesterday will be our dream of glory
And each tomorrow will be as we hope.

 I find this work very pleasing – I particularly like the image of the piper sailing his boat through the tune and safely into port – and I am surprised that it has not received more publicity among pipers.
 Norman MacLean is the son of a Tiree father and a mother from North Uist. Born in Ibrox, Glasgow, he was sent as a child as a war evacuee first to his great-uncle in Strathan, Lochaber, and then to Benbecula, where he spent much of his childhood. On his return to Glasgow he went to Bellahouston Academy, the College of Piping and Glasgow University, and became a teacher of English and mathematics – is there anything this man cannot do?
 In 1967 he achieved the double at the Mod: he won both the Bardic Crown for the best Gaelic poem and the Gold Medal for singing. He has written other poems, and numerous articles, as well as two novels in Gaelic, and between 1976

and 1991 he was well-known as one of the funniest comedians of the century.

To see him live on stage with a mixed audience of tourists and local people is an experience never to be forgotten, as he plays the pipes, sings, dances and tells incomparable stories, using not only Gaelic and English but most of the languages of the visitors, from Swedish to Japanese. I remember watching a group of local teen-aged boys in Barra, who thought they were too sophisticated to enjoy the humour of one so old; it was fascinating to see the reluctant grins creep over their faces, followed by an outright laugh, and in the end they succumbed, as they had to, and they ended up rolling on the floor, weak with laughing.

Norman was a great success on television, too, his impersonation of an Inverness Free Church elder being particularly memorable.

His brilliance has its price, of course, and at times his hold on his mood-swings has slipped; stories of his exploits when in a manic phase have added to the legend. But his humour and his sincere love of his native language endear him to the Gaidhealtachd, and there is no doubt that he is unique. The words brilliant, intelligent, gifted and funny will always be mentioned when anyone speaks of Norman MacLean.

Norman MacLean who made the modern Gaelic piobaireachd poem Maol Donn in 1967.
(PHOTOGRAPH BY COURTESY OF THE COLLEGE OF PIPING)

SOURCES
Notices of Pipers
Derick S. Thomson: *Selected Poems of Alasdair Mac Mhaighstir Alasdair*,
The Rev. A. and the Rev. A. MacDonald
Derick S. Thomson: *Alasdair Mac Mhaighstir Alasdair's Political Poetry*,
Derick S. Thomson: *An Introduction to Gaelic Poetry*
Ed. Ronald Black: *An Tuil*

PIPER AT DRIMNIN, MORVERN

IN 1792, THE FIFTH LAIRD of Drimnin, Allan MacLean, died at the age of 68, leaving his faithful piper, whose name was Duncan, with no alternative but to emigrate. The local minister many years later, the Revd. Norman MacLeod, wrote of this:

'Poor Duncan Piper had to expatriate himself from the house which had sheltered him and his ancestors. The evening before he sailed, he visited the tomb of his old master, and played the family pibroch while he slowly and solemnly paced round the grave, his wild and wailing notes strangely disturbing the silence of the lonely spot. Having done so, he broke his pipes, and laying them on the green sod, departed, to return no more'.

As this account was written around 1867, its accuracy has to be in doubt, and it seems more likely that the departing Duncan would have taken his pipes, possibly his most valuable asset, with him. But we must allow for artistic licence.

Duncan has not been identified – if indeed this was his name – but the rent rolls of 1779 list 12 men called Duncan in the parish, any (or none) of whom might have been the piper. At Fernish, the township closest to the Laird's house, there was Duncan MacEachern, and he may have been the one; was he related to the piping MacEacherns of Islay? Or was MacEachern a patronymic, meaning only that his father's name was Hector?

KAID SIR HARRY MACLEAN was born in 1848, of the family of the MacLeans of Drimnin, Morvern, Argyll, the family mentioned by the minister in the above account. Around 1890 he became head of the army of the Sultan of Morocco, a post he held for 19 years. Wanting pipers to go out to teach his men to be pipers, he approached P/M R.Meldrum of the 93rd and Duncan Campbell of the 79th, but they declined. He finally persuaded a piper (- who was it?-), and the Sultan ordered a gold-mounted set of pipes costing £500 from Peter Henderson's in Glasgow. It is not clear who was to be the recipient.

Sir Harry had had a distinguished career in the army. In 1869 he was an Ensign in the 69th Foot, and went on the Red River Expedition in Canada. He resigned his commission in 1876, for a more adventurous life as Instructor in Drill and Discipline in the Moorish Army, an appointment which led him to the top, with the title of Kaid. He was himself a player, taught by Donald MacKay, piper to the Prince of Wales. H. Forsyth composed a 2/4 March with one part, called *Kaid Sir Harry MacLean's Moorish Salute*.

Some of the Lawrie or Laurie families in Appin had strong links with Ardnamurchan, and especially the district around Acharacle and Strontian (see above).

DUGALD CAMERON of Acharacle makes pipes from native oak which he fells himself, seasons, treats with additives under great pressure and finishes in the normal way. The mounts are polished aluminium which he reckons stays bright longer than silver. The pipes are an unusual light brown colour, reminding us of the MacCrimmons' Maol Donn, their Brown Sweetheart, presumed to mean brown drones made of laburnum wood.

ALASTAIR FLETCHER, Glasgow pipe-maker and piper comes of an Ardnamurchan family, his father Donald having been born there. Alastair was a pupil of Angus J. Maclellan, at the College of Piping. Recently he donated a silver-mounted pipe as a raffle prize, to help raise funds for the College Building Fund. The lucky winner was Ian Macleod, in Kirkwall.

BIBLIOGRAPHY

[TGSI = Transactions of the Gaelic Society of Inverness]

BAILEY, Geoff B. 1996: *Falkirk or Paradise!*
BIGWOOD, W.F.L. 2001: Edicts of Executry, Records of the Commisary Court of Argyll, and Records of the Vice-Admiral Court of Argyll, 1685-1825
BLACK, Nancy 1999: *From a Hollow on the Hill: History and Tales of Lorn and Fortingall Families*
BLACK, Ronald (ed.) 1999: *An Tuil*, An Anthology of 20th Century Gaelic Poetry
BRANDER, Michael 1971: *The Scottish Highlanders and their Regiments*
BROWNE, James 1847: *A History of the Highlands and of the Highland Clans*. 4 vols
BUCHANAN, Robert 1871: *The Land of Lorne*, 2 vols
CAMPBELL, Archibald of Kilberry 1984: *Side Lights on the Kilberry Book of Ceol Mor*. 1986: *Further Side Lights on the Kilberry Book of Ceol Mor*
CAMPBELL, Jeannie 2001: *Highland Bagpipe Makers*
CAMPBELL, J. F. 1880: *Canntaireachd: Articulate Music*. 1890: *Popular Tales of the West Highlands*
CAMPBELL, Marion: unpublished notes on Kilnaish Mausoleum. 1977: *Argyll, The Enduring Heartland*
CANNON, Roderick 1988: *The Highland Bagpipe and its Music*. 1994: (ed) Joseph MacDonald's *Compleat Theory of the Scots Highland Bagpipe* (c.1760). 1997: General Preface to the Piobaireachd Society Collection
CHARLES, George 1816: *History of the Transactions in Scotland in the Years 1715-16 and 1745-46*, 2 vols
CHEAPE, Hugh 1999: *The Book of the Bagpipe*
CLAN CAMPBELL ABSTRACTS, documents concerning the Campbells, taken from the Sheriff Court Books and Books of Council and Session, in Inveraray. 6 volumes, published 1913-18. The series was started by the Rev. Kenneth Palmer, and then taken over by Major (later Colonel) Sir Duncan Campbell
COLLIE, William 1908, reprint 1992: *Memoirs of William Collie, a 19th Century Deerstalker*
CRAIGNISH, early 18th century: Manuscript history of the Campbells of Craignish, Misc. Scot. Hist. Soc. vol iv
DALYELL, Sir J.C. 1849: *Musical Memoirs of Scotland*
DONALDSON, William 2000: *The Highland Pipe and Scottish Society 1750-1950*
DRUMMOND, John of Balhaldie (ed) 1842: *Memoirs of Sir Ewen Cameron*
FAICHNEY, Alexander Mailer 1902: *Oban and the District Around*
FAIRWEATHER, Barbara 1971: *Living in Old Glencoe, A Social History of the Glencoe and Ballachulish Areas* (booklet)
FAUJAS, B., de Saint Fond 1907: *A Journey through England and Scotland and to the Hebrides 1784*, 2 vols
FERGUSSON, J. 1951: *Argyll in the Forty-Five*

FIONN (Henry Whyte) 1904: *The Martial Music of the Clans*
FRASER, Alexander 1964: *North Knapdale in the XVII and XVIII centuries*
FRASER, Dr Alexander Duncan 1906: *Some Reminiscences and the Bagpipe*
FRASER, The Rev. James 1905: *The Wardlaw Manuscript, Chronicles of the Frasers 916-1674*. Published by the Scottish Historical Society
FRASER, Simon, ed. B.J. Maclachlan Orme 1979: *The Piobaireachd of Simon Fraser with Canntaireachd*
GASKELL, Philip 1968: *Morvern Transformed. A Highland Parish in the 19th Century*
GIBSON, John 1998: *Traditional Gaelic Bagpiping 1745-1945*. 2002: *Old and New World Highland Bagpiping*
GLEN, David 1880-1907: *A Collection of Ancient Piobaireachd*. 1900: *Music of the Clan MacLean*
GORDON, Seton 1935: *Highways and Byways in the West Highlands*
GRAHAM-CAMPBELL, David 1978: *Portrait of Argyll and the Southern Hebrides*
GRANT, Mrs, of Laggan 1807: *Letters from the Mountains*, 2 vols
HADDOW, Alec 1982: *The History and Structure of Ceol Mor*
HIGHLAND PAPERS 1916: Volume II 1240-1716, published by the Scottish Historical Society
HILL, J. Michael 1993: *Fire and Sword, Sorley Boy MacDonnell and the Rise of Clan Ian Mor 1538-90*
HISTORY of Lochfyneside, Furnace, Crarae and Minard (anon), undated
The HOUSE of Argyll and the Collateral Branches of the Clan Campbell from the Year 420 to the Present Time. (anon) 1871
HUNTER, Charles 1984: *Oban, Kilmore and Kilbride*. 1993: *Oban Past and Present*
INNES, C (ed.) 1859: *The Book of the Thanes of Cawdor, 1236-1732*
LIVINGSTONE, Alastair of Bachuil, AIKMAN, Christian and HART, Betty Stuart 1984: *Muster Roll of Prince Charles Edward Stuart's Army 1745-46*
MACARTHUR–MACGREGOR MANUSCRIPT: ed. Buisman, Frans and Wright, Andrew 2001
MACDONALD, Alexander 1914: *Story and Song from Lochness-side* (with translations and music). Re-issued 1982
MACDONALD, Alexander 1998: *The MacDonalds of Glencoe*
MACDONALD, The Rev. A., Killearnan, and the Rev. A., Kiltarlity. 1900: *The Clan Donald*, 2 vols. 1924: *The Poems of Alexander MacDonald (Mac Mhaighstir Alasdair)*
MACDONALD, Colin 1950: *History of Argyll*
MACDONALD, Donald of Castleton 1978: *Clan Donald*
MacDONALD, Stuart 1994: *Back To Lochaber*
MACDOUGALL, Allan 1798: *Collected Poems*
MACDOUGALL, Jean 1984: *Highland Postbag, The Correspondence of Four MacDougall Chiefs 1715-1865*
MACFARLANE, James 1922: *History of the Clan MacFarlane*
MACFIE, J.W.S. 1938: *John MacFie of Edinburgh and his Family*

MACINTOSH, Peter 1861: *History of Kintyre*
MACKAY, Angus 1838: *A Collection of Ancient Piobaireachd*
MACKAY, William 1893: *Urquhart and Glenmoriston, Olden Times in a Highland Parish*
MACKENZIE, Alexander 1884: *History of the Camerons*
MCKERRAL, Andrew 1948: *Kintyre in the 17th Century*
MACKNIGHT, James (ed) undated: *Memoirs of Lochiel*
MACLEAN, Marianne 1991: *The People of Glengarry, Highlanders in Transition 1745-1820* (MacGill University)
MACLEOD, the Revd. Norman 1867: *Morvern, A Highland Parish, based on Reminiscences of a Highland Parish*, first published 1867, re-issued, edited by Iain Thornber in 2002
MACMILLAN, Somerled 1952: *The MacMillans and their Septs*
MACROBBIE, William 1999: *Achgarve*
MARSHALL, J.S. 1986: *The Life and Times of Leith*
MARTIN, Angus 1984: Kintyre, *The Hidden Past*
MATHESON, William 1938: *The Songs of John MacCodrum*. 1951: Notes on Mary MacLeod, in TGSI 41
MUDIE, Robert 1822: *A Historical Account of His Majesty's Visit to Scotland*
MUNRO, Neil 1896: *The Lost Pibroch and other Shieling Tales* (re-issued 1996)
MURRAY, W.H. 1968: *The Companion Guide to the West Highlands of Scotland*
NEWTON, Norman 1999: *Kintyre*
PEKAAR, Robert L. 1990: *An Encyclopaedia of Tunes for the Great Highland Bagpipe* (an Index rather than an Encyclopaedia)
PREBBLE, John 1966: *The Massacre of Glencoe*. 1975: *Mutiny, Highland Regiments in Revolt 1743-1804*. 1988: *The King's Jaunt*
ROBERTSON, D. 1915: *The Bailies of Leith*
ROBERTSON, James 2001: *The Mull Diaries of James Robertson 1842-6*, transcribed by J.B. Loudon
RUSSELL, John 1922: *The Story of Leith*
SANGER, Keith: 'MacCrimmon's Prentise – A Post Graduate Student Perhaps' Piping Times 44/6, March 1992
SANGER, Keith and KINNAIRD, Alison 1992: *The Tree of Strings*
SCOTT, Archibald B. 1918: *The Pictish Nation, Its People and Its Church*
SCOTT, James E. 1969: Notes on Muckairn and Glenlonan, in TGSI Vol 46
SHEDDEN, Hugh 1938: *The Story of Lorn, Its Isles and Oban*
SIMPSON, Douglas 1958: *Dunstaffnage Castle and the Stone of Destiny*
SKENE, W.F. 1880: *Celtic Scotland*
STEVENSON, David 1980: *Highland Warrior, Alasdair MacColla and the Civil Wars*
STEWART, John of Ardvorlich 1974: *The Camerons, A History of Clan Cameron*
STEWART, COLONEL DAVID OF GARTH 1822: *Sketches of the character, Manners, and Present State of the Highlanders of Scotland*, 2 vols
SUNART OAKWOODS RESEARCH GROUP 2001: *The Sunart Oakwoods, A Report on their History and Archaeology*

THOMSON, Derek 1974: paper 'Niall Mor MacMhuirich', in TGSI vol 49. 1974: *An Introduction to Gaelic Poetry* (re-issued 1999). 1983: (ed) *The Companion to Gaelic Scotland*. 1989: paper 'Alasdair Mac Mhaighstir Alasdair's Political Poetry' in TGSI Vol 56, pp.185-213. 1996: *Selected Poems of Alasdair Mac Mhaighstir Alasdair*
THOMSON, Frank 1984-6: paper on J.F.Campbell, in TGSI Vol 54
WALLACE, Joyce 1997: *The Traditions of Trinity and Leith*
WATSON, William 1926: *History of the Celtic Place-names of Scotland*
WHYTE, Henry – see FIONN
WILLIAMS, Ronald 1984: *The Lords of the Isles*

INDEX OF PEOPLE

CT = Campbeltown
JMG = John MacDougall Gillies

All names beginning with Mac, Mc
or M' are treated as Mac-.

Alasdair MacColla - see MacColla
Alasdair Mac Mhaighstir Alasdair-
    see MacDonald, Alexander
Alasdair, son of Angus Mor of Islay 4
Albert, Prince 130-1
Allan, G.S. 1
Allanby, Major, Ardrishaig 105
Anderson, Campbell, drummer, CT 60
Angus Mor of Islay 4
Antrim, 1st Earl of (Ranald MacDonnell)
    4,5,6
Antrim, 2nd Earl of 5,6,10,11
Antrim, 3rd Earl of 5
Antrim, Earl of (1720s) 190
Antrim, Earls of 29,36
Antrim harpers 6
Archibald of Keppoch (Gilleasbuig na Ceapaich)
    15
Argyle or Argyll, 7th Earl of (1584-1638)
    (Archibald Campbell) 90,120
Argyle or Argyll, 8th Earl and Marquis of
    (1638-1661) (Archibald Campbell)
    6,10,11-13,90,119-123
Argyle or Argyll, 10th Earl of (1685-1701)
    (Archibald Campbell) 253; 1st Duke of
    (1701- 03) 23,123-5
Argyll, Dowager Duchess (1890s) 64
Argyll, 3rd Duke of (1743-1761)
    (Archibald Campbell) 8,9,20
Argyll, 5th Duke (1770-1806)
    (John Campbell) 21,127,191
Argyll, 7th Duke of (1839-1847)
    (John Campbell) 144
Argyll, 8th Duke of (1847-1900)
    (George Campbell) 64,118,128,130,141
    2,144,145,151,155-6,214
Argyll, 9th Duke of (1900-1914)
    (John Campbell) 66,74,144,155,158
Argyll, 11th Duke (1950s) 138,157,285
Argyll, 13th Duke of (1993) 214
Argyll and Sutherland Highlanders
    106,133,156-7,159-163,234,237,
    265,267
Argyll Fencibles (1745) 155,159
Argyll Highlanders (91st Regiment) 159
Argyllshire Volunteers 156,159,267
Argyllshire Gathering, list of Gold Medallists
    217-20
Armstrong, Chris 291
Astley, Constance and Gertrude 216
Atholl, Countess of (1705) 124
Atholl, Duke of (1830s) 222
Attlee, Clement 284

Bain, Andrew 108
Bain, Peter, Portree 229
Ballantine, John, Jacobite 174
Bannatyne, Charles 295
Barbreck, Laird of 97
Barrie, James 75
Barrie, William 88, 166, 276
Bartholomew, Sheriff John 115-6
Beaton, Lewis 107, 275
Beatson, Captain 26
Bell, Henry 99
Bissett, Marjorie 4
Bissett, Mr (1746) 195
Black, John, Kilberry (1898) 38
Black, Nancy, Oban 176,178,256
Black, Ronald 92,298-9,303
Black Watch 19,20,207,235
Blackie, John Stuart 118
Bohuntin, Domhnall Donn of 15
Bonaparte, Napoleon 39,192,255
Bowman, D. 241
Boyd, Agnes, CT 35
Boyd, Anndra Mac an Easbuig xv
Boyd, Andrew xv
Boyd, Jean xv
Boyd, Sandy, Largs 229
Boyd, Thomas, Lord xv
Breadalbane Fencibles 225,257
Brown, Bessie 222
Brown, Robert U. 37,109,222
Buchanan, John (1800) 99
Buchanan, Katrine 28
Buchanan, Robert 201
Buchanan, Roddy 80
Buie, Marion, Jura 280
Burgess, John D. 58,89,111
Burnett, James 85

Caird, Dr Colin 270,276
Caithness and Bute Volunteers 225
Callander, Lairds of 123
Callender, Captain, Seaforths 153
Cameron, A.K., Montana 275
Cameron, Alexander, brother of Donald 143
Cameron, Alexander, son of Donald 63, 67,
    70-1,95,101,105-6,160,268-71,274
Cameron, Alexander, 3rd of Dungallon 288-9
Cameron, Allan, 16th of Lochiel 288
Cameron, Allan of Erracht 288
Cameron, Angus (1790s) 222-3
Cameron, Archibald, 1st of Dungallon 288-9
Cameron, Charles 161
Cameron, Donald 42,95,105,143,146,153,160,
    268,274-6
Cameron, Donald, son of Allan 288
Cameron, Donald Dubh, 15th of Lochiel 288
Cameron, Dugald, Acharacle 308
Cameron Sir Ewen of Lochiel 288-9
Cameron, Ian C. 74
Cameron, J. 241

Index of People

Cameron, Jean 288
Cameron, John xiv
Cameron, John of Callert 225
Cameron John of Glendessary 288
Cameron, John, 2nd of Dungallon 287-9
Cameron, Keith, son of Donald 276
Cameron, Major Kenneth 65-6
Cameron of Lochiel (1790s) 222
Cameron, William W. 160
Camerons (family) 68,71
Campbell - see also Argyll, Dukes of
Campbell, Alistair of Airds 125
Campbell, Angus, sailor (1812) 43
Campbell, Angus, son of Archibald 65,68,106
Campbell, Ann (1778) 26
Campbell, Ann, Oban 113,115-6
Campbell, Archibald of Kilberry 25, 37-8, 63-72,
  83,93,115,154,185,270,272,275
Campbell, Archibald, 6th of Lochnell 195
Campbell, Lady Archibald 156
Campbell, Lord Archibald (1870s) 74,118,
  154-6,175
Campbell, Archie, Milngavie 168
Campbell, Bruce 285
Campbell, Captain, at Killian, Inveraray 99
Campbell, Captain, of Glenfeochan 178
Campbell, Captain, of Glenlyon 116
Campbell, Catherine, Dalmally 244
Campbell, Colin, army piper (1854) xvi
Campbell, Colin of Ballimore 195
Campbell, Colin of Boghole, Nairn 124
Campbell, Mr Colin - see Campbells of
  Breadalbane
Campbell, Colin, brother of Young George of
  Cawdor 124
Campbell, Captain Colin of Carwhin 113-5
Campbell, Colin, son of Archibald 65,68
Campbell, Colin Mor 37, 113-6,196,198
Campbell, Colonel, Fort Augustus (1745) 195
Campbell, Craig and Iain 80
Campbell, D., composer 73
Campbell, Daniel of Shawfield 196
Campbell, Sir Donald of Ardnamurchan 221
Campbell, Donald, 14th Captain of
  Dunstaffnage 173
Campbell, Donald Dubh (1745) 20,125,160
Campbell, Donald (1815), son of Donald,
  Nether Lorne 114-5
Campbell, Donald, Nether Lorne, father of
  Colin Mor 113-6
Campbell, Dougal, 13th Captain of
  Dunstaffnage 172-3
Campbell, Dugald of Kintarbert 19-24,26,28-30,
  39,45,277
Campbell, Duncan, Foss 25
Campbell, Duncan, Oban (1870) 202
Campbell, the Rev. Duncan (1960s) 97
Campbell, Duncan, 79th Regiment 308

Campbell, Sir Duncan, 8th of Lochnell 160,190,
  195-6
Campbell, Duncan of Sunderland, Islay 26
Campbell, the Hon. Elspeth 66,74,156
Campbell, Major F.C.G.. 40th Pathans 65
Campbell, General Sir Frederick 65
Campbell, George of Airds 93,171,221
Campbell, Young George of Cawdor
  123-5,221,289
Campbell, Sir Hugh of Cawdor 124-5
Campbell, Isabella MacNeill of Kintarbert
  22,26,28-9
Campbell, James (1745) 195
Campbell, James, son of Archibald of Kilberry
  64,68-9,70,72,81-2,275
Campbell, James, brother of Archibald of
  Kilberry 66
Campbell, James C., the Queen's 2nd piper
  105,119
Campbell, Janet, the Black Bitch of
  Dunstaffnage 93,171,193,221
Campbell, Jeannie 50,55,136,138-40,154,174,
  205,208,210,226,267-9,272,285,287
Campbell, J.F., folklorist 114-8,126,128,130-3,
  145,152
Campbell, Colonel Jock (1940s) 107
Campbell, Colonel John of Barbreck (1778)
  98,163
Campbell, Sir John of Cawdor 126
Campbell, John, Dunstaffnage 172
Campbell, Sir John of Glenorchy 242
  (see also Earl of Breadalbane, 1680)
Campbell of Glenorchy, Lady (1662) 242-3
Campbell, John of Innergeldie (1675) 243
Campbell, John, 10th of Kilberry ('Big Jock')
  father of Archibald 63,66-795
Campbell, John, 11th of Kilberry, brother of
  Archibald xvii, 63,65-6,68,106
Campbell, John (Islay), son of Donald,
  Nether Lorne 114-7,196
Campbell, Lachlan MacNeill of Kintarbert
  21-4,26-7,29,45
Campbell, Laurie, photographer 197
Campbell, Margaret of Kintarbert 21-3,26,29
Campbell, Margaret of Shawfield 196
Campbell, Marion xvii, 259
Campbell, Mary of Glenfeochan (1773) 180
Campbell, Neil (1608) xv
Campbell, Niall, Strachur 74
Campbell, Peter, Kintyre (1812) 43
Campbell, Captain Robert of Glenlyon (1692)
  253,255
Campbell, Lt Col Robin 161
Campbell, Lt Ronald xvi
Campbell, Walter, Islay 116
Campbell, Walter F., Islay 114-7,119
Campbell, William, Queen's piper 101,105
Campbell, William, son of Donald,
  Nether Lorne 117
Campbell, W.J. 1

Campbells in Argyll :
Campbells of Achallader, Orchy 123
Campbells of Airds 95,170,221, 223-4
Campbells of Ardmaddy 113 = Campbells of
  Carwhin or of Mochaster 113,114,116
Campbells of Argyll 11,12,92-3,187
Campbells of Barcaldine 223
Campbells of Breadalbane 104,113,126,146,
  184,225,241,243,269
Campbells of Cawdor 91-2,123-4,221,243
Campbells of Craignish 97,99
Campbells of Glendaruel 267
Campbells of Glenfeochan 178
Campbells of Glenlyon 242
Campbells of Glenmacrie 189
Campbells of Glenorchy 242-3
Campbells of Inverneill 103
Campbells of Jura 104
Campbells of Kilberry 9,63-72
Campbells of Knock (1794) 196
Campbells of Lochawe 225
Campbells of Lochnell (1794) 196 (1830) 200
Campbells of Skipness 120
Campbeltown, burghers of 30
Cannon, Roderick 25,45,47
Carruthers family, Kilberry 40,63
Carruthers, Helen 205,207
Carruthers, Jeannie 207
Carruthers John 37-8,64-5,205
Carslaw, Dr Stewart 47
Casey, Mr, CT Grammar School 60
Cassidy, Lucy 52
Chapman, Annie 149
Charles I, King 122
Charles II, King 120
Cheape, Brigadier, of Tiroran 95
Cheape, Hugh 98,163
Clark, George 139
Claverhouse - see Dundee
Clerk, Dugald xvi
Cockburn, Lord 222-3
Collie families in the Great Glen 254
Collie, Mary, mother of William Ross 255
Collie, William, father of Mary 255
Contullich, Laird of 10
Cordiner, Janet, CT 35
Cousin, Alistair,CT 58
Cousin, Lorne 58
Covenanters 11,91
Cowie, Alex 139
Crawford, Janet 140
Cromwell, Oliver 120
Cummings pipers 89
Currie, John, Mull 228
Currie, Malcolm 139

Dalrymple, Sir John 253-4
Dalyell (Memoirs) 116
Darroch, John, Jura 278
Darroch, Mary, Jura 278,280,282

Davidson, Duncan, of Tulloch 153
Davidson, Emily 56
Dedo, Dr Herb 239
Dighton, David (1822) 252-3
Docherty, Isabella 136
Donald Ban (in poem) 15-17
Donald of Islay 4
Donald, 2nd of the Isles 4
Donaldson, Brian 58
Donaldson, William 33,44,68,70,117,143,181-2,
  223,257
Douglas, Thomas 119,277
Dugald, son of Somerled 4
Duncan, Archie 1,36,42
Duncan, Ian 51
Dundee, Viscount of, = James Graham of
  Claverhouse = Bluidy Clavers xv,3,48
Dunmore, Earl of 264
Dunn, Kenneth, Inveraray 155
Dunn, Malcolm, Inveraray 155

Edward VII, King 102,105
Eglinton, Earl of xv
Empster, Elizabeth 263
Eunson, Mr, from Leith 283

Fairweather, Barbara 256
Falconer, Agnes 260
Ferguson, Sir Alex 167-8
Ferguson, Donald 49-50,136
Ferguson, Dougie 80
Ferguson, Isabel, Skye 261
Ferguson, Pipe Major, Argylls 275
Fergussone, Captain James 19
Fettes, Alexander 60,267-9
Finlay, John, Glasgow 34
Finlayson, Calum 235
Finlaysons at Achilty 150
Fionn - see Whyte, Henry
Fisher, Donald (1783) 225
Fleeming, Jean, CT 35
Fleming, Ron 1,56,57,63
Flemings in CT 7,35
Fletcher, Alistair 59,309
Fletcher, Donald 309
Flockhart, Jean 230-2
Forbes, Sir Charles of Newe 24-5
Forsyth, Henry 160,286,308
Fraser, Dr Alexander Duncan 161
Fraser Highlanders (78th Regiment) 98
Fraser, Marjorie Kennedy 283
Fraser, Simon, Lord Lovat (1746) 19-20
Fraser clan 19
Frimley Volunteers 106

Galbraith, Flora CT 133,136
Galbraith, John CT 51
Galbraith, Neil 49-50,136
Garroway, John 238
Gayre of Gayre and Nigg, Lt Col 51,88-9

Index of People

George IV, King 44,46,252
Gibson, John 20,116-8,182
Gilleasbuig na Ceapaich 15
Gillies, Alasdair 101,165
Gillies, Alexander, brother of JMG 272
Gillies, Alexander,Strachur, grandfather of JMG 269
Gillies, Alistair MacDougall, son of JMG 269
Gillies, Allan, uncle of Arthur 166
Gillies, Arthur 86,89,101, 164-8,170,220
Gillies, Barbara, wife of Arthur 166,168
Gillies, Duncan, father of John 103
Gillies, Gilbert, brother of John 103-4
Gillies, Ian MacDougall, son of JMG 269
Gillies, Isabella, sister of John 104
Gillies, Jessie, mother of Arthur 165
Gillies, Jessie, sister of John 104
Gillies, John, Glendaruel, father of JMG 267
Gillies, John MacDougall 60,63,67,69-71,95, 100-1,104-5,160,194,205,208,238, 267-76,281,284-5
Gillies, John, Scots Guards100-3, 105,165, 268,276
Gillies, Kate, daughter of John 102
Gillies, Malcolm, father of Arthur 165
Gillies, Neil, Edinburgh 100,267,270,276
Gillies, Norman 58,101,165
Glasgow Highlanders 144
Glen, Alexander 143
Glen, David 91,277
Glengarry's Regiment 251
Glenorchy, Lady - see Campbell
Glensmen of Antrim 3
Gordon, Col Bertie 160
Gordon, Duke of (1770s) 99
Gordon, General (1804) 191
Gordon Highlanders 89,222,237,266
Gordon, John xiv,105-6,211
Gordon, Seton 13,68
Graham, John 3
Graham Campbell, Dugald 73
Graham Campbell, Jock 73,81,91
Grainger and Campbell, pipemakers 80
Grant, Annie, Dunoon 285
Grant, George 241,266
Grant, Iain of Rothiemurchus (1960) 64, 107
Grant, Sir James 251
Grant, John 119
Grant, Sheriff J.P. of Rothiemurchus (1920s) 117
Grant's Fencibles 251
Gray, William 91,112,274,276
Gregson, Mr, of Tilliefourie 278
Grieve, William 162
Gunn, William, pipemaker 50
Guthry, Bishop 12

Haddow, Alec 76,79,84,90-93
Hamilton Jim 241
Hamilton, Elizabeth 136

Harkness, Isabella 280
Harkness, John Currie 280
Harkness, Sarah 280
Hayes, John, Torrisdale 49
Henderson -see also MacEandric, MacEnrich
Henderson, Alistair, brother of Jim 181
Henderson, 'Big', of the Chanters 241
Henderson, Christian 244
Henderson, Duncan, Arivean 242
Henderson, Ewen, Scots Guards 147
Henderson, Jim 278,280-1
Henderson, Joe 242
Henderson, John, brother of Jim 281
Henderson, Murray 89
Henderson, Neil, father of Jim 281
Henderson, Peter or Pat, Arivean 242
Henderson, Peter, pipemakers 139,204,208, 230,269,271,274,308
Hendersons, pipers in Glencoe 241-2
  – see also MacEandric
Higgins, Lizzie, singer 222
Highland Light Infantry (H.L.I.) 270,277
Hume, R.W., Leith (1822) 44
Hunter, Charles K. 177
Hunter, James 263
Huntly, Marquis of (1715) 188, (1838) 226,268, (1880s) 274
Hurst, Iain, Oban 220

Inglis, William Laidlaw 283
Irish lord at Duart 287
Irishmen from Antrim 3

Jackson, James, Alness 261,266
Jackson, James, Argylls 263
James III and VIII, King 188
Jeffrey, Charles and William 281
John of Islay (Iain Ileach) (1385) 4
Johnson, Catherine 263
Johnston, Archibald, CT 59
Johnstone, Duncan 230
Johnston, Hector, Coll 116
Johnstone, James 230
Johnstone, John, Islay 111
Johnstone, Malcolm 282

Kennedy, Hugh, Tiree 111
Kenneth, Archie xiv,1,46,63,68,71,73,81-88,95, 116,164,168
Ker, Lord Mark's (regiment) 124
Kerr, Daniel, Inveraray 155
Kerr, John, Imverary 155
Kerr, John (1950s) 162
Kilcolumkill minister, Kintyre 10
King's Own Scottish Borderers 138

Lamont, Alexander (1785) 277
Lamont, Duncan, Cowal 277
Lamont or Lamond, Katherine 183
Lamonts in Cowal 120, 277

Lang, Catherine CT 136
Lang, Neil CT 136
Langwill, Patric 48
Laverty, Mary, Antrim 55
Lauder, Sir Harry 284

[The names Lawrie, Laurie, Lowrie and Lourie are here all treated as Lawrie]

Lowrie, Alexander, Ardnamurchan 234,260
Lawrie, Angus ('Old Toasty') 234-5,237
Lawrie, Angus, Largs xiv,234-6,238
Lawrie, Ann (1864) 262
Lourie, Christian 234,260
Lawrie, Christina (1853) 262,264
Lawrie, Donald (1856) 262
Lawrie, Donella 264
Lawrie, Dugald (1855) 262,264; his two children 264
Lawrie, Flora (1857) 262
Lawrie, Gordon, Dunbarton 234,260,263
Lawrie, Graeme 263
Laurie, Hugh (1847), father of William 260,262-3 Hugh's six children 263
Lawrie, Iain, son of William 51,237,241, 265
Lawrie, Ian (1912), father of Colin 263
Lowrie, James, Ardnamurchan 234,260,263
Lourie, James 1821 234,261
Lawrie, James, Oban (1859) 233-4,263
Lawrie, James (1859) 262
Lawrie, James (1859) Ballachulish and Luss 262-4
Lawrie, James (1860) Strontian 263
Lawrie, James (1870) Ballachulish 264
Lawrie, James (1894) 234
Lawrie, James, son of James,Luss 264
Lawrie, James ('Jack') 237
Lawrie, Jane, wife of Dugald 264
Lowrie, John, Ardnamurchan 234,260,263
Lourie, John 1808 234
Lawrie, John, Appin (1849) 234
Lawrie, John (1876) Ballachulish 264
Lawrie, Kenneth (1901) 234
Lawrie, Kenneth, brother of Ronald 234-5
Lawrie, Dr Kenneth, son of Angus 235
Lawrie, Margaret (1891) 234
Lawrie, Martin (1899) 234
Lawrie, Mary (1897) 234
Lawrie, R.G., pipemakers 55,78,208
Lawrie, Ronald, Oban 57,164,168,220,234-5, 237-9,263
Lourie, Thomas, Strontian 234,260,262; his six children 234
Lawrie, Thomas, brother of William, Ballachulish 264
Lawrie, William, son of Thomas 262
Lawrie, William (1850), son of William 262
Lawrie, William, son of James (1859) 263
Lawrie, William, died 1916 xiv,56,89,95,106,163 170,205,211,233-4,241,260-66,281,285

Lawrie, William (1893), son of Ann 262
Lawries in Ardnamurchan 233
Leitch, Donald and John 271-2,277
Leitch, Jock 57
Leitch, Mrs 272
Leslie, General 11-13,120,174
Leyden, Dr John 201
Liddell, Stuart 36
Limbu, L/Cpl, Ghurkas 85-6
Lindsay, Hugh, Jura 131,280-1
Lindsay, Neil, Jura 281
Lindsays at Lagg, Jura 280
Livingstone, Agnes, grandchild of Hugh 264
Livingstone, Ann or Agnes (1807) 234,262-3
Livingstone, Archie, son-in-law of Hugh 264
Livingstone family on Scarba 99
Livingstone, Sarah, Moleigh 183
Logan, James 33-4,38,253
Longwill, Janet 48
Longwill, Peter 48
Longwills in CT 48
Lorne, Marquess of 141,154,159,214
Loudon, James 160
Loudon, Lord (1745) 195
Louise, Princess 141,144,154,159,214,285
Lovat Scouts 103,229,232
Low, Margaret, wife of JMG 269
Lynch, Pipe Major 93rd regiment 275

MacAlister, Agnes (1837) 35
MacAlister, Alexander of Loup and Torrisdale (1844) 41
MacAlister, Angus of Loup (1761) 21
MacAlister, Archibald, CT 55
MacAlister, Archie, Ardrishaig 79-80
MacAlister, Betsey (1833) 35
MacAlister, Angus, brother of John 29
MacAlister, ?Donald, possible brother of John 29
MacAlister, Duncan, brother of John 29
MacAlister, Ellen, CT 55
MacAlister, Godfrey 34
MacAlister, Hector, of Loup 12
MacAlister, Isabella (1835) 35
MacAlister, Janet (1824) 35
MacAlister, Jean (twin 1826) 35,40
MacAlister, John, champion piper 9, 28-34, 36-7,39-40; his wife 32
MacAlister, Malcolm (1831) 35
MacAlister, Margaret (1823) 35
MacAlister, Mary (twin,1826) 35,39
MacAlister, Mary, daughter of Ronald, Garvachy 40
MacAlister pipers 24,28,46
MacAlister, Ronald, Dunskeig (1790) 34-6,40
MacAlister, Ronald, Garvachy (1790) 35, 40
MacAlister, Ronald (1829) 35
the MacAlisters in CT 3,6-7,24,34-5,37,39,41
the MacAlisters of Loup 4, 6-9,28,30,34
Macandoirie, Donald, fiddler 7

Index of People

MacArthur, Alexander, Lerags 226
MacArthur, Angus 8
MacArthur, Archibald, Ulva 287
MacArthur, Bell, Lerags 226
MacArthur, John, 'the Professor' 8,33,34,223
MacArthur, John, Balvicar 127
MacArthur, John, piper to Craignish 97
MacArthur, John Ban, uncle of the Professor 8
MacArthur, John, drummer, Inveraray 156
MacArthur, Katherine 40
MacArthur pipers (1780s) 32
the MacArthurs of Loch Awe 97,127
the MacArthurs of Skye/Edinburgh 39
Macartney, Paul 56-7
MacAulay, Alexander 175-6,183
MacAulay, Angus, South Uist 55,107,230
MacAulay, Dr Flora 58,59
MacAulay, Fred 250
MacBean, John 213
MacBeth of Cawdor 124
MacCaig, Norman, poet 221
MacCallum, Archibald 35
MacCallum, Archibald (1860) 35
MacCallum, Archibald (1883) 36,157
MacCallum, Hugh (1882) 35-6
MacCallum, Hugh (1960s) 35,41-2,58-9,133-5
MacCallum, James (1792) 35,40,46
MacCallum, Lachlan 35
MacCallum, Malcolm (1867) 35
MacCallum, Margaret (1857) 35
MacCallum, Marion (1886) 36
MacCallum, Mary (1731)
MacCallum, Mary (1852) 35
MacCallum, Mary, wife of Donald MacLean, CT 39
MacCallum, Neil, senior 35
MacCallum, Neil (1825) 35,40
MacCallum, Nicol (1935) 162
MacCallum, Peter, brother of Ronald MBE 157
MacCallum, Ronald MacAlister (1854) 45
MacCallum, Ronald MacAlister (1880) 36
MacCallum, Ronald, CT Pipe Band (1930s) 51
MacCallum, Ronald, MBE 55-7,59,157-8,
MacCallum, William, son of Archie 35,39
MacCallum, William (1863) 35
MacCallum, William (1880), father of Hugh 36
MacCallum, William senior, father of William (2000) 57-9
MacCallum, William, Glasgow x,24,36,42,58
the MacCallums in CT 3,6-7,34-5, 40-1,48
MacCallums in Dalnahassaig 96
MacCambridge, Flora 12
MacCaog, Duncan, Molighe 177
MacCodrum, John, bard 15-18
MacColl, Allan 211
MacColl, Angus, Oban ix,58,164,211,220,238
MacColl, Archibald Robertson 210
MacColl, Dugald, father of John 202
MacColl, Dugald, son of John 210
MacColl, Duncan 58-9

MacColl, Evan 138
MacColl, Hugh 264
MacColl, John, Appin (1745) 202
MacColl, John, Appin (1781) 202
MacColl, John, Oban xiv,37-8,40,43,50,55-6,
    63-5,67,70,89,106,108,112,157,160,
    163,170,202-210, 223,225,228-9,233,
    264-5,274
MacColl, John Carruthers 207-8,210
MacColl, Mary, Kenmore 138
MacColl, Mr, Scottish Pipers 111
MacColla, Alasdair (MacDonald) 4,6,11,13,
    90-4,120
McComb, William 162
MacCormick, Andrew, Antrim 55
MacCormick, Catherine, Antrim 55
MacCorquodale, piper to Barbreck 98
the MacCorquodales 163
MacCrimmon, Donald Ban 17, 41,162,297
MacCrimmon, Donald Donn 162
MacCrimmon, Donald Mor 4,6,98
MacCrimmon, Donald Ruadh 31
MacCrimmon, Ey Malcolm, CT 31
MacCrimmon, Iain Dubh 31
MacCrimmon, Malcolm 162,297
MacCrimmon, Patrick Mor 6,32
MacCrimmon, Patrick Og 114,162
MacCrimmon. Peter 162
the MacCrimmon pipers 18,39,113,125,243,
    291,309
MacCulloch, John, Molighe 183
MacCulloch, Maggie, wife of JMG 269
MacDiarmid, Annie, wife of Calum Piobaire 222
MacDiarmid, Flora 140
MacDonald, A., Pipe Major 119
MacDonald, Alasdair of Dunyveg 5
MacDonald, Alasdair MacColla - see MacColla
MacDonald, Alasdair, 16th century 10
MacDonald, Alexander, Glencoe (1745) 241
MacDonald, Alexander (Alasdair mac Mhaighstir Alasdair) 15,257-9,292-7
MacDonald, Allan, Glenuig 53,295,133
MacDonald, Andrew 1
MacDonald, Angus (1880s) 50
MacDonald, Angus Ileach 10
MacDonald, 'Big Angus', Scots Guards 166-7,238
MacDonald, Dr Angus, Glenuig 133
MacDonald, Annie, wife of Robert MacKinnon 50
MacDonald, Archibald, Inveraray (1786) 73
MacDonald, Coll Ciotach, father of Alasdair 4,5,13,90-2
MacDonald, D., 93rd Regiment 161
MacDonald, Donald of Laggan 245,288
MacDonald, Donald, pipemaker 20,35,39,45-48,
    93,200,225 253
MacDonald, Donald, son of the pipemaker 252-3
MacDonald, Lt Donald (1746) 195

MacDonald, Donald, Benbecula 229
MacDonald, Donald of Kinlochmoidart 33
MacDonald, Donald Stewart 216
MacDonald, Flora (1745) 296
MacDonald, Flora, sister of Joseph 180
MacDonald, George, Dunoon 275,281-2,285
MacDonald, H.L. of Dunach 95,205
MacDonald, Iain, Glenuig 133
MacDonald, Iain Mor of the Isles 4,10
MacDonald, Iain Og (MacIan), 1st of Glencoe 242
MacDonald, Sir James of Dunyveg and the Glens 92
MacDonald, Jane 292-3
MacDonald, John Cathanach 10
MacDonald, John, 42nd Regiment 252-3
MacDonald, John, Tongue (late 18th century) 98-9
MacDonald, John, son of Donald 40
MacDonald, John, Inverness 55,63,66-8,70-1, 108-10,157,208,211,225,255,270-1, 275
MacDonald, John 'Roidean' 108-10,210,238
MacDonald, Joseph, Durness 29,37,71,93,180
MacDonald Lords of the Isles 3-4,29,36,41,91, 242
MacDonald, Margaret, daughter of Donald 35,40,46
MacDonald, Mary (1817) 40
MacDonald, Mary, wife of Iain Ciar 185-90,192
MacDonald of Glenaladale 114,116
MacDonald of Largie (1745) 4,7-9,13,36
MacDonald of Sanda, Archibald Mor 10-11,13, 91-2
MacDonald of Sanda, Archibald Og 10,13
MacDonald of Sanda, infant grandson 11
MacDonald of Sleat, Lady (1930s) 229
MacDonald of Sleat, Lord (1880s) 64,145,152-4
MacDonald of Sleat, Sir Donald (1715) 187
MacDonald, the Rev Patrick 37,179-82
MacDonald, Pipe Major, Sydney 241
MacDonald, Roderick 'Roidean' 109-10,230-1,238
MacDonald, Ronald of Keppoch 181
MacDonald, Ronald, Ulva near Taynish 80
MacDonald, William, Benbecula 229
MacDonald, William, Gruids 109,229
MacDonald, William M. 78,239,241,255
the MacDonalds in CT 3,4
the MacDonalds of Colonsay 4
the MacDonalds of Dunach 264
the MacDonalds of Sanda 4,10,12
the MacDonalds of Sleat 5
MacDonnell, Alasdair Dearg of Glengarry 245,288
MacDonnell, Alasdair Ronaldson of Glengarry 225,245,248,251-3,256
MacDonnell, Barbara 182
MacDonnell, Colla nan Capull 5
MacDonnell, Duncan, Kilmonivaig 251
MacDonnell of Glengarry, Lady 253
MacDonnell of Keppoch, 16th Chief 182

MacDonnell, Sir James of Dunluce 5
MacDonnell, Sorley Buy, Antrim 4-6
MacDonnells of Keppoch 98
MacDougall, Alasdair Mor 13,173-4
MacDougall, Alexander, Dunollie 23rd Chief 191
MacDougall, Alexander, Molighe 183
MacDougall, Allan, blind piper, Glencoe (1745) 55,174-5,
MacDougall, Allan, blind poet, 174,176,245, 250,253,255-6
MacDougall, Allan, Dunollie 184
MacDougall, Allan, son of Iain Ciar 189
MacDougall, Ann, Dalmally 245
MacDougall, Anne, daughter of Iain Ciar 190
MacDougall, Bell, sister of Capt. Sandy MacDougall 194
the MacDougall clan 4; MacDougalls of Dunollie 172,175-6,184; of Lorne 13
MacDougall, Donald (1750) 174-5,182-3
MacDougall, Donald, on Comet I (1820) 99
MacDougall, Dugald, Gallanach 174
MacDougall, Dugald or Dougal, Molighe 182-3; his 7 children 183
MacDougall, Duncan, Dunollie 11
MacDougall, Duncan (Perthshire) 175
MacDougall, Elizabeth, wife of Ranald Mor 183
MacDougall, Gavin, Perthshire 175
MacDougall, Hope 178
MacDougall, Hugh, Molighe 183; his 3 children 183
MacDougall, Iain Ciar,Dunollie, 22nd Chief 10,174,176,179,185-90
MacDougall, Jane, Benderloch 227
MacDougall, Jean 185
MacDougall, John, Dunollie, 24th Chief 184,192,262
MacDougall, John, Kincraig 56
MacDougall, John, Molighe 183
MacDougall, John, Perthshire 175
MacDougall, Johnny, son of Iain Ciar 189
MacDougall, Ketty, daughter of Iain Ciar 188-9
MacDougall, Margaret 177
MacDougall, Mary, Molighe (1789) 183
MacDougall, Mary, Molighe (1794) 183
MacDougall, Mary, Strachur 267
MacDougall of Lunga, Captain (1917) 106
MacDougall of Lunga, Colonel (1900) 105-6
MacDougall of Lunga, Major Stewart (1903) 106,264
MacDougall of MacDougall, Madam 176
MacDougall of Melford, Colin 192
MacDougall, Neil 183
MacDougall pipers at Moleigh 13,39,173-9,196, 226
MacDougall, Ranald Ban174-5,179,182,185, 187,190,256
MacDougall, Ranald Mor 174,177,182-3,192, 194,256
MacDougall, Ranald Og 177,183
MacDougall, Robert, Argylls 160

Index of People

MacDougall, Captain Sandy, Dunollie 179,184,190-4
MacDougall, Sarah, Molighe 183
the MacDougalls of Lorne 13
the MacDougalls of Reray 113
MacDowell, Angus J. xiv
MacEachern, Duncan 308
MacEachern, Neil, Islay 235,238
MacEandric - see also Henderson
MacEandric, Iain Breac 241
MacEnrich, Archie, nephew of Donald 241-2
MacEnrich, Donald, Glencoe 241-2
MacEwen bards 120-1
MacFadyen brothers 290
MacFadyen, Hector 238
MacFadyen, Iain 89
MacFadyen, John 58, 78-9,,88,111,139
MacFadyen, John of Melfort 112,207
MacFarlan, Robert, Dunbarton 271,277
MacFarlane, Andrew, Flodden 272
MacFarlane, Archibald, Dalmally 244
the MacFarlane clan 272
MacFarlane, Donald (1911) 226
MacFarlane, Dugald, late 19th century xvi
MacFarlane, George (1776) 244
MacFarlane, Hugh, Oban 226
MacFarlane, Janet (1823) 105
MacFarlane, John, Dalmally 176,243-53
MacFarlane, John, Inverioch 244-5,250
Macfarlane, John, Inveraray 143,251
MacFarlane, Mary or Sarah, mother of Donald, Glasgow 140,142-3
MacFarlane, Walter xiv,83
MacFarlane William, father of John 243-4
MacFarlane ?William? Dalmally 244
MacFarlane. William (1823) 143
MacFater, John, Kilberry 37-8
MacFederan, John, North Carolina 143
MacFederan, Mary 143,251
MacFie, Bob 139
MacGeachie, Margaret 35
the MacGeachies in CT 3
MacGibbon, Neil, Inveraray 22
MacGillivray, Margaret, Jura 104
MacGlasrich pipers, Mid-Argyll 98
McGloan, T.P. 286
MacGregor, Archibald, Glenlyon (1783) 223
MacGregor, John, Glenlyon (1783) 223
MacGregor, John, Loch Fyne 74, 156
MacGregor pipers (1783) 32,223
MacGregor, Rob Roy 159,189-90,195
MacHenry, Dougal, 11th century 242
the Maclans of Ardnamurchan 120
the Maclans of Glencoe 241,253-4, 292; 3 sons of the chief (1692) 255
McIlrodich, John 195,198
MacIndeor, Dugald (or Donald) 131-2
the MacIndeor family 7
MacInnes, Angus, Appin 203,225-6
MacInnes, Elizabeth, mother of John MacColl 203
MacInnes, Iain 164
MacInnes, Paul (1780s) 203,225
MacInnes, Rachel, sister of Sarah 234
MacInnes, Sarah, wife of James Lawrie, Oban 233-4,263
MacIntosh, Peter 3,7-9,31-33
MacIntyre, Donald Ruadh 33,243
MacIntyre, Dugald, Lorne (1790s) 222
MacIntyre, Duncan Ban, poet 50,256-9,293, 295-6,298
MacIntyre, Duncan, Islay 229
MacIntyre, George M. xiv,1,51-5,57-8,88-9,237
MacIntyre, Henry, drummer, Inveraray 156
MacIntyre, Isobel, wife of George M. 51,53
MacIntyre, John (1697) 113,222,243
the MacIntyres in CT 3
the MacIntyres of Skipness 50,257
the MacIver clan 243
MacIver, Donald, Vancouver 105
MacIver, Finlay 243
MacIver, James 108
MacKay, Angus, Raasay 1,24-5,32-3,38,42, 44-5,47,83,93,115,119, 123,132,167, 184,194,196,198-9,252-3,262,288
MacKay, Donald, brother of Angus 184
MacKay, Donald, nephew of Angus 308
MacKay, Donald Duaghal, 1st Lord Reay 6,290-1
MacKay, Hugh (marches) 42
MacKay, Iain Dall 10,189,257-8,295,298
MacKay, James (1895) 160
MacKay, John, Argylls 160
MacKay, John, brother of Angus 184-5,262
MacKay, John, Raasay, father of Angus 24-5,45,145,184
MacKay, John Roy, Gairloch 105
MacKay, Kenneth 83
MacKay, Mary, mother of John Ban 126,147
MacKay, Rob Donn, poet 258
the MacKays in CT 3,34
MacKay-Scobie, Major Ian 159
MacKellar, Alexander (1860s) 73
MacKellar, Catherine, Kenmore 138
MacKendrick - see Henderson
MacKenzie, Alexander, Achilty (1820) 147; possibly brother of John Ban 146-7,150
MacKenzie, Ann, Achilty 146-7, 150-1
MacKenzie, Anne (Nancy), Inveraray (1837) 128
MacKenzie, Christian, Achilty 147
MacKenzie, Christian, Ardmaddy 126-7,136
MacKenzie, Colin, Achilty (1820) 147
MacKenzie, Diana 149
MacKenzie, Donald, son of John Ban 45,131,145
MacKenzie, Duncan, Ardmaddy 126,128
MacKenzie, Duncan, Inveraray (1833) 128
MacKenzie, Elizabeth, Achilty (1829) 147
MacKenzie, Farlane 112
MacKenzie, Sir Francis, Gairloch 105
MacKenzie, Sir Hector, Gairloch 105
MacKenzie, Isabella, Achilty (1815) 147

MacKenzie, Isabella (Bell) Inveraray (1835) 128-30,137-8,156
MacKenzie, Lady Isabella 196
MacKenzie, Janet, Inveraray (1831) 128
MacKenzie, Janet, Urray 147
MacKenzie (or MacKinnon), Hugh, Glencoe (1692) 255
MacKenzie, John Ban xvi,41,45,47,64,113,118, 126,131,136,144-8,150,153-4,156,184, 290
MacKenzie, John, Loch Fyne 113,118,126-31, 133,136-7
MacKenzie, John, Caledonian Schools 147,150-1
MacKenzie, John M., Victoria School xiv,1,40, 50,55,57-9,130,133-7,211,235,238-9; his wife Margaret 135-6; his daughters 135-6
MacKenzie, JohnDon 168
MacKenzie, Kenneth, Ardmaddy 113,126-7, 136-8
MacKenzie, Kenneth, Inveraray (1825) 128,133, 136
MacKenzie, Kenneth, Loch Tay 126; his 5 children 127
MacKenzie or MacLennan, Murdo, Strathconon 146,150
MacKenzie, Neil, grandfather of John M. 136
MacKenzie, Neil L., father of John M. 136
MacKenzie, 'Pook', Portree 232
MacKenzie, Ronald, brother of John Ban 147
MacKenzie, Ronald, Ord, Skye 106,205
MacKenzie, Ronald 'Seaforth', nephew of John Ban xvi,101,147,151,153-4
MacKenzie, Sarah, Inveraray (1828) 128
MacKenzie, William, father of John Ban 126-7,147
MacKenzie, William (1815) 146
MacKenzie, William Dubh, Appin 223
MacKenzies in Ardnamurchan 234,263
MacKenzies in Kenmore, Loch Tay 126
MacKerral fiddler, CT 7,35
MacKerral, Ian, CT 52,60
MacKerral, Malcolm 35
MacKerral, Mary 35
the MacKerrals in CT 3,7,34
MacKillop, James 66,275
MacKinnon, Lt Col A.C.B., India 65
MacKinnon, J., composer 111
MacKinnon, Robert 49-50,142,257
MacKinnon, Walter, India 65
MacKinnon, William, pipemaker 50
MacLachlan, Ann or Agnes 105,140,142
MacLachlan, Colin, Crinan 105
MacLachlan, Duncan, Nova Scotia xvi
MacLachlan, John, brother-in-law of Donald MacPhedran 73,95,101,105,142-3
MacLachlan, John, Ballindalloch (1881) 105
MacLachlan, four brothers, war service 162
MacLaren, Anne 227-8

MacLauchlan, Catherine 263
MacLauchlan, Colin xiv,73
MacLauchlan, John, Vittoria 73,105
MacLean, Alexander Esq of Ardgour 287
MacLean, Allan, Ardgour 223,287
MacLean, Allan, 5th of Drimnin 308
MacLean, Allan, Ardrishaig 77-9
MacLean, Angus (1913) 108
MacLean, Ann, Ardmaddy 126
MacLean, Ann, Loch Tay 127
MacLean, Archibald, Invercarnan (1841) 228
MacLean, C.A.H., of Pennycross 66
MacLean, Donald, CT (1790s) 38-9,40,46
MacLean, Donald junior, CT 39
MacLean, 'Big Donald', Lewis 164,226
MacLean, 'Wee Donald', Oban 170,210,211, 226-33
MacLean, Duncan, Ardrishaig xiv, 77-80,250; his brothers on Scarp 77
MacLean, Duncan, Benderloch (1818) 227-8
MacLean, Sir Fitzroy 74
MacLean, Kaid Sir Harry 308
MacLean, Hector, bishop xv
MacLean, Hector (1890s) 223
MacLean, Hector (1930s) 111,223,225
MacLean, James, Skye 227-8
MacLean, John, Mull bard 15
MacLean, John, Benderloch 227
MacLean, John, Benderloch 227-8
MacLean, John, CT 136
MacLean, John, Invercarnan (1841) 228
MacLcan, John (1950) 232
MacLean, Lachlan, Jura 280
MacLean, Lachlan mhic Iain, bard 15
MacLean, Marion, mother of John M.136
MacLean, Margaret, daughter of Wee Donald 232
MacLean, Mrs Donald, mother of Wee Donald 227
MacLean, Murdo(ch), Glasgow 116,287
MacLean, Neil, Airds (1783) 223-5,287
MacLean, Norman 259,298-307
MacLean, William, Creagorry 95
MacLean of Duart (16th century) 287
MacLean, 13th Laird of Coll 288
the MacLeans in CT 3
MacLellan, Angus J. 89,309
MacLellan, Annie, Dunoon 280
MacLellan, Archie, Dunoon 280
MacLellan, Archie, Islay 280
MacLellan, Iain 238
MacLellan, John, Dunoon xiv, 1,73, 89,280,112 (?),119,161,277-85
MacLellan, Captain John A., Edinburgh Castle 112 (?),238,282
MacLellan, Margaret, Dunoon 280,282
MacLellan, Neil, brother of John 280-1
MacLellan, Neil, father of John, Dunoon 278,280
MacLellan, Sarah, Dunoon 280
MacLennan, Alexander, Inverness 147, 205

Index of People 323

MacLennan, Alister, Oban 220
MacLennan, Ann, Strathconon 146
MacLennan, Donald, Scatwell 146
MacLennan, D.R. 96,111,265,269,282
MacLennan, Elizabeth, nee Stewart, mother of G.S. 222
MacLennan, George, son of G.S.25, 237
MacLennan, G.S. 25,43,66,73,96,146,222,237, 265-6,274
MacLennan, Jane, Strathconon 146,150
MacLennan, Jessie, wife of George 25
MacLennan, John, Scatwell (1817) 146
MacLennan, Lt John, father of G.S. 25,43-4, 174,222
MacLennan, Peggy, wife of Duncan MacLean 78
the MacLennans, Black Isle 35
MacLennan, William 43,50,207,274
MacLeod, Angus, Skye 274
MacLeod, Bobby, Tobermory xiv
MacLeod, Donald, Lewis xiv,1,43,77,80,109, 170,232,277
MacLeod, Iain 89
MacLeod, Ian, Kirkwall 309
MacLeod, John of Contullich 10
MacLeod, N. 170
MacLeod, Neil of Gesto 152,289
MacLeod of Kintarbert 26,28
MacLeod, Roderick 58
MacLeod, Ruairidh Halford 195
MacLeod of Talisker, Mrs 288
MacLeod, Peter, senior 232-3 ; junior 137, 229,231,233,
MacLeod, the Rev 283
MacLeod, the Rev Norman 308
MacLeod, Victor 109
the MacLeods of Dunvegan 5,6,32,196
MacLeolan (MacLellan), Largie (1745) 7-8
MacMhuirich, Niall Mor 14-5,17-18
the MacMhuirich family 9,15
MacMichall, Donald, CT (1820s) 40
MacMichall, John 40
the MacMichalls in CT 3,34
MacMillan, Angus, Lergnahensian (1898) 37-8, 64-5
MacMillan, Duncan, brother of Angus 37
MacMillan, Duncan of Dunmore 21,28
MacMillan, Geilis of Dunmore 21-2,29
MacMillan grandfather of Angus 37
MacMillan, Neil, brother of Angus 37-8
MacMurchy, William (1745) 7-9,15,36-7,39; his wife 9
the MacMurchies in CT 3,9,15,24, 34,36-7,39
MacMurphy, John, Kilberry 37
MacNab, Archibald, drummer, Inveraray 156
MacNab, Archie 108-12,163,238
MacNab, Colin 225
MacNab, Donald 225
MacNab, Duncan 225
MacNab of MacNab, Francis 225

MacNab, John 225
MacNab, Robert, Inveraray 155
MacNeil, Captain N.A. 112
MacNeill, Alexander, cousin of Seumas 210
MacNeill, Andrew, Oronsay 232,264
MacNeill, Archibald ('Blind Archie') 80,156,170, 226-8,274
MacNeill, Dennis 235
MacNeill, Dugald 70-1,232
MacNeill, Dugald of Kintarbert 22,25-6,28
MacNeill, Duncan, brother of Captain Hector 26; his children 28
MacNeill, Hector F., CT 59
MacNeill, Hector of Ardmeanish in Gigha 21,23, 29,45
MacNeill, Captain Hector, R.N., of Drumdrishaig 22-3,26,29,45
MacNeill, Malcolm, Jamaica and Skipness 26
MacNeill, Mary (1831) 26
MacNeill, Sandy, Kilberry 37-8
MacNeill, Seumas xiv,53,58,76,84,88-9,108,110, 139,202,210,232,268, 291
the MacNeills in CT 3,34,92
the MacNeills (or MacNeals) of Ugadale 55,211
MacNicol, the Rev Donald 258
MacPhail, Ann (1791) 149
MacPhail, Dr William 106-8
the MacPhails in Islay 254
MacPhee, Bell, wife of Donald 226
MacPhee, Carradale fiddler 7
MacPhee, Donald, Glasgow 119,142,204,226, 228
the MacPhees of Colonsay 4
MacPhedran, Dr A., Ontario 138
MacPhedran, Alexander, Inveraray (1867) 129
MacPhedran, Archie, Glasgow 137-9,230,269, 275
MacPhedran, Archie 'Coll', Kenmore 138
MacPhedran, Colin, father of Donald 140,142-3
MacPhedran, Colin (1853), son of Donald, Glasgow 140
MacPhedran, Donald, Glasgow xiv,73,94,105, 131,137,139-44,251
MacPhedran, Donald, Inveraray (1870) 129,137, 153-5
MacPhedran, Donald, grandfather of Donald, Glasgow 140
MacPhedran, Dugald (1914) 138
MacPhedran, Duncan, Inveraray (1866) 129,153,155
MacPhedran, Duncan (1914) 138
MacPhedran, John, Kenmore 129,137,156
MacPhedran, John, Kenmore, g.g.father of Archie 138
MacPhedran, John, son of John and Bell (1865) 129
MacPhedran, John, son of Donald, Glasgow 142-3
MacPhedran, Kenneth, Inveraray (1873) 129
MacPhedran, Marion (1914) 138

MacPhedran, Mary, daughter of Donald, Glasgow 142
MacPhedran, Neil, Inveraray (1877) 129
MacPhedran, Neil, Ontario 153-4
MacPhedran, Peter, Inveraray (1868) 129
MacPhedrans in Knapdale 41
MacPherson, Angus Cam, father of Calum Piobaire 225
MacPherson, Angus, son of Calum Piobaire 149,221
MacPherson, Calum Piobaire 71,149,152,161, 216-7,222,225,290
MacPherson, Christian 260
MacPherson, Donald 58,139,170,231-2,274, 291
MacPherson, Donald, Glenelg xvii
MacPherson, Donald, Scots Guards 147
MacPherson, Iain, father of Iain and Donald 274
MacPherson, Iain, brother of Donald 139,274
MacPherson, James (Ossian) 47
MacPherson, Robert, 5th HLI 139
MacPhie or MacFie, Bailie in Leith 44,46
the MacQuilkans in CT 3,34,40
MacRae, Angus 63,67,70,205,274
MacRae, Captain Colin 66
MacRae, Finlay, Dingwall 227-9,231-3
MacRae, Finlay Dubh 243
MacRae, Malcolm 85
MacRae, William Boa 206
MacRaes at Achilty 150
MacRaes of Kintail 18
MacShannon, Dugald 59
MacShannon, Ronald 36
MacSporran, Duncan 162
MacVicar, Anne (Mrs Grant of Laggan) 180
MacVicar, Janet, Inveraray 127,133,136-7
Main, Donald 230
Maitland, Charles, Inveraray 74,145,153,155-6
Maitland, Peter, Inveraray 155
Major, Hugh, Appin 234
Malcolm of Duntrune, Zachariah 91,94
Malcolm of Poltalloch, Lord (1890s) 95,104
Malcolm of Poltalloch, Lt Col George (1960s) 95
Malcolm of Poltalloch, Lt Col J.Wingfield 95
Malcolm of Poltalloch, Neil (1850) 94,100,105, 132,143,268
Malcolm of Poltalloch, Robert 94
the Malcolms of Poltalloch 92-4
Marr, Earl of (1715) 188
Martin, Angus 3,49,144
Martin, Mary, Skye 227
Masson, John 73
Mather, D.C. 73,105-6,119,158
Matheson, Niall 291
Matheson, William 17
Mauchline, James (1836) 73
Meldrum, Robert 63,71,95,147,153,160-1,163, 194,272,308
Meldrum, Ronald, son of Robert 161,204-5

Melford, Colin - see MacDougall
Melford, Jeremiah (fictional) 172
Millen, Janet, CT 55
Mitchell, Agnes 136
Montgomery, Robert xv
Montrose, Earl of (James Graham) 6,11,90,92, 120,288
Morocco, Sultan of 308
Morrison, Catherine, Dalmally 243,251
Morrison, Donald, Oban 178
Morrison, Neil Rankin, Mull 8
Morrison, Iain 168
Morrison, John, Dalmally 245
Morrison pipers, South Uist 178
Morrison, Ronald 229
Moss, Major Eric 241
Mudie, Robert 45-6
Munro, Archie 170,225-6,253
Munro, Catherine, stepmother of Calum Piobaire 226
Munro, Donald, pipemaker 55
Munro, Neil 18,74-5,123,125
Munro, Sir Robert of Foulis 32-3
Murray, Lt Col David 265
Murray, Ian K. 42,135,283
Murray, Sir John MacGregor 116-7
Murray, William 268,272

Nevoy, Mr John 13
Nicol, Angus 214
Nicol, Robert, Balmoral 109,222

O'Donnell, Hugh of Tyrconnell 5,11
the O'Donnells of Tyrconnell 5
O'Neill, Alice 5
O'Neill, Con, Earl of Tyrone 5
O'Neill, Hugh, Earl of Tyrone 5,11,29
O'Neill, Lady (1925) 5
O'Neill, Mary 5
the O'Neills of Tyrone 4
O'Rourke, Tom 51

Pearston, Thomas 58,139,232,238,289
Pennant, Thomas 122
Peterson, Captain R.C. 267,286
Philip, Prince, Duke of Edinburgh 135
Pincet, Jacques (Jackie) 88
Pitkeathly, Andrew 163
Pollock, Ruth, wife of Young George 124
Pont, Timothy 128
Prebble, John 245

Queen's Own Cameron Highlanders 109
Quigley, Joseph 284

Ramsay, Sir Douglas of Banff 64
Ramsay, Sir James of Banff 64, 275
Ramsay, Sir John (1780s) 180
Rankin, Sarah, Lerags 226
Rankin (16th century), Mull 287

Index of People

Rankin pipers at Kilbrennan 8,39,76,113,243
Reay, Lord - see MacKay, Donald Duaghal
the Red Robber, Ulster 190
Reid or Reed, Hugh, CT 48
Reid, Hugh, son of Peter 48
Reid, James Robert, son of Peter 48
Reid, Jessie, daughter of Peter 48
Reid, Margaret, daughter of Peter 48
Reid, Mr, bookseller, Leith 46
Reid, Peter 10,43-48,119,185,225
Reid, Robert 108,133,231,238,270,273-4
the Reids in CT 48
Riddell, Donald, Kiltarlity 230
Robb, William 160
Robertson, Hugh, pipemaker 257
Robertson, James, Tobermory 1-2,26
Robertson, J.B. 106,108
Robertson, Jeannie, singer 222
Rodger, Annie 227
Rodger, Mr, father of Annie 227
Ross, Alec, brother of Willie 276
Ross, Alexander, brother of Duncan 50,64, 145-6,148,150-2
Ross, Alice (Mrs MacPherson of Inveran) 149
Ross, Andrew 149,150
Ross, Angus, Scots Guards 149,150
Ross, Annie, wife of Duncan 151-2
Ross, Annie, daughter of Duncan 151
Ross, Donald, Skye, father of Angus 149,150
Ross, Dr Donald F. (1930s) 74
Ross, Duncan, Inveraray 64,142,145-55
Ross, George, Royal Highlanders (1890s) 50
Ross, George, Argylls (1912) 281
Ross, J.George, Black Watch 50
Ross, John, Achilty 146,150-1; his 9 children 150-1
Ross, John, waiter 146,150
Ross, Roderick, Brora 151,154
Ross, Violet, daughter of Duncan 152
Ross, William, Queen's piper 149,150,199
Ross, William, Edinburgh Castle 43,63,66-7,74, 82,109,207,213,229,237,241,255,286
Ross, William, HLI 218
Ross, William Alexander, son of Duncan 152
Royal Highlanders 50
Royal Scots 31,225

Sanger, Keith 9,36-7,113,225,242-3
Schell, George E. 239
Scots Guards 100-2,138,147,149,213
Scott, Charlie 110
Scott, James E. 49
Scott, John W. 170
Scott, Samuel 277
Scott, Walter 47,76,123,194,272
Scottish Horse (regiment) 207
Seaforth, Earl of (1715) 188,196
Seaforth Highlanders 103,151,278

Semple, James 168
Shaw, Allan, shepherd 85
Shaw, Marion 278
Shedden, Hugh 163,170
Shedden, Stuart 58
Sillar, William, surgeon 36
Sinclair, David 232
Sinclair, Jessie, mother of John Gillies 103-4
the Sinclairs in Caithness 242
Smith, Captain Charles 277
Smith, Ernest, Inveraray 155
Smith, Isabella, mother of JMG 267
Smith, J. 163
Smith, Pipe Major Argylls 275
Smollett, Tobias, writer 172-3
Sobieski brothers 117
Somerled of Argyll 4
Stevenson, Robert Louis 75,123
Stewart, Alexandra, wife of George 222
Stewart, Andy, entertainer 60,267
Stewart, Donald (1825) 222
the Stewart family 222
Stewart, General, of Garth 98
Stewart, George, Golspie 222
Stewart, James, Banff 222
Stewart, John (1835) 222
Stewart, John, uncle of G.S. MacLennan 222
Stewart, Margaret, wife of Peter Reid 48
Stewart, Robert, Inveraray 155
Stewart of Appin 190
Stewart of Fasnacloich 203,226
de St Fond, Bartholemy Faujas 201
Stoddart, Margaret 106-9
Stuart, Prince Charles Edward 8,288,296
Sutherland Highlanders (93rd Regiment) 159,161
Sutherland, James 106-9

Taylor, George D. 1
Taylor, William 278
Taylors, Skipness 40
Thomason, General C.S. 48,67,93,105,143, 185,275
Thomson, Dr Bruce E. 170,241
Thomson, Colin 161
Thomson Derick 14,17,257-8,295,297
Thomson, J. 1
Thomson, John, piper to Loup 41
Thomson, Malcolm, Inveraray 74
Thomson William, CT 55,157,211
Townsley, Jock xvii
Townsley, old Mrs xvii
Townsley pipers xvii
Trigge, David (1783) 223

Urquhart, Hector 128

Venus 17-18
Victoria, Queen 50, 94,105,130-3,140-2,144, 149,151,154,159,160,214

Wales, Prince of (later King Edward VII) 308
Walford, Karl 170
Walker, Gordon 58,72,214
Wallace, Robert 58
Ward, Frank Kingdon 82
Ward, Lord, at Glengarry 184,262
Ward, Mr, Glasgow 101,104
Wark, James 1,56
Watson, W.J. 121
Weatherston, John 139
Wellington, Lord 192,194
Whistlebinkies (folk-group) 85
Whyte, Henry ('Fionn') 2,76-7,91
Wilhelm II, Kaiser 103
Wison, Archie, killed, N.Africa 56
Wilson, Greg, N.Z. 58
Wilson, J. 1
Wilson, James 281,285
Wilson, James (1905), son of Wm III 56
Wilson, John, went to Canada 51,78,257
Wilson, John, Strathclyde Police, son of Wm IV 56
Wilson, Mrs Katrine 57
Wilson, Lord, Hydro Board 165
Wilson, Mary (1910), daughter of WM III 56
Wilson, Tony (1932) 56-7
Wilson, William I, Antrim 55
Wilson, William II, Antrim and CT 55
Wilson, William III, drowned 1919 55
Wilson, William IV, father of John 56-7,59,157, 211
the Wilsons in CT 3.40,55
Wood, John, Leith (1822) 44

Yardley, Pipe Major, Cambuslang 275
Young, David xiv
Young, John, Edinburgh 191
Young, Margaret 149-50
Yule, Alexander MacQueen 162

INDEX OF PLACES

CT = Campbeltown

Aberdeen 7,217,267-9
Aberdeenshire 25,160,278
Aberfeldy 174,194
Aboyne 274
Achallader, Bridge of Orchy 123
Achamore, Cowal 283
Achaneilt 260
Acharacle 286,308
Ach(a)rossan 19,21,29,277
Achilty 126,141,146-7,150-1,154
Achnamara 78
Add, river 96
Aden 73
Africa 162
Airds 93,95,124-5,171,221,223-4
el Alamein 162

Aldershot 81,106
Allandale, Stirlingshire 162
Allangrange, Black Isle 154
Allt Dearg 175
Almanza, Spain 124
Alness 266
Altimarlach, Wick 243
Altnabreac, or Altananbreac 126,146-51,153
America 31,98,163,234,261,263
Amhuinnsuidhe, Harris 77
Angus 219
Antarctica 129
Antrim 3-6,10-11,29,41,55,91,190,255
Appin 190,202-3,220-39,260-4,308
Applecross 141,217
Arbroath 219
Ardchattan 244
Ardfern 106
Ardgour 223-4,261,263,286-309
Ardkinglas 128
Ardlamont 277
Ardmaddy, Loch Etive 113
Ardmaddy, Nether Lorne 97,113-16,126-7,136, 141,222
Ardmeanish, Gigha 21,23,29
Ardmucknish Bay, Benderloch 196,227
Ardnamurchan ix, 80,120,165,221,233-4,241, 257,259,260-3,286-309
Ardrishaig 77-81,104-5,133
Ardtornish, Morvern 216
Ardvasar, Skye 84
Argyll(shire) ix-x,xiii-xviii,6-7,9,12-13,24-5,36-8, 41,45,57,64,66-7,74-5,82-2,89-92,105, 118-20,123,126-30,132,141-5,148,154-5, 157,159,161-2,164-5,174-5,190,195-6, 205,211-14,216,220,225-6,237,253,257, 267-8,272,276,283,285-6,297,308
Argyllshire Gathering Ground, 215
Argyll Arms, CT 58
Argyll House, London 152
Argyll Street, Dunoon 285
Arisaig 297
Arivean, Glenlochy 242,244
Armadale, Skye 152-4
Arnhem 236
Aros, Mull 104
Arrochar 244-5,250
Asgog Bay, Loch Fyne 277
Atholl 124,174,221
Australia 162,210,217,232,235-6,285
Ayrshire xvii,3,6-7,48

Baddan, Lochgilphead 80
Badenoch 230
Baillieston, Glasgow 101,104
Ballachulish ix,210,222,225,227-8 233-4,237, 241-266;
Ballachulish Road 263-4
Ballimore 195
Ballindalloch 105

Index of Places

Ballycastle, Antrim 55
Ballyhennan, Loch Lomond 245
Balmoral 37
Balvicar, Seil Island 127,141
Banff, Canada 103
Banff, Scotland 64,222,275
Barbados 190
Barbreck 97-8,127,163
Barcaldine 223
Barmolloch, Inveraray 143
Barnton, Edinburgh 100,268
Barony (parish), Glasgow 140
Barra 282,307
Bearsden, Glasgow 219
Beaufort Castle, Beauly 217
Beauly 217,230
Beinn Buidhe, Glen Shira 159
Beinn Cruachan 165
Beinn Doaig 241
Beinn Dobhrain (Ben Dorain) 258
Bellahouston, Glasgow 306
Bellshill, Glasgow 119
Benbecula 219,229,306
Benderloch 196,227-8
Berwick-on-Tweed 197
Birnam 208
Bishopton, Renfrewshire 219
Blackburn, Strathconon 151
the Black Isle, Easter Ross 35,146,149,154
Blair Atholl 221
Blawberg xvi
Blythswood, Glasgow 140
Boghole, near Nairn 124
Bohuntin 15
Bonawe 204,217
Bonhill, Stirlingshire 140
the Borders 233
Boreraig, Skye 125
Borrodale, Ardnamurchan 288
Brackley, Kintyre 50
Braemar 269
Brae Road, Ardrishaig 78
the Braes of Lochiel 299,303
Braigo, Islay 278,280
Bravallich, Inveraray 143
Breadalbane 104,113-5,126,146,148,225,241-3,
    269,274
Bridgend, Islay 114-15
Bridge of Allan 88,219
Bridge of Orchy 123
Brisbane 57,210
Britain 39,230; British Isles 82
British Columbia, Canada 102-3,276
Brittany 88
Broom Wood 24
Brora, Sutherland 151
Brown Street, Glasgow 50
Brussels 255
Bute, Isle of 220,225,276
Buzancy, France 281

Caithness 39,225,242
Calder - see Cawdor
Caledonian Schools, London 147,150-1
Calgary, Canada 162
California, USA 281
Callander 123
Callert 225
Calton Mor 95
Camberley, Surrey 160
Cambridge 63-4,67,205
Cambuslang, Glasgow 218,275
Campbeltown x,2,7,9,12,14,20-2,24,26,29-31,
    34-6.38-41,44,46,48,50-2,55-61,132-3,
    136,141,157,159,206-7,211,238
Campbeltown Loch 36
Canada xvi,98,100,102-3,127,138,149,151,
    153-4,162,261,264,287,308
Canna, Isle of 297
Cape of Good Hope xvi
Capilano Cemetery, Vancouver 103
Cardross 269
Carlisle 33,174
Carradale, Kintyre 7,43,49-50,58
Carrbridge 217
Carwhin 113-15
Castle Gardens, Dunoon 282
Castle Grant 89
Castle Kilchorn (Kilchurn) 113,225
Castle Sween 92
Catlodge, Laggan 161,216
Cawdor 91-2,123-6,221,243,289
Charlotte Street, London 55
China 82
Cill = Kilkerran = Campbeltown 9
Ciudad Rodrigo, Spain 192
Clachan, Kintyre 7,29-30,34
Claddens Quadrant, Glasgow 208
Cladich 97
Cleigh, near Oban 180
Cluny, near Newtonmore 149
Clyde, river 156,263
Clydebank 220
Clynder 167
Cnoc-an-Lin 16
Coll, Isle of 15,116,217,287-8
Collagan, near Oban 183
Colonsay, Isle of 4,23,90,287
Conaglen, Ardgour
Conisby, Islay 263
Connaught 5
Cononbridge, Easter Ross 149
Contin, Strathconon 64,146-8,150,152
Corby, England 51-2
Cork, Ireland 225
Corran Halls, Oban 213
Corrieairick Pass 226
Corryvullin, Ardnamurchan 292
Coupar Angus 163 ; Cupar 220
Cowal 59,95,100,120,165,210,231,268,271-2,
    275,277-85

Cowcaddens, Glasgow 142
Craignish 97-9,106,108,110-111,127
Craignish Place, Dunoon 280
Crathie, near Balmoral 218
Creagorry, Benbecula 95
Crear, near Kilberry 21,23
Crete 281
Crieff 167
Crinan 90,105,131-3,142
Crinan Bay 131
Crinan Canal 94,99,131,133
Croit a'Phiobair, Kilbride 173
Cromarty 278
Cromdale 89
Culfail Hotel, Kilmelfort 112,207
Culloden 19,33,98,113-14,174,188,195,202,296
Cumbernauld 219

Daileag, near Taynuilt 170
Dalilea, Loch Shiel 292
Dalintober, CT 31
Dalmally 201,242-5
Dalnahassaig 96
Dalriada 96
Danna, Isle of 80
Davaar Island, CT 36
Dingwall 153
Doncaster Street, Glasgow 142
the Dorlinn, CT 36
the Dorus Mor, Crinan 99
Drill Hall, Oban 214
Drimnin, Morvern 308
Drimvore, Kilmartin 96
Druim Liaghart, Glenorchy 257
Drumdrishaig 21-4,26,29,45
Drummond 24
Duart, Mull 104,27-8
Dumfries 219; Dumfries-shire 260
Dunach, near Oban 95,205,217,264
Dunadd, Kilmartin 96
Dunaverty, Kintyre 6,10-13, 90-2,120,174
Dunbarton 140,260,271,277;
Dunbartonshire 269
Dunblane 88,130,133,162
Dundee 25,217,219
Dungalan, Colonsay 287
Dungallon, Sunart 125,287-9
Duniquaich 158-9
Dunkeld 44
Dunluce 5
Dunmore, Knapdale 21,27-9,37,264
Dunollie, Oban 11,13,172-4,262
Dunoon 74,89,161,234,237,275,277-85
Dunskeig, Kintyre 7,29-30,34-5,37-8,40,61
Dunstaffnage 93,171-3,187,221
Duntroon or Duntrune 4,90-4,171
Duntulm, Skye 187
Dunvegan, Skye 5,196,238
Dunyveg, Islay 4-5,10,90-2
Durness, Sutherland 179

Duror 202,228
Easdale 76,115,234,263
Eassie, Angus 219
Easter Ross 35,146-7,149,217
East Kinkell, Urquhart 146
East Laroch, Ballachulish 260
East Lothian 260
East Sutherland 222
Ecuador 74
Edendonich, Dalmally 243-5
Edinburgh xiv,8,19-20,24-5,32-3,35,38-41,43-6,
  61,73-4,86,98-101,106,109,111,115,116,
  120,123-4,131,133,143,154,156,162,174,
  182,184,191,201,203,207,218-20, 222-3,
  225-6,242-3,252-3,255-6,258,260,268,
  275, 277-8,282,287
Edward Street, Dunoon 280
Egilsay, Orkney 78
Eglinton xv
Egypt 99
El Alamein 162
Ellon, Aberdeenshire 160
Elmbank Street, Glasgow 139,232
England 18,69,74,81,88,127,151-3,207,222
Epsom, Surrey 112
Erracht 288
Erskine Ferry 49-50
Eton College 117
Eyre, Raasay 24

Falkirk 8,32-3, 50,223,255-7
Fascally, Pitlochry 217
Fasnacloich, Appin 203,225-6
Feochan, river 180
Fernish, Morvern 308
Fife 60
Fingal's Cave, Staffa 155
Fionn Eilean, Loch Awe 163
Firth of Lorne 106
Flanders 99
Flodden 272
Fort Augustus 19,195,226
Fort George 111
Fort William 19,99,132,219,253,255-6,286
Foss, Perthshire 25
Foulis, near Dingwall 32-3
France 51,75,81-2,103,138,189,201,237,265,
  274,278,281-2,296
French Farland, near Inveraray 130
Frimley, Surrey 106-7,109
Fruin 263
Furnace, Loch Fyne 88

Gairloch 59,105
Gallanach, Oban 174,182-3,206
Gallipoli 81
Garrioch Drive, Glasgow 139
Garscube Road, Glasgow 142
Garth, Perthshire 98
Garvachy, CT 7,34-7,40,61

Index of Places

Gayre 51
George Street, Edinburgh 66
Germany 78,165,168
Gifford 162
Gigha, Isle of 2-3,7,23,29,45,80
Glaonaig, Kintyre 49
Glasgow x,xvii,25,34,36,40,42,44-6,48-50,57,70,
    74,76,78,80,99,101,104-5,108,110-11,
    116-17,136-44,154,156-7,160,162,164,
    168,187,204-5,208,210,217-19,225-30,
    235-8,263-4,269,272,274-5,283,287,298,
    306,308-9
Glassary 98
Glenahurrich 288
Glenaladale 114,116
Glen Aray 74
Glencoe 3,174,176,233,241-66,292
Glencruitten, Oban 201
Glendaruel, Cowal 67-78,284
Glendessary 288
Glenelg xvii,6,195
Glenfeochan, near Oban 178,180
Glengarry 176,184,225,244-5,251-3,256,260-3,
    288
Glenhinnisdale, Skye 39
Glenlyon 242,253,255
Glenmore 101
Glenmore, Oban 208
Glenorchard 115-16
Glenorchy 50,113,222,241-66
Glen Sallach 204
Glenshiel 189
Glenshira 159
Glens of Antrim 3-5,91
Glenuig 133,297
Glenurquhart 254-5
Golspie, Sutherland 161,222
Gorebridge 88
Gourock xvii
Govan xvii,154,168,281
Grangemouth 274
Grantown-on-Spey 89
Gravesend, Kent 190
Great George Street, Glasgow 48
the Great Glen 254
Great Western Road, Glasgow 269
Greenhill Cottage, Kilcoy 149
Greenhill Cottage, Munlochy 146
Greenock 43,226,278,280
Greyfriars, Edinburgh 258
Gruids, Lairg 229
Gylen, Kerrera 188

Haddington(shire) 260-1,263-4
Hamilton, Ontario 138
Hamilton, Scotland 217
Harkness Cottage, Dunoon 280
Harris, Isle of 77-8,289
Harrogate, Yorkshire 163
Harrow, school 67,205

Hebrides (Western Isles) 3-5,7,29,36,41,91,207,242
Helensburgh 74,261,263-4
Helmsdale 291
Henderson Stone, Glencoe 242
High Aird, Saddell, Kintyre 43
Highlanders Institute, Glasgow 210,232
the Highlands 6,67,117-18,236
High Street, Edinburgh 143
High Street, Oban 205-6,233
Hillhead, Glasgow 45,48
the Himalayas 82
Holyrood, Edinburgh 45
Hong Kong 185
Hope Street, Glasgow 204,269
Huntly 188,226,268,274

Ibrox, Glasgow 306
India xvi,37,63-5,67,69,70,73,160,162,180,278
Innergeldie 243
Inveran, Sutherland 141,149,221
Inveraray xvii,8-9,11,22,57,60-1,64,73-4,
    119-159,160,165,187,201,207,219,253
Invercarnan, Ballachulish 228
Inverioch 244-5
Inverlochy, Fort William 11,120-1,180,253,256
Inverneill, near Ardrishaig 103-4
Inverness 14,41,55-6,70,73,92,95,97,105,108,
    110,130,132,147,157,160-1.163,167,
    205-6,208,210-12,217-20,225,228,230,
    233,237,255,265,269,274-5,287,307
Inverness-shire 153,161,260,286,292
Invershin 218
Iomaire na Spaidsearachd 173,176,178
Iona, Isle of 155
Ireland 3,5-7,11,13-14,17,48,92,190,207-8,225
Irish Sea 130
Islandfinnan, Loch Shiel 292
Islay 3-4,7,10,14,17,26,29,80,90-2,111,114-17,
    127,130-3,167,219,221,235, 238,254,
    263,275,278,280,308
Islay House, Bridgend 114-15
the Isles - see Hebrides
Italy 162

Jamaica 26
Jamestown, Bonhill 140
Jersey, Channel Islands 191-2
Jib, Benderloch 227
John O'Groats, Caithness 19
Johnstone, Renfrewshire 219
Jura, Isle of 3,91,104,132-3,256,263,278,280-1

Keil, Benderloch 227-8
Keills, Jura 278
Kelvinbridge, Glasgow 143,269,275
Kenmore, Loch Fyne 113,127-30,133,136-8
Kenmore, Loch Tay 126-7,150
Kensington Gardens, London 117
Kentallen, Appin 202-3
Kenya 68

Keppoch 15,98,116,182
Kerrera, Isle of 183,188,190
Kersland Street, Glasgow 45,48
Kilberry xvii,9,11,21,23,26,37-8,63-72,95,106,
    145,152,154,185,205,270,275
Kilbowie Cottage, Oban 206
Kilbride, Oban 173-4,176-80,182-3,194,227
Kilcalmonell Parish 29,34
Kilchoan, Ardnamurchan 287,292
Kilchoan, Loch Melfort 121
Kilchoman, Islay 278
Kilchrenan, Loch Awe 164,166,168,219
Kilchurn 225
Kilcolumkill, Kintyre 10
Kilcoy, Easter Ross 149-50
Kilkerran (=CT) 9,52
Killean, Kintyre 7
Killen, Strathconon 146,151
Killian 99
Killiecrankie xv,241
Killin 104
Kilmartin 11,96,99,100,106,108,142,162,165,
    268
Kilmelfort or Kilmelford 111-112
Kilmichael Glassary 11,103
Kilmodan, Argyll 267
Kilmonivaig 250,260,262
Kilmore, Oban 177-80,182
Kilmory, Ardnamurchan 292
Kilmuir, Skye 227-8
Kilmun, Loch Fyne 144
Kilnaish, near Kilberry 26 8
Kiltarlity 230
Kincraig, Badenoch 231
Kingshouse, Glencoe 242
King's Park, Edinburgh 44
Kinkell, Easter Ross 149-50
Kinlochleven 261,265
Kinmylies, Inverness 255
Kintail 18
Kintarbert 19,21-9,45,277
Kintyre ix,1-61,82,90,92,133,174,255,257
Kirkintilloch 80
Kirkwall, Orkney 309
Kirn, Dunoon 277,285
Kirriemuir 219
Knapdale 4,11,23-4,41,63-72,82,92
Knock 196
Knockbain, Easter Ross 150
Knoydart 297
Koungaur 128
Kyleakin, Skye 24

Lacon, France 265
Lagg, Jura 280
Laggan, Glengarry 245,288
Laggan, near Newtonmore 50,149,152,180,216
Lahore, India 63
Lambhill Street, Glasgow 142
Lanarkshire 50,119,233,260

Langbank, Renfrewshire xvii
Largie 4,7-9,11,13,36
Largieside 8
Largs, Ayrshire 229,234
Laroch, Ballachulish 262
Laventie, France 281
Leadhills 233,260
Le Havre, France 78
Leith 44-6,255,283
Lerags, near Oban 176-8,226
Lergnahensian, near Kilberry 37
Le Tuport, France 138
Lewis, Isle of 164,166,219,226
Liberia 74
Limecraigs, CT 20-22,31
Linnvale Gardens, Glasgow 48
Lismore 263
Little Scatwell, Strathconon 151
Liverpool 141,160
Lochaber 98,131,161,165,182,221-2,306
Loch Achilty 147-51
Lochaline 78
Loch Awe(side) 74,97,99,127,163,165,225
Loch Caolisport 23
Lochcarron 217
Loch Creran 211,223,225-6
Loch Crinan 92
Lochearn 190
Loch Eil 262
Loch Etive 113
Loch Fyne 19,26,49,55,73-90,99,113,118-9,
    126-7,130-1,136,138,144-5,156,159,
    167,267,277
Lochgelly 60
Lochgilphead 73-4,79-80,96,98-101,104,112,
    132-3,161,218
Lochiel 222,288-9
Loch Katrine 140
Loch Leven, Ballachulish 256,260
Loch Linnhe 120
Loch Lochy 241
Loch Lomond 245,263
Loch Melfort 112,121
Lochnell 160,177-8,190,195-200
Loch Ness 254-5
Loch Shiel 115,288,292
Loch Sunart 287-8
Loch Tay 126-7
Loch Tromlee 163
London 19,44-5,55,63,67,70,95,106,117-8,120,
    128,147,149,151,160,163,190,212,223,
    230,256-7,275,284
Londonderry 171
Loch Tummel 25
Longsdale, Oban 236
Longstop Hill, North Africa 55
Loos 161,285
Lorne ix,13,128,141,159,172,174-5,190,196,
    208,214,220-39
Lorne Street, CT 136

Index of Places 331

Loup 4, 7-9,12,21,24,28-30,34,41
Lunga 105-6,211,264
Luss, Loch Lomond 60,263

Macharioch, Kintyre 10,157
Malaya 68
Malta 281-2
Maltland, Inveraray 151-2
Manchester 167
Marr 188
Maryhill, Glasgow 139,156,274
Maryhill Road, Glasgow 142
Maryland, USA 220
Melfort 112
Melness 218
Mid-Argyll ix, 78,80,82,90-111
Middleton Hall, Gorebridge 88
Millhall 275
Mingary, Ardnamurchan 292
Milngavie, Glasgow 157,168
Minard, Loch Fyne 51,88-9,235
Mochaster 113
Moidart 2,116
Moleigh (Molighe) 99, 173-8, 182-3,194,196,256
Monadh-leigh 176
Montana,USA 275
Monte Cassino 162
Montreal, Canada 229
Morar 19-20,297
Moray Firth 123; Morayshire 278
Morocco 308
Morvern ix,78,216,263,286-309
Mossfield Park, Oban 213
Moy, Inverness-shire 153,217,297
Moy, Strathconon 146
Muckairn 113
Muir of Ord 218
the Mulbuie, Easter Ross 146-7
Mull, Isle of xv,14-15,76,80,104,113,165,190, 219-20,228,137,243,286-7
Mull of Kintyre 11,57,131
Munlochy, Black Isle 146
Murrayfield, Edinburgh 133
Musdale, Kilmore 180

Nairn 123-4
Nant Power Station, Ben Cruachan 165
the Netherlands 251
Nether Lorne 112-19,168,196,198
Newe, Aberdeenshire 25
Newgate Prison 190
New Guinea 236
New World 1
New York, USA 126
New Zealand 217-19
Nigg 51
North Africa 56,162
North Berwick 219
North Carolina, USA 143
North Uist 306

Norway 52
Nottingham 78
Nova Scotia, Canada xvi,98,105

Oban ix,13,40-1,50,55-6,66-7,71-2,74,78-80,83, 99,108,111-13,116,132,142,154-5,157, 160,162,164-8,170-221,225-7,230,232-8, 245,253,255,261,263,265,269,274,278
Ontario, Canada 138,153,219-20
Ord, Skye 205,217
Orkney 78,198
Otago Street, Glasgow 227,230,291
Oxford 233,265

Paisley 219
Palestine 274
Paris, France 206
Partick, Glasgow 110
Pembroke College, Cambridge 64,67
Pennycross, Mull 66
Pennyghael, Mull 219
Perth 188 ; Perthshire 25,127,146,174-5,177, 183,222,269
Peterhead 191-2
Phantelands 163
Piper's Cave, CT 14
Piper's Hill, Taynuilt 170
Pitt Street, Glasgow 230
Plymouth 185
Polmont, Edinburgh 66
Poltalloch 93-6,100-1,104-5,132,143,268
Portavadie, Loch Fyne 277
Portree, Skye 154,229,232
Port Selma, Benderloch 227
Portugal 99,192
Preston, Lancashire 78
Prince Edward Island, Canada 98

Quatre Bas, Waterloo 255
Queen Victoria School, Dunblane 130,133,135, 162
Queen's Cross, Glasgow 142
Queensland, Australia 210,232

Raasay, Isle of 24,126,141,145,217
Ramshorn Theatre. Glasgow 42-3
Red River, Canada 308
Renfield Street, Glasgow 78
Renfrew 208,210,234,263
Renfrewshire xvii,49,210
Reray 113
Rest-And-Be-Thankful, hill pass 167
Rhodesia (Zimbabwe) 133
Rhone, river 201
Rhunahaorine, Kintyre 11
Rio de Janeiro 185
Rob Roy's House, Glen Shira 159
the Rockie Mountains 103
Rome, Italy 5
Rose Street, Edinburgh xvi

Rosneath 167
Ross and Cromarty (= Ross-shire) 41,64,126, 136,146-50,152
Rothesay, Bute 39
Rothiemurchus 64,107
Rubh Garbh, Appin 260
Russia 158
Rutherglen 157
Rwanda 283

Saddell, Kintyre 21,23,25-6,43
Salen, Ardnamurchan 288
Salen, Mull 104
Sanda 4,10-12,92
San Francisco, USA 239
Sanntaig, Arisaig 297
Saughton Prison, Edinburgh 43
Scarba, Isle of 99,106
Scarp, Isle of 77
Scatwell, Strathconnon 146,151
Scone 120
Scotland 7,14,25,31,36,39,44,69,117,120-1,127, 130,133,181,204,207-8,230,233,285,291
Seaforth 188,196,219
Seil Island 113,127
Seil Sound 113,127
Shawfield 114-5,117,196
Sheriffmuir 174,176,187,272
Shetland 198
Shirvan 73,81,95
Shotts 219
Sighthill Cemetery, Glasgow 44,48
Simla, India 65
Skipness, Kintyre 26,40,49-50,120,257
Skye 5,10,17,24,39,42,64,80,113,125,127,145, 149-52,154,187-8,205,217,220,225, 227-9,243,253-5,261,274-5,296,297
Sleat, Skye 152,154,187,229,291
Sligo, Ireland 5
Sound of Mull 132
Sound of Sleat 75
South Africa xvi,100-02,160-1,217-18,281-2
Southend, Kintyre ix,10,14,34,46,55,58
Southern Ocean 129
South Uist 37,110,165,175,178,220,230,296
South Wales 58
Spain 5,73,99,105,124,179,192-4
Spey, river 89; Strathspey 255
Springbank Distillery, CT 58
Springburn Road, Glasgow 48
Springfield Gardens, Inverness 232
Srathan 299 = Strathan 303,306
Staffa, Isle of 155
St Andrews Street, Dunoon 280
St Andrews University 120
St Blimont, France 51
St Catherine's, Loch Fyne 138
St Fillans 44
St Helena 185
Stiallaig, Loch Fyne 277

Stirling 44,165; Castle 106
Stirling University 135
Stirlingshire 162
St John's Church, Ballachulish 264
St Lourence, Haddington 264
Stornoway, Lewis 189
Strachur, Loch Fyne 19,74,99,267
Stranraer 78
Strathclyde 56,168,219,235-61
Strathconon 146,148,151
Strathearn 44
Strathendrick 168
Strath Halladale 254
Strathlachlan, near Strachur 99
Stronachullin 81-2,164
Stronmilchan, Dalmally 243-4
Strontian 233-4,260-1,263,308
St Valery-en-Caux, France 51,78,235,237,265
Sunart 233,288
Sunderland, Islay 26
Surrey 107
Sutherland 98-9,105,151,161,218,277

Talisker, Skye 288
Tarbet, Loch Lomond 245
Tarbert, Loch Fyne 26,49,55,277
Tasmania 230
Tayinloan 2
Taymouth 104,113,115,126,141,144,146,151, 174-5,182,184,194,204,269
Taynish 80
Taynuilt, near Oban 170,187
Tayside 225
Teigh-an-Ratha, Inveraray 140
Texas, USA 219
Theatre Royal, Glasgow 269
Thistle Street, Glasgow 226
Ticanderoga, USA 252
Tigh Bhroinein, Barbreck 98
Tigh na Piobairean, Kilbride 173,176
Tilliefourie, Aberdeenshire 278
Tiree, Isle of 218,306
Tiroran, Mull 95
Tobermory, Mull 1,26,76,83,132
Tom a' Phiobaire, Glen Shira 159
Tomnahurich, Inverness 233
Tongue, Sutherland 99,218
Toranduch, Islay 278,280
Torosay, Mull 239
Torrisdale, Kintyre 41,49,136
Townhead, Glasgow 104
Trieste, Italy 111
Trotternish, Skye 227
Tulloch, Dingwall 153-4
Tulloch Gorm, Loch Fyne 89
Tullochgorm, Speyside 89
Tyndrum 242
Tyrconnell, Ireland 5
Tyrone, Ireland 5,236
Ugadale, near CT 55,211

Index of Music 333

the Uists 255,296
Ulster xv,11,236
Ulva, Isle of, Mull 80,127
Ulva, Isle of, near Taynish 80
Union Arcade, Glasgow 204
Urquhart, Black Isle 146-7
Urray, Easter Ross 147

Vancouver 100,102-3,105,220
Vittoria, Spain 73,105

Weem, near Aberfeldy 146
Wembley, London 284
West Highlands 58,82,199,201
West Indies 257
West Loch Tarbert 7,21,28,34
West Lothian 88
Westminster Abbey 43
Whitestone, Kintyre 49,136
Wick, Caithness 243
Worcester, England 32

INDEX OF MUSIC

This index does not include those tunes given in lists in the text, but the composers and the associated places are listed here.

M=March, R=Reel, S=Strathspey, J=Jig, HP= Hornpipe, RM=Retreat March, P=Piobaireachd, SM=Slow March, SA= Slow Air

M	Abercairney Highlanders 143
	A mhnathan nan glinne gur mithe dhuibh eirigh 3
M	Angus MacColl 168
M	Angus MacInnes 168
SM	Archibald Campbell of Kilberry 63,205
J	Archie MacNab 111
	Ardnamurchan, list of tunes 286
	Argyll and Sutherland Highlanders, list of tunes 163
	Argyll, list of tunes xiv
M	The Argyllshire Gathering 210
M	Armstrong's Welcome 36
HP	Arthur Gillies 168
J	Arthur Gillies 168
M	Arthur Gillies 168
	Arthur Gillies 168
M	The Atholl and Breadalbane Gathering 284
M	The Badge of Scotland 160
M	Ballochyle 284
P	Barisdale's Salute 147
M	The Barren Rocks of Aden 73
SA	The Battle Is O'er 160
P	The Battle of Auldearn 13
P	The Battle of Glenshiel 189
P	The Battle of the Pass of Crieff 71

P	The Battle of Sheriffmuir 243
M	The Battle of the Somme 265
M	The Bells of Malta 282
P	The Bells of Perth 71
P	Beloved Scotland 1
	Bencorrum 284
M	Benderloch Bay 227
M	The Bens of Jura (The Road to the Isles) 282
	Bessie MacIntyre 284
J	Bha Mi Aig Bhanais Air Bhail' Inneraora xvii
HP	The Blackbird 284
P	Black Donald's March 13,180
P	The Blind Piper's Obstinacy 231
RM	The Bloody Fields of Flanders 282
P	The Blue Ribbon (or Riband) 167
M	Bonnie Anne 143
SA	Bonnie Argyll 106
	Bonnie Dunoon 282
SM	Bonnie Strathyre 78
P	Breadalbane's March 255
J	The Bride's Jig (Lord Dunmore) 143
M	Brigadier General Lorne Campbell V.C. of Akarit 221
	The Brolum 284
	Burnbank 143
M	The Burning Sands of Egypt - see The Bens of Jura
	Cabar Feidh xvi
S	The Caledonian Society of London 142
J	The Campbells Are Coming xvii, 8
M	Campbeltown Loch 60
song	Campbeltown Loch, I Wish You Were Whisky 60,267
P	Captain Campbell of Glenlyon's Lament 116
S	Captain Duncan MacGregor 208
P	The Carles Wi' the Breeks 242
P	Carwhin's Lament 116
M	Charles Edward Hope de Vere 42
S	Chasing De Wet 282
P	Cha Till Mi Tuille 159,182
P	Chisholm's Salute 10,185
M	The Clan MacColl 208
P	Clanranald's March 225
P	Cogadh no Sith (War or Peace) 33-4,83, 182
	Coirechoille Blend 212
	Colonel MacLean of Ardgour 282
M	The Conundrum 231
P	Corrienessan's Lament 295-6
M	Cowal Society 282
M	The Crags of Stirling 42
RM	Creag Ghuanach 160
P	Cronan nan Cailleach 256
P	Cumha Fir Sundaigh - see Lament for MacDonald of Sanda
P	Cumha na Cloinne 32

P?	Da laimh 'sa piob, lamh 'sa chlaidheamh 175	M or S	The Haughs of Cromdale 89
S	Dalnahassaig 96	RM	The Hawk That Swoops On High 160
P	The Daughter's Lament 14	M	Hello Archie Kenneth ! 88
P?	The Day of Dunaverty 13		Her Golden Hair 64
R or S	The Devil In The Kitchen 142	RM	The Heroes of Vittoria 282-284
		J	The Herring Wife 142
RM	The Dhorlinn 36	RM	The Highland Brigade at Magers-fontein 282
R	Doctor MacPhail's Reel 108		
J	Donald, Hugh and his Dog 158	M	The Highland Brigade Depot 158
R	Donald MacLean (RMS Athenia) 229	M	The Highland Brigade's March to Heilbron - see The Bens of Jura
M	Donald MacLean's Farewell to Oban 80,226		
		M	The Hills of Argyll 51
M	Dovecote Park 284	RM	Hugh A. MacCallum 42,158
M	Dr E.G. MacKinnon 43		
	Dr Flora MacAulay 58	P	Iain Ciar's Lament 10,174,179,185,190
M	Dugald MacColl's Farewell to France 284	P	Iain Ciar's Salute 174
M	The Duke of Roxburgh's Farewell to the Blackmount Forest 42	M	Iain Morrison, Stornoway 168
		P	I Got a Kiss of the King's Hand 208,230
R	Duncan MacIntyre (RMS Athenia) 229	S	Inveraray Castle 265,284
M	Duncan MacNeil's Farewell to Melfort 112		Inveraray, list of tunes 119
P	Dungalan's Lament 289	S	Inveraray Schoolhouse (=The Caledonian Society of London) 142
	Dunoon and Cowal, list of tunes 277		
M	Dunoon Home Guard 282	M	Inverlochy Castle 43
R	Duntroon 94	P	Isabel MacKay 71,295-6
P	Duntroon's March 91	S	The Islay Ball 142
P	Duntroon's Salute 91		
P	Duntroon's Warning 91	M	Jeannie Carruthers 207
		M	John Bain's Sister's Wedding 149
M	The Earl of Mansfield 142	M	John MacColl's Farewell to the Scottish Horse 207
P	The Earl of Seaforth's Salute 71,243,269		
P	The End of the Great Bridge 152,271	M	John MacColl's March to Kilbowie Cottage 212,265
P	Ewen of the Battles 13		
		M	John MacDonald of Glencoe 265
M	The Fall of Port Arthur 282	S	John MacDougall Gillies 276
M	Farewell to the Creeks 284	M	John MacFadyen of Melfort 112,207
P	Farewell to the Laird of Islay 167	S	John MacFadyen of Melfort 112
P	His Father's Lament for Donald MacKenzie 131	M	John M. MacKenzie (SPA, Glasgow) 137
		J	John Patrick's Jig 168
P	A Favourite Piece 38		
S	The Fiddler's Joy 284	M	Kaid Sir Harry MacLean's Moorish Salute 308
P	The Finger Lock 182		
P?	Fir Chinntire 8	M	Kantara to El Arish 110
P	The Fishers of Geogh Brodinn 199	S	Kelvingrove 143
	Fleming, Ron, list of compsitions 57		Kenneth, Archie, list of compositions 86-88
P	Frasers' March 20		
M	Frimley 106		Kilberry, list of tunes 63
		SA	Kilkerran 52
M	General Thomason's March 277	P	The King's Taxes 174-5
P	George Brodin 199		Kintyre, list of tunes 1
P	George Campbell Yr of Calder's Salute - see Young George's Salute		
		P	Lachlan MacNeill Campbell of Kintarbert's Fancy 24
P	A'Ghlas 93		
J	The Ghurkas' Joy 265	P	Lachlan MacNeill Campbell of Kintarbert's Salute 24
	Glen Caladh Castle 282		
	Glencoe, list of tunes 241	S	Lady Campbell of Longsdale 235
M	Glendaruel Highlanders 60,267	R	Lady MacIntosh's Reel 212
	Glendaruel, list of tunes 267	S	Lady Madelina Sinclair 143
P	Glengarry's Lament 225	P	The Laird of McLachlan's March (=Mary's Praise) 277
P	The Glen Is Mine 10,185,190		

Index of Music

P	Lament for Airds 125,221	P	MacFarlanes' Gathering 157,271-2,217
P	Lament for Alasdair Dearg MacDonnell of Glengarry 288	P	MacGregors' Salute 225
P	Lament for the Bishop of Argyll xiv	P	MacIntosh's Lament 182,200
P	Lament for Captain MacDougall 71,174,183,194,256		MacIntyre, George M., list of compositions 52,54-5
P	Lament for the Castle of Dunyveg 14,93	P	MacIntyres' Salute 243
P	Lament for the Children 32,71,210		MacKenzie, John M., list of compositions 136-7
P	Lament for the Clans 32	P	MacKenzie of Gairloch's Lament 105
P	Lament for Donald Ban MacCrimmon 41,271		MacLean, Duncan, Ardrishaig, list of compositions 79
P	Lament for Donald of Laggan 288	P	MacLeod of Gesto's Lamentation 289
P	Lament for the Earl of Antrim 4-5,13	P	MacLeod of Raasay's Salute 70
P	Lament for Hugh 4-5,13,41	M	Madam Gayre, Baroness of Lochore 88
P	Lament for Iain Ciar 10,174,185,190,256	S	Madam Gayre of Gayre and Nigg's Strathspey 88
P	Lament for the Laird of Contullich 10,48		
P	Lament for the Lord of Connaught 287	P	MacNabs' Gathering 47
P	Lament for MacDonald of Kinlochmoidart 33	S	Maggie Cameron 142
		M	The Maid of Glendaruel 143
P	Lament for MacDonald of Sanda 4,10-14, 48,91-2	song & M	The Maid of Morvern 287
P	Lament for Munro of Foulis 33	P	Maol Donn - see MacCrimmon's Sweetheart
P	Lament for Neil MacEachern of Conespie Islay (1933) 212		The Marquis of Argyle's Salute (The Marquis's Welcome) 119-123
P	Lament for Patrick Og MacCrimmon 271		
P	Lament for Samuel 4-5,13	M	Martin Kessler 168
P	Lament for the Viscount of Dundee 14	waltz	Mary Darroch 282
P	Latha Dunabharti 13,174	P	Mary's Praise 277
	Lawrie, Angus, list of compositions 236-7	P	The Massacre of Glencoe 253,255
	Lawrie, Iain, list of compositions 237	P	Melfort's March 116
	Lawrie, Ronald, list of compositions 239	P?	The Men of Kintyre 8
	Lawrie, William, list of compositions 266	P	The Men Went To Drink 2,269
P	Leaving Kintyre 1	P	Menzies' Salute 243
M	Leaving Lunga 106,211	M	Minard Bay 88
P	The Little Spree (The Wee Spree) 69,233,271	M	Minard Castle 88
		M	Miss Elspeth Campbell's March 277
M	The Lochaber Gathering 78	M	Miss Forbes' Farewell to Banff 42
SA	Lochaber No More 161	P	Moladh Moraig – see In Praise of Morag
RM	Lochanside 282	M	Morar Sim (or Morair Simi) 19,233
P	Lochend's March 116	M	Mrs Barbara Gillies (or Mrs Arthur Gillies)168
	Loch Fyne, list of tunes 73		
P	Lochnell's Lament 115,178,190,196,198	M	Mrs Donald MacLean 227
J	Lorna's Slipper 168	M	Mrs H.L. MacDonald of Dunach 205,212,264
P	Lovat's March 19-20		
M	Lt Col Gayre, Baron of Lochore 88	S	Mrs MacDonald of Dunach 205,264
J	Lt McGuire's Jig 284	song	Mull of Kintyre 57
HP	Lucy Cassidy 52	P	My King Has Landed In Moidart 243
P? M?	MacAlistrum's March 13	M	The 91st at Modder River 111
			Oban, list of tunes 170
	MacColl, John, list of compositions 211-12	S	The Oban Strathspey 225
		R	The Old Man's Address (= The Sheepwife) 142
P	MacCrimmon's Sweetheart (Maol Donn) 16,38,298		
		P	The Old Men Went To Drink 1-2,269
P	MacDonald's Salute (=Duntroon's Salute) 91	P	The Old Woman's Lullaby 256
P	MacDougall of Lorne's Lament 182	P	The Park Piobaireachd 225
M	MacDougall of Lunga 106	M	The Pass of Melfort 112
P	MacDougalls' Gathering 175		People of this Glen - see Women of this Glen
P	MacDougalls' Salute 174-5		

M	Pipe Major Angus MacInnes Lawrie of Oban 235	P	Gathering Too Long In This Condition 70,98,270,272
R	Pipe Major A.W.Wilson 57	RM	Torosay Castle 237
M	Pipe Major J. Lawrie 237	M	Tug Argan Gap 135
M	Pipe Major John Stewart 222	S	Tulloch Gorm 89
HP	Pipe Major R. MacCallum MBE 158		
M	Pipe Major William Lawrie's Favourite 266	P	The Unjust Incarceration 43
M	Pipe Major William Wilson, Campbeltown 56	P	The Vaunting 270
M	Pipe Major Willie Wilson 56	P	War or Peace 33,83,182
P	Pipers Meeting 116	song	Wee Donald Ban 49
P	The Piper's Warning to his Master 14,90-1,93	P	Weighing From Land 1
M	Poltalloch House 95,105,143	song	We Will Take The High Road 241
S	Poltalloch House 95	RM	When The Battle Is O'er 160
M	Portree Bay 284	M	William Sillar, FRCS 36
P	In Praise of Mary 277	SA	Women of this Glen 3,242,255
P	In Praise of Morag 295-6		Woodside 143
P	The Prince's Salute 113,243,277,295-6		
M	The Prophet (The Earl of Mansfield) 142	P	Young George's Salute 123-5,221,289
		P	The Young Laird of Dungallon's Salute 125,287-8
M	The Raasay Highlanders 284		
M	Rab's Wedding 162		
R	The Reel of Tulloch 143,223		
M	The Road To The Isles 282-3		
song	The Road To The Isles 103		
RM	Ronald MacShannon 36,158		
S	Ronnie Lawrie (Oban) 239		
J	Ronnie Lawrie's Rant 239		
P	The Rout of the MacPhees 4,14		
	The Royal Secret Society 245		
P	Salute to Captain MacDougall 174,190		
SA	Samantha's Lullaby 166		
M	The Sands of Cairo - see The Bens of Jura		
P	Scarce of Fishing 178,198,200		
M	The Seven Pipers of Simla 65		
M	The 71st's Farewell to Dover - see The Bens of Jura		
R	The Sheepwife 142		
	The Shepherd and the Goat 143		
M	Sir Alex's Glorious Return to Govan 168		
P	Sir Ewen Cameron of Lochiel's Salute 14		
J	The Skyeman's Jig 284		
P	The Sound of the Waves Against Duntroon Castle 91,94		
M	South Hall 282,284		
song	South of the Border 234-5		
P	Stewart's White Banner 5		
P	Stiallaig 277		
S	Stumpie 143		
RM	Sunset on the Somme 266		
M	The Surrender of Cronje 282		
M	The Sweet Maid of Glendaruel 143		
M	The Taking of Beaumont Hamel 282,284		
	Tigh Bhroinein 97-8		
P	Togail nam Bo - see MacFarlane's